SCHOOL CHOICE TRADEOFFS

School Choice Tradeoffs

LIBERTY, EQUITY, AND DIVERSITY

R. Kenneth Godwin
and Frank R. Kemerer

 University of Texas Press, Austin

First edition, 2002

Requests for permission to reproduce material from this work should be sent
to Permissions, University of Texas Press, Box 7819, Austin, TX 78713-7819.

⊚ The paper used in this book meets the minimum requirements of
ANSI/NISO Z39.48-1992 (R1997) (Permanence of Paper).

Library of Congress Cataloging-in-Publication Data

Godwin, R. Kenneth.
    School choice tradeoffs : liberty, equity, and diversity / R. Kenneth Godwin
and Frank R. Kemerer.—1st ed.
        p.   cm.
Includes bibliographical references (p.   ) and index.
    ISBN 0-292-72842-5 (alk. paper)
    1. School choice—United States.   2. Education and state—United States.
3. Educational equalization—United States.   I. Kemerer, Frank R.   II. Title.
    LB1027.9   .G63   2002
    379.1′11′0973—dc21

2001005081

To the inner-city children

Contents

Figures

Tables

Preface

AN OPTIMAL EDUCATIONAL POLICY in a liberal democracy goes beyond teaching literacy and numeracy. It also supports the learning of moral reasoning, political tolerance, respect for diversity, and citizenship. Educational policy should value individual liberty and equality of opportunity for all people, and it should create mechanisms to foster efficiency and to hold educational institutions accountable. *School Choice Tradeoffs* examines how these goals are in a state of tension with each other when government affords parents the means to select the schools their children attend. It shows how school choice offers a rare opportunity to make significant advances toward equality of opportunity and ethnic integration. While the concept of school choice is simple, seemingly small changes in program design substantially alter policy outcomes. If policy is poorly designed, school choice can threaten the basic values that a liberal democratic society holds dear. Thus, while school choice represents an important policy opportunity, it also presents serious policy risks.

School Choice Tradeoffs grows out of our four-year study of public and private school choice in San Antonio that was funded principally by the U.S. Department of Education and the Spencer Foundation. The study enabled us to investigate firsthand the consequences of allowing parents to choose schools for their children. It also prompted us to begin a broader study of school choice from the philosophical, political, and legal perspectives, for we quickly realized that school choice represents a fundamental change in the way we educate children.

In recent years, a spate of books have been published on school choice. Most emphasize the empirical evidence that supports the author's preferred policy. Proponents argue that school choice will result in educational gains for choosing students, improved economic efficiency, enhanced parental rights, and the introduction of a competitive academic

market that will stimulate all schools to improve. Opponents assert that school choice will harm nonchoosing students, increase segregation and social inequality, and ultimately destroy the public school system. Several factors set *School Choice Tradeoffs* apart from existing books in this field. First, the book places the topic in a broad theoretical framework based on the idea of opportunity cost. Second, the book anchors the discussion in the conflicting educational goals of such liberal democratic theorists as John Locke, John Dewey, and John Rawls to demonstrate how their different priorities have affected thinking in this country about the role of the state versus the parent in schooling. Third, the book encompasses available scholarly research in economics, education, law, and politics. Fourth, the book shows how federal and state constitutional law has great influence over the design and functioning of school choice programs, and how policy design and functioning determine outcomes.

School Choice Tradeoffs is not about a "single best policy." We seek to offer a balanced perspective that goes beyond rhetoric and ideology to provide readers in general and public policymakers in particular insight into the complex tradeoffs that are inherent in the design and implementation of school choice policies. While all policies create winners and losers, the key questions concern who these individuals are and how much they gain or lose. By placing school choice within a broader context, the book stimulates reflective thought by all readers.

School Choice Tradeoffs first considers the many dimensions that school choice takes and what we know about its consequences. Then the book discusses underlying values at stake, with primary emphasis on liberty, equity, and diversity. Included among the questions the book explores are: How much liberty should parents have to control their children's education? Does education for effective democratic citizenship require that the state both provide a uniform system of public schooling and regulate alternatives? Should a liberal democratic society allow students to be educated in ways that eschew such liberal values as gender equality, the priority of rationality, and individual autonomy? Are private schools more or less effective than public schools at teaching political toleration? Would a market-based educational system be more efficient and equitable? How would it affect educational funding? Does federal and state constitutional law permit the state's use of public money to enfranchise parents with the opportunity to select religious private schools? Will school choice programs balkanize the learning environment into mutually exclusive enclaves along racial, religious, and socioeconomic lines, and, if so, would this be harmful to democratic citizenship? How can the state assure that every parent has an equal opportunity to choose without dis-

criminating on the basis of race? Does state constitutional law permit the deregulation and privatization of schooling? Is educational privatization possible without subjecting schools to federal and state constitutional constraints? The book concludes with a specific proposal that we believe makes a reasonable tradeoff among the competing values and reflects our priorities for an educational policy that exhibits a strong commitment to pluralism, equality of educational opportunity for all children, parent rights, and institutional autonomy.

We owe a strong debt of gratitude to many organizations and individuals who have assisted us in the research leading up to this book. First, we thank the U.S. Department of Education; the Spencer Foundation; and the Covenant, Ewing Halsell, and USAA foundations in San Antonio for funding the San Antonio School Choice Research Project. Encompassing a multifaceted look at both public and private school choice, the study was conducted under the auspices of the Center for the Study of Education Reform at the University of North Texas from 1992 to 1996. Both the Children's Educational Opportunity (CEO) Program in San Antonio, which sponsored the private school choice program there, and the San Antonio Independent School District were willing participants. We are especially grateful to Robert Aguirre, director of the CEO program, and to the San Antonio I.S.D. school board and the two superintendents we worked with, Victor Rodriguez and Diana Lam, for their cooperation and support. We also thank the Spencer Foundation for funding the toleration study, whose findings are reported in Chapter 2, and the National Center for the Study of Privatization in Education at Teachers College, Columbia University, for underwriting part of the research on the legal aspects of privatization reported in Chapter 7. Our commissioned research paper for the National Research Council of the National Academy of Sciences facilitated our understanding of the likely policy outcomes of different types of choice policies. We thank the John Templeton Foundation for providing funding for us, together with our colleague Richard Ruderman, to teach a unique interdisciplinary course on educating the liberal democratic citizen that enabled us to think through many of the topics discussed in this book. Finally, we are indebted to Chancellor Alfred Hurley and the University of North Texas for both financial support and encouragement throughout this research.

Numerous individuals have helped with facets of this study. First and foremost is Valerie Martinez, who served as co-principal investigator with us in the San Antonio study and was instrumental in orchestrating the survey research. Richard Ruderman, our coauthor in Chapter 3, advanced significantly our understanding of the philosophical dimensions of school

choice. Jennifer L. Kemerer became a collaborator with us through her research on school choice and racial segregation, and we acknowledge her contribution by adding her as coauthor of Chapter 4. We owe a strong intellectual debt of gratitude to Henry Levin, Terry Moe, Stephen Sugarman, and John Witte, all of whom assisted us at one point or another in the research and writing of this volume. Kay Thomas, Carrie Ausbrooks, and Alice Miller, doctoral students in educational administration at UNT, served as research assistants during the San Antonio project and based their dissertations on the study. Casi Davis also worked as a research assistant and drew on the study to complete a master's thesis in public administration. University of Texas School of Law students Elizabeth González, Kristine Tidgren, and Patricia Esquivel assisted with legal research, as did Marc Gracia of St. Mary's School of Law in San Antonio. UNT doctoral student Catherine Maloney assisted with charter school research. Eric Juenke read an earlier draft of the book and made valuable contributions. Finally, we are indebted to the students in our graduate courses and seminars who helped us think through many school choice issues with their critical comments and insights. To these individuals and the many others who offered assistance during the researching and writing of this book, we offer our deepest gratitude.

School choice is a disputatious subject. Coming from different academic disciplines, we began with different opinions on the value of both public and private school choice. Many times over the course of our collaboration, we have argued intensely about school choice and its policy implications. These differences helped keep us honest, and as we learned more about school choice, the differences narrowed. We hope that this book will stimulate serious thought about the tradeoffs that are inherent in designing a school choice policy that is compatible with the fundamental goals of a liberal democratic society.

R. KENNETH GODWIN
FRANK R. KEMERER

SCHOOL CHOICE TRADEOFFS

School Choice Options and Issues: An Overview

WHEN IT COMES TO EDUCATION POLICY, Americans want it all. We demand better test score results for all students, greater equality of opportunity, respect for diversity, preparation for good citizenship, efficiency, regulatory accountability, the development of autonomy in students, and preparation for jobs in a postindustrial society. But it is impossible to maximize educational performance in all these areas at the same time. This book is about the tradeoffs involved in any school choice policy. All decisions make tradeoffs among desirable goals, and education policy is no exception. It cannot simultaneously maximize efficiency and equity, educational outcomes for the most- and the least-advantaged students, or the rights of parents and the rights of the community. We hope that by examining the many tradeoffs that are a necessary part of education policymaking we can clarify the issues involved in answering the question, "What school choice policy is best?"

Selecting the most desirable education policies requires that we first identify the most important goals for education. Three educational goals enjoy the support of almost everyone who lives in liberal democratic societies such as the United States and Canada. Students should learn the economic skills necessary to become economically independent, the political skills and understandings necessary to support the democratic process and to participate rationally in it, and the moral reasoning required to understand what constitutes ethical behavior and why such behavior is the cornerstone of a good society.

The justifications for economic skills and political judgment are self-evident in the words "liberal democratic society." To have full liberty, an individual must have the capability to be economically independent. For democracy to work, people must be able to participate meaningfully in the political process. But why give moral reasoning equal status? Some

who prefer a strict wall of separation between church and state might argue that moral reasoning is outside the purview of public education. We think a moment's reflection will convince readers that schools have an obligation to develop moral reasoning in every student. While the U.S. Constitution prohibits the state from teaching religious beliefs in public schools, it does not prohibit teaching the principles of justice that are fundamental to a civil democratic society. Reasoned political decisionmaking depends heavily on the ability to engage in moral reasoning. More important, moral reasoning is the key variable leading to moral behavior, an outcome that all of us desire.[1] The issue, therefore, is not whether schools should teach moral reasoning, but how they should teach it.

We argue that liberal democracy requires one other fundamental policy goal—equal educational opportunity. Liberalism holds that social, political, and economic rewards should result from the combination of reason, skill, and hard work. Contemporary liberalism[2] maintains that public funding of education is the chief mechanism the state uses to reduce the inequalities in economic and social rewards created by the circumstances of birth and childhood. If the rational application of skills is a necessary condition for achieving rewards, then a just education policy will provide students with equal opportunities to develop rationality and to obtain skills.

WHY CHANGE CURRENT POLICIES?

There are many other legitimate and important educational policy goals. Most Americans want an educational system that is efficient, respects diversity, assists economic growth, provides accountability to citizens, and gives parents reasonable control over the values their children learn. Americans also want an education that encourages individual autonomy and respect for the common good. In our discussion of these various goals, we make three fundamental assumptions. First, no educational goal has absolute priority. Second, resources spent on any goal are subject to diminishing marginal returns. And third, every goal conflicts with at least one other. If these assumptions are true, then policymakers must constantly make difficult tradeoffs as they allocate scarce resources.

The United States has an education system that most of the world would love to emulate. We make available free public education to all residents and spend more per pupil than any other country. Graduates of our public schools attend colleges and universities that are among the best in the world. Public opinion polls indicate that most parents are reasonably

satisfied with the schools their children attend. Why should we change such a system? The most important reasons are that current policies create highly unequal educational opportunities and that most inner-city children do not receive an adequate education. Current policies discriminate against low-income families and ethnic minorities. They institutionalize this discrimination through the assignment of students, teachers, and resources to individual schools. Some of these inner-city schools are so bad that former President Clinton's Secretary of Education Richard Riley stated that they should not even be called schools.[3]

To illustrate the inequality of opportunity, we ask you to join us in a brief thought experiment. Assume that we are policy analysts from another country. Our government hires us to recommend policies that will result in more equal educational opportunities for students. As U.S. education journals often discuss that goal, we decide to visit the United States to analyze its education policies and outcomes. Our review of the empirical research finds that the four sets of variables shown in Figure 1.1 are the primary factors that influence educational outcomes. Of these four, the characteristics of classmates and the attributes of schools are the most relevant because policymakers can alter them to a far greater degree than they can change student and parent characteristics.[4]

The existing research on the effects of classmates on learning finds that students learn more when their classmates value education highly and are easy to teach. The research also demonstrates that students are more likely to have these characteristics if they come from high socioeconomic status (SES) families and live in neighborhoods with a high percentage of non-Hispanic whites. Putting it in economic terms, students from higher SES families and from neighborhoods populated largely by non-Hispanic whites tend to create positive spillovers (externalities) that increase the learning of their classmates. Therefore, policies that cluster students by income and ethnicity disadvantage students assigned to schools with high concentrations of low-income and minority students.

Our review of the education literature also indicates that the monetary resources that schools receive are correlated with the income and ethnicity of their students. Schools populated by whites from high SES families have more resources than schools where students are predominantly from minority and low-income families. Per pupil expenditures in many states differ drastically from one school district to another, and, even within school districts, some schools receive far greater resources than other schools. Some schools are well staffed while others are overcrowded. Some schools have a stable faculty of highly experienced teachers while others have constant turnover and teachers with little experience. Unfor-

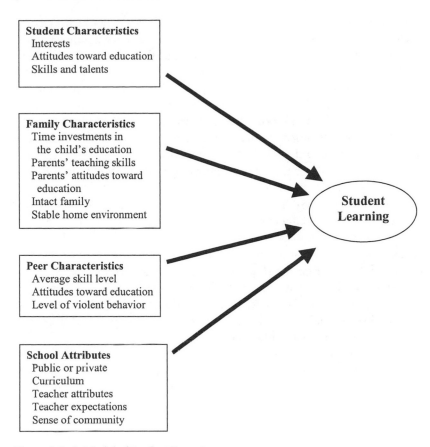

Figure 1.1. A Model of Student Learning.

tunately, these inequalities in resources penalize minority and low-income students.[5]

Our visit to the United States would lead us to conclude that segregating students by income and ethnicity is certainly the result, if not the intent, of current public policies. Assigning students to schools on the basis of housing price segregates students by income. Real estate, banking, and government housing practices tend to segregate students by ethnicity.[6] Therefore, the current school choice policy—assigning students to schools based on where they live (henceforth called "residence choice")— creates enormous inequalities in the spillovers students receive from their classmates and in the resources available to their schools. Many school districts exacerbate these inequalities by separating the most and the least

academically advantaged students into classes for the "gifted and talented" and the "academically challenged."

If we actually had made this hypothetical fact-finding tour of the United States we probably would conclude that although Americans may pay lip service to equality of educational opportunity, their policies often exacerbate rather than reduce existing inequalities. When we returned home to advise the Minister of Education, what policies could we recommend? What politically feasible policies would reduce existing inequalities while not lowering the overall quality of education in our country?

WHY USE SCHOOL CHOICE TO PROMOTE EQUITY?

Among the reasons that increasing school choice emerged as a policy option is the failure of other policies to integrate schools and to achieve acceptable educational outcomes for inner-city students.[7] Every year that these students remain in their neighborhood public schools they fall further behind their suburban counterparts.[8] Since 1973, the segregation in public schools has increased,[9] and most states and school districts have been ineffective in achieving equity in school funding.[10]

The difficulties in achieving funding equity are likely to increase. States that moved toward funding equity across school districts generally have done so not by taking money from rich districts and giving it to poor ones, but by increasing state funding in needy districts more rapidly than in wealthy districts.[11] This has been possible because over the last fifty years real per pupil expenditures in public schools have risen by 500 percent.[12] But the baby boom generation will soon retire, and the yearly increases in per pupil expenditures are not likely to continue. Future improvements in education must come from increased productivity, not from doubling per pupil spending every twenty years.

The most daunting challenge to equality of educational opportunity is the achievement of equal positive spillovers from classmates. Unlike funding, where it is not necessary to directly take from the more advantaged to improve the position of the less advantaged, equalizing spillovers requires the redistribution of students who are most likely to create positive spillovers. Past efforts to use government coercion to achieve this have failed. We need only to recall public reactions to forced busing to see that voluntary approaches are the only politically acceptable mode of achieving the desired redistributions. We will argue that achieving greater equality of educational opportunity requires a radical expansion of school

choice. But expanded choice can increase inequalities. Therefore, choice policies must be combined with incentives that encourage the redistribution of educational resources from upper-middle-class schools to schools for low-income and working-class children.

TYPES OF SCHOOL CHOICE

If one conceives of choice policies as a continuum, the option with the least choice is a policy where families choose a public school by taking up residence in its attendance zone. At the next level is the school-within-a-school. For example, a school may offer a special math and science academy for students whom the school designates as gifted and talented. Qualified students who attend the academy would continue to take other courses with regular students. A more expansive version of this approach is the magnet school. Originally an incentive to school integration, the magnet school concept is evident in today's thematic schools that attract students from across the school district. Thematic schools emphasize special subjects such as foreign languages, the arts, math, or science. Students within the district may enroll in the school of their choice so long as they meet district-determined qualifications. Recently some states have adopted statewide open enrollment policies that allow students to enroll in public schools outside their own district.

The newest form of public school choice is the charter school. A charter school is, in effect, a new public school started by teachers, parents, or private organizations with the approval of a state-designated authority. Since Minnesota enacted the first charter school legislation in 1991, more than two-thirds of the states have introduced charter schools. But charter school laws vary considerably. Some states allow only existing public schools to convert to charter schools, while others permit the creation of new schools as well. In a few states, private schools can convert to charter school status. Although charter schools are classified as public schools, in several states private for-profit organizations operate these schools through subcontracts with public entities. A good example is the Boston Renaissance Public Charter School, one of the largest charter schools in the country, with over 1,200 students. Boston Renaissance is operated by the for-profit Edison Schools. The autonomy of charter schools varies from state to state. At one extreme is Arizona, where charter schools operate virtually unfettered by state regulations, teacher organizations, and continuing oversight. At the other extreme is Rhode Island, where teachers' unions virtually control the charter schools.

The most extensive form of school choice would be a state-funded voucher that students may use to attend any public or private school to which they gain admission. Schools would be free to select students using any constitutionally valid criteria. A school might or might not accept the voucher as full payment of tuition and fees. Most proposed voucher policies are not so inclusive. Some restrict vouchers to nonsectarian schools, to low-income students, or to students whose public school has failed to achieve acceptable educational outcomes. To reduce the possibility that private schools would discriminate on the basis of ethnicity, gender, or other unacceptable basis, some voucher proposals require participating schools to use a lottery to select new students. Such a provision also reduces the likelihood that private schools would admit only students who are easily taught and who produce positive spillovers for their classmates.

Experience with public school choice shows that the higher a family's socioeconomic status, the more likely it is that the children will participate in choice programs. This pattern results, at least in part, because of the greater difficulty low-income families have in obtaining information about choice programs and arranging transportation to schools outside their attendance zone. To reduce the likelihood that only higher SES families would participate in voucher programs, many proposals include transportation subsidies and parent information programs. Other proposals are designed to facilitate integration and equality of educational opportunities. These plans often require that schools which accept vouchers recruit a quota of low-income students.

To see how increased choice can affect equality of opportunity either positively or negatively, imagine two schools in contiguous attendance zones. The majority of students in Zone A are upper-middle-class and produce positive spillovers for their classmates. The majority of students in Zone B come from low-income families and create negative spillovers. To the extent that better classmates (i.e., those that create positive academic spillovers) increase learning, then a student who attends school in Zone A will learn more than an identical student enrolled in the Zone B school. What happens if the school district creates a math and science academy in the Zone A school and allows Zone B students who are in the top 20 percent of their class to transfer into that academy? Such a policy would accentuate inequalities in opportunities to learn because it would increase the concentration of students who create positive spillovers. But increasing school choice need not increase inequalities. Suppose both schools become thematic academies, with Zone A's school emphasizing math and Zone B's school emphasizing foreign languages. To the extent that families choose on the basis of curriculum and these choices are un-

related to the positive spillovers students create, then increased choice will lessen inequalities by reducing the concentration of students who create positive spillovers.

MAJOR ISSUES IN THE CHOICE DEBATE

Debates over school choice involve numerous empirical and philosophic issues. Among these are: Who chooses? Why do they leave their attendance-zone schools? What are the impacts of choice on the students who attend choice schools and on the students who remain behind? Does democratic control of schools cause them to become inefficient and ineffective? What choice policy is most compatible with liberal democratic ideals and practices? How much influence should parents have over what their children will learn? How much authority should the state claim? Will increased choice increase the costs of education? If so, who should pay these costs? Are vouchers constitutional? What state regulations should apply to private schools that accept vouchers? The goal of this book is to examine each of these questions and to reach a conclusion concerning what policy options make the best tradeoffs among competing educational goals.

Why families choose is an issue of intense debate among opponents and supporters of expanded choice. Opponents claim that white students often leave attendance-zone schools to avoid schools with large numbers of minority students. Certainly much of the data on public school choice programs and on private school attendance is consistent with this hypothesis.[13] Research on magnet schools and open enrollment programs shows that unless a choice policy includes provisions that prevent it, white parents will choose schools that enroll a lower percentage of minority students than the school their children left.[14] Similarly, minority parents tend to choose schools where their child is in the majority group, and all ethnic groups try to avoid schools where their children constitute a small minority.[15] If these results from public school choice policies predict what will happen if school choice includes private schools, then, in the absence of steps to prevent it, expanded choice will lead to greater ethnic segregation and greater inequalities in educational opportunities.

Even if families receive adequate information and transportation is available, increasing school choice may enlarge the diversity among schools, and this may produce greater ethnic and socioeconomic sorting. Henry Levin has argued that lower SES parents will choose schools that emphasize traditional values and the memorization of basic skills. In contrast, higher SES parents will choose schools that emphasize abstract think-

ing and the development of problem-solving skills.[16] Schools that emphasize bilingual education programs will draw students predominantly from families where English is not the first language. Schools that use an Afrocentrist curriculum are more likely to attract African American students. Vocational schools tend to attract students from working-class families. And, to the extent that religious affiliation is correlated with socioeconomic status, then allowing parents to choose sectarian schools may increase SES segregation.

Proponents of expanded school choice maintain that the goal of parents who exercise school choice is not to achieve segregation, but to improve educational opportunities for their child. Surveys that ask choosing parents why they decided their children should leave their attendance-zone school uniformly show that the primary reasons are expected academic excellence, safety, and, in the case of private school choosers, religious instruction.[17] When magnet and thematic schools provide clear educational incentives, parents will place their children in these schools even if they are more ethnically diverse than the schools the students leave behind. Many parents send their children to sectarian schools that are more integrated than the attendance-zone school their children would have attended. These patterns suggest that how policymakers design a choice program will determine whether it increases or decreases economic and ethnic segregation.

The likelihood that greater economic and ethnic segregation will occur if the diversity of schools increases and if parents select schools on the basis of religious or cultural values leads to a critical policy question: "Is having a diverse and responsive educational system worth the cost of increased segregation and increased inequality in educational opportunities?" For example, if a voucher policy allows Native American, African American, Jewish, or Baptist families to send their children to schools that stress the particular worldview preferred by the parents, this may result in greater inequalities in educational outcomes. Similarly, if Levin is correct and low SES families send their children to schools that stress memorization while higher SES children learn problem-solving skills, this too will lead to greater inequalities in outcomes. How do policymakers weigh the costs of these inequalities against the benefit of having a more diverse set of schools that respond to the demands of parents and students?

Educational Outcomes

Do private schools achieve better academic outcomes than public schools? This question has sparked the most controversy in the choice debate.

Chapter 2 examines this question and the issue of whether private schools are more efficient than public schools. If any single book energized the school choice debate it was *Politics, Markets and America's Schools.*[18] Written by political scientists John Chubb and Terry Moe and published by the Brookings Institution, the book uses data from a longitudinal study of high school students to show that students in private high schools learn more than children in public high schools.

As we shall discuss in detail in Chapter 2, there are four major sets of influences on student learning: the characteristics of the student, the parents, the classmates, and the school (see Figure 1.1 above). If students with higher cognitive ability or greater interest in academic pursuits are more likely to attend private schools, then observing that private school students learn more does not mean that private schools are better. It may mean only that private schools have students who learn more easily. If parents teach their children at home and induce them to work hard in schools, this improves learning. As parents of private school students value education sufficiently to pay for their children's schooling, it seems reasonable to expect that those same parents teach their children more at home and induce them to work harder in school. Thus, a positive association between private school attendance and better educational outcomes may be caused by differences in parents rather than differences in schools. Similarly, students in private schools may learn more because their classmates create a more positive learning environment. Again, it is not the characteristics of the school that lead to improved learning. If we could take the same student body and place it in a public school, the student might have learned as much or more.

Chubb and Moe maintain that democracy is a primary cause of inefficient and ineffective public schools. They claim that private schools outperform public schools because public schools are bureaucratic and inefficient, and respond to organized political interests rather than to parents and students. *Politics, Markets and America's Schools* shows that public school institutions, curricula, and pedagogies are not the product of producers attempting to increase efficiency and quality nor are they responses to the educational demands of parents and students. Rather, they are the result of endless bargaining among political interests and reflect the political power of those interests. School districts choose policies because politically powerful groups desire them rather than because the policies lead to better educational outcomes. In contrast, private schools must respond to the discipline of the market and to the demands of students and parents. Chubb and Moe created a stir in the policy community not only because they found that private high schools appear to outper-

form public high schools, but also because they claimed that democratic control of schools makes public schools *inherently* inferior to private schools. An example may clarify their argument.

During the final days of the congressional session in 1998, President Clinton demanded that the Republican-controlled Congress pass a bill that would increase federal aid to public schools for the purposes of reducing class size and hiring more teachers. The Republicans opposed this proposal, but the president ultimately won the policy battle. Smaller classes, Clinton claimed, would improve student learning. In the spring of 1999, the Republicans attempted to allow school districts to use the money for purposes other than reducing class size and hiring new teachers. Once again, President Clinton prevailed.[19] How might Chubb and Moe view Clinton's policy to reduce class size?

They might suggest that Clinton's policy provides a perfect example of why democratic control leads to inefficiency. Smaller classes, Chubb and Moe might respond, do not improve educational outcomes so much as they meet the political demands of teacher organizations. Money spent to reduce class size might better be used in purchasing new technology, funding after-school tutoring programs, providing remedial classes during the summer, or providing merit pay to teachers. If there is a shortage of quality teachers, then requiring smaller class sizes may harm learning by reducing the quality of teaching.[20]

Why do legislators and presidents seek smaller classes rather than allowing schools and school districts to determine how to use the available resources? Because teacher organizations are perhaps the most important supporters of elected officials in the Democratic Party,[21] and these organizations lobby hard for class-size regulations.[22] Teachers are like everybody else; they prefer higher wages and more pleasant working conditions. Regulations that reduce class size guarantee that few teachers who have state certification will be unemployed. A shortage of teachers also puts pressure on state and local governments to increase salaries to attract new teachers into the profession. Finally, even if smaller class sizes do not improve learning, they improve the working conditions of teachers. Chubb and Moe might argue, therefore, that Clinton's policy victory provides just another example of democracy creating inefficient outcomes.

On the other hand, if Chubb and Moe are correct in their analysis that government control of schools leads to inefficiencies, this inefficiency may be a price worth paying. Improved test scores and higher graduation rates are not the only important results of education. We also expect schools to produce citizens who understand and appreciate democratic government and behave in morally responsible ways. Such distinguished

policymakers and scholars as Horace Mann and John Dewey have argued that public schools are more likely to achieve these results. Mann and Dewey believed that public schools teach a common core of democratic values, develop political tolerance, and help overcome parental prejudice and superstition. Public school advocates claim that private schools are more likely to teach the parochial and prejudiced values of parents and to stress individual success rather than the common good.[23] Proponents of private school choice contend that private schools are more likely to teach the moral reasoning and judgment that lead to moral behavior and respect for the rights of others. We examine the empirical research on these competing claims in the next chapter.

Another reason to accept democratic control is that it may be necessary for public accountability and the development of democratic institutions. Democratic control of local schools provides an opportunity for citizens to learn political participation and develop a stronger political community.[24] There may be an important tradeoff between efficiency and better academic outcomes on the one side and developing tolerance, democracy, and community on the other.

Liberal Democratic Theory and Education Policy

The question of how well schools teach tolerance, respect for the common good, and moral judgment leads us to two of the most fundamental issues in school choice policy. First, what is the appropriate content of education in a liberal democratic society? Second, how should control over that content be divided between parents and the state? Chapter 3 examines these issues. John Locke, the father of liberalism, advocated parental control and an education that stressed the teaching of rationality, moderation, civility, toleration, and moral judgment. Because Locke's great concern was government tyranny, he rejected giving government the power to socialize students by controlling the content of their education. Locke argued that the essential characteristics of a liberal state are its limited power and a restriction on using the state's power to force one conception of the good life and the good person on those who hold different beliefs. By design, therefore, the liberal state is forbidden to advance a positive concept of virtue. But teaching virtue is essential to education. Our understanding of virtue tells us why we should become educated. It makes clear education's ultimate purposes and helps us make morally correct judgments. Therefore, if we require state neutrality among reasonable worldviews, then state control over the content of education must be minimal.

Dewey, the father of progressive education, took an opposing view.

He argued that public schools constitute a better culture than any from which the students are likely to come. It is better because it is more democratic, tolerant, and universal. Leaving the education of children under the control of their parents allows parental prejudices to go unchallenged by science and reason. Dewey feared that parents would discourage their children from embracing a scientific outlook that was critical of religious tradition. Without science, what would protect the students from superstition? What would prevent them from holding the undemocratic beliefs of their parents and from repeating their mistakes? From Dewey's perspective, if the teachings of school and home conflict, democratic progress requires that the school wins. Dewey also saw public schools as places to build a community in which students from diverse backgrounds would learn not only reason and science, but also democracy and respect for diversity.[25]

The opposing views of Locke and Dewey lead us to the tradeoff between encouraging cultural diversity and encouraging the liberal values of democracy, equality, and autonomy. If aspects of students' cultures or traditions are undemocratic, should schools attempt to weed out those practices? If a student's culture demands acceptance of beliefs that conflict with current scientific evidence, should schools force the student to examine critically her beliefs? Parents who are faithful to nonscientific beliefs may argue that forcing students to apply the scientific method and the Enlightenment's conception of rationality threatens the souls of their children and the survival of their culture. If liberalism truly respects diversity, should it not facilitate the survival of all reasonable cultures, even those that have illiberal elements?

Parental Rights and Equality of Opportunity

The claim that education demands rational and critical self-reflection should not be easily dismissed. Teaching autonomy, the ability to critically reflect upon issues and to rationally choose among reasonable conceptions of the good life, is a cardinal goal of a liberal education and has been so since John Stuart Mill and Immanuel Kant. By teaching their children that certain rational conceptions of life are wrong or by limiting the child's education in ways that grossly limit future alternatives, are parents unreasonably restricting their children's freedom to choose among meaningful lives?[26] While parents have the right to believe irrational and unscientific ideas, do they have the right to prevent their children from developing the intellectual tools that allow them to critically evaluate their beliefs?

Publicly funded education creates an inherent tension between the

right of parents to transmit their culture to their children and the right of society to use the educational system to produce the values that society believes are critical to its continuance. We begin Chapter 4 by exploring how courts have made these difficult tradeoffs, paying special attention to the struggle between parent rights and the desire of the state to socialize children. We then review how courts have attempted to balance the egalitarian requirement of equal educational opportunity with the demands of parents and local communities to control education according to their own values. Finally, we examine the constraints today's courts are likely to place on attempts to achieve greater equality of opportunity. We do this by studying how the courts previously have reacted to policies designed to achieve ethnic integration and greater equality in funding.

The Constitutionality of Vouchers and Tax Credits

Whether a choice policy that includes vouchers is constitutional is a complex question. Not only are there questions of federal constitutionality, but also state constitutions vary widely in their degree of restriction on state involvement with sectarian organizations. But if school vouchers encompassing sectarian private schools cannot pass constitutional muster, they cease to be of value as a school reform. Adding to the complexity of the constitutionality issue is a lack of consensus among judges concerning how vouchers affect the relationship between state and religion. For example, despite almost identical state constitutional provisions, trial judges reached opposite conclusions on the constitutionality of the Milwaukee and Cleveland voucher programs.

In 2002, the U.S. Supreme Court will rule on the constitutionality of the Cleveland voucher program. As written, the program encompasses suburban public school districts and both religious and nonreligious private schools. However, because the public school districts and most of the nonreligious private schools chose not to participate, the U.S. Court of Appeals for the Sixth Circuit struck the program down as an unconstitutional advancement of religion. If the Supreme Court affirms the lower court ruling, what are the implications for voucher program design? If the Supreme Court upholds the program, will the Justices allow states to apply their own constitutional provisions to the queston? States with more stringent anti-establishment provisions would be able to exclude religious private schools. Or might the Justices indicate that such exclusion would violate the rights of parents and discriminate against religion?

Drawing upon our intensive examination of constitutional provisions, interpretive judicial and state law in all fifty states, and research on

issues of federalism, Chapter 5 explores the likely outcome of litigation over school vouchers and tax credit programs at both the federal and state levels. Based on this discussion, the chapter sets forth the design features a voucher program should have to pass constitutional muster.

The Economics of Choice

Chapter 6 reviews the economic tradeoffs involved in the selection of a school choice policy. Too often academic debates over education neglect important economic concerns. This neglect is unfortunate because costs are always important to policymakers. When confronting a policy proposal that raises substantially the costs of education, it is a rare elected official who does not ask where the money is going to come from. Education is the biggest item in the budget for local and state governments. A small percentage increase in the costs of elementary and secondary education typically requires either new taxes or large cuts in other programs. Neither option is one that elected officials embrace willingly.

One of the frustrating aspects of studying public policy is that commonsensical policies can lead to unanticipated and highly undesirable outcomes. For example, relying on local property taxes to fund schools leads to substantial inequalities in funding across districts. An obvious solution to reduce these inequalities is to have the state rather than local school districts raise and allocate funding for education. Many economists believe that this reform harms education by reducing voter support for education taxes. Imagine for a moment that you have no school-age children. If you believe your property taxes improve the schools in your district, then you may support these taxes despite the fact that you have no children attending public schools. The reason for your support is that if your district's schools decline, so too will the value of your property. If, however, all funding comes from the state level, then the taxes you pay for education are unrelated to the quality of *your* neighborhood schools. For this reason, cuts in taxes for education will not reduce the value of your property. In this situation, you may choose to support candidates who promise lower taxes. Proposition 13 in California, a measure that greatly reduced the state's ability to fund schools, may be an example of what happens when a state divorces the funding of public schools from their local financial base.[27]

Another situation in which common sense may prove incorrect is the claim that private schools will lower the costs of education. Milton Friedman argued vouchers would impose the discipline of the market on producers. This would force schools to look for production-enhancing in-

novations and would reduce wasteful bureaucracies.[28] David Boaz and Morris Barrett of the libertarian Cato Institute attempted to show that Friedman's faith in market discipline was justified. They compared the tuition that private schools charge with the per pupil expenditures of public schools. As the latter are generally much higher than the former, Boaz and Barrett claim that Friedman was right and that vouchers would lower educational costs.[29] Other economists claim that this comparison is inappropriate. Sectarian schools often receive subsidies from their religious organizations, do not pay the market value for teachers who are members of religious orders, and typically do not pay the costs of transportation. In addition, private schools do not have the same number of specially challenged or at-risk students, students that cost considerably more to educate. Economists Henry Levin and Cyrus Driver maintain that a voucher system, rather than reducing the cost of education to taxpayers, would increase those costs substantially.[30]

Accountability versus Autonomy

How should choice schools be held accountable to parents and to the state for the education that they provide at public expense? Too much accountability produces the same plethora of regulations that have created the rule-bound traditional public school. Too little allows unscrupulous entrepreneurs to benefit at public expense. The tradeoffs are particularly apparent when school choice programs encompass private educational organizations. Here there is a narrow and mostly unmarked public policy channel between state constitutional law that restricts the delegation of public schooling to private organizations and federal constitutional law that allows parents to choose private schools, protects freedom of religion, and prevents unreasonable private school regulation.

In Chapter 7 we examine how the complexities of the legal framework for holding choice schools accountable create an inevitable tension with institutional autonomy. The sources of regulation are many: state constitutions, statutes, regulations issued by state and local agencies, charters and contracts, and judicial decisions. Failing to stop school choice outright, opponents often can exert tremendous influence over the design of school choice programs through the exercise of both political clout and litigation. But without autonomy, choice schools are handicapped in fulfilling their missions and offering an alternative to the one-size-fits-all public school. Where should the line be drawn between overreaching accountability and unfettered autonomy? Our examination of the account-

ability versus autonomy tradeoff in Chapter 7 sets the stage for the proposal we present in the last chapter.

DESIGNING A CHOICE PROGRAM
THAT PROMOTES EQUITY

Analyses of existing public and private choice programs show that the design features of a program tremendously affect its policy outcomes. The question, of course, is whether or not it is possible to design a program that is politically feasible, that can improve equity and diversity, and that allows more diverse schools to prosper while encouraging efficiency and maintaining an acceptable level of public accountability.[31] To understand which future policy options are politically feasible, we must examine the politics that currently surround the choice debate. In the first part of Chapter 8 we review the positions of various interest groups. We pay special attention to teachers' unions and the Christian Right and to their relationships to the Democratic and Republican parties.

After reviewing the political feasibility of various policy options, we propose a school choice policy that we believe makes appropriate tradeoffs among competing educational goals. The proposal gives incentives to families and choice schools to behave in ways that promote public goals, particularly equality of educational opportunity and ethnic and income integration. The incentives to parents are greater opportunities to choose the education they prefer for their children and dramatically reduced costs for attending choice schools. The incentives to private schools are the substantial reduction in the tuition and fees they must charge and a substantial increase in the demand for their services. As we stress throughout the book, all policies must make tradeoffs among desirable goals. The policy we propose is no exception. We believe, however, that the tradeoffs we make are ones that a liberal democratic society should find acceptable.

The Outcomes of School Choice Policies

IN WILLIAM STYRON'S powerful and poignant novel *Sophie's Choice*, a concentration camp guard forces Sophie to choose which of her two children will have a chance to live and which one will not. Opponents of expanding school choice assert that increasing school choice creates a similar choice for our society. Increased choice raises the question "Which disadvantaged children will receive increased educational opportunities and which ones will have their few existing opportunities reduced?" This choice occurs, opponents argue, because any policy that encourages the relatively more advantaged children and more active parents to leave their neighborhood school reduces the opportunities of the most disadvantaged children in that neighborhood. School choice is a zero-sum game. Peers who learn easily and parents who are most active and knowledgeable about education are important educational resources for their classmates and their schools. Whatever one child gains by moving to a choice school another child loses through the parting of the more educationally able student and her parents.

To determine whether school choice is Sophie's choice we first must examine the arguments that increased choice will improve academic outcomes for all children, including the most disadvantaged, and the claims of those who expect increased choice to harm students. We then can deduce the testable hypotheses from both sets of arguments and review the results of existing research that relates to those hypotheses. Such an analysis provides substantial insight into the likely outcomes of alternative school choice policies.

WHY PROPONENTS EXPECT CHOICE TO IMPROVE ACADEMIC OUTCOMES

Choice proponents believe that greater choice will improve outcomes through three causal mechanisms: (1) competition will force low-performing schools to either improve or close, (2) greater choice will improve student outcomes by increasing parental involvement and matching students' interests and aptitudes to a school's pedagogy and curriculum, and (3) choice will reduce the harms caused by political control of schools by eliminating much of that control. We review each of these causal arguments and discuss the evidence for and against them.

The Effects of Competition

Many choice proponents hypothesize that schools would improve if only they had to compete for customers. Adam Smith showed in *The Wealth of Nations* that in the absence of collusion by firms or intervention by government, the real winner in a free market is the consumer. Competition forces all producers to look for ways to improve the product or for a way to lower the cost of production. Either change allows the producer to increase sales and, in the short term, profits. But competition forces all other producers to improve their products or lower their costs. If all producers are selling goods of equal quality, then consumers will seek out the lowest price.

To see how competition works, take the example of cars. During the 1950s and early 1960s, almost all automobiles sold in the United States were produced by four automakers—General Motors, Ford, Chrysler, and American Motors. The average life of a car produced in this period was only about fifty thousand miles, and its reliability and gas mileage were low. The American automakers engaged in price collusion, and they relied on government to protect them from foreign competition. When the government lowered its trade barriers, Volkswagen, Toyota, Datsun (now Nissan), and Mercedes invaded the U.S. market. These cars had life spans of over a hundred thousand miles, were significantly more reliable than their American rivals, and had better gas mileage than comparable cars made in the United States. Within a short time, enough consumers switched to foreign-built cars to force American automakers to improve the quality of their cars and to lower their prices. American Motors was unable to meet the foreign competition and went out of business. Proponents of increased choice, particularly proponents of public funding for

private school choice, argue that what happened with automobiles would happen with schools if the public school monopoly were ended.[1] If forced to compete, schools would look for ways to improve their product and lower their costs.

Increased Parental Involvement and Better Matching of Students and Schools

Proponents of choice believe that giving families greater choice will improve student performance in two ways. First, choice will empower parents by making them consumers of education rather than targets of social policy. This will encourage parents to become involved in their children's education, and research shows that greater parental involvement increases the academic success of students. Second, parents can match the learning style and interests of the student with the pedagogy and curriculum of the school. This also improves academic outcomes.[2] The increase in parental involvement in schools may have another advantage: it can build social capital. Social capital is the web of trust, cooperation, and communication that allows societies to function efficiently and civilly. Social capital encourages people to cooperate on collective action problems. A basic building block of trust among citizens is the voluntary association in which people give their time and energy for the common good. Mark Schneider and his colleagues at the State University of New York at Stony Brook have argued that increasing the level of school choice available to parents increases their trust in each other and in social institutions.[3] Such trust is particularly important in low-income communities in the inner city where social capital is extremely difficult to build. To the extent that school choice increases participation in voluntary associations and increases parents' satisfaction with the social institutions that supply collective goods, then society is better off.

Democratic Control and Bureaucratic Inefficiencies

Two political scientists, John Chubb and Terry Moe, developed the best-articulated argument of why school choice that includes publicly funded vouchers or privatizes schools will improve academic outcomes.[4] In *Politics, Markets and America's Schools,* Chubb and Moe claim that the problem with past educational reforms was that they directed their energies at the wrong questions. Past policy debate discussed how public control should be exercised, but the problem with public schools is that they are

controlled by the public through the institutions of democratic government.[5] But democratic government is more likely to produce ineffective schools. Effective schools have clear goals, vigorous leadership, autonomous teachers, rigorous academic goals, and an orderly environment. Democratic control of schools produces inconsistent missions, unclear goals, weak principals, and dependent teachers.[6]

To see the logic of the Chubb and Moe argument, assume for the moment that you are chair of the Senate Education Committee in your state legislature. You are a Democrat, the governor is a Democrat, and your party controls both legislative chambers. You want to improve public schools in your state, and you have been convinced that reducing class size in elementary schools to fewer than sixteen students per class is essential to improving educational outcomes. You also believe that this will be of particular help to low-income and minority students. What will you choose to do? Will you propose a bill that requires all public elementary schools to have only small classes, or will you simply increase the education budget so that school districts (or individual schools) can reduce class size if they believe that smaller classes are the most effective use of the additional funds?

If you recommend a new law requiring all elementary schools to have class sizes of sixteen or fewer students, then you are opting for greater regulation of schools. You are attempting to make schools more effective by imposing controls on them. In the abstract, most of us object to large bureaucracies and value principal and teacher autonomy. But when we have the opportunity to impose *our* favorite law, we almost always are willing to limit the very autonomy we claim to support. One of the great insights of *Politics, Markets and America's Schools* is that while any single law or regulation may help schools, the long-term accumulation of such laws inevitably harms schools by bureaucratizing them. Each new law restricts the autonomy and flexibility of principals and teachers, and it increases the likelihood that public educators will face conflicting goals and rules.

Chubb and Moe argue that as different parties and interests replace each other in state government, the list of rules and regulations that govern education will grow. For example, one year the legislature may rule that all public high school students must take a course in environmental policy. The following year a new legislature may decide that each student must take a course on free enterprise. This year the legislature may choose to require sex education. Next year the legislature may choose to exempt the children of parents who object to the sex education course and require

that the schools provide alternative classes for those children. This year the legislature may require that biology classes teach that evolution and creationism are simply differing theories and that neither has been proven superior to the other. The following year the legislature may require that biology classes teach only the explanation of current life forms that has the backing of the scientific community.

The state legislature is only one of many locations where new regulations originate. Almost every state has a commissioner of education, a state board of education, and an education agency that has the power to make rules (administrative laws) that are binding on all public schools. In addition, the federal government creates rules concerning the use of funds that it provides and enacts such statutes as the Individuals with Disabilities Education Act. Both the state and federal courts may choose to impose legal restraints on schools. Local school boards, local superintendents, and school-based management teams also make new rules and regulations.[7] The result of this political process is a large and contradictory set of state laws and regulations. In Texas, for example, the combined length of the Texas Education Code and the Texas Administrative Code governing K–12 education totals 1,473 double-column pages.

The contract negotiated between teachers' unions and school districts is another source of school regulations. The agreements that unions reach with school boards have the same effect as laws passed by the legislature. Union contracts determine teacher qualifications, teacher assignment and transfer policies, the relationships between teachers and their principals, teacher duties, and evaluation procedures.[8] The 1995 contract between the Milwaukee teachers' union and the Milwaukee Public Schools illustrates the extent to which union contracts take away the autonomy of principals and teachers. The contract was more than 150 pages long and included 26 pages governing what the school district or principal could require a teacher to do, 19 pages concerning leaves of absence and absenteeism, and 5 pages on grievance procedures.[9]

Teacher organizations often are in a particularly advantaged position to protect themselves from the repeal of regulations they support because teachers typically are the most powerful electoral force in school board elections. Thus, the people who collectively bargain with the teachers' unions concerning new regulations are the elected representatives of those teachers. These collective bargaining agreements prevent schools from achieving productive efficiency and keep low-performing teachers from being released. For example, the teachers' union in Milwaukee has made it almost impossible for a principal or a school district to fire bad teach-

ers. In a school system of more than 5,800 teachers, an average of only 1.5 teachers a year are terminated or forced to resign because of unsatisfactory evaluations.[10]

The Particular Problems Facing Inner-City Schools

There is general agreement among proponents and opponents of increased choice that the worst schooling takes place in the inner cities, and this schooling is particularly bad for low-income, minority children. Chubb and Moe argue that a major reason that inner-city schools are so bad is that these are the schools where bureaucratic regulation is greatest. Chubb and Moe construct their argument as follows. The inner cities of large metropolitan areas are "teeming with diverse, conflicting interests of political salience—class, race, ethnicity, language, religion—and their schools are plagued by problems so severe, wide-ranging, and deeply rooted in the urban socioeconomic structure that the situation appears out of control and problem filled in the extreme."[11] When a school is in such an environment, unions are likely to be stronger and more militant. They will demand more protections and use their political power to create procedures, rules, and regulations concerning how each particular problem will be solved. This generates "a vicious circle of problems and ineffectiveness."[12] Thus,

> where the problems are the greatest—in poor urban areas—and thus where strong leadership, professionalism, clear missions, and the other aspects of effective organization are most desperately needed, public authority will be exercised to ensure that schools are highly bureaucratized. There will be little discretion to allow for strong leadership. Teachers will be unable to participate as professionals. . . . Unions will insist on myriad formal protections. Principals will be hamstrung in their efforts to build a cooperative team. And so on.[13]

For Chubb and Moe, the fundamental obstacle to the effective organization of the urban public schools is not their problem-filled environment. It is democratic control.

In summary, proponents of school choice see public schools as having all the problems inherent in the monopolistic production of goods and services. To be effective, schools must be freed from the regulations that now make it difficult for a public school to have a clear mission and the autonomy to pursue that mission. Autonomy and competition can combine to solve the most serious problems in education.

WHY OPPONENTS EXPECT CHOICE TO
LOWER ACADEMIC OUTCOMES

Opponents of expanded school choice, particularly of choice that includes public funding for private schools, disagree strenuously with the conclusion reached by Chubb and Moe. To see why opponents of increasing choice argue that it will harm society's most disadvantaged children, we use the 1996 book *Who Chooses? Who Loses?* Edited by two opponents of private school choice, Richard Elmore and Bruce Fuller,[14] the book reviews past research on school choice and forecasts the most likely results of increased choice.

Elmore and Fuller suggest that the exacerbation of existing student segregation by race, social class, and cultural background is the most likely result of expanding school choice. This will occur because the value families place on education correlates highly with race, class, and cultural background. Elmore and Fuller then make the Sophie's choice argument. The separation of choosing and nonchoosing families into different schools will injure those children whose families are less supportive of education and less knowledgeable concerning choice alternatives. This will reduce the quality of classmates for those low-income and minority students who already are most vulnerable, and it will remove the most politically active parents from neighborhood schools and thereby reduce pressure on these schools to improve.

Another likely outcome of greater choice is that average educational outcomes will not improve. Elmore and Fuller believe that proposed choice policies pay too much attention to school governance and too little attention to reforming what goes on *inside* the classroom. Without reforming curriculum, pedagogy, and teacher quality, the competition that Chubb and Moe desire would be irrelevant. An additional problem with market competition among schools is that consumers of education are not sufficiently informed or rational to make value-maximizing choices. Information has always been the Achilles heel of choice programs, and without highly informed and highly motivated consumers, the competition among schools cannot improve them.[15]

Can choice programs overcome these problems? Elmore and Fuller argue that a good choice policy requires great attention to the details of the program. If policies do not include regulations or incentives that force integration, then segregation will increase. If choice programs only respond to the choices of parents who already are choosers, then the programs will not help children in families where the parents are unwilling or unable to choose. If choice programs do not consider ethnic and cultural

aspects of different students, then minorities are less likely to choose. If policies exempt private and charter schools from the Individuals with Disabilities Education Act (IDEA), then those schools will not develop programs that facilitate participation by students with disabilities. For Elmore and Fuller, the only acceptable choice programs require substantial government regulation to ensure that schools do not exclude those who are educationally disadvantaged.

Opponents of choice do not limit their attacks to those listed by Elmore and Fuller. They argue that any choice policy that includes sectarian schools will have four highly negative consequences. First, it would violate the constitutional barrier between church and state that has played a significant and largely positive role in America's political and social life.[16] Second, if a child's teachers and peers share the parents' religious and cultural prejudices, this will imperil the political tolerance and respect for diversity that are important in a multicultural democracy.

Opponents argue that a third problem with allowing private school choice is that private schools may not develop a key attribute of a liberal democratic citizen, autonomy. Autonomy has been an important goal of liberalism[17] since John Locke and is an important part of a liberal democratic education. Autonomy, along with tolerance and respect for diversity, is essential if America is to maintain and improve its democracy.[18] Allowing parents to shield their children from competing cultural ideas and values will inhibit their development of autonomy and leave them less able to assume the burdens of citizenship in a democratic society.

The fourth problem with private schools is that they will emphasize private values such as success in the competition for social advancement. In contrast, public schools will stress collective goods and collective values. Schools respond to their constituents. As parents and students who are interested in getting ahead in a competitive job market are the constituents of private schools, private schools will concentrate on teaching the necessary skills to achieve that goal. But the constituents of public schools are the entire citizenry, and they will require schools to teach the collective values that are important to the maintenance of community and democracy.

EMPIRICAL HYPOTHESES CONCERNING THE IMPACTS OF CHOICE

One of the best aspects of the choice debate is that it provides us with empirically testable propositions. Proponents make the following hypotheses:

1. Parents choose schools to obtain higher academic outcomes and to place their children in a particular type of school. We should be able to test this hypothesis by asking parents why they chose an alternative school and by comparing the schools they chose with those their children left behind.

2. Increased choice will increase parental involvement and student satisfaction. We can test this by observing whether parents who move their child from attendance-zone to choice schools become more involved and students become more satisfied.

3. Democratic control of schools leads to unclear missions and goals; reduces teamwork among administrators, faculty, and staff; and lessens teacher autonomy and satisfaction. We can test this hypothesis by examining the degree to which teachers and administrators agree on their school's central mission, checking the extent of cooperation in the pursuit of their mission, and asking teachers about their control over their classrooms and their satisfaction with their work.

4. Schools in a more competitive environment will be more productive and more efficient. We can test this in two ways. First, we can compare the cost and effectiveness of public schools in environments where there are many school districts with public schools in areas with few districts. Second, we can compare the costs and effectiveness of public and private schools.

5. Democratic control of schools reduces school productivity and increases costs. We can test this by determining if, after controlling for the effects of other variables, private schools adopt more effective teaching practices and achieve higher academic outcomes than public schools.

The opponents of school choice also have put forth testable propositions.

6. Choosing is difficult for low-income, low SES parents and non-English-speaking parents. We can test this by seeing if choosing parents have higher socioeconomic status and English-language proficiency than nonchoosing parents. We also should observe whether higher SES parents are better able to match their preferences with choice schools.

7. Increasing school choice will lead to increased segregation by socioeconomic status and by ethnicity. We can test this by comparing the segregation in school districts with high levels of choice and school districts with low levels of choice. We also can determine if choice schools are more segregated than the attendance-zone schools in the same district.

8. Parents who are not African Americans will choose schools to avoid

African Americans. We can test this by comparing the percentages of African American students in the school a student left and the school the student chose.

9. Students in private schools will show less support for democratic norms, political tolerance, and concern for the common good. We can test this by comparing student attitudes and behaviors in public and private schools.

10. Increasing school choice will harm the most disadvantaged students. We can test this by looking at the test scores of students in districts with high and low levels of choice. If the test scores of the students in the lowest quartile are lower in districts with substantial choice than in districts with little choice, then we can conclude that choice is harming the most disadvantaged students.

11. The differences in the educational outcomes of public and private schools are the result of differences in the resources of students, parents, peers, and schools rather than whether the school is public or private. We can test this by controlling statistically for the differences in resources.

What does existing research tell us about the validity of each set of claims?

SCHOOL CHOICE AND SEGREGATION

Many of the most important services people receive from their government (police protection, water and sewage, transportation, and education) are financed by local taxes, and local governments decide how much of each service citizens will receive. In most states, the single largest local expenditure is elementary and secondary education. Studies of how families choose their residence indicate that the quality of local schools is an important influence on the choice of residence for about half of all families whose children attend public schools.[19] As their income rises, parents demand more education for their children.[20] This means that wealthier families tend to choose houses in school districts where per capita spending for public schools is higher and poorer families tend to choose residences in districts where that spending is lower. Because income and ethnicity are highly correlated, sorting students by the price of their homes segregates them by race and ethnicity. This sorting process has been exacerbated by racially motivated real estate and home mortgage practices and by the preference of most ethnic groups to locate in areas where the percent-

age of African Americans is small. In short, the current system of school choice through residence choice has developed a system of highly segregated public schools that clusters disadvantaged students in the same schools and does not provide them with an easily available opportunity to escape.

When we examine the likely impacts of alternative choice policies on ethnic and income sorting, it is important to keep in mind that the current practices have created a system of highly segregated schools. Gary Orfield and John T. Yun of Harvard University's Civil Rights Project have found that since 1986 the percentage of blacks in schools with a majority of whites has declined from 43 percent to 35 percent and the percentage of African Americans in schools that are over 90 percent minority has increased slightly from 32.5 percent to 35 percent. The trend in the segregation of Hispanics is even more pronounced and has been going on for a longer time. In 1970, the average Latino student attended a school where 43.8 percent of the students were non-Hispanic whites. By 1996, that percentage had dropped to 29.9 percent.[21] Segregation in the Northeast is particularly pronounced; over half of all black students attend schools that are 90 percent or more minority students.[22] Recent research concerning residential choice and schools indicates that a primary reason that many families move to the suburbs or send their children to private schools is to avoid schools with large numbers of African American students.[23]

Segregation by income is also very high, and this reinforces the racial and ethnic segregation. Orfield and Yun found that African American and Hispanic students were eleven times as likely to attend schools with concentrated poverty. The correlation between the percent black and Hispanic in a school and the percentage of students eligible for a free lunch is 0.66.[24] Because the income difference between the richest and poorest families in America has increased since 1996, it is likely that school segregation by income is increasing.

How will increasing school choice affect segregation by income and ethnicity? We saw above that both the proponents and opponents of choice have hypotheses concerning who chooses, why they choose, and the effects of choice on segregation. There are three ways that we can study these hypotheses. We can compare the patterns of segregation in areas with high and low levels of choice; we can compare the schools students choose with those they leave behind; and we can ask families why they chose or did not choose an alternative to their neighborhood school.

Because the dominant means of school choice is residential choice, we can explore how increasing the opportunity of individuals to choose

alternative school districts affects segregation. Harvard economist Carolyn Hoxby studied the effects of having multiple school districts in a metropolitan area. She reasoned that having many school districts makes it easier for families to exercise school choice by changing districts. Hoxby found that having more school districts did increase ethnic and income segregation, but this effect was small.[25]

Do public choice programs increase or decrease segregation? Magnet schools were originally developed to decrease segregation in metropolitan areas, but to a large degree they have been unsuccessful. Magnet schools nationwide are equally as segregated as neighborhood schools in the same school district.[26] However, magnet schools may have had a small effect on preventing further segregation in school districts.[27] Because charter schools are so new, very little data exist concerning their impact on segregation, but the available data indicate that charter schools are slightly less segregated than other public schools.[28] Studies of open enrollment programs indicate that while white and higher socioeconomic status families participate at higher levels than nonwhite and lower socioeconomic status families, the net effect of these programs on income and ethnic segregation is negligible. For example, a study of open enrollment programs in Massachusetts found that they slightly increased the percent minority in both the sending and receiving districts.[29]

When we look at voucher programs outside the United States, the effects of choice on segregation are unambiguous. Studies in Chile, France, Great Britain, New Zealand, and the Netherlands all indicate that vouchers increase ethnic and socioeconomic segregation.[30] Regardless of the country, whites tend to avoid schools populated predominantly by people of color. Because religion is correlated with ethnicity and social class, allowing sectarian schools to receive public funds increased both ethnic and religious sorting. In all of these countries the size of vouchers is unrelated to family income, and the voucher policies do not attempt to use incentives or regulations to achieve income and ethnic balance.

In the United States there are only two publicly funded voucher programs that have been in place for a sufficient length of time to study their impacts on segregation. These programs are in Milwaukee, Wisconsin, and Cleveland, Ohio. Because both programs limited participation in the voucher program to low-income students, neither program increased socioeconomic segregation. And, except for schools specifically designed to attract a particular minority ethnic group, the schools in Milwaukee and Cleveland did not increase ethnic segregation. The numerous privately funded voucher programs around the United States also limit financial assistance to either low-income families or to families in low-income

areas, and, because of this, they have not increased segregation by income or ethnicity.[31]

Although current school choice programs in the United States have not significantly increased ethnic and income segregation, they may sort students and families in other ways. The key hypothesis in the Sophie's choice argument is that choice will sort students such that high-performing children attend choice schools while low-performing children will remain behind in their neighborhood schools. This sorting harms the low-performing students because the quality of one's peer group matters in the learning process. The sorting process also will place active and involved parents in choice schools, and this will deprive neighborhood schools in low-income and minority neighborhoods of the parents who are most likely to pressure policymakers for resources necessary to improve the schools. We tested these hypotheses by examining the differences between choosing and nonchoosing students and families.

San Antonio, Texas, provided a natural laboratory for answering many questions concerning public and private school choice programs. In 1992 the privately funded Children's Educational Opportunity (CEO) program offered partial scholarships to low-income children in grades 1–8 who wished to attend a private school or a public school in another district. Only students who resided in the San Antonio metropolitan area and qualified for free or reduced-price lunches were eligible. The scholarships covered approximately half of a school's tuition up to a maximum of $750. CEO provided 936 students with scholarships for the 1992–1993 school year. Half of the scholarships went to families whose children attended public schools in the previous year and half went to families whose children already were enrolled in private schools. CEO selected both sets of recipients on a first-come, first-chosen basis. Of the total enrollees, approximately 60 percent enrolled in Catholic schools, 30 percent in Protestant schools, 9 percent in other denominational schools, and 1 percent in nonsectarian schools. None chose public schools outside their home district.

At the same time that CEO was introducing its scholarship program, the San Antonio Independent School District (SAISD) had an ongoing public choice program, called the multilingual program. The multilingual program was a continuous seven-year curriculum of intensive foreign-language instruction beginning in the sixth grade. Students applied in the fifth grade and gained admission based on superior academic performance as evidenced in test scores, grades, and teacher recommendations. The program included instruction in the same essential elements required of all Texas public schools as well as language enrichment through honors

classes, accelerated pacing, and individualized instruction. For the 1992–1993 school year, SAISD admitted 675 students. Because of space limitations, the district had to reject almost 300 students who met the requirements and applied to the program.

The authors of this book requested permission to evaluate these choice programs, and both the CEO directors and the San Antonio Independent School District granted us the necessary access to do the evaluations. The San Antonio study included five sets of students and their families: (1) CEO participants who used the scholarship to switch from a public to a private school, (2) CEO participants who were in private schools the year prior to receiving the scholarship and remained in private schools, (3) participants in the SAISD multilingual program, (4) students who applied to the multilingual program and met the eligibility requirements but were rejected because of space limitations, and (5) a random sample of SAISD students in grades 1 through 8 who enrolled in their neighborhood schools and who did not apply to any choice program. We label the students and families of the first four groups "choosers" and the students and families in the fifth group "nonchoosers."

To investigate differences among the five groups of families we sent mail questionnaires in both English and Spanish to each family in the four choosing groups and conducted phone interviews with the sample of non-choosing families. The survey asked parents for standard socioeconomic and demographic information as well as their opinions regarding the children's educational experiences, the extent of their involvement in their children's education, and the importance of education relative to other goals. In addition, the survey asked choosing parents what factors were most important in the decision to have their children leave the neighborhood public school. The most frequently mentioned reason for public and private choosers was the quality of the alternative school. The second most important variable for private school choosers was school safety. For multilingual school choosers, the second most important factor was the special language program. For parents who moved their child from a public to a private school, 62 percent named frustration with the child's previous public school as a very important consideration in their decision. These findings correspond closely with results from other choice programs.

Do choice programs skim higher socioeconomic status families and more active and involved parents from attendance-zone schools? Yes. Looking at the San Antonio choice programs we can see substantial differences between choosing and nonchoosing families. Table 2.1 shows these differences. The first and second columns in Table 2.1 show that even

among these predominantly low-income families, parents that send their children to choice schools are more likely to be better educated, are more likely to be employed, and are less likely to be on federal assistance programs than parents who do not attempt to enroll their children in choice schools. Choosing parents also have higher educational expectations for their children and attend church on a more regular basis. One other characteristic of choosing families stands out: they tend to have fewer children.

Did the choice programs accentuate segregation by income and ethnicity in San Antonio? Very slightly. Table 2.1 shows that families whose

Table 2.1. Mean Scores for Characteristics of Nonchoosers, All Choosers, Public Choosers, and Private Choosers[a]

Variables	Non-choosers	All Choosers	Public Choosers	Private Choosers
Demographic characteristics				
Female parent education	2.82	4.15***	3.74	4.32***
Male parent education	2.89	4.11***	3.81	4.24***
Family income	4.22	4.53***	4.71	4.45
Female parent employment	.35	.48***	.57	.45***
Male parent employment	.73	.89***	.80	.80
Receiving federal assistance	.35	.15***	.16	.15
Two-parent family	.48	.61***	.61	.61
Number of children	3.51	2.92***	3.00	2.90
Gender of student	1.38	1.56***	1.65	1.53
Anglo	.03	.14***	.06	.18***
Latino	.82	.71***	.73	.71
African American	.10	.08	.14	.06***
Family values				
Educational expectation	3.47	4.43***	4.43	4.43
Importance of religion	1.58	1.90***	1.80	1.95***
Importance of ethnic values	1.50	1.67***	1.60	1.70**
Religious attendance	2.41	2.87***	2.46	3.03***
Parental involvement in education				
Help at home with homework	5.43	7.29***	5.23	8.15***
Contacts with school	4.01	4.80***	3.05	5.53***
Activity in child's school	1.85	2.77***	1.98	3.09***
Child's education				
Child's test scores	62.10	108.83***	109.60	93.14***
Evaluation of past school	3.18	3.08***	3.44	2.33[b]
N	1,375	1,311	433	878

[a] Comparisons are between Nonchoosers and Choosers, and between Public School Choosers and Private School Choosers.

[b] Includes only those CEO families who moved from public to private schools ($N = 262$).

** p < .01 (one-tailed test).

*** p < .001 (one-tailed test).

children attend the SAISD multilingual program have the highest incomes and children in SAISD neighborhood schools have the lowest incomes. In all choosing groups, non-Hispanic whites were overrepresented and Hispanics were underrepresented. Among private choosers, African Americans were slightly underrepresented. Once we controlled statistically for parent education, however, there were no significant differences in ethnic group participation, but given the overwhelming percentage of students in both public and private schools that are Hispanic, it was unlikely that ethnic segregation could have increased.

Did the San Antonio choice programs skim the better students from their neighborhood schools? Again the answer is yes. Students in choice programs had higher achievement test scores before entering the program than did nonchoosing students. The average score for nonchoosing students in SAISD schools was the 27th percentile in both math and reading. In sharp contrast, students who were accepted by the SAISD multilingual program scored in the 56th percentile for math and the 57th percentile for reading! The students who applied to the multilingual program but were rejected averaged the 48th percentile in math and the 46th in reading. Children who used the CEO private scholarship to move from a public to a private school averaged the 44th and 48th percentiles on math and reading in the year prior to their move. Overall, the average test scores of children in all choosing groups were more than a full standard deviation higher than the average scores of children in nonchoosing families!

Large-scale surveys of choosing and nonchoosing parents allow us to identify those parent and student characteristics that best predict choosing behavior. In our San Antonio research we used probit regression, a technique that is appropriate when predicting an individual's choice between two alternatives, to discover those characteristics. Our results showed that mother's education was the most important predictor of who would choose an alternative to attendance-zone schools. Parents' educational expectation for their child also was an important variable in the choice process. Two other variables influenced the decision to apply to the SAISD multilingual program, the child's standardized test scores and the amount of parent involvement in the child's education at home. The most important variables in predicting whether a family would apply for a CEO scholarship included higher church attendance and parental dissatisfaction with the child's previous public school. While only 57 percent of nonchoosing families and 64 percent of multilingual families reported attending church at least once a week, 76 percent of families who moved their child from a public to a private school and 85 percent of families whose child already was in a private school reported weekly church atten-

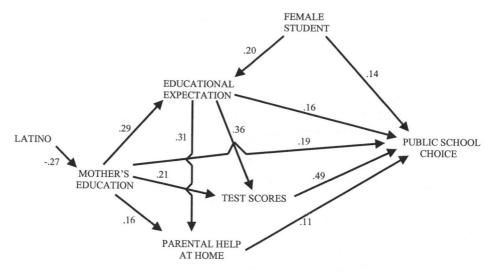

Figure 2.1. Path Diagram of the Decision to Choose a Public Multilingual School.
SOURCE: Valerie Martinez et al., "The Consequences of School Choice: Who Leaves and
Who Stays in the Inner City," *Social Science Quarterly* (1995).

dance. Similarly, while 81 percent of nonchoosing and 90 percent of multilingual families gave their previous public school either an A or a B for
its overall performance, only 43 percent of families who moved their child
from a public to a private school evaluated their previous public school
that highly.

We can get a visual representation of the variables that affect choosing by using another type of multivariate statistical technique, path analysis. Figure 2.1 shows the path diagram for public school choosers, and
Figure 2.2 shows the diagram for private school choosers. These figures
show that public and private choosers have a lot in common. For both programs, mother's education has a positive effect on parental expectations
about their children's future education, test scores, parental help at home,
and the likelihood that the child will attend a choice school. When a child's
mother has more education she appears to be more willing to search out
the best educational alternative for her children, and she is more able to
seek out information on alternatives to neighborhood schools. More educated mothers are more likely to expect their children to attend college,
and they are more willing and able to help their children achieve these
educational goals by helping their children with schoolwork at home
(multilingual school choosers) and by participating in activities at their
children's schools (private school choosers). Children of more educated

mothers have higher test scores, a factor that was important in applying
to the multilingual program. In San Antonio, Latina mothers tend to have
significantly less education, and, for that reason, Latinos are less likely to
participate in either public or private school choice.

Are the San Antonio results representative of other choice programs?
Very much so. Research on magnet schools, charter schools, interdistrict
open-enrollment public choice, private voucher programs, and publicly
funded voucher programs finds that choosing parents and their children
will have the characteristics that encourage educational involvement by
parents and educational achievement by students.[32]

How do the above findings fit with the projections of the opponents
and proponents of choice? Given the socioeconomic characteristics of
choosers, it seems clear that low-income and less educated families have
difficulty in exercising choice. It seems equally clear from evidence of
voucher programs outside the United States that unrestricted voucher
programs lead to greater ethnic and socioeconomic segregation. Past research also indicates that non–African Americans choose their schools
to reduce the percentage of their children's classmates who are black. At
the same time, the research also indicates that parents who choose are
doing so largely for reasons related to academic excellence. When parents
use open enrollment opportunities to change schools they almost always

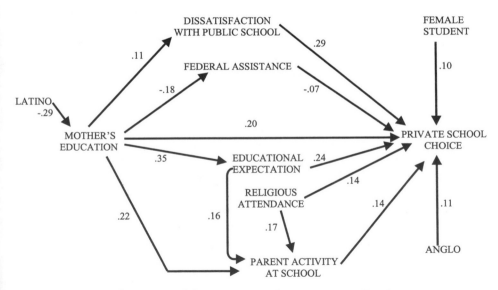

Figure 2.2. Path Diagram of the Decision to Choose a Private School. SOURCE:
Martinez et al., "The Consequences of School Choice."

choose a school with a lower student-teacher ratio, higher standardized test scores, a higher percentage of graduates entering college, and higher per capita spending than the school left behind. When parents choose magnet, thematic, or private schools they look for schools that appear safe and schools with a clear academic program.

Before we decide that increasing choice must lead to skimming and segregation, it is useful to compare the skimming of the school choice programs in the San Antonio inner city with the skimming that occurs through residential choice. When we compared choosing families in the inner city with families who had exercised choice by moving to the suburbs, we found that the average income and education of parents in the suburbs are much higher than those of either multilingual or CEO families. We also found that the percentages of CEO and multilingual families who were from minority ethnic groups are much higher than the percentage minority in suburban schools. In addition, the average test scores of suburban children are equal to those of the multilingual students and higher than the CEO private school choosers. In other words, residential choice was much more likely than either the CEO or multilingual program to segregate students and families.

Although many choice programs have increased segregation between high- and low-achieving students and segregation between more- and less-involved parents, these are not necessary outcomes. One way to prevent choice programs from increasing segregation is to use incentives and regulations that make sorting by income, ethnicity, and student ability less likely. In his analysis of the effects of magnet schools on ethnic segregation in Montgomery County, Maryland, Jeffrey Henig argued that whether school choice increased segregation depended on the design of the program. "[I]t is in large measure the institutional framework—the specific design of the choice program and the will and capacity of the educational bureaucracy to implement its provisions—that determines whether choice will complement or confound the pursuit of racial integration."[33] Henig refers to programs that use incentives and regulations to reduce sorting as "managed choice." The tools of managed choice include limiting transfers to choice schools to only those transfers that improve racial balance and choosing students by lottery rather than on the basis of student ability.

There are three key issues in designing an effective managed choice policy. A legal issue concerns whether approaches to managed choice that attempt to balance student bodies by using ethnicity or family income in admissions decisions can withstand challenges on grounds of impermissible discrimination. We explore this concern in Chapter 4. A political issue concerns whether managed choice policies that include restraints on

ethnic and income segregation could gain approval by state legislatures and local school boards. We explore that issue in Chapter 8. The third issue concerns understanding why some parents choose and others do not. We need to know a good deal more about the process of choice to design programs that lead to integration rather than segregation. It is to this issue that we now turn.

How Do Parents Choose?

School choice is not a behavior that occurs in a single moment of time, as does the decision to purchase a refrigerator. Rather, choosing behavior is related to cultural predispositions and ways of looking at the world. Some parents see themselves as active consumers of education while others see their role as passive participants in an educational process where teachers, principals, and other experts decide what schools and classes are best for their child. To obtain better information about this decision process, members of our San Antonio research team conducted focus group sessions with parents of children in public neighborhood schools, in the multilingual program, and in the CEO program. We also conducted focus groups with parents of students who dropped out of their choice schools and returned to attendance-zone schools and with nonchoosing parents. We combined these data with in-depth interviews by Amy Stuart Wells of African American families in the St. Louis inner city and with Robert Bulman's lengthy interviews with families in two San Francisco suburbs.[34] Taken together the three sets of interviews provided substantial insight into the cultural factors that lead families to become choosers and into the decision to drop out of choice schools and return to neighborhood schools.

Both Wells and Bulman use the concepts of "habitus" and "cultural capital" to help explain why some families engage in choice and others do not. Habitus is a system of lasting predispositions or internalized understandings that people use to navigate the social world and to take action within it.[35] Cultural capital consists of the skills and resources that individuals acquire through school and family within a habitus. Habitus limits the goals an individual can pursue, and the person deploys her cultural capital to achieve the goals she selects from the available set.[36] The importance of habitus and cultural capital is that even if extensive school choice is available and parents have the money, time, and information to exercise choice, they still may not become choosers. They will remain nonchoosers because their way of looking at the world (their habitus) precludes them from seeing that school choice is an avenue open to them, and because

their cultural capital does not include skills necessary to make choices among schools.

The San Antonio, St. Louis, and San Francisco interviews all found that a family was more likely to exercise choice if one of the parents had attended a choice school. That experience created a habitus in which adults see themselves as consumers of educational services rather than as passive targets of bureaucratic expertise. Past experience in choice schools also helped to create the cultural capital necessary for parents to become actively involved in their children's education. Wells found that the African American parents whose children attended suburban public schools were far more attentive to their children's education, were more achievement oriented, assertive, and demanding. They perceived themselves as quite capable of making educational choices and saw this as part of their parental role.[37] Wells also found that students who transferred to the suburban schools adopted the achievement orientation of their parents and were far less bound by the habitus of inner-city, minority life.

Our interviews with San Antonio parents discovered similar patterns. Whether selecting a private or public choice school, choosing parents tended to be aggressively involved in their child's education. These parents frequently contacted their child's school and teachers to ensure that the schools were responding to the needs of their child. In addition, children in choosing families who remained in their choice schools often were highly involved in the choice decision.[38] In sharp contrast, parents who did not consider alternatives to their neighborhood schools did not see education as a "commodity" over which they could exercise power as consumers. Nonchoosing parents often expressed the idea that a teacher knows better than the parent what type of school is best for the child. All of these factors led to a habitus that did not include high levels of parental involvement in educational choices.

While our research team and that of Amy Stuart Wells interviewed low-income, largely minority families, Bulman interviewed parents in middle- and upper-class suburbs of San Francisco. Despite these demographic differences, Bulman's results were quite similar to those found in St. Louis and San Antonio. Bulman found that "nonchoosing" parents typically gave a cursory investigation of public schools in various neighborhoods before moving into their current residence. After the move these parents rarely sought out information about either their child's public school or about alternatives that might be available. This created a situation where most nonchoosers had highly inaccurate information about their child's public school.

The cost of private schools was a major issue in both San Antonio

and San Francisco. The families that originally received a CEO scholarship but did not enroll their child in the school named the cost of the school not covered by the scholarship as the primary obstacle to their child's enrollment. In San Francisco, even though most nonchoosing parents could afford private schools, parents often mentioned that the difference between public and private schools was not worth the cost of private schools.

Perhaps the most interesting families were those whose child enrolled in a choice school and then returned to the neighborhood school. Both Wells's study in St. Louis and our study of San Antonio included in-depth interviews with these parents and students. Wells found that the African American parents of students who initially transferred from inner-city to suburban schools and then returned to their inner-city school were less involved in their children's education and were less supportive than were the parents of transferring students who remained in the suburban schools. More important, Wells believed that the returning students were more bound by the habitus of the inner city. Some of these students felt "pushed out" by the suburban schools either through the schools' disciplinary process or through poor grades, but more students returned to their neighborhood school because of their lack of comfort in predominantly white suburban schools.[39] Their inability to fit in with the white culture led them to return to the more comfortable surroundings of their inner-city schools.

The San Antonio picture of returning students was somewhat different in that the ethnic makeup of the neighborhood, multilingual, and private schools did not differ significantly. Nevertheless, both the multilingual schools and the CEO program had high dropout rates. More than 20 percent of the multilingual students dropped out in their first year; one-third left before the end of the third year. Only one-third of the multilingual students actually stayed in the program through high school graduation. Dropouts were also high in the CEO private choice program. Among families who used the CEO scholarship to transfer from public to private schools, the student dropout rate over the three-year period was 50 percent. CEO students were most likely to withdraw from the program either during their first year or when they moved from middle school to high school.

Parents of students who dropped out of the multilingual program during their first year indicated that the school generally initiated the dropout decision. Typically, the teacher would tell the student or her parents that she was unlikely to be successful in the program, and the teacher then encouraged the student to take the less demanding curriculum of her

neighborhood school. Another cause of dropping out was the absence of close friends in the multilingual school. A student whose closest friend remained in attendance-zone schools was more than twice as likely to return to the neighborhood school as a student whose closest friend attended the multilingual school.

Our focus groups found that parents whose child remained in the CEO program were products of sectarian private schools and they typically made the decision to send their child to religious school either before or shortly after the child was born. In contrast, parents of students who dropped out rarely had private school experience. Parents who removed their child from the CEO program cited the cost of tuition and fees and travel difficulties as the most important reasons for their decision. Many parents who moved their child from a public to a private school made their decision to enter the CEO program in response to frustration with public schools. For the parents of students who returned to their public schools, the sacrifice of consumer goods that they had to forego plus the costs of transportation became greater than the benefits they believed their child received in the private school. Unlike the students who dropped out of the public school choice programs, however, no CEO parents whom we interviewed indicated that their child was uncomfortable in the private schools or that their child lacked friends there. In addition, there was no evidence that a teacher had encouraged a family to take its child out of the private school.

In summary, the in-depth interviews reported above suggest that several variables are important in the choosing decision, but the two most important are whether at least one of the parents attended a choice school and whether the parents see themselves as active consumers of education. The first of these factors tells us whether or not the habitus of a family includes a perception of parents as consumers of education. The second indicates whether or not parents perceive themselves as having the necessary skills and resources to make a good decision about their child's school. When families were deciding whether to remain in or drop out of a choice program, the child played a major role in the decision. If the child had been involved in the original decision, had the same ambitions as the parents, and had close friends in the choice school, then the family was likely to remain in the program.

Policy Implications

The above research provides a picture of the choice process that has substantial implications for the design of public policy. The in-depth inter-

views indicate that because many parents have a habitus of nonchoosing, school policies should place the burden of recruiting students on schools rather than on parents. Public policies must provide incentives for schools to encourage parents to think of education as a consumer good rather than a government service guided by education experts. Policies also should encourage schools to seek out students from families where parents are likely to think of themselves as unable to make good choices about the schools their children should attend or where the parents are likely to be unaware of the opportunity. While information centers and other outreach efforts may be useful in spreading the word about choice programs, the information may only be useful once the parents have been convinced by advertising that choice is possible and that they can choose effectively.

The experience of minority students who moved to predominantly white schools in suburban St. Louis, as well as the experiences of students in San Antonio's multilingual program, indicates that choice schools must work hard to integrate students into the initial choice decision and then to ensure that they have sufficient academic and nonacademic support services to prevent them from dropping out.

The multivariate analyses of who chooses also have clear policy implications. Because entrance into the San Antonio multilingual program was based on past academic achievement, the SAISD public choice program took the very best students out of their attendance-zone schools. A policy could reduce skimming by limiting the use of standardized test scores in the admissions process, by using a lottery to determine admission, and by setting quotas for the number of students who must come from low-income families. Because CEO gave scholarships to low-income students on a first-come, first-accepted basis and these scholarships could be used in religious schools, families who attended churches associated with religious schools were far more likely to learn about the CEO program and to apply early enough to obtain a scholarship. Families who were not religious or who did not attend churches associated with a parochial school were less likely to know about the program. This caused sorting among students on the basis of their religion and their religiosity. Once again, a lottery method of admitting students would help alleviate this problem. Finally, because the CEO vouchers covered only one-half of the private school tuition and none of the fees, few of San Antonio's very poor families participated in the program, and those that did tended to drop out.

DO PRIVATE SCHOOLS TEACH PUBLIC VALUES?

Critics of private school choice hypothesize that public subsidies for private schools create a substantial threat to democratic government. The threat is that students will fail to learn democratic norms and tolerance, and they will learn to pursue private rather than public values. But without tolerance, multicultural societies cannot maintain democracy and peace.[40] Without a concern for the common good, it will be impossible to overcome the free-rider problem that is inherent in the production of the common good.

Unfortunately for democracy, intolerance seems more instinctive than tolerance. The effortless way that people acquire negative stereotypes and attribute danger to those who are stereotyped suggests that, in the absence of strong efforts to prevent it, intolerance is a natural and universal development.[41] How can liberal democracies discourage this process? It turns out that education is the best antidote to intolerance.[42] And, in America, public schools have been considered *the* critical location for learning political tolerance.[43] Public schools, the argument goes, are the single institution that brings together citizens of different ethnicity, culture, gender, socioeconomic status, and conception of the collective good. Public schools provide the diversity of friendships and acquaintances through which students realize that having a different worldview or culture does not necessarily make a person evil or dangerous.[44]

Opponents of private school choice are especially critical of fundamentalist Christian schools.[45] David Blacker's 1998 article "Fanaticism and Schooling in the Democratic State" maintains that fanatics should not be allowed to establish schools or to home school their children. Who are the fanatics? They are members of right-wing militias and some Christian fundamentalist sects. Blacker claims that members of these groups should not control the education of a child because they have worldviews that are so comprehensive and single-minded that students will not learn to tolerate and respect alternative worldviews, religions, and cultures.[46] Despite the frequency with which their advocates assert the superiority of public schools, little research has examined whether public schools do a better job than private schools in engendering political tolerance.[47] The only direct empirical research on this issue is that by R. Kenneth Godwin and his colleagues, who tested the model of tolerance development implicit in the writings of those who see private schools as inferior educators of democratic citizens. Figure 2.3 presents that model. Its premise is that public schools, by virtue of their diversity, reduce the threat that students feel from those who are different. Diverse public schools also encourage re-

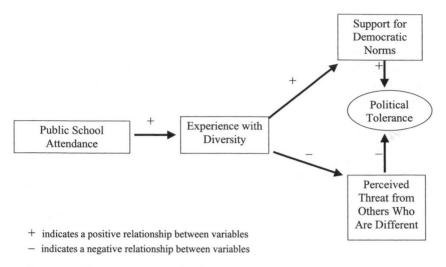

Figure 2.3. The Development of Tolerance by Public Schools.

spect for alternative cultures, religions, and worldviews, and this fosters support for democratic norms. Because a low perception of threat and a high appreciation for democratic norms lead to political tolerance, students in public schools should develop greater tolerance than students in private schools.

To test the above model, a research team surveyed more than two thousand students in eighth grade social studies classes in public and private schools in New York City and Fort Worth, Texas.[48] The research team placed schools and their students into three categories: public, nonevangelical private, and evangelical private. To obtain measures of the variables in the above model, students completed a written questionnaire previously shown to accurately measure an individual's perception of threats from others, support for democratic norms, and political tolerance.[49] Students first chose the political group that they liked least from among the American Nazis, the Ku Klux Klan, advocates for the rights of women, advocates for the rights of people of color, Christian fundamentalists, atheists, advocates of abortion rights, and opponents of abortion rights.[50] Students also had the option of selecting a group that was not on the list. Students then indicated their willingness to allow members of their least-liked group to make public speeches, to hold public demonstrations, and to teach in public schools; and the students recorded whether they believed that the government should tap the phones of group members and outlaw the group. The questionnaire measured perceived threat by the

degree to which students believed their least-liked group was dangerous, bad, untrustworthy, and violent. The survey also included items that measured a student's support for such democratic norms as free speech.[51] Because other factors might affect a student's tolerance, the survey contained questions concerning parents' income, education, religion, and religiosity, as well as the student's gender, current grades, interest in politics, and self-esteem. To measure the interethnic climate in a school, the questionnaire asked students to indicate their level of agreement with two statements: "Students make friends with students of other racial and ethnic groups at my current school" and "Fights often occur between different racial and ethnic groups at my current school." Diversity was measured by subtracting from 100 the percentage of the student population who were members of the largest ethnic group in the student's classroom. For example, if a classroom is 80 percent Hispanic, the diversity score would be 20. If the classroom is 49 percent Hispanic and no other ethnic group was as large, the diversity score would be 51.

The greatest obstacle to comparing different types of schools is the self-selection of students into those schools. Suppose we observe differences in the levels of tolerance between public and private school students. How can we determine if those differences are the product of the school or are the result of what students learned elsewhere? Many of the same factors that lead parents to choose private schools probably affect the tolerance they teach their children. Less tolerant parents might choose a specific private school because they expect the school to instruct students that *only* the parents' worldview is legitimate. More tolerant parents might choose a public school because they want their child to learn to appreciate diversity by interacting with students whose worldviews differ from their own. If a statistical analysis does not correct for the self-selection of families into a particular type of school, then it will overestimate the impact of schools on tolerance.[52] Fortunately, statistical techniques allow the separation of family and school effects and minimize the impact of selection bias.[53]

The results of the above research showed that students in private schools have greater knowledge about American institutions and American politics, and students in evangelical schools have the highest levels of political knowledge. These differences are statistically significant and remain even after controlling for socioeconomic status and selection bias.[54] With respect to support for democratic norms, nonevangelical private schools have a stronger positive impact on their students than do either public schools or evangelical private schools. The comparison between public and evangelical school students, however, shows no difference be-

tween the two groups' support for democratic norms. The most important research finding was that the type of schools students attend is unrelated to their level of political tolerance.

One reason that public schools may not be more effective in teaching tolerance is that increasing diversity within a school does not increase political tolerance or support for democratic norms, and it does not reduce the threat students perceive from their least-liked group. Having friends of a different ethnic group does increase support for democratic norms, but students in private schools tend to have more interethnic friendships than students in public schools.

What do the above findings mean for the teaching of democratic values? Two conclusions seem clear. First, public schools currently are not outperforming private schools when it comes to teaching the attitudes and values central to democratic citizenship. Second, simply increasing ethnic diversity within a classroom does not increase tolerance or support for democratic norms. In fact, greater diversity in schools tends to increase the threat students perceive from their least-liked group. Although ethnic diversity does not increase support for democratic norms, interethnic friendships do have that effect. The critical question is: how can schools encourage interethnic friendships?

Although the private schools in this study are, on average, less ethnically diverse than the public schools, private school students report a higher incidence of interethnic friendships at their schools. This finding is consistent with past research.[55] Perhaps when parents and students voluntarily choose a school, they have greater confidence that other parents and students share their values. These shared values may encourage interethnic friendships. For example, parents and students who choose a religious school expect that other students at the school come from homes that stress values similar to their own. This expectation may help students overcome racial stereotypes. If the voluntary character of integration is important, then an examination of magnet, thematic, and charter schools should find greater numbers of interethnic friendships and greater student support for democratic norms than occur in attendance-zone schools. For similar reasons, research at the high school level should investigate whether students who participate in such ethnically diverse extracurricular activities as band, athletics, and theater have more interethnic friendships and, if so, whether this increases their support for democratic values.

Are opponents of choice correct in hypothesizing that students who attend private schools will learn to maximize their own private values and neglect the common good? Jonathan Kozol stated this expectation most succinctly: "[Choice] will fragmentize ambition, so that the individual

parent will be forced to claw and scramble for the good of her kid, and her kid only, at whatever cost to everybody else."[56] To our knowledge there has been only a single published article testing this hypothesis, that of Jay Greene.[57] Using data from the National Educational Longitudinal Study (NELS) of 1992, Greene studied both attitudinal and behavioral measures of concern for the common good. High school students were asked how important it is to help others and how important it is to participate in volunteer activities. With respect to the first question, 36.2 percent of private school students responded that it was very important to help others and 47.2 percent thought it was very important to do volunteer work. The corresponding figures for public school students were 32.6 percent and 34.8 percent. These differences were statistically significant, and they remained so after controls for the socioeconomic characteristics of the students. Similarly, when these students were asked if they had done volunteer work in the past two years, 63.2 percent of private school students reported having done so compared to only 45.6 percent of public school students.[58]

We attempted to replicate the NELS data on volunteer activity in our study of eighth-grade students in New York and Texas. We found that students in private schools were 21 percent more likely to report that they participated in volunteer activities than were students in public schools; and among those students who did volunteer, private school students spent almost 50 percent more time in the activity than did public school students.

It would appear, therefore, that critics of private school choice are incorrect in their expectation that public schools will do better than private schools in teaching tolerance and respect for the common good. To the extent that different types of schools affect democratic citizenship, the small differences we observed favor private schools. Of course, it is possible that the use of behavioral measures of tolerance might yield different results. There may be a huge gap between paper-and-pencil measures of tolerance and the actual behavior required of democratic citizens. In addition, it may be that the greater ethnic diversity of public high schools will facilitate interethnic friendships in extracurricular activities and these friendships will lead to increased tolerance. Nevertheless, the above findings suggest that private schools do a slightly better job of encouraging interethnic friendships and developing support for democratic norms. Private school students are more likely than public school students to think volunteering for the common good is important, to volunteer for community service, and to volunteer for more hours.

THE EFFECTS OF CHOICE ON
TEACHERS AND PRINCIPALS

The proponents of choice argue that increasing school choice will lead to more effective schools. To test this hypothesis Chubb and Moe used a large national database, High School and Beyond (HSB).[59] The HSB database is a random sample of approximately one thousand public and private high schools and seventy thousand students. The database includes changes in student scores from the tenth to the twelfth grade; whether students graduated from high school, attended college, and graduated from college; and the wages of students after they finished school. These data were then supplemented by a survey of the principals, teachers, and staff members in approximately half of the original HSB schools.[60] The database also includes the characteristics of the school district in which a high school was located.

Chubb and Moe measured school performance by computing the average change in schools on the standardized tests from the tenth to the twelfth grades and then selecting the schools in the top and bottom quartiles. They hypothesized that schools in which students had greater test score changes would have: (1) fewer bureaucratic constraints, (2) clearer missions and goals, (3) principals with greater control over the school's affairs and commitment to teaching, (4) more professional teachers who had more autonomy in the classroom, and (5) a stronger sense of community and harmony among the principal, faculty, and staff.[61] Chubb and Moe found substantial support for these hypotheses, and they found that private schools were much more likely to have the attributes of effective schools.

To what degree have the findings of Chubb and Moe been replicated by other researchers? Several scholars have used different theoretical frameworks to study the HSB data. Education sociologist Jane Hannaway of the Urban Institute used the perspective of organizational sociology to compare levels of autonomy for principals and teachers in public and Catholic schools and to examine the degree to which environmental variables affected the management practices in the two types of schools.[62] She found that Catholic school principals and teachers had significantly higher levels of autonomy than did public school teachers. This difference remained large even after Hannaway statistically controlled for the socioeconomic status of the students, size of school, level of urbanization, and student test performance. In fact, the levels of autonomy for principals in public and Catholic schools were so different that their distributions on the autonomy scale barely overlapped.

Just as principals have greater autonomy in Catholic schools, so too do teachers. Hannaway discovered that teachers in Catholic schools had substantially higher job satisfaction, a greater sense of collegiality and community, and higher personal efficacy than public school teachers. Catholic school teachers also reported a much broader range of professional responsibilities in their school, and they exercised more control over both school-level policy and classroom practices. Catholic school principals observed substantially less teacher absenteeism and a greater sense of teacher commitment than did public school principals.[63]

In her examination of management practices, Hannaway observed that the practices of public schools were similar regardless of the schools' political, environmental, or organizational context. She argued that the inability of public schools to respond and adapt to local conditions implies "that there is something about public educational institutions that restricts their adaptation to local conditions."[64] This lack of responsiveness in public schools was particularly surprising given the level of decentralization in American education; yet decentralization of authority appears to stop at the level of the school district. In discussing her findings concerning the organization and management of public and private schools, Hannaway concluded that

> even if we changed public schools in terms of their clients, their organizational and political contexts, and the characteristics of their principals, these schools would still not be managed the way private schools are managed. [The findings] suggest the reasons for management differences in the two sectors are closely associated with the very "public" and "private" nature of these schools.[65]

Another research effort carried out with the HSB data was by Anthony Bryk, Valerie Lee, and Peter Holland. They found that Catholic schools had distinctly better outcomes for low-income and minority children than did public schools.[66] They attributed these outcomes to the clearer missions, more communal orientation, and less bureaucratic organization of Catholic schools, and to the fact that Catholic schools place almost all of their students in an academic (precollegiate) track rather than allowing students to choose a less demanding curriculum.

In more recent work, one of the most outspoken opponents of school choice, education professor Valerie Lee, led a research team that examined science and math learning in more than 9,600 students from 789 high schools in the National Educational Longitudinal Study (NELS) data set. This research attempted to discover what organizational characteristics

of high schools led to greater learning and a more equitable distribution of learning. Lee and her colleagues found that high schools with a clear mission, less bureaucracy, more satisfied teachers, and a more demanding curriculum for all students improved educational outcomes.[67] Although Lee and her colleagues did not address specifically whether public or private schools were more likely to have the characteristics that improved science and math outcomes, the features that they describe as characterizing effective schools were almost exactly those identified by Chubb and Moe. Lee also looked at instructional practices and divided schools by whether they used innovative or traditional practices, or had no clear pattern of instruction. Schools that had innovative instructional practices had the greatest success in teaching math and science, while schools that had no clear instructional pattern were the least successful. Fifty-five percent of private schools had innovative instructional practices, while only 1 percent had no clear instructional pattern. The corresponding numbers for public schools were 44 percent and 13 percent.[68]

Several authors have suggested that the greater teacher autonomy, more positive job-related attitudes, and cooperative behavior observed in private schools are the products of the choice-school environment, where the students and parents select the school and the school then chooses among the applicants. In other words, the observed differences in teacher attitudes and behaviors are not the result of a school being private or public but reflect instead the fact that private schools are schools of choice. If this is the case, then we would expect the teachers in the San Antonio multilingual schools will be more similar to those in the private schools in our study than to teachers in the attendance-zone public schools. We tested this possibility by comparing the teachers in private middle schools not only with those in attendance-zone middle schools, but also with the teachers in the multilingual public choice program. We surveyed 206 middle-school teachers and 1,871 middle-school students at nine middle schools.[69]

Table 2.2 shows that both being a choice school and being a private school create better organization and improve teachers' attitudes and behavior. But of the two, being private is the more important. Private schools have clearer goals and priorities, and experience greater teamwork among the teachers; and the private school teachers are more likely to perceive that their administration supports them. In each case, attendance-zone schools score lower than multilingual schools. In contrast to previous findings at the high school level, teachers in public attendance-zone schools do not perceive themselves as having less control than private school teachers. Multilingual teachers report having the least

Table 2.2. Comparisons among Attendance-Zone, Public Choice, and
Private Middle Schools

	Attendance-Zone	Private	Public Choice
Percent of teachers strongly agreeing that			
School goals and priorities are clear	9	55	31
All school personnel work closely as a team	2	32	6
Teachers are not supported when they enforce discipline rules	20	4	18
Percent answering that teachers have moderate or a great deal of influence over			
Establishing the school curriculum	52	58	43
Establishing school staffing patterns	15	19	5
The selection of textbooks and instructional materials	44	74	45
Determining the content, topics, and skills taught	83	80	75
Percent of teachers agreeing or strongly agreeing that their school's learning environment is not conducive to student achievement	59	11	22
Percent of teachers who expect a majority of their students to be reading at grade level at the end of the year	35	73	79
Percent of teachers who give less than 15 minutes of homework per class period	65	14	35
Percent of teachers who do *not* meet the majority of students' parents	46	2	24
Students usually do their homework (from student survey)	42	63	56
Number of respondents	54	73	79

control over curricular matters, probably because of the thematic character of the schools.

The clearest difference among the three types of schools occurs in teachers' agreement with the statement "The school learning environment is not conducive to student achievement." *A majority of teachers at attendance-zone middle schools agreed with this statement!* In contrast, only 22 percent of multilingual school teachers and 11 percent of teachers in private middle schools perceived the atmosphere in their school in such a negative light. One reason that the atmosphere in attendance-zone middle schools may be so negative is the absence of parental involvement. Fifty-four percent of teachers in attendance-zone middle schools reported *no* contact with parents of the majority of their students during a typical school year! Only 2 percent of teachers in private middle schools and

22 percent of teachers in multilingual schools reported having no contact with the majority of parents.

A second reason for the absence of an achievement atmosphere in attendance-zone public schools may be the low expectations that teachers have for their students. Only 35 percent of teachers in attendance-zone public schools expected the majority of their students would be reading at grade level by the end of the academic year. In sharp contrast, 79 percent of multilingual school teachers and 73 percent of private middle school teachers expected the majority of their students to be reading at grade level. While these expectations are realistic given that the average reading score of SAISD seventh-grade students is the 29th percentile, the teachers' expectations may be self-fulfilling. Sixty-five percent of attendance-zone middle school teachers assigned less than fifteen minutes of homework per class period. Only 35 percent of multilingual teachers and 14 percent of private middle school teachers reported assigning so little. In addition, a majority of students at public attendance-zone schools reported that students do not do the little homework that they are assigned. In the multilingual schools this figure falls to 46 percent, and the private schools figure is 36 percent.

Given the repeated research findings that private schools have a much clearer organization, that private school teachers work together in a setting of teamwork and cooperation, and the perception of many public school teachers that their schools do not have an environment conducive to learning, why do public school teachers so uniformly oppose policies that would increase the availability of private school opportunities? Here the answer is quite clear. Nationwide, public school teachers have 36 percent higher salaries than private school teachers. Public school teachers also have much greater job security because of tenure protection, union contracts, and the greater likelihood that a given public school will remain open from one year to the next.[70] Thus, while the learning environment and working conditions in private schools may be better than in public schools, these differences are not sufficient to encourage teachers to leave the public sector. In fact, although national surveys show that private school teachers report significantly greater job satisfaction than public school teachers, the rate of turnover for private school teachers is 33 percent higher than for public school teachers![71]

In summary, the research concerning the organizational characteristics of public and private schools supports the hypotheses of those who expected that choice schools would outperform traditional schools and that private schools would surpass public schools in their academic outcomes. These results were found by researchers who used different theo-

retical perspectives and different data sets. While public choice schools scored better than public attendance-zone schools on school organization and atmosphere, clear differences exist between public choice and private schools, and these differences favor the private schools.

THE EFFECTS OF CHOICE ON PARENTS

Both proponents and opponents of choice agree that the people who matter most in the success of any choice policy are the parents. Do they have the skills necessary to choose effectively? Are they satisfied with the experiences of their children? Do they become more involved in their child's education? Data on choice programs show that parents who have chosen their children's school are significantly more satisfied with the schools than are parents whose children attend neighborhood public schools.[72] Part of this increase in satisfaction stems from parents' sense of empowerment. This sense is greatest when there is compatibility between the school's publicized specialty and the parents' perception of what is special about the school.[73]

Supporters of greater choice claim that a substantial benefit of greater parent satisfaction is greater involvement of parents in their children's education. This is important because parental involvement has strong, positive effects on student achievement.[74] Our research in San Antonio found that parent satisfaction increases involvement, and this increased involvement leads to still greater parent involvement. The San Antonio research did find a significant problem with the public choice program. Parent satisfaction with the public schools dropped when students were rejected by the multilingual program. Focus group interviews with these parents found that they believed that the public school system treated their child unfairly.[75] The unfortunate result of this dissatisfaction was not only a substantial decline in the parents' involvement with their children's schools, but also a decline in how much time parents spent on their child's education at home.[76]

In summary, the available research concerning the impacts of increased choice on the producers of education (teachers and principals) and the consumers of education (students and parents) supports the hypotheses of choice supporters. Principals and teachers in choice schools have more autonomy, work together more closely, and have more clearly defined missions and goals. Students in public and private choice schools tend to outperform students in attendance-zone schools whether the out-

come measure is the level of political tolerance and support for democratic norms or parental satisfaction and involvement. However, not every study finds positive results, and many of the observed outcomes may be partially the result of selection bias. In addition, existing voucher programs outside of the United States have increased segregation by ethnicity, religion, and social class. These studies make clear that if America adopts a full-scale voucher program, policymakers should design the program to encourage integration rather than segregation.

THE EFFECTS OF CHOICE ON ACADEMIC OUTCOMES

The aspect of the school choice debate that receives the most attention is whether or not increasing school choice will improve student outcomes generally and the outcomes of disadvantaged and at-risk children particularly. One of the difficulties with the existing research is that at the time of this writing there are only three publicly funded voucher programs in the United States, and each of these is too small and too new to allow definitive conclusions. In addition, the outcomes of a voucher or tax policy will vary extensively with the design of the policy. Some policies may include only secular private schools, while others may include sectarian schools as well. Some policies may include only low-income children, while others might make vouchers available to all income groups. Some policies might provide transportation to private schools, while others would not. Each of these options will have substantial implications for the policy outcomes.

Researchers have attempted to overcome the absence of existing programs in the United States in three ways: (1) examine the impacts of competition within the public sector, (2) compare the effectiveness and efficiency of public and private schools, and (3) study the existing public and private voucher programs in the United States. Each of these approaches has its strengths and weaknesses, and we will review each set of studies in turn.

The Effects of Competition

Carolyn Hoxby, an economist at Harvard, has done much of the research on the effects of existing competition among public schools and between public and private schools. Hoxby examined the effects of public school choice as measured by the enrollment concentration of students within school districts in metropolitan areas. She reasoned that if there are many

school districts within a metropolitan area, then it is easier for families to exercise school choice by changing school districts. It is also easier for upper-income families to cluster together. To analyze student outcomes, Hoxby used the National Longitudinal Survey of Youth (NLSY)—a panel study of 12,676 men and women, aged fourteen to twenty-two in 1979, who have been surveyed every year since 1979. These data allowed Hoxby to control for the respondents' ethnicity, sex, number of siblings, birth order, parents' education, and religious affiliation. NLSY students took the Armed Forces Qualifications Test (AFQT), and Hoxby used those scores, high school graduation, highest grade of school attained, and wages at age twenty-four as her measures of educational outcomes.[77]

Hoxby's results show that increasing the number of school districts did increase ethnic and income segregation. However, it decreased educational costs and improved all student outcome variables. The greatest improvements occurred among the more advantaged students. When Hoxby added data on private schools to her study, she found that when religious institutions increase their subsidy to private education and when enrollment increases in private schools, the educational outcomes for *public school students improve.[78] These results, Hoxby argues, indicate that competition among educational producers decreases costs and improves educational outcomes. Because Hoxby's data contained information only on the metropolitan area in which students resided rather than on the schools they attended, we must be careful in generalizing from her results. Hoxby could not examine the effects of student-body composition or other school effects on individual students or sets of students. Nevertheless, her results suggest that competition and decentralization improve learning outcomes.

Kevin Smith and Ken Meier, two political scientists, also have looked at the impact of private school enrollment on public school performance. They examined educational outcomes among school districts in Florida and found that as private school enrollment increases, public school performance declines.[79] Unfortunately, the equations they use to estimate student outcomes are misspecified. Smith and Meier omit from their regression equation the variables percent black and percent minority. But almost every study of educational outcomes has found these variables to be important predictors of educational outcomes, and their omission by Smith and Meier leads to serious mistakes in their analyses. In Florida, the percentage of students enrolled in private schools is highly related to the percent black. This means that the negative correlation between percent in private schools and student achievement observed by Smith and Meier is an artifact of leaving out a critical variable.

Comparing Public and Private Schools

In the absence of large-scale experiments with vouchers or tax credits, many researchers have looked to comparisons of public and private school outcomes to gain insights into whether or not expanding private school choice would increase educational outcomes. There are four difficulties with this approach. First, almost all available data are limited to high schools. We cannot know, therefore, whether the comparisons are valid for the earlier years, a time when the learning curve for students is steepest. Second, most such comparisons suffer from selection bias. As we saw above, families that send their children to private schools and to public choice schools differ in important ways from nonchoosing families. The parents in choosing families have higher educational expectations for their children and higher involvement in their children's education at home and at school. Third, private schools can select their students. It may be that experienced principals and teachers can identify students whose goals and motivation fit with the pedagogy of the private school.[80] Finally, even if we were to find that private schools are more effective, this would not mean that new private schools would be as effective as existing schools. As 78 percent of all private school students attend sectarian schools where profits are not a primary motivation, we cannot generalize safely from today's private schools to those that would enter the market if there were a voucher system. Despite these difficulties, comparing the outcomes of public and private schools can tell us if the many problems that critics allege make public schools ineffective actually make them less successful than the supposedly more productive private schools.

High School and Beyond. Among the earliest efforts to compare public and private schools were those of James Coleman and his colleagues, who used the High School and Beyond (HSB) data.[81] Coleman and his colleagues found that the average change in test scores from the sophomore to the senior years was greater in private than in public schools. This difference remained statistically significant even after controlling for prior test scores, socioeconomic status, classmates, and other relevant variables. As we saw above, Chubb and Moe used the HSB data and more sophisticated methodologies to replicate the findings of Coleman and his colleagues. Many researchers, however, challenged the HSB findings. They argued that Coleman's research failed to account for sampling problems in the HSB survey and neglected to correct for selection bias, prior learning, and courses taken.[82] Another problem was that there was very little difference between the tenth- and twelfth-grade test scores. The av-

erage twelfth-grade student improved by only 6 questions on a test with
115 items. On the math portion of the test, the average gain was only
0.27 items on a 10-item test.[83] Such small gains (an average of only 0.1
standard deviations over two years) may have no practical policy relevance.[84] The analyses did not control sufficiently for the courses students
took and students' socioeconomic status.[85] University of Wisconsin professor John Witte argued that the simplest explanation of the HSB results
was that Catholic schools simply admit better students. This allowed the
schools to place more of their students in the college preparatory track
and to maintain a better learning environment. Thus the slightly greater
achievement of Catholic schools was not due to the school being private,
but to the students being better prepared and more motivated.[86]

One way around the problem of little change in the tenth- and twelfth-
grade test scores is to use as measures of a school's success whether or not
its students graduate from high school, enter college, and graduate from
college. Here, too, the findings have been mixed. Economists William
Sander and Anthony Krautmann found that while Catholic school students were more likely to graduate from high school than similar students
in public schools, Catholic school students were no more likely to attend
college.[87] University of Maryland professors William Evans and Robert
Schwab used a slightly different statistical model and determined that
Catholic school students not only were more likely to graduate from high
school, but they also were significantly more likely to attend a four-year
college.[88]

Results from Other National Databases. To overcome the limitations
of the HSB data, Derek Neal of the University of Chicago used the National Longitudinal Survey of Youth to compare Catholic school and public school students.[89] Using a statistical approach that allowed him to correct for selection bias, Neal's analysis found striking advantages for urban
minorities who attend Catholic high schools. After correcting for selection
bias and controlling for relevant socioeconomic and demographic variables, Neal found that urban minority students were 245 percent more
likely to graduate from college if they attended a Catholic school rather
than a public school![90] Attending a Catholic school also increased wages
after schooling for urban minority students.[91]

Given the very large gains to urban minorities who attend Catholic
schools, the question arises as to whether the gains stem from students being in a private school or whether the gains are enjoyed by students in all
choice schools. The two papers that have addressed this question reached
slightly different conclusions. Using the National Educational Longitudi-

nal Study (NELS) and using statistical techniques to correct for selection bias, Adam Gamoran found that magnet schools increase test scores more than do Catholic schools, and that secular private schools actually do worse than attendance-zone public schools after correcting for the socioeconomic status of the students and their classmates and for the number of academic courses students take.[92] In contrast to Gamoran's findings, Stephen Plank and his colleagues at the University of Chicago used the same NELS data and found that although magnet schools did almost as well as private schools, the private schools still had a slight advantage.[93]

Evaluations of Existing Choice Programs

We turn to studies of choice programs in individual cities to gain further insight into the impact of private schools on academic outcomes. There are three major types of choice school evaluations: those that examine the effects of magnet schools, those that look at publicly funded voucher programs, and those that assess privately funded voucher programs. The most complete evaluations of magnet schools use the National Educational Longitudinal Study (NELS). The data for publicly funded vouchers for private schools come from voucher experiments in Milwaukee, Wisconsin, and Cleveland, Ohio. The data on privately funded voucher programs come largely from studies carried out by a group headed by political scientist Paul Peterson of Harvard.

Despite the relatively long history of magnet schools as tools of desegregation, few researchers have studied their academic outcomes. We saw above that existing analyses of the NELS data indicate that students in magnet schools learn more than students in attendance-zone schools, and these differences remain significant after controlling for socioeconomic and demographic variables and for selection bias. Our study of the multilingual public choice program in San Antonio found that students who participated in that program had significantly higher test score gains than nonchoosing students who remained in their neighborhood schools and students who applied to the program but were not admitted.[94] These differences remained significant after controlling for socioeconomic and demographic variables, parental involvement, and educational expectations.

By far the most heated debates over choice take place over the appropriate interpretation to place on results from the voucher experiments in the United States. In 1990, Milwaukee, Wisconsin, initiated the Milwaukee Parental Choice Program (MPCP). The program allowed low-income families (up to 1.75 times the national poverty line) who were not in pri-

vate schools during the prior year to apply for vouchers equal to the state aid that would have gone to the Milwaukee Public School System (MPS). The program was limited to nonsectarian schools until 1995.[95] John Witte, a political science professor at the University of Wisconsin, was hired to evaluate the program. For four years Witte gathered outcome data on the students who received a voucher, a random sample of more than five thousand students in the MPS, and students who applied for the voucher but were unable to participate in the MPCP because the private school they chose was already fully enrolled. Witte's group also sent surveys to the parents of all students in the study requesting the standard socioeconomic and demographic information as well as information about the parents' involvement in their children's education and their educational expectations for their children.[96]

In his fourth-year report, Witte compared the test scores of students in the voucher program with a random sample of all Milwaukee public school students and with a subsample of low-income MPS students. Witte concluded that although parents were more satisfied with private schools, the voucher students learned no more in private schools than did the control group of students in public schools.[97]

Paul Peterson and several of his graduate students at Harvard have challenged Witte's finding. The Harvard group argued that Witte's methodology was severely flawed in that more than 80 percent of the students had missing data and Witte did not control appropriately for family background variables. As an alternative to the comparison groups used by Witte, Peterson argued that the appropriate comparison group would be the students who applied to the voucher program but were unsuccessful in their application.[98] When using this control group, Peterson found that students in private schools had significantly better academic outcomes than the students who remained in the public schools.[99]

Cecilia Rouse, an economist at Princeton, prepared a third evaluation of the Milwaukee data.[100] Rouse concluded that while the Witte group underestimated the impact of private schools, the Harvard group overestimated that impact. Rouse replicated and corrected the methods of both sets of researchers. She found that voucher students gained between 1.5 and 2.3 percentile points per year in math more than public school students, but that neither the public nor the private schools had a consistent advantage in reading scores.[101]

An apparent benefit of the Milwaukee voucher program has been its impact on the Milwaukee Public Schools (MPS). Carolyn Hoxby studied what happened to the MPS as the Milwaukee voucher program expanded

in size and included sectarian as well as nonsectarian private schools. (In 2001 the program included approximately ten thousand students.) Hoxby compared those MPS schools that were most at risk of losing students to the voucher program with other public schools in the MPS district and with a control group of public schools outside the district. She found that the schools most at risk improved substantially more than other MPS schools, and both sets of MPS schools improved significantly more than did the control schools outside the MPS district.[102] While it is not possible to prove that the voucher program was responsible for the MPS gains, Hoxby's results suggest that competition from private schools did not harm the public schools generally, and it especially did not harm the schools that lost the most students to the voucher program.

Cleveland, Ohio, also has a publicly funded voucher experiment. As in the Milwaukee program, only low-income students are eligible. But from the very beginning the Cleveland program allowed the voucher students to enroll in sectarian as well as nonsectarian private schools. As was the case in Milwaukee, different researchers have found different results. The Peterson group found that the test scores of voucher students were significantly higher than those in the public schools. A research group from Indiana University's School of Education concluded that although the scores of students in sectarian schools were higher than those of public school students, the gain in test scores of private school students who enrolled in secular schools started in response to the voucher program were lower than the gains of public school students.[103] Peterson and his colleagues have argued that the Indiana group not only omitted important data from their analysis, but they also used highly questionable data in reaching their results.

The State of Florida also has a publicly funded voucher policy, the Florida A-Plus Accountability and School Choice Program (hereafter called the A-Plus Program). In 2000 the Florida legislature decided to require the Florida Comprehensive Assessment Test (FCAT) of all public schools in the areas of mathematics, reading, and writing. Based primarily on the FCAT results, the state assigns each school one of five grades (A, B, C, D, F). Any school that receives two grades of "F" in a four-year period becomes eligible for action from the Florida Department of Education. One action is that students of those schools can receive a voucher for use at private schools or they may transfer to another public school.

Seventy-six schools received F grades in 1999, and had they received a second F grade in 2000, their students would have been eligible to receive a voucher. None of the seventy-six schools received an F grade in

2000. Jay Greene, an analyst at the Manhattan Institute for Policy Research, carried out an evaluation of the A-Plus Program for the State of Florida.[104] Using schools as his unit of analysis, Greene compared the changes in test scores for the seventy-six schools that scored F with the changes in test scores for the Florida schools that had received very low D grades. He found that the schools with F grades improved significantly more than the schools with D grades. Greene concluded that the threat of losing students to vouchers probably was responsible for a major portion of the improved performance by the F schools.

Greene's conclusions have not gone unchallenged. Gregory Camilli and Katrina Bulkley of the Rutgers University Graduate School of Education used students as the unit of analysis, a slightly different sample of student scores, and different statistical methods to analyze the A-Plus Florida Program. Camilli and Bulkley found that while the schools may have improved, the changes were not nearly as large as those claimed by Greene and may have been related to aspects of the accountability program other than the threat of vouchers.[105]

Privately Funded Voucher Experiments. Over thirty cities have privately funded scholarship or voucher programs for low-income children, and several of these have been evaluated. Our analysis of the San Antonio privately funded voucher program found that the test scores of students who participated in the voucher program remained largely unchanged from one year to the next. On average, for every year that a voucher student attended a private school her standardized test score dropped by 0.14 percentiles in math and increased by 0.44 percentiles in reading. These outcomes were markedly superior to the corresponding changes for students in San Antonio attendance-zone schools. The average student in those schools lost over 2 percentiles per year in math and 1 percentile in reading.[106] If our results are generalizable to other programs, they are quite significant. However, the small size of the San Antonio private voucher program and the likelihood of selection bias make generalizations from the study risky.

Paul Peterson and his Harvard research group have evaluated private scholarship programs in New York City, Washington, D.C., and Dayton, Ohio. All students in these studies initially were in public schools and all applied for a scholarship to move to a private school. As the result of a lottery, some students received scholarships and transferred to private schools, while other students did not receive a scholarship and remained in the public schools. The Peterson studies obtain baseline scores on all

students who apply for the scholarship by having them take a nationally normed standardized test prior to the lottery. Then each year both winners and losers in the lottery take a nationally normed achievement test. Because the Peterson group administers the standardized tests only to children from families who applied to the scholarship program and because the winners of the scholarships were chosen randomly, the control group of students (those who lost in the scholarship lottery) is much more similar to the treatment group (the winners of the lottery) than was the case in our San Antonio study. Peterson is comparing students in choosing families who were able to move from a public to a private school with students in choosing families who desired to make that move but were unable to do so.

In general, Peterson's results show that the students who move from public to private schools experience higher test score gains than students who remain in the public schools.[107] Perhaps Peterson's most interesting and important finding is that African American students typically gain far more from the private school experience than do non-Hispanic whites. In Dayton, Ohio, for example, African American students who received scholarships and attended private schools scored 7 percentiles higher in math and 5 percentiles higher in reading than the African American students who remained in the public schools. For non–African Americans in Dayton, however, private school attendance did not improve their test scores.[108]

THE EFFECTS OF CHOICE ON CHILDREN WHO REMAIN BEHIND

We began this chapter asking whether or not school choice necessarily was a type of Sophie's choice. Does it help some students while simultaneously hurting others? A fair summary of the above research on the effects of school choice on choosing students would be that students who attend choice schools, whether public or private, tend to have better academic outcomes than students who attend neighborhood schools. These positive outcomes remain significant even after controlling for the socioeconomic characteristics of families, past achievement by students, and selection bias. Thus, we can conclude that choosing helps the choosers. But what does increased choice do to students who remain in their attendance-zone schools? If more academically able classmates improve student outcomes and students who attend choice schools are, on average, more academi-

cally able than students who remain behind, it seems reasonable to expect that students who remain in attendance-zone schools will learn less.

To our knowledge, only one empirical study of academic achievement has addressed this issue. That study is our own analysis of the impact of the public choice program on neighborhood school students in San Antonio. The San Antonio Independent School District provided a good location to study the effects of choice on students left behind, because at the time of the study, the district had only one choice program that enrolled a significant number of above-average students. SAISD invites all students who are in the top quintile of their class in the fifth grade to apply to the multilingual program. In 1992, the year we began our study, more than seven hundred students applied to the program and approximately four hundred students enrolled in the multilingual schools at the beginning of the sixth grade. The loss of these students to a choice program meant that more than one-third of the highest-performing students left their attendance-zone schools in the sixth grade. If a substantial loss of high-performing classmates has an impact on the students left behind, then the test scores of students who remain in neighborhood schools should show a steeper drop in the sixth grade than in the fifth grade.

To test whether this expected loss occurred, we compared the change in standardized test scores of students in neighborhood schools from the end of the fourth grade to the end of the fifth grade with the changes in their scores from the fifth to the sixth grade. We found that members of our random sample of SAISD students dropped 0.48 percentiles in reading from the end of the fourth grade to the end of the fifth grade. The corresponding drop from the fifth to the sixth grade was 1.06 percentiles. This difference was not quite statistically significant. The math score drop, however, was statistically significant. Students lost an average of 1.93 percentiles during the fifth grade and 5.63 percentiles during the sixth grade. The San Antonio Independent School District's records for all students indicate that the score decline between one grade and the next is greater between fifth and sixth grade than for any other year in both math and reading.[109] The negative impact of losing students to the multilingual choice program appears, however, to be short-lived. Although two-thirds of the students who enter the multilingual program continue in it during the seventh and eighth grades, there does not appear to be a negative impact on students who remain in their neighborhood schools. The standardized test scores for students attending attendance-zone schools for these grades do not decline more rapidly than in other years. In fact, they decline slightly less rapidly.

SUMMARY AND CONCLUSIONS

What do the above outcomes tell us about the impacts of school choice on education? First, choosing families and students differ significantly from their nonchoosing counterparts, and these differences relate both to the socioeconomic status of the families and the academic skills of the students. If increased choice is to avoid segregating students on the basis of either their academic abilities or the involvement of their family, then policymakers must design choice programs in ways that reduce such segregation. Among the approaches that might work would be to use a lottery system to choose among applicants, to exclude test scores from admissions criteria, and to have a quota of low-income students for each choice school.

The second impact of school choice appears to be to improve the school environment for teachers. Faculty in choice schools experience a stronger sense of mission, greater teamwork among teachers, increased autonomy, and an improved learning atmosphere. These effects are greatest in private schools, but they also occur in public choice schools. Related to the improved environment is the impact of school choice on the involvement of parents in their children's education. Not only are more involved parents more likely to be choosers, but also choice increases that involvement. Because increased parent involvement improves student outcomes, the process of choice may improve student outcomes even if there are no important differences in the curriculum and pedagogical approaches of attendance-zone and choice schools.

When we turn our attention to the impacts of choice on students we find that, contrary to the expectations of the critics of private school choice, private schools do not have a negative impact either on students' support for democratic norms or on their level of tolerance of disliked groups. This holds true even for evangelical schools.

Of course, the major concern of most readers will be how choice affects academic outcomes—for both choosing and nonchoosing students. Is school choice Sophie's choice? Although there is substantial disagreement about the magnitude of the private school advantage, it does appear that private schools do improve outcomes for their students. This is particularly true for minority students in the inner cities. National data show that minority students who attend Catholic schools in the inner city are more likely to graduate from high school and they are much more likely to attend and to graduate from college. Data from the private voucher programs indicate that minority families are those who are most likely to benefit from attending private schools. Both the local

and the national data indicate that increased choice does little for suburban whites. Thus, to the extent that the least advantaged in our society become choosers, school choice reduces current inequalities in educational opportunities.

Unfortunately, there are almost no data on what happens to the students whom choosers leave behind. In addition, until a city, school district, or state embarks on a full-scale voucher program that potential suppliers of schooling expect to be permanent, we have no idea of how many students will become choosers or what types of private schools will emerge. Currently 25 percent of students attend either public or private choice schools.[110] If that percentage increased to 50 or 75, then the impacts of choice might be quite different than their current effects. In addition, the design of the choice program would have a critical impact on any results. A program that provided a large voucher to all children and did not attempt to prevent increased sorting by income or student skill would be likely to increase ethnic and socioeconomic segregation. A program that required all choice schools to have a quota of low-income students probably would have the opposite effect.

In conclusion, current outcomes of choice policies validate neither the nightmares of choice critics nor the dreams of choice proponents. It may be, therefore, that the case for or against increased choice rests on the tradeoffs school choice makes among other social values. These include parent and family rights, student autonomy, the separation of church and state, and the costs of alternative programs. We turn to these issues in the following chapters.

THREE

Political Theory and School Choice

THE PREVIOUS CHAPTER dealt with such empirical questions as what is the current situation of low-income children in the inner cities, who chooses alternatives to attendance-zone schools, and what have been the outcomes of those choices. For these questions to have meaning for public policy we must place them in a normative context. We want to know what education develops the best human beings and what education is best for our society. But identifying the "best education" requires that we know the goals we want to pursue and that we assign a priority and a weight to each. The purpose of this chapter is to analyze educational goals and their ordering.

Before laying out our argument we would like you to participate in another thought experiment, one suggested by Stephen Gilles.[1] Gilles asks you to pretend that you are behind John Rawls's veil of ignorance. This is an imaginary location where you are one of several representatives who will choose the rules their society will use to promote justice. Those rules include deciding whether a child's parents or the state[2] should decide the content of the child's education and how to present that content. You, like all other representatives, are rational and know that when you step from behind the veil you will live either in the United States or Canada. But you do not know in which geographic area you will live, when you will live there, or the characteristics you will have.[3] You may be rich or poor, a fundamentalist Muslim or secular humanist, a feminist or a paternalist, smart or stupid, and you could be a member of either a majority or minority ethnic group. To whom will you give principal control over curriculum and pedagogy, the child's parents or the state? Will you give the majority the right to use government to determine the values and beliefs that

Richard Ruderman is a coauthor of this chapter.

all students must learn? If so, will the government's decisionmaking power be at the national, state, or local level?

Your answers to the above questions are critical to deciding which school choice policy you prefer. If you decide that parents should control the content of their child's education, then a voucher policy would be a logical choice. Parents could review the available schools and select the one that best suits their preferences. Or, if no school is acceptable to them, they could start a new school or home school their child. On the other hand, if you think that the majority should control education policy through its elected representatives and appointed agents, then you would require either substantial state regulation of private schools and home schooling or the elimination of private schooling.

Why might you decide that parents rather than the majority should control education? Because you fear government tyranny. Tyranny occurs in democracies as well as in authoritarian regimes. The United States and Canada have used the public schools to force children of minority groups to learn values to which their parents object. The "Great School Wars" were fought over the efforts of the politically dominant Protestants to use public schools to mold Catholic and Jewish children into cultural Protestants.[4] In the name of the common good or cultural coherence, whites have forced their beliefs on Native Americans, African Americans, and Latinos. Professional educators in the United States have supported providing inferior education to ethnic minorities, particularly African Americans.[5] Many members of fundamentalist religious groups argue that the values of professional educators currently work to destroy their religious culture by denigrating its teachings and beliefs.[6] Persons who believe that their lives should be governed by knowledge gained through faith rather than through science object to an education that requires their children to critically examine their most deeply held beliefs. They see such an education as encouraging thoughts and behaviors that may lead to their child's eternal damnation.

But allowing parents to control the education of their children also has dangers. If the political toleration of beliefs and behaviors with which one disagrees is essential to democratic government, then the preservation of democracy may require that students be exposed to ways of life that their parents find objectionable. If a child's religion or tradition teaches intolerance, racism, sexism, or other illiberal ideas, then should not the state instruct the child on why such worldviews are unreasonable? If parents teach their children that scientific findings that conflict with their religious teachings are wrong, is it not the obligation of the state to expose those children to the scientific method and to scientific evidence that

may contradict those religious teachings? What should the state do if parents systematically deprive their children of the knowledge and skills that would allow them to leave the traditions and beliefs of parents? Do not liberty and freedom for the child require that the state prevent parents from severely limiting the choices of their children?

If you were behind the veil of ignorance, what guides might you use to decide how to divide parental and state control? One way of approaching the question would be to examine how liberal democratic theorists have answered it. A number of eminent thinkers have wrestled with this question. What can we learn from their analyses?

LIBERAL DEMOCRACY

The United States and Canada are democracies based largely on a political philosophy developed by John Locke. That philosophy, called "liberalism," provided the American Founders many of their ideas about government, including the principle that the appropriate goal of the state was to protect life, liberty, and property. We assume that liberalism and democratic theory provide the boundaries within which any education policy must fit. Liberal democratic societies are founded on several key values, among which are political equality, personal liberty, and limited government. An essential attribute of liberalism is its acceptance that the good is plural; therefore society must tolerate a plurality of ways of life. Traditionally liberalism has advocated a neutral state, one that prohibits any group from using coercion to impose its conceptions of the good life and the good person on others.[7] This state neutrality grew out of the desire to end the religious wars between Catholics and Protestants, but it continues to prove itself an important principle for achieving compromise, moderation, and toleration in democratic politics.

The combination of liberty, limited government, and tolerance for different ways of life dictates that liberal democracy recognize a private sphere of life, one generally off-limits to government intervention. This sphere includes an individual's choice of ultimate goals, family life, occupation, and matters of personal taste. Although it recognizes that religious and family institutions have political implications, liberalism places a heavy burden on the state to justify its intervention in the private sphere. The first philosopher to place these ideas together in an attempt to justify a liberal society under liberal government was John Locke (1632–1704). While Locke is the progenitor of liberal theory and perhaps its greatest thinker, liberalism has changed substantially since his death. Among the

more significant changes are a growing emphasis on democracy, individual autonomy, and equality of opportunity, and a widespread acceptance of government guaranteeing an economic threshold below which no one should fall. These changes are logical extensions of Locke's liberal ideas of the inherent equality, liberty, and worth of every human being. They require, however, substantially greater government intervention than Locke envisioned.

The philosophic underpinnings of liberalism require that education develop in students the three capacities designated in Chapter 1: the ability to be economically productive, the competence to participate in democratic government, and the capacity to make moral judgments. Liberalism also requires that individuals be able to choose among competing conceptions of the good life. The development of these four capacities requires that education encourage rationality, tolerance, and a degree of personal autonomy. Although these goals and competencies set the broad outlines of a liberal education, several important issues remain unresolved.

- Is the education of a child within the public or the private sphere? Should parents or the state have the final say concerning what a child will study?
- Does liberal democracy's emphasis on rationality require that schools teach students to critically evaluate their own moral and religious beliefs? Stated differently, does the goal of developing personal autonomy—the ability and willingness for sustained rational examination of self, others, and social practices—take precedence over liberalism's respect for all reasonable comprehensive views, including those based in faith or tradition?
- How does education in a liberal society deal with traditions or cultures that include such illiberal practices as treating men and women unequally? Should education attempt to weed out illiberal practices or should the state allow cultures with some illiberal traits to survive and prosper?
- Does government neutrality among competing worldviews allow the state to subsidize secular education while refusing the same subsidy to an education that stresses religious values?

LIBERAL ARGUMENTS THAT EDUCATION IS IN THE PRIVATE SPHERE

One of the most interesting aspects of the school choice debate is that most citizens who conceive of themselves as "liberals" perceive expanded parental choice as the illiberal policy and state control as the liberal solu-

tion. Yet the greatest of liberal thinkers, John Locke, proposed home schooling for families for whom this was possible. He would have abhorred the idea of government-controlled education. Similarly, John Stuart Mill (1806–1873) argued in *On Liberty* that while the state should provide funding for education, it should never control the content of that education except to assure basic literacy and numeracy. Why were classical liberals opposed to state control? What factors led many contemporary liberals to stand that position on its head?

Like many earlier proponents of education, the classical liberals sought to use education to free the mind of prejudice and conformism. To achieve this they sought to stake out a moderate, middle ground between the extremes of the authoritarian, patriarchal family and the full-scale replacement of the family by the state. Classical liberals chose this position because it was congruent with their views concerning human nature and the purpose of society. Locke made his argument for a liberal society by asking his readers to imagine what life was like before government. He argued that in the state of nature each person was free and equal—meaning, in practice, that everyone was equally free to attempt to live by the "laws of nature," their rules worked out by reason. The state of nature, however, neither provided material plenty nor protected reasonable persons from the assaults of those who were unreasonable. Foolish, vain, or greedy people coupled with material scarcity turned the state of nature into a state of war. This situation placed security at the top of everyone's agenda.

Human life and liberty, Locke maintained, could be secured only by entering into a social contract, whereby individuals granted some of their previously unlimited natural rights to the state. That state must have adequate power to secure the life, liberty, and property of all citizens. Locke knew that a liberal society required more than a government kept limited through such institutions as separation of powers and checks and balances. He saw that liberal institutions would require liberal citizens to maintain and preserve them. Because Locke expected that liberal citizens would arise only through education, he believed that a liberal state had a manifest interest in the education of its citizens. Such citizens would be more likely to understand the lessons of the state of nature and of past government tyrannies. But despite the state's obvious interest in education, Locke argued that education belonged in the private sphere. He believed that, whenever possible, parents should home school their children because authorities other than parents generally lack the particular concern that parents have for their children. Where tutors

or schools might concern themselves only with the academic skills of students, parents would be concerned not only with skills, but also with virtue.

How do these insights lead to Locke's insistence on parental control over education? Locke does not view the family as the benevolent "union of love and discipline."[8] Many of Locke's writings, particularly the *First Treatise*, read as if they were an argument against parental control. Locke did not see instinct or a natural moral sense as ensuring sound parental care. He cites evidence not only of parents who abuse their children, but even of whole societies that do this.[9] However, except in cases of genuine physical abuse, Locke does not support the right of the state to intervene in what parents teach their children or how this teaching occurs. And, unlike contemporary liberals such as John Dewey and Amy Gutmann, Locke does not allow the state to weed out illiberal activities within the family. Locke takes a slower route to autonomy, one that begins by enticing the family to liberalize through such policies as easier divorce and encouraging parents to become friends of their children. Locke also emphasizes that both parents, not only the father as was formerly the case, should educate their children.

From an educational perspective, Locke's claim that there are no "innate moral ideas" is critical. Unlike older traditions, Locke recognized neither a natural end (as the classics did) nor a revealed end (as Christianity did) to humanity. This claim implies that each human being must regard her life as a free project, a unique opportunity to engage in what John Stuart Mill termed "experiments of living."[10] Reason coupled with intellectual and moral education provides the necessary tools to carry out this project. But are parents or the state more likely to develop these tools? Locke unambiguously answers, "Parents." The state's ability to propagandize, to enforce conformity, and to repress criticism impressed Locke (and later Mill) far more than its ability to safeguard each individual's experiment in living from the sometime retrograde forces of family and culture. This is why Locke prohibited the state to concern itself with such things as the "good of souls."[11] For Locke, control of education clearly fell in the private sphere of family life. Nathan Tarcov, a scholar who has written extensively on Locke's recommendations for education, argues that his grant of educational authority to parents rather than the state was "the fundamental separation of powers."[12]

But what about autonomy, the development of a child's ability to choose her own goals and methods of attaining those goals? What saves students from being forced to accept the superstitions and prejudices of

their parents? Because Locke saw so little in human nature that resists socialization, the possibilities of molding and remaking humans through education and propaganda were substantial. While more revolutionary thinkers looked upon the malleability of human nature as an exhilarating opportunity to create the ideal citizen through the use of state power, Locke threw his weight entirely in the opposite direction. He strictly limited government, encouraged rational conduct, and taught vigilance in the name of freedom. By stressing an education that developed the rational working out of our desires, Locke hoped to provide a fence beyond which socialization (or indoctrination) would be unable to pass. He expected that a liberal education would encourage children to develop a sense of independence toward parents. As we shall see below, there are many who fear that parental indoctrination will inhibit the development of autonomy unless the state can actively override parental preferences. Locke acknowledged that such parental efforts occur, but he saw the danger to society of government tyranny as much greater than that posed by parents attempting to indoctrinate their own children.

Mill, building upon Locke's ideas and, like the Founders, fearing oppression by government and public opinion, stressed the immense social value of good education. He urged the state to "require for every child a good education," while denying the state the right to *provide* it.[13] He asserted that a "general state education is a mere contrivance for molding people to be exactly like one another," and that rather than a single state monopoly, there should then be "many competing experiments" in education.[14] Because Mill saw that few parents could spare the time or expense to educate their children directly, he gave the liberal imprimatur to school choice, including, he expressly noted, the choice to attend any sort of religious school.[15]

The aim of the classical liberal model of schooling was not to make students into philosophers, but to develop citizens who would be competent in a range of practical social tasks revolving largely around business and self-government. While Locke directed his original treatise on education only to the elites who could afford private tutors and had the leisure and the educational training to educate their own children, he states expressly that the virtues of his sort of liberal education are for "a man" and a "lover of truth" as well as "a gentleman."[16] The goal of inclusiveness received a significant boost when Mill argued that government should help "pay the fees of the poorer classes of children, and [defray] the entire school expenses of those who have no one else to pay for them."[17] However, Mill's premise with respect to education was that, insofar as there

was a necessity for parents to cede educational control to schools, the latter would act in loco parentis. Schools would teach skills and knowledge beyond what the parents could themselves (in most cases) teach, but teachers would defer to the parents' express wishes for their children, above all in the realm of religion. For Mill, as for Locke, control over education, particularly as it pertained to conceptions of what constitutes the ends of life, belonged in the private sphere.

In summary, Locke and Mill recognized the importance of education to the development and preservation of a liberal society. Each saw education as appropriate to the private sphere because a good education must be guided by a conception of the good person and the good society. Parents can provide this critical aspect of education that classical liberal theory forbids the state from attempting. As education unguided by a concept of virtue cannot develop moral reasoning, parents must control what their children will learn. Locke and Mill viewed the state as something to fear, and, by forbidding it to control the socialization of children, protected their liberty and autonomy. For Locke, the separation of parental from political power was the basis of legitimate, liberal government. To secure liberty, parents must be denied political power and the state must be shorn of its tendency to paternalize citizens. We think that were Locke alive today he would see that the former principle has been firmly established, but the latter has not. He would argue that the contemporary liberal state, in the belief that what it imposes is necessary for toleration and autonomy, is unable to recognize its own paternalism.

LIBERAL ARGUMENTS FOR INCLUDING
EDUCATION IN THE PUBLIC SPHERE

Despite Locke's arguments for placing education in the private sphere, all liberal democracies have supported public schools and, for the most part, public control of education. What is the liberal rationale for putting education in the public sphere? Why have governments disregarded the advice of Locke and Mill? Many contemporary theorists would argue that while classical liberal ideas concerning education may be interesting, today they are irrelevant. When Locke and Mill were writing, the state was something to fear. With the development of the liberal democratic state, however, the best way to prevent tyranny is to educate people to become fully autonomous citizens and to discourage illiberal and undemocratic institutions and values. Today education need not worry so much about preventing government tyranny. Rather, it can concern itself with increasing

equality, encouraging greater respect for minorities and alternative ways of life, and improving democracy. Two important theorists who make these arguments are John Dewey and Amy Gutmann.

John Dewey and Progressive Liberalism

Lockean theory challenged both classical and religious conceptions of human nature in that each postulated a permanent, positive core to human nature. If Locke's understanding of human nature is correct, education can make and remake students as a sculptor molds clay. Because of the awesome potential for socialization implied by this, Locke and Mill were vigilant in limiting the capacity of the state to do the socializing. In time, however, the temptation to turn liberalism from the wary defense of individual rights against intrusions by the state into an ambitious attempt to mold citizens into genuine liberal democrats proved too great. Locke's liberalism gave way to one in which purely self-directed moral autonomy and thoroughgoing democratic institutions became the primary goals. For education to accomplish these goals, it needed the power to remove the obstacles created by parents and their prejudices. If parents have any positive role in the education of their children, it is, in the felicitous phrasing of one observer, "strictly in loco societatis."[18] The good parent will reinforce rather than contest the teachings approved by the state.

Though not the first philosopher of education to argue along these lines, John Dewey (1859–1952) was the most influential to do so. Rather than treat public schools as neutral grounds on which children from various cultures and traditions could meet and learn to accept the minimal liberal code of public civility, Dewey advanced the argument that the public schools constitute a competing culture which is more universal and, therefore, better than any from which the children are likely to come. Should the teachings of school and home conflict, school deserved to win out. Leaving educational oversight in the hands of partisan, prejudiced parents obstructed the onward march of universality (chiefly scientism) and creativity.

Dewey was convinced of the essentially historical nature of human beings and their continuing improvement. He argued that to improve humans and their society, the state has the duty to control the arbitrary preferences of parents. Dewey saw even less at the core of humanity than Locke, and he rejected the idea that there was an internal person not formed by socialization. Dewey also rejected the idea that in modern society a successful culture could be based on spiritual values.

And the idea of perfecting an "inner" personality is a sure sign of social divisions. What is called inner is simply that which does not connect with others—which is not capable of free and full communication. What is termed spiritual culture has usually been futile, with something rotten about it, just because it has been conceived as a thing which man might have internally—and therefore exclusively. What one is as a person is what one is as associated with others, in a free give and take of social intercourse.[19]

As Dewey's contemporary exponent Richard Rorty writes, there is "nothing to people except what has been socialized into them."[20] We are, and can only be, children of our society. In Locke's view of human nature, students still possessed an independent rationality and could attain a certain capacity to resist or ward off social or state influences. Dewey's democratic students have no natural ground from which to resist socialization. Therefore socialization is no longer limited to teaching the civility required to allow diverse people to live and learn peacefully together. It is the very construction of identity, and it should provide the universal values that hold society together.

Another way in which Dewey's liberalism differs from Locke's classical liberalism was Dewey's use of public schools to achieve equality of opportunity. Classical liberals recognized the importance of providing all persons with an education sufficient to exercise their basic rights, to choose their conception of the good life, and to amass property. But classical liberals did not see creating equality of opportunity as an appropriate task for education. In fact, Locke's educational prescriptions would reinforce existing inequalities. Because Locke urged the home schooling of children whenever possible and saw education by schools as inherently inferior, the differences in the resources and abilities of parents would lead to substantial differences in educational outcomes. Dewey's ultimate goal for education was to create an increasingly democratic society, and he believed that society could become more democratic only if it became more egalitarian.[21] Therefore, education must eliminate inherited class differences and see to it that there was true equality of opportunity.

Steven Rockefeller, a disciple of Dewey, argues that he saw liberal democracy not first and foremost as a political mechanism, but as a way of life. It was a distinct moral faith that would transform society into a more participatory and more equal place.[22] Dewey viewed liberal democratic politics not as a set of procedural rules, but as "a mode of associated living where the quality of democracy depended on the number and variety of interests members of society held in common."[23] In this view, democracy is strong and healthy only when its spirit pervades all institutions

in society, including the family and the church. Should a particular culture or institution conflict with democracy, then it must be reconstructed to become an instrument of democratic growth and liberation.

The implications of Dewey's views for school choice are dramatic. They move control over education from the parents to the state. Locke could look forward to a parent-controlled education because he still allowed for a small, albeit reactive, component core to human nature. Given the opportunity, everyone, including parents, would liberalize as the mystifications of older religious and philosophic views faded away. Human beings would become industrious and rational creatures. Counting on rational self-interest to keep people hard at work, Locke encouraged his readers to be skeptical of all claims to authority over them. Locke expected parents, when educating their children, to instill those habits and teachings that would be of greatest use to them in a liberal society: industriousness, rationality, and skepticism toward those who might abridge liberties. Parents would teach their children to be kind, liberal, and civil to others as well as to take care not to transgress the rules of justice.[24] But Dewey, impressed by the diversity within American society and the fragility of reason and of human identity itself, feared that society would not hold together unless children were taught a common core of democratic values. It became the task of education, therefore, to socialize students to a common culture that would form democratic citizens and forge a liberal democratic society. For Dewey, this common core included the priority of science over religion and the submission of truly individualistic ideas to those developed in association and intercourse with other members of society. Public schools were the location where this intercourse would take place.

Dewey did not imagine that parents would encourage their children to embrace a scientific outlook that might be critical of their spiritual tradition, nor did he expect parents to welcome schools that would create, through stimulation with diverse ideas and associations, a new identity that might replace their traditions and values. But Dewey believed that without science nothing would protect children from superstition. Without the creative self-realization engendered by interactions with students from diverse cultures and backgrounds, nothing could save children from blindly repeating the mistakes of their parents.

Dewey saw humanity as requiring more nurturing than Locke had expected, and the state, through public education, was the obvious candidate to take on the task. He did not seek a single type of school that would produce regimentation. Instead, his enlightened public schools would enable people from all cultural backgrounds to participate in an experiment

in self-creation. They would teach creativity and promote a new kind of individualism. Whereas a person's attachment to values learned at home (or in a school of like-minded adherents of the same values) might shield students from confronting a wide array of conflicting and challenging viewpoints, Dewey's public schools would encourage diversity and novelty as a means of challenging thought and developing the skill of critical deliberation.[25]

Dewey praised public schools for initiating the cause of "social engineering." But what do such ominous-sounding words portend? Again, Rorty is helpful: Dewey's "social engineering" was to be a "substitute for traditional religion."[26] Dewey understood that such an experimental approach could be dangerous. But his desire to create a universal culture based on science that would use education to perfect the human race allowed him to equate the state's development of shared cultural values with democratic progress. This, of course, is exactly what Locke and Mill feared. The state, in its efforts to perfect individuals and improve democracy, would create a new conformity.

Sharing Educational Responsibility: The Ideas of Amy Gutmann

Any current defense of the state providing a democratic education must reject the simple equation of education and state-directed social engineering proposed by Dewey but, nevertheless, justify restricting the influence of the family. Amy Gutmann attempts to do just this, and she is the most influential current liberal theorist to argue that the priority given to parental rights by Locke is inappropriate for a democratic state. Where Locke promoted democracy for the sake of liberty, Gutmann considers personal autonomy and democracy to be the very things that give value to liberty. And because autonomous choice combined with democratic deliberation creates value, the purpose of education is not liberty, but the development of autonomous individuals who can engage in such deliberation.

Gutmann follows Dewey in rejecting the priority claims of the family. She argues that because students are members of both their families and their polity, the two institutions should share educational authority. In the liberal tradition of creating checks and balances, the family and the state each limit the power of the other. Within its domain, each authority has legitimate, though not complete, control over the values it teaches. In a child's earliest years the family may promote its values. Once formal schooling begins, the state, and the professional educators who are its agents, have the authority and the obligation to promote what Gutmann calls the core value of democracy: conscious social reproduction. The key

to Gutmann's argument is that "social reproduction" does not mean keeping basic social structures and values intact—the unexceptionable goal of virtually every society. Her goal is the same as Dewey's, the transformation of society into one that is increasingly democratic and populated by autonomous, participatory citizens who respect all views and ways of life that are both reasonable and rational.[27] Gutmann claims that the one goal we all share is a commitment to collectively re-create and make more democratic the society that we share. Public schools are the key agency in this transformation.

Gutmann does not limit the authority of the family so that children can choose among all reasonable conceptions of a good life. She recognizes the impossibility of this and insists that because rationality is a fundamental value of liberalism, liberals need not accommodate nonrational ways of life. Proper liberal toleration, Gutmann maintains, requires that the state accomplish two goals: teach children only those conceptions of the good life based on rationality and critical deliberation, and correct any prejudices directed against such rationality that parents may teach their children.[28] If parents teach their children that some ways of life based on critical deliberation are wrong and unworthy of private respect, then the state must use its educational curriculum and teachers to destroy these prejudices.[29]

Gutmann's goals in preventing the transmission of parents' prejudices to their children are to further individual autonomy, teach respect for minority viewpoints based on rationality, and provide cultural coherence in a diverse and democratic society. The liberal state should not be neutral among competing ways of life. It has a duty to shape the character and to bias the choices of children to encourage democracy.[30] Gutmann argues that democratic societies must go beyond toleration and teach mutual respect for reasonable differences of moral opinion. This requires a "willingness to accord due intellectual and moral regard to reasonable points of view that we cannot ourselves accept as correct."[31] Gutmann, like Dewey, sees democracy "not merely (or primarily) as a *process* of majority rule, but rather as an *ideal*."[32] Because such democratic institutions as local school boards and state boards of education may encourage illiberal prejudices, to achieve the democratic ideal the state must at times deny the democratic process and prohibit elected local representatives from allowing schools (both public and private) to teach views that deny scientific rationality or that lead to the disrespect of any reasonable lifestyle.[33]

But what constitutes a "reasonable lifestyle"? Here Gutmann departs from classical liberalism and many modern liberal theorists such as John Rawls and William Galston. For Rawls, a reasonable lifestyle is one that

does not reject basic moral or liberal norms on which there is a general consensus among reasonable people.[34] Similarly, Galston argues that liberals should treat as reasonable any comprehensive view that acknowledges the importance of normal human development, embraces civic toleration and respect for law, and acquiesces in our basic constitutional arrangement.[35] As we shall see below, Rawls and Galston would allow as a reasonable lifestyle one such as the Old Order Amish even though their society is patriarchal and they limit their children's formal schooling to eight grades. Gutmann rejects this lifestyle because it does not meet her standard of rational capacity and critical deliberation. For Gutmann, rational critical deliberation is the litmus test for liberal reasonableness. If parents restrict the future options their child may choose by limiting the child's education, the parents are unreasonably restricting the child's freedom to choose among meaningful lives.[36] Even if parents teach their child that a certain way of life must be tolerated but not respected, they are unreasonably restricting the child's freedom because they are teaching that certain rational conceptions of life are wrong or less worthy.[37]

The most important and controversial of Gutmann's claims is that there is a social consensus that social reproduction (which for her means social transformation) is the ultimate goal of education.[38] This claim of consensus allows her to reverse the traditional presumption of liberalism that the state must justify its taking of rights from individuals and can do so only by showing that the individuals' actions are harming others. By claiming a social consensus, Gutmann is arguing that all reasonable persons agree on what children must learn with respect to a liberal society. Therefore, the state need not prove that a particular private action is creating a harm in order to ban it in schools. It must prove only that the action does not further social reproduction.[39] Gutmann requires that schools teach children to privately tolerate and respect all (and only) those lifestyles based on rationality and critical deliberation. In this way we collectively create a more democratic, and therefore a better, society. As Gutmann points out, this requirement to respect such lifestyles paradoxically means that to improve democracy neither "children [nor] parents have a right of free exercise of religion or of free speech within schools."[40]

DIVERSITY OR AUTONOMY

Respect for diversity is a key goal of liberalism, and Gutmann expects her proposed education to encourage diversity by reducing students' preju-

dices, particularly the prejudices against minority lifestyles so long as they are not traditional. To ensure this she suggests a constitutional provision that prohibits any school from using education to restrict rational deliberation of differing conceptions of good lives and societies. She further fosters diversity by combining the principles of nonrepression and nondiscrimination to protect minority rights. These principles require that society educate all children and that their education include rational and critical deliberation of minority and majority lifestyles. Gutmann argues that repression and discrimination have been used by more powerful groups, including democratic majorities, to repress the capacity and desire of disfavored groups of children to participate in politics. In particular, repression and discrimination commonly were (and are) used against ethnic minorities and women.[41]

Gutmann's educational proposals violate one of the core principles of classical liberalism: the neutrality of the state. She freely acknowledges this.

> Although a democratic state permits adults to live unexamined lives as well as examined one [sic], it does not support education that is neutral between these two options nor does it claim that the two ways of life are equally good. Democratic education cannot be neutral between these two options and still educate citizens (or public officials) who are capable of exercising good political judgment.[42]

But on what grounds can Gutmann ask citizens who believe in a life based on faith to support an education policy that will teach their children that the life their parents lead is not as good as the one promulgated by the schools? Can a liberal society force parents to accept an education they believe may lead their children to eternal damnation? To classical liberals, it would appear that Gutmann is resurrecting the battleground on which Protestants fought Catholics in order that secularists can fight, and defeat, sectarians.

Comprehensive Liberalism versus Political Liberalism

Gutmann's proposals for democratic education fall within the contemporary branch of liberalism called "comprehensive liberalism." Its proponents include Kant and Dewey; its hero is Socrates; and its motto is his famous dictum "For humans, the unexamined life is not worth living." But there are two problems with Gutmann's proposals: they limit rather than increase diversity in society, and they may decrease rather than in-

crease true autonomy. In fact, it is questionable whether Gutmann's perspective is fully consistent with either liberalism in politics or cultural diversity in education.

Two individuals who have argued that Gutmann's approach is not liberal are John Rawls and William Galston. They advocate a type of liberalism known as "political liberalism." Rawls argues that in a pluralistic society such as the United States, one where reasonable people endorse religious and nonreligious as well as liberal and illiberal comprehensive doctrines, it is necessary to adopt a political conception of justice that preserves rather than represses reasonable conceptions of life. To demand that all citizens in a liberal society accept moral autonomy and critical self-reflection as the best way of life forces a comprehensive doctrine on individuals whose ultimate values conflict with this demand.[43] While liberalism must reject worldviews that teach political intolerance and wish to use the state to implement that intolerance, it can accept most reasonable doctrines, even those that include some illiberal ideas and practices.[44]

The court cases *Wisconsin v. Yoder* and *Mozert v. Hawkins County Board of Education*[45] provide examples of where comprehensive and political liberals disagree and show many of the consequences of the two liberalisms for education and social diversity. In the *Yoder* case, the Amish argued that a high school education was incompatible with the Amish way of life and therefore infringed upon their freedom of religion. They wanted to remove their children from school at age fourteen. But this practice conflicted with a Wisconsin law which mandated that students remain in school until they were sixteen. Most political liberals would argue that the Amish should have the right to remove their children; most comprehensive liberals would argue that they should not. As we discuss in Chapter 4, the United States Supreme Court agreed with the Amish parents that Wisconsin's compulsory education law violated the Free Exercise Clause of the First Amendment.

The tradition of the Old Order of Amish violates many basic liberal ideas. It is patriarchal, discourages its members from applying rational criticism to their religious beliefs, and restricts their children's economic opportunities by curtailing their formal education. In addition, the Amish refuse to participate in politics outside of their community. Despite these illiberal and undemocratic practices, most political liberals would maintain that the Amish lifestyle meets the requirements of a "reasonable way of life." It allows people to exit the community, protects its members' constitutional rights, and does not attempt to use the state to force others to accept the Amish worldview. As their way of life is reasonable, the state

should allow the Amish to protect it, even if this includes illiberal practices and limits the formal education of their children.

Comprehensive liberals argue that while Amish adults may choose a culture that is reasonable but illiberal, their decision to severely limit the education of their children is unacceptable. The decision is illegitimate because it reduces their children's opportunities to choose ways of life outside the Amish community and it prevents them from learning the skills necessary to participate fully in democratic politics. For comprehensive liberals, the religious freedom of adults does not "extend to exercising power over their children so as to deny them the education necessary for exercising full citizenship or for choosing among diverse ways of life." [46] Thus comprehensive liberals would deny the Amish the power to restrict their children's education even though this denial might end the Amish way of life and reduce cultural diversity in America.

The case of *Mozert v. Hawkins County Board of Education* [47] stretches the limits of political liberalism in that it involves a clash between the religious values of parents and the state's authority to teach children values that many see as essential to a democratic society. The *Mozert* case involved a group of fundamentalist Christian parents who claimed a right to exempt their children from the basic reading curriculum of the public schools. A stated goal of the readings was to encourage students to use their imaginations and to exercise critical judgment so that they could learn to understand and respect ways of life not their own. The *Mozert* parents objected to, among other things, exposure to evolution, feminism, and supernatural ideas not based in the parents' religion. They objected to these materials because they feared their children might doubt their beliefs and might think critically about issues on which the Bible provides The Answer. The U.S. Court of Appeals ruled that the required reading did not violate the free exercise rights of the *Mozert* students. The majority of the judges asserted that the free exercise exemption from curricular requirements was not warranted when the students were not required to affirm or deny a religious belief or required to engage in a practice prohibited by their religion.

Comprehensive liberals argue that what the *Mozert* parents want for their children is unacceptable because a liberal democracy expects citizens to exercise critical judgment, to respect reasonable points of view that they personally reject, and to obey public policies from which they dissent. Learning these skills and obligations requires exposure to ideas that differ from one's own. If, for example, students are to learn to deliberate about such ideas as why privacy protects civil liberties or why government must

protect the freedom of all religions, then education must expose them to ideas that differ from their own beliefs and values. This may be uncongenial to parents, but it is essential to civic education. Eamonn Callan makes this argument succinctly in his book *Creating Citizens: Political Education and Liberal Democracy*.

> The attempt to understand the reasonableness of convictions that may be in deep conflict with doctrines learned in the family cannot be carried through without inviting the disturbing question that these convictions might be the framework of a better way of life, or at least one that is just as good. That question is unavoidable because to understand the reasonableness of beliefs that initially seem wrong or even repellent I must imaginatively entertain the perspective those very beliefs furnish, and from that perspective my own way of life will look worse, or at least no better than what that perspective affirms.[48]

Comprehensive liberals further argue that the *Mozert* parents wish to deny moral education to their children. Students are educated as citizens and as autonomous moral actors by being required to take heed of the ideas of others. Students learn that part of being moral is to give serious consideration to those ideas. Not to give respect to the lifestyles and worldviews of others while claiming it for one's own ideas is to make an illegitimate demand and to fail to honor the humanity of others. In short, for the comprehensive liberal a refusal to take seriously the ideas of others is an immoral act.[49]

Many political liberals do not find this argument compelling. Liberalism, Galston asserts, should not attempt to change the educational practices within a community unless those practices restrict a constitutional right, impede the physical growth and maturation of children, or systematically disenable the development of a rationality that is necessary to participate in the society, economy, and polity. A decision to throw state power behind the promotion of individual autonomy and critical deliberation undermines the ways of life of those who cannot organize their affairs in accordance with autonomy without destroying the deepest sources of their identity.[50] The *Mozert* parents, for example, see their identity defined as people who are obedient to the word of God as manifested in the Bible. For them, to doubt biblical teachings is a sin. For teachers to urge these children to question the beliefs that the parents perceive as necessary for salvation forces young children to choose between the dictates of their religion and the instructions of their teachers. It also may reduce the ability of their culture to survive. The Old Order of Amish and Christian

fundamentalists are far from the only cultures based on beliefs that conflict with science and the rationality of the Enlightenment. Any tradition that encourages the sacrifice of individualism to the claims of faith, community, tribe, or nation may offend comprehensive liberalism.

If diversity means differences among individuals or groups over such matters as the nature of the good life, sources of moral authority, and reason versus faith, then comprehensive liberalism diminishes diversity because it reduces the survival rates of ways of life based on faith or cultural traditions. Galston writes, "[T]o place an ideal of autonomous choice . . . at the core of liberalism is in fact to narrow the range of possibilities within liberal societies. In the guise of protecting the capacity for diversity, the autonomy principle in fact represents a kind of uniformity." [51]

A problem with Galston's perspective is that educating students to unreflective ways of life may stand in the way of learning democratic citizenship. Does not an intense and unreflective commitment to one's own way of life conflict with the requirements of citizenship in a liberal society? Comprehensive liberals give an affirmative answer to this question. They insist that unless we use our capacities for imagination and empathy so that we can, at least in our mind, place ourselves into the cultures of others and thereby understand and respect the bases for their positions, we cannot adequately judge the merits of their policy preferences. [52] Political liberals reject that claim. They maintain that it is possible to have an intense and unreflective commitment to one's own beliefs and to be a good citizen in a liberal democracy. There is a difference, they argue, between learning to tolerate other comprehensive worldviews and requiring respect for those views. An atheist need not attempt to place herself in the position of a Buddhist, Muslim, or Christian in order to tolerate the political policy preferences that are informed by religious beliefs. Political liberals maintain that a citizen need only respect the right of others to have a different conception of the good and to advocate peacefully for it. In any pluralist society there are bound to exist groups loathsome and contemptible from our particular point of view. Liberalism does not require that a feminist respect the views of a patriarchalist any more than during the Reformation it required a Catholic to respect the beliefs of a Protestant. Liberalism requires only that we tolerate other points of view and recognize that we cannot use the state to force our views on others. Using the *Mozert* example, students need not become acquainted with worldviews that conflict with their own or to respect such views. It is sufficient that they understand that toleration for their own religious beliefs requires that they tolerate the views of others.

There is an additional problem with Gutmann's analysis: she believes

that those who live a life of obedience or who sacrifice their individual wants to the demands of their community cannot be autonomous. Callan makes a similar claim in his discussion of how fundamentalist religious groups may create children who are not autonomous but are "ethically servile."[53] Yet, as Jeff Spinner-Halev has argued, when a person rejects a life of individuality, this does not mean that the person is not autonomous. More than most Americans, the religious conservative is aware of the life he has chosen.[54] Theorists who relentlessly stress individual choice and opportunity as the basis of autonomy restrict the opportunities that people have to choose a life of obedience.[55] Lorraine Smith Pangle and Thomas Pangle, the foremost authorities on the American Founders' views of education, argue that the great synthesis of republican and liberal principles that characterized the Founders has been disappearing from our public school curricula and therefore from our moral horizon over the past fifty years. The cause of this, they assert, is the emphasis of liberalism on maximizing individual choice at the expense of civic duty and community obligation.

> [L]aw, and public education sanctioned by law, has been instilling with intensifying moralism that specific moral outlook that requires the liberation of the individual from all ties of solidarity, responsibility, tradition, and obligation that are not autonomously chosen. The balances delicately articulated in our original, founding public philosophy have been decisively tilted: rights have eclipsed responsibilities, freedom has obscured virtue, tolerance has rendered suspicious the passing of moral judgments, and concern for autonomous choice has come to outweigh concern for human fulfillment found in dedication and devotion.[56]

SCHOOL CHOICE AND COMMUNITARIAN THOUGHT

One answer to comprehensive liberalism and its emphasis on autonomy has been communitarianism. Arguments against increased school choice frequently include the recommendation that schools put less emphasis on teaching individualistic values and pay greater attention to developing public values, respect for the common good, and a sense of community. For example, Anthony Bryk, Valerie Lee, and Peter Holland argue in their book *Catholic Schools and the Common Good* that Catholic schools are more successful because they create a sense of community among students, parents, faculty, and staff. Bryk and his colleagues maintain that public schools should develop a similar spirit, one that places greater em-

phasis on public rather than private goals.[57] James Comer, a professor of child development at Yale, has started an entire public school movement based on communitarian ideas. He calls attention to the importance of community with the title of his 1996 book, *Rallying the Whole Village: The Comer Process for Reforming Education.*[58] Comer believes that if students are to maximize their potential, then they must sense that they belong to a community. This occurs when families, schools, and community organizations work together to achieve the common good of better educated, more community-spirited children.[59]

The theoretical underpinnings of the calls for community come from those who reject liberalism's view of human nature, society, and the state. While accepting the liberal ideals of democracy and political equality as well as the basic liberal rights of life, liberty, and due process, communitarians reject liberalism's argument that society should be (or can be) founded on a social contract for mutual benefit among rational, self-interested individuals.[60] Communitarians might summarize liberal theory as follows: (1) Individuals are antecedent to the society into which they are born and to the ends that they choose. (2) Society is composed of individuals who have their own aims, interests, and conceptions of the good, and they enter into society as autonomous beings seeking a cooperative venture for mutual advantage.[61] And, (3) the state's role is to guarantee individual rights and to place limits on what can be done to individuals for the sake of the common good.[62]

Communitarian theory claims that such an understanding of the self, society, and state denies the very elements that make civilized society possible. We do not come into the world as "unencumbered selves," but as "situated members" of families, religions, ethnic groups, classes, and nations. These inherited ties provide our values, goals, and communities. They are part of who we are, and they are essential to our understanding of ourselves. We cannot realistically step back and accurately examine these aspects of our lives. We are the product of narratives between ourselves and our communities, and the language we use for our narratives comes from interactions with other members of our communities. These narratives teach us that virtue sustains traditional practices, and this historically defined virtue enables us to overcome temptations and to achieve knowledge of the good.[63] Therefore, what is good for the individual must be closely related to the community's definition of what is good for a person who inhabits the role inherited from the clan, ethnic group, or religion.[64]

Because the person begins as a member of communities and because what is a good life is historically defined, communitarian theorists argue

that the idea of a state where neutral representatives make the laws is a disastrous myth. Charles Taylor writes that liberalism is far from the neutral set of difference-blind principles that political liberals defend. Rather, liberalism reflects one hegemonic culture that suppresses communal identities and discriminates against minority cultures.[65] Because communitarians reject the possibility of a neutral state, they believe the state should own up to its biases. By so doing, it openly can encourage citizens to support the common goals that they have democratically chosen.

Taylor uses the current law in Quebec as an example of how a regime may pursue a common good without violating basic human rights. The government in Quebec helps the French-speaking culture survive (the common good) by requiring, among other things, that all French-speaking and immigrant children attend schools taught in French. The purpose of this rule is to create new Québécois and to maintain their majority status.[66] Taylor claims that organizing society around the majority's definition of the good life allows the state to recognize the importance of inherited ties to the creation of individual identity and community. Supporting one conception of the good life does not allow the state to deprecate those citizens who do not share that conception. All regimes must respect the fundamental rights of life, liberty, religion, and due process. But to pursue the majority's vision of the common good the state may abridge such less essential rights as the right of parents to determine the culture their child will learn in school.[67]

Given their emphasis on the importance of communities based in tradition, religion, ethnicity, and ideology, we might expect that communitarians would support policies that allow families to choose schools that build and reinforce these communities. For example, parents for whom being an African American, a Catholic, or a supporter of gay and lesbian rights is an essential part of their identity could send their child to a school that stresses African American accomplishments, Catholic beliefs, or gay and lesbian rights. Despite these possibilities, communitarians not only reject vouchers, they often reject all types of school choice that are not based on geography.

Two communitarian theorists who have written extensively on education are Michael Walzer and Benjamin Barber. Both writers demand state control of education because improving democracy is the primary common good that the state should pursue, and democracy is best served in local communities where citizens learn it by practicing it.[68] Debating what values children must learn increases citizen participation. Participating in that debate helps neighborhood residents define who they are and what they stand for. Walzer and Barber maintain that all of the good

things that liberalism wants—freedom, justice, equality, and autonomy— are products of democracy.[69]

Communitarians reject vouchers because they believe the invisible hand of the market is a poor substitute for public deliberation and decision. Vouchers would not stimulate political judgment, but would contribute to its atrophy. They would harm the development of community because they allow "self-interested clients" to displace "community-minded neighbors."[70] Barber, after indicating that he likes many things about vouchers such as empowering citizens and encouraging them to become more involved in their children's education, ultimately rejects them.

> [A voucher system] speaks exclusively to their private interests as parents and thus as consumers of parental goods (such as education). . . . [It] transforms what ought to be a public question ("What is a good system of public education for our children?") into a personal question ("What kind of school do I want for my children?"). It permits citizens to think of education as a matter of private preference and encourages them to dissociate the generational ties that bind them to their own children from the lateral ties that bind them (and their children) to other parents and children.[71]

Walzer writes that while vouchers might reinforce existing communities, it is more likely that they would create a society without a strong geographic base. The result would be a society with

> [a] large and changing variety of ideological groups—or better, of groups of consumers brought together by the market. Citizens would be highly mobile, rootless, moving easily from one association to another. . . . Citizens could, in Albert Hirschman's terms, always choose "exit" over "voice."[72]

Walzer expects a voucher system, compared to a system of neighborhood schools, to decrease diversity within the schools and to provide less opportunity for personal growth. Vouchers also expose children to "entrepreneurial ruthlessness and parental indifference."[73] Walzer recognizes that existing housing patterns mean unequal schools, but he claims that neighborhood schools are preferable to all alternatives because politics always are geographically based.[74]

We believe there are critical defects in the above arguments. Walzer and Barber commit the error that Stephen Carter has labeled "geographic essentialism," i.e., all communities of political importance are geographically constructed.[75] If, however, "community" includes groups of individuals who define themselves according to a set of understandings that

may differ radically from the larger society, then the most common form of community in America is religious. And, as nearly 80 percent of private schools are religious, private schools could provide a strong foundation on which to build stronger communal ties. Why does Walzer omit religious communities? Because only by so doing does his vision of nomadic, rootless consumers make sense.

Walzer and Barber expect vouchers to decrease diversity. They base this expectation on their belief that public schools are more diverse than private schools and are more likely to teach tolerance of diversity. However, as the empirical data in Chapter 2 showed, the median private school is more ethnically diverse than the median public school. Private school students are more likely than public school students to have friends who are of a different ethnicity, and private school students are at least as tolerant as public school students. If shared values and traditions are the bases of community, if preparation for democracy means the development of tolerance, and if "diversity" denotes meaningful interaction among different ethnic groups, then currently private schools are more likely than public schools to achieve communitarian objectives.

Additional problems with the arguments of Walzer and Barber include their expectation that local control will result in participatory democracy and in the furtherance of equality. Citizen participation in local politics is notoriously low, and education politics are not bastions of democracy but citadels of interest group liberalism. Such organized interest groups as teachers' unions and the Christian Right are far more likely to dominate the politics of education than are ordinary citizens, particularly citizens who lack extensive personal resources. Barber recognizes this problem. He writes that "public schools . . . are run by a routinized union of educational bureaucrats whose certification and tenure rules give them a greater interest in security and tranquility than in education." [76] Inner-city public schools "are little more than the compulsory private domain of those trapped in poverty." [77] In addition, the empirical reality of popular control at the local level is that it generally works against political equality, ethnic and socioeconomic integration, equality of opportunity, and other liberal goals. [78]

Clearly Walzer and Barber do not advocate state control of education because they believe current education politics and current public schools stimulate democracy and community. Rather, they await a restructured polity based on participatory democracy at the neighborhood level, one in which whites do not participate more than nonwhites, where the rich do not vote more frequently than the poor, and where the better-organized few do not defeat the less-organized many. How do Walzer and Barber

expect this restructuring of politics to occur? One step in this process is to prohibit students from attending any school other than the neighborhood public school. Exit must be denied, Walzer argues, because private schools violate the principle of distributive justice, reduce political pressure to improve public schools, deny positive spillovers to students whom choice would leave behind, and reduce diversity.[79]

Walzer's reasons for denying families the right to exit are credible, but flawed. He is correct that the current education system creates inequalities in parental rights by giving high-income families choices denied to those with low incomes. But this is not a critique of vouchers. If a voucher provided full funding to low-income families, then inequalities in parental rights would decrease sharply. Walzer may be correct that allowing families with higher education and income to exit public schools reduces pressure on the public schools to improve and deprives the students who remain behind of positive spillovers. He fails to mention, however, that the majority of students who might create positive spillovers for inner-city children left long ago for suburban school districts. Neighborhood public schools simply do not and cannot address the problem of segregated housing, the institution that is the primary cause of inequities in all types of student resources.

Perhaps the most serious problem with communitarian educational proposals is their denial of the right to exit neighborhood schools. This allows the majority of politically active citizens to choose a vision of the good society and the good citizen and allows them to force this vision on the children of minorities and those who are not active politically. As Judge Boggs pointed out in his concurring opinion in *Mozert,* although neighborhood governments and school districts cannot violate students' constitutional rights, they have a wide berth to socialize students in ways that may disparage the lives their parents wish them to lead. Even Gutmann, a strong proponent of public schools and neighborhood democracy, argues that allowing children of intensely unhappy minorities to exit to private schools is preferable to forcing them to attend public schools. Allowing dissenting families to exit, she maintains, not only accords them an important liberal right, it also encourages public schools to become more tolerant.[80]

The denial of the right to exit is part of a larger danger, the curtailment of autonomy, that accompanies communitarians' desired polity. Comprehensive liberal Anthony Appiah and political liberal Nancy Rosenbaum argue that communitarian politics force people into roles they may have inherited but do not wish to have as part of their "public self." Appiah writes that requiring people to bring their ethnic identity or sexual pref-

erence into the public sphere makes public and private life difficult for those who may wish to treat their skin color and their sexual body as private dimensions of the self.[81] Similar arguments could be made about other inherited characteristics. Rosenbaum shows that being "situated" or "embedded" in an inherited, community-determined role is not always a positive thing. Members who inherit inferior roles may wish to escape those roles.[82]

Autonomy demands that people choose the roles or scripts that they wish to follow in their public life. By insisting that inherited characteristics define who we are as public citizens, communitarians encourage students to conform to socially defined roles rather than to become autonomous choosers. Taylor's discussion of Quebec unintentionally illustrates this problem. Denying immigrant children the right to exit schools that teach in French and which emphasize the French-speaking culture reduces the diversity that immigrants bring to Quebec. It also reduces autonomy by allowing schools to socialize children to a single cultural tradition rather than allowing families and children to choose among numerous reasonable alternatives.

DISCUSSION

Table 3.1 summarizes the conceptions of classical liberals, political liberals, progressives, comprehensive liberals, and communitarians concerning the goals of the "best education" and the appropriate division of power between the state and parents. The table shows that liberalism after Locke changed to advocate a more extensive role for government in society and a greatly enlarged state influence in education. This has led to a corresponding reduction in the rights of parents to control what their children will learn. John Stuart Mill and political liberals allow the state to fund education and to participate in its provision. They also see educational opportunity as an important aspect of increasing political and social equality. This view is consistent with their endorsement of a greater state role in social welfare. Comprehensive liberals have more ambitious expectations. They would like the state to encourage greater economic equality and to ensure political equality. To eliminate discrimination and to guarantee that parental prejudices do not go unchallenged, comprehensive liberals would adopt constitutional rules to prohibit certain types of practices and speech in schools. Most important, comprehensive liberals view a life based on faith as inferior and would use publicly funded schools to socialize students to that idea.

Table 3.1. Alternative Views of the State's Role in Education

	Parent Rights Strongest ⟶				⟶ State's Rights Strongest
	Classical Liberals	Political Liberals	Comprehensive Liberals	Progressive Liberals	Communitarians
Leading proponents	Locke & Mill	Rawls & Galston	Gutmann	Dewey and his disciples	Walzer & Barber
Role of the state in society	Limited to protecting life, liberty, and property	Protect constitutional rights and promote pluralism & autonomy	Protect constitutional rights, promote autonomy, and develop participatory citizens	Create a deliberative and egalitarian democracy with multiple shared values	Provide the structure through which the community creates the values it will promote
Role of the state in education	For Mill, the state should fund, but not provide. State tests for literacy and numeracy, but no other control.	Fund and regulate. The state can provide, but not as a monopoly. Minimal regulation of private schools.	Fund and provide public schools while stringently regulating private schools	Fund and provide as a monopoly	Fund and provide as a state monopoly. No private schools.
Goals of education	Practical skills for economic self-sufficiency and political self-government. The development of tolerance and (for Mill) autonomy.	The development of tolerant citizens and the necessary skills for self-government, economic self-sufficiency, and the performance of citizen duties	The development of autonomous, rational, and participatory citizens. The elevation of reason over faith. The elimination of political inequality.	Develop shared common values that emphasize science, creativity, participatory democracy and political and economic equality. Practical skills for economic self-sufficiency.	The development of participatory citizens who share common values chosen democratically by the citizens. The recognition of duties to the community.
Role of parents in education	Control the content, particularly that dealing with virtue	Control that portion of education dealing with what constitutes a good life and a good person	Teach children virtue at home and have the option to exit public schools if the teachings of the state are unacceptable	Support decisions made by the state and professional educators	Support those decisions made by the community through deliberative democracy

Among liberals, Dewey and the progressives give the state the broadest educational goals, and they give it almost total control over schooling. Progressive liberals want the state to root out illiberal practices within the various cultures that exist in liberal societies. Education in common public schools would be a primary tool in achieving this goal. The state's role is even greater for communitarian theorists. While the state guarantees that individuals maintain many liberal rights, communitarians consider it inappropriate (and impossible) for a citizen to choose independently her own conception of the good person and the good life. Rather, citizens collectively use state institutions to deliberate and develop social conceptions of these ideals. The government then uses education to socialize people to accept and to pursue those socially created goals.

We are now ready to return to our thought experiment with the veil of ignorance. We have seen that advocates for parental control and those who support state control have reasonable grounds for their choice. Now pretend that you are back behind the veil. Which claims convinced you? Gilles maintains that rational individuals behind the veil would reach a consensus that the state will fund education, but that parents will decide the content of their child's education. Why? Because we care more about what values our own children learn than we care about socializing to our point of view the children of others. Gilles believes that almost everyone can imagine stepping from behind the veil to discover that you have one set of values and the majority of active citizens hold values diametrically opposed to yours. You might be a feminist and a secular humanist stuck in a school district or state controlled by the Christian Right. Will your local school board be reasonable concerning what your child learns about history, biology, race relations, and appropriate sex roles? Alternatively, you might step from behind the veil to find yourself a Native American in a white culture. Would you accept a situation in which your local school board decides to teach that your traditions are illiberal superstitions? Gilles claims that representatives behind the veil would not choose an educational system that allows proponents of one worldview to impose their values on the children of those who do not share their beliefs. Why? Because the disadvantages of losing the struggle for political control over education far outweigh the advantages of being on the winning side.

The thought experiment that Gilles suggests is an extension of the argument proposed by Rawls when discussing the principle of religious toleration.[83] According to Rawls, people behind the veil of ignorance who are ignorant of their own religious practices would choose a policy that gave all persons an equal right to freedom of religious conscience and practice. But are religious freedom for adults and parents' control of their

children's education equivalent? In the former case individuals decide their own practices. In the latter situation one set of people (parents) choose for other people (their school-age children). Clearly the cases are different. Is a policy of parental control likely to achieve the appropriate balance between the sometimes competing interests of the child, parent, and state?

How you decide the veil-of-ignorance question depends upon how complete you believe parents' domination of their children is likely to be if they are in control of their child's education, whether you believe that cultures with illiberal practices are unacceptable in a liberal society, and your faith in the state and its professional educators to socialize students to more democratic and more autonomous lives. Below we provide our answer to these questions. Needless to say, many reasonable people are likely to disagree with us.

Dewey's ideal state demands shared values, a common culture, and the elimination of all illiberal aspects of communities and subcultures. Progressive liberals justify this liberal dominance because illiberal practices limit individual autonomy and encourage inequalities based on such characteristics as race or gender. However, neither autonomy nor political equality requires that all communities within a pluralistic society provide their members with a wide range of options and political equality. So long as the larger society contains a range of choices and political equality and the members of the illiberal community are free to exit, the members of that community have autonomy and the option (if they choose it) of political equality.[84] If liberals truly accept that the good is plural and that a liberal democratic society should strive for pluralism and diversity, then liberals must reject Dewey and his progressive liberalism.

Comprehensive liberals argue for state control for two major reasons. First, they argue that if parents raise their child so that the child sees as wrong and wrongheaded ideas that disagree with the parents' values, then the parents have made the child "ethically servile," as she has no ability to reject the parents' teachings. If the child has no ability to reject the parents' teachings, then the child will be unable to take on the burdens of judgment necessary for self-government in a democratic society when she becomes an adult.[85] Attendance of public schools, where children will learn to critically examine their own beliefs, prevents parental brainwashing. Notice that this argument depends on the truth of two empirical hypotheses: (1) parents can effectively socialize their children to such a degree that even in a pluralistic, liberal society the child is psychologically incapable of choosing any course other than the one preferred by the parents; and (2) a large number of parents will socialize their children to ethical servility (otherwise there would be no justification for reducing the

liberty of parents). Callan adds a third hypothesis: ethical servility is most likely to occur in families who look toward religious revelation rather than rationality to obtain truth. This makes them less likely to critically reflect upon their values and beliefs.

We believe that the above hypotheses are empirically false. In a society so completely pluralistic as our own, it is almost impossible for parents to socialize their children to ethical servility. This is particularly true for families who practice fundamentalist faiths in North America. Whether they are Jews, Christians, or Muslims, fundamentalists know that they are different from the mainstream society. American society encourages people to discover and fulfill their desires, but the religious fundamentalist lives a life that attempts to deny those desires. When one practices a life that is so different from the dominant culture, it is impossible not to think deeply about the life one has chosen.[86] Living a restrictive life takes a depth of commitment, character, and autonomy that most people lack. It is Nietzsche's Last Man who lacks autonomy, not the deeply religious man or woman.

Many readers may accept that the parents who would send their children to private schools are unlikely to socialize them into ethical servility, but reject public support for private schooling. They might argue that only public schools should receive public funds because public school students come in direct contact with people who do not share their worldview and values. This will make them more likely than private school students to understand, tolerate, and respect the viewpoints of others. Spinner-Halev makes this argument:

> For students to see other ways of life up close, they must talk on a regular basis with people who are different; they must befriend those with different ideas. Schools with a diverse student population give children the opportunity to learn about others in a real way, not just through books. Diverse schools enable students to learn how to cooperate with others and the importance of compromising with those who are different.[87]

The difficulty with this argument is that it is an empirical claim about educational outcomes that lacks empirical support. We know of no research that shows persons who attended public schools are more likely than private school students to cooperate with persons whose worldview differs from their own.

Communitarians Walzer, Barber, and Taylor join comprehensive liberals in rejecting state neutrality, because they believe the state cannot and should not be neutral. Communitarians believe the state should use local

participation in setting educational policy to improve democracy and to build community. Local participation in the formation of education policy encourages democracy by allowing citizens to choose the core values for their community. Schools then reinforce community by teaching students the values that citizens have democratically chosen.

From Sparta to the present, communitarian thinkers have searched for The Good. From Jean-Jacques Rousseau forward, a goal of communitarian education has been to prepare people to participate democratically in the search for that good and to understand that their desires must reflect the values that the community has chosen. But for liberals The Good is plural, and a goal of a liberal education is to develop in students the capacity to frame, revise, and pursue alternative conceptions of the good life and good citizen.[88] The liberal perspective, therefore, encourages multiple communities and requires that individuals be able to change communities as their conception of a good life evolves. But communitarians reject the right of exit and insist that inherited characteristics are constituent parts of our public selves. This negates liberalism and makes the achievement of liberal autonomy impossible. Therefore, so long as we believe that The Good is plural and expect education to foster the ability to choose among the competing conceptions of the good life, good person, and good citizen, we must reject the communitarian vision of education.

Does our rejection of the ideal communitarian education require that we reject all communitarian contributions to education theory? Not at all. Communitarians have attempted to bring back the republican spirit and the concept of duty into a society that often appears to care only about rights. They remind us that the American Founders saw that an ideal education creates citizens who recognize not only the benefits of living in a liberal democratic society, but also the corresponding personal and civic obligations.

CONCLUSION

It should now be clear that progressive and comprehensive liberals' portrayals of parental choice as illiberal make important tradeoffs. To guarantee that the education that all students receive is directly accountable to the state and to ensure that all students receive an education devoted to participatory democracy and a conception of individual autonomy based solely on rationality, they are giving up greater cultural diversity, government neutrality among competing worldviews, a lower probability of government tyranny, and a significant set of parental rights.

These tradeoffs represent a dramatic shift from a muted, Lockean political liberalism devoted to keeping citizens tolerant and industrious to an ambitious liberalism dedicated to a highly controversial ordering of values and goals. The fact that their vision is controversial does not make it wrong or any less a contender for the best possible human type. But their vision does invite the state to define what constitutes a good life.

There is an important, though often unrecognized, danger that occurs when attempting to use the state to implement any ambitious educational goal: the political reaction of those who oppose that goal. Recent political battles with both the Christian Right and postmoderns suggest that comprehensive liberals will have to fight these groups in order to win control over the state's educational apparatus. And herein lies a great danger to liberalism. The forces arrayed against comprehensive liberalism are—and, we suspect, will always be—stronger than those promoting it. Those who fight at the local school board level on behalf of comprehensive liberalism will lose, whether to the forces of egalitarianism (in some locales), postmodernism (in others), or "traditional family values" (in still others).

Why should more moderate liberals worry about comprehensive liberals fighting and losing? Because the likely result of such battles is not the status quo ante, but the loss of previously held liberties. Liberals must not pick unnecessary (and unwinnable) political fights. If we demand of parents that their children be handed over to the hostile (from the parents' viewpoint) public schools, the parents will evade or assail this system. At worst, aroused by the efforts of comprehensive liberals, opponents of liberalism will mobilize to take control of the state and use it to promote their view of the best life. Those who doubt such an outcome need only review how public schools in the United States have taught, and in many places continue to teach, creationism, racism, sexism, nativism, Protestantism, and relativism.

We agree with Rawls that an education based on justice as fairness would not cultivate any comprehensive doctrine. A liberalism that values diversity and recognizes that The Good is plural must treat equally all reasonable conceptions of the good life, whether based on faith, tradition, or reason. An educational system that treats diverse conceptions of life fairly does not choose to subsidize only the education that the state prefers. Therefore, the policies that best protect diversity and provide the greatest liberty are those that subsidize all reasonable approaches to education and allow families to choose freely among them.

But what would happen to the common core of liberal democratic values? When the American Founders developed the liberal arrangement embodied in the Constitution and the Bill of Rights, they agreed to put

religious differences in the private sphere. They also agreed to support a common public culture that included not only the basic liberal rights, but also their common identity as citizens of the United States. It seems to us that if Americans agree to give parents and not the state the principal control over education—requiring only that schools teach tolerance and the illegitimacy of using coercion to force one comprehensive view on others—there remains within the public life of Americans a substantial common history as well as an uncommon commitment to diversity, liberal democratic principles, and the American experiment.[89]

Parent Rights, School Choice, and Equality of Opportunity

IN THE PREVIOUS CHAPTER, education philosophy constituted the lens through which we viewed tradeoffs inherent in considering the claims of parents versus the state for controlling the education of children. In this chapter, constitutional law is our lens for looking at tradeoffs inherent in balancing parents' right to control the education of their children against society's interest in assuring that school choice programs pursue democratically chosen social goals in an environment that assures equality of opportunity.

Following the logic of the classical liberalism espoused by John Locke and John Stuart Mill, the federal judiciary for the first third of the twentieth century supported the idea that governmental intrusions into private lives required considerable justification. This was the era of the sanctity of private property and rugged individualism. In the context of education, the U.S. Supreme Court ruled in the early 1920s that parents have a constitutional right to control the upbringing of their children, including the right to send them to private schools. At the same time, the Court was reluctant to intrude on the authority of school officials to operate public schools. By the 1950s, deference to parent rights and school board authority faded, as the Supreme Court began the long effort to advance equality of opportunity by ending school segregation. But the pursuit was only partially successful and now is in retreat. Public policymakers worry that school choice will only aggravate the balkanization of education by race and class unless steps are taken to assure equality of opportunity through a system of integrated schools.

Can policymakers foster equality of opportunity in education by requiring that choice schools must be racially and economically integrated

Jennifer L. Kemerer is a coauthor of this chapter.

without violating the rights of choosing parents? This chapter explores this question from legal and empirical perspectives, beginning with a discussion of parent rights.

PARENT RIGHTS IN EDUCATION

Americans generally assume that they have a constitutional right to control the upbringing of their children. Encompassed within this assumed right is the desire to pass on a cultural tradition, to inculcate religious beliefs, to foster an understanding of the good life, to promote certain values and attitudes—in short, forming the character of their children. Most parents want the schools their children attend to support and reinforce these goals. Parental rights, however, are not mentioned anywhere in the U.S. Constitution. Parents sometimes discover that their rights are relatively weak when it comes to challenging the authority of public school officials to determine where their children should attend school and under what circumstances. At the same time, school choice implies that parents, not government officials, should make these decisions.

How Fundamental Are Parent Rights?

As a matter of constitutional law, parent rights in the context of education were first recognized in 1923 in the case of *Meyer v. Nebraska*.[1] The case involved a state law forbidding the teaching of foreign language in a public or private school to any child who had not successfully passed the eighth grade. A private school teacher was convicted for doing so and challenged the constitutionality of the law. The U.S. Supreme Court struck the measure down as a violation of the "teacher's right to teach"—a right that the Court has been reluctant to support in later cases—and the parents' right to "control the education of their own." The Court found these rights to emanate from the word "liberty" of the Fourteenth Amendment, which reads in part, "nor shall any State deprive a person of life, liberty, or property without due process of law."

Two years later, the Court revisited parent rights in the context of an Oregon law that required all children to attend public schools. The practical effect of the law was to put private schools out of business. Two private schools sued, claiming the law violated their property rights under the Fourteenth Amendment. In the *Pierce v. Society of Sisters* decision, the high court agreed.[2] Not only did the law constitute an "arbitrary, unreasonable, and unlawful interference" with the operation of private schools,

it also "unreasonably [interfered] with the liberty of parents and guardians to direct the upbringing and education of children under their control." The unanimous Court pointed out in a key passage that "the fundamental theory of liberty upon which all governments in this Union repose excludes any general power of the state to standardize its children by forcing them to accept instruction from public school teachers only. The child is not the mere creature of the state; those who nurture him and direct his destiny have the right, coupled with the high duty, to recognize and prepare him for additional obligations." The *Pierce* ruling is particularly important to school choice because it recognizes the right of parents to select a private school for the education of their children. But the decision conveyed no support for the idea that the state must provide the financial means to exercise the choice. And, as we discuss in Chapter 5, many states ratified constitutional provisions that forestall the provision of state aid to both private schools and parents. So, as a practical matter, most parents have been forced by economic reality and by compulsory attendance laws to send their children to assigned public schools.

Meyer and *Pierce* are seminal decisions that have triggered considerable debate in the legal community. It has been argued that the Court considered children as chattel in the decisions, a view that fits well within the property rights protectionism philosophy of the Court during the pre-Depression years.[3] After the Court's retreat in the 1930s from expansively interpreting the Fourteenth Amendment's Due Process Clause as a source of unenumerated constitutional rights, doubt arose as to the precedential value of these cases. In *Wisconsin v. Yoder*, a 1972 decision to be discussed below, the Court observed that *Pierce* provides "no support to the contention that parents may replace state educational requirements with their own idiosyncratic views of what knowledge a child needs to be a productive and happy member of society."[4] A year later in *Norwood v. Harrison* the Court ruled that Mississippi could not provide textbooks to students in segregated private schools.[5] The thrust of *Pierce*, the Court observed, was only to affirm the right of private schools to exist. The decision said nothing of any supposed right of private or parochial schools or of parents to share with public schools in state largesse.

In the 1976 case of *Runyon v. McCrary*, the Court upheld the application of a federal civil rights law, 42 U.S.C. §1981, to prohibit a private school from practicing racial discrimination in admissions.[6] The school argued that the statute interfered with the right of parents to have the choice of sending their children to a private school that practices racial segregation. The Court disagreed. Writing for the majority, Justice Potter Stewart noted that nothing in the Constitution restricts the ability of the

government to regulate the implementation of parental decisions concerning a child's education. Here the elimination of racial segregation practiced by a commercial private school that advertised in the Yellow Pages clearly took precedence over any intrusion on parent rights to control the education of their children. That same year, the Court recognized that children have rights independent of their parents. Writing for the majority in deciding that neither parents nor husbands can have veto power over the right of a woman under the age of eighteen to secure an abortion, Justice Harry A. Blackmun observed that "Constitutional rights do not mature and come into being magically only when one attains the state-defined age of majority. Minors, as well as adults, are protected by the Constitution and possess constitutional rights."[7]

In the spring of 2000, the Supreme Court breathed new life into the *Meyer* and *Pierce* rulings by affirming the Washington State Supreme Court's ruling that a statute giving state judges the authority to order child visitation over the objections of parents violates parent rights.[8] Writing for three colleagues, Justice Sandra Day O'Connor noted that the liberty interest of parents in the care, custody, and control of their children is "perhaps the oldest of the fundamental liberty interests recognized by this Court." Several other Justices wrote approvingly of parent rights but were less inclined to read them as expansively as Justice O'Connor. What the ruling might portend for parent rights in the context of education remains to be seen.

Coupling Parent Rights with Free Exercise of Religion

Are parent rights strengthened when combined with the First Amendment right of parents to free exercise of their religious beliefs? In the first case involving both, the Supreme Court was not supportive. In *Prince v. Commonwealth of Massachusetts* in 1944, the Supreme Court decided against a parent who maintained that she had a right to have her nine-year-old child sell religious magazines on public streets despite a state law prohibiting the practice.[9] Noting that neither parent rights nor rights of religion are beyond state regulation, the Court observed that the state has a wide range of authority for limiting parental freedom and authority in things affecting the child's welfare and that state power is not nullified by claiming interference with religious freedom.

However, in 1972 members of the Old Order Amish faith were successful in contesting a state law requiring two years of education beyond the eighth grade.[10] Chief Justice Warren E. Burger's majority opinion in *Wisconsin v. Yoder* noted the need to balance the interests of the state

against the interests of parents "with respect to the religious upbringing of their children." Burger ignored the fact that the *Pierce* decision was not limited just to the religious aspect of child rearing. Burger acknowledged that Wisconsin's interests in compulsory schooling beyond the eighth grade were important. However, they were not so compelling as to override the right of the Old Order Amish to control the education of their children. The majority recognized that the separatist nature of the Old Order Amish religious heritage made a convincing case, "one that probably few other religious groups or sects could make."[11]

More recent developments have cast doubt on the viability of the *Yoder* decision. In 1990 the high court handed down a ruling in which it declined to give religion a favored position with regard to exemptions from neutral governmental programs *(Employment Division, Department of Human Resources of Oregon v. Smith)*.[12] In so ruling, the Court upheld denial of unemployment benefits to a worker who was terminated for using peyote, an illegal hallucinogen, in a Native American religious ceremony. But the Court did not overrule the *Yoder* decision. Writing for the Court, Justice Antonin Scalia noted "hybrid" claims where religion was joined with other constitutional rights to tilt the balance in favor of the individual against the state. As a case in point, he cited *Wisconsin v. Yoder,* noting that the claim involved both the free exercise of religion and the right of parents to control their children's education. We explore in Chapter 7 what the implications of the *Smith* ruling might be for regulating publicly funded voucher programs encompassing religious private schools.

Contemporary Developments

In the absence of legislation, parent rights in education remain weak, as courts generally defer to the interest of public authorities in educating the child for the best interests of the child and for society in general. An Illinois couple discovered this in the early 1970s when they claimed a constitutional right to educate their children at home. A federal district court rejected the contention, pointing out that the *Pierce* decision did not enfranchise parents with a right to educate their children "as they see fit" and "in accordance with their determination of what best serves the family's interest and welfare." Such claims, the court ruled, do not rise above a personal or philosophical choice and are not constitutionally protected.[13] Similarly, parents were unsuccessful in challenging a school district's mandatory community service program for their children.[14]

The "*Yoder* exemption" also has been unavailing. In one of the leading cases involving claims arising under the Free Exercise Clause, Christian fundamentalists were unsuccessful in asserting a right to have their
children exempted from reading the Holt, Rinehart, and Winston reading
series. As we noted in the previous chapter, parents contended that reading the series introduced their children to a number of ideas and practices
that conflicted with the family religious views and thus undermined both
the free exercise of religion and parental rights. The U.S. Court of Appeals
for the Sixth Circuit held that to prove a violation of the Free Exercise
Clause, it must be established that the government compelled or coerced
a person either to affirm/disavow beliefs or to do/not do acts that are forbidden or required by the person's religion.[15] Mere exposure to religiously
objectionable material did not constitute an infringement on the students'
right to freely exercise their religion. "There was no evidence that the conduct required of the students was forbidden by their religion. Rather, the
witnesses testified that reading the Holt series 'could' or 'might' lead the
students to come to conclusions that were contrary to teachings of their
and their parents' religious beliefs. This is not sufficient to establish an
unconstitutional burden."

In 1995 the U.S. Court of Appeals for the First Circuit decided
against parents who contended that requiring their children to attend an
explicit AIDS awareness program violated both their parental and free
exercise of religion rights.[16] Finding no right of parents to "dictate the
curriculum at the public school to which they have chosen to send their
children," the judges also observed that combining parent rights with free
exercise rights did not bring the case within the "hybrid" exception advanced by the U.S. Supreme Court in *Employment Division v. Smith*. The
judges noted that the parents were not alleging that a one-time compulsory attendance requirement at the AIDS awareness program "threatened
their entire way of life," as was the case with the Old Order Amish in
Wisconsin v. Yoder. More to the point, the U.S. Court of Appeals for the
Tenth Circuit observed in a 1998 decision that merely invoking the parental rights doctrine and then combining it with a free exercise claim
will not suffice. "Whatever the *Smith* hybrid-rights theory may ultimately
mean," the judges wrote, "we believe that it at least requires a colorable
showing of infringement of recognized and specific constitutional rights,
rather than the mere invocation of a general right such as the right to
control the education of one's child."[17] The Tenth Circuit Court thus rejected the claim of parents who home schooled their child to a right to
send their child to public school on a part-time basis.

One of the reasons for these decisions is uncertainty among judges regarding the extent of parental rights in the context of schooling. Congress tried to infuse parent rights with more weight through legislation in 1995. Called the Parental Rights and Responsibilities Act, the measure recognized the "fundamental right of parents to direct the upbringing of a child" and required the state to show a compelling state interest before the parent's role could be "usurped." The right of a parent encompassed such actions as making health care decisions, disciplining the child, and directing the religious teaching of a child. The bill was not enacted. Constitutional amendments or statutes have been proposed in several states, including Colorado, Kansas, North Dakota, and Virginia, that would recognize the right of parents to direct the upbringing and education of their children.[18] None has been successful.

Congress did pass a law in 1993 that restored a favored position for religious exemptions, following the U.S. Supreme Court's *Employment Division v. Smith* decision. The law required that whenever government substantially burdens a person's religion, it must establish a compelling reason to do so. Further, the government must show that there is no less intrusive way to accomplish the purpose. The intent of the law was to restore religion as a favored right deserving of exemption from governmental requirements. However, the U.S. Supreme Court, in a 6-3 decision in 1997, declared the law unconstitutional as an infringement on the high court's prerogative to determine the nature of a constitutional right.[19] In 1999, a similar measure called the Religious Liberty Protection Act passed the House of Representatives but was scaled back significantly in the Senate. Retitled the Religious Land Use and Institutionalized Persons Act, the bill was passed by both houses and signed into law by President Clinton in September 2000. The act prevents state and local governments from enacting zoning laws that substantially burden religious exercise and from imposing a substantial burden on the religious rights of persons confined in prisons and hospitals.

In sum, aside from the right to select private schools, parent rights to control the education of their children generally are subordinate to those of the state. This makes choice programs all the more important for those parents who lack the means to escape inferior public schools or to find an educational program that is philosophically suitable. At the same time, the state has a strong interest in assuring equality of opportunity for all choosers regardless of race or income. The dilemma for the state is how to do this without engaging in impermissible discrimination against parents and students and without diminishing the choice opportunity.

RACIAL AND ECONOMIC SEGREGATION IN TRADITIONAL PUBLIC SCHOOLS

The struggle for racial and economic equality in education is one of the major social movements of the twentieth century. It wasn't too long ago that states were instrumental in perpetuating a segregated public school system. First the federal judiciary and then Congress intervened to end state-sanctioned racial apartheid. Later, some of the same strategies were tried to ameliorate economic disparities. Because the passage of time inevitably dims recollection of the massive struggle waged to achieve racial and economic justice in education, we briefly highlight events from 1954 onward. We show how school choice was part of the strategy of resistance and the extent to which racial and economic inequalities continue in public schooling. The resulting historical perspective will show why there is a tradeoff to be made between unfettered school choice and fostering equality of opportunity and what role the federal judiciary is likely to play in efforts to maintain a balance between the two.

Racial Segregation

In 1954, the Supreme Court recognized the evils inherent in a segregated school system, heralding a monumental change in judicial reasoning and in American education. By unanimously declaring in *Brown v. Board of Education* that "in the field of public education the doctrine of 'separate but equal' has no place," the Justices overturned over half a century of state-maintained segregation and created the legal justification and much of the impetus for the school desegregation movement of the past four decades.[20] *Brown* rightfully earned its place in civil rights history by eliminating the legal underpinnings of institutionalized racial inequality that the Court had upheld in its 1896 *Plessy v. Ferguson* decision.

But the decision was not without ambiguity. Was the mandate to end state-maintained school segregation or to bring about school integration? Prohibiting segregation and promoting integration are not the same. The former assumes that segregation is harmful because it is a form of government validation of racial discrimination, while the latter presupposes that segregation is harmful because racially balanced learning environments are beneficial for students. The Justices first relied upon the thrust of the Fourteenth Amendment Equal Protection Clause to conclude that all students have an equal opportunity to an education "where the state has undertaken to provide it." Then, in a controversial passage that cited social

science evidence on the harmful effects of racial segregation, the Court added, "Separate educational facilities are inherently unequal." Did this mean that anytime students are segregated in education, whether the result of state action or not, they are deprived of equal educational opportunity? Lack of clarity over the reach of the decision, coupled with the absence of a timetable to implement it, left schools and policymakers unsure how to proceed.

One year later, in the second *Brown v. Board of Education (Brown II)*[21] case, the Court announced that school authorities were to be the primary designers of desegregation plans, and federal district courts were responsible for seeing that they were implemented. The Court announced a flexible time frame, stating that federal judges must proceed with "all deliberate speed." Vagueness in the language in *Brown II* compounded the ambiguities of *Brown I*. Federal district courts were left without guidance on how to evaluate desegregation plans or to devise remedies in case they were deficient. Schools, especially those protesting *Brown I*'s ruling, took advantage of the flexibility in the phrase "all deliberate speed" by postponing, often indefinitely, their desegregation plans. The majority of Southern states embarked on a program of massive resistance, enacting legislation countering *Brown*'s holding, either by denying the Court's power to overturn *Plessy* or by hindering school desegregation. In a number of school districts, authorities only made token efforts to desegregate, falsified attendance reports, or simply closed the schools. To avoid a desegregation court order in Little Rock in 1958, voters approved turning the city's school system over to a private corporation to be operated on a segregated basis. The lease was later declared invalid. Many Southern federal judges also engaged in attempts to subvert the *Brown* rulings.[22] Furthermore, President Eisenhower remained silent, refusing to explicitly endorse or condemn the Court's rulings in *Brown I* and *II,* thereby implicitly allowing resistance. Ten years after *Brown,* 98 percent of Southern black children were still in totally segregated schools.

Meanwhile, the Northern states remained almost entirely untouched by the *Brown* decisions. Both cases invalidated government-enforced segregation, which was interpreted to apply to dual school systems—primarily a Southern phenomenon. In the North, many students were also segregated by race and ethnicity, but districts did not explicitly maintain dual schools. Other factors, such as residential segregation, largely were responsible. Industrial cities were populated by minorities and suburban communities by whites, thus making neighborhood schools racial and ethnic enclaves. Notably, the Court did not address segregation in schools outside of the South until two decades after the initial *Brown* decision.

Eventually, views about race relations in America began to change. The increased focus on civil rights drew attention to the lack of Southern compliance with *Brown I* and *II,* a situation that dramatized the need for congressional action. By 1964, events in the South, particularly the violence against blacks, which was being shown on television news programs, solidified public opinion in the North and helped prod a reluctant Congress to action. The 1964 Civil Rights Act empowered the Department of Health, Education, and Welfare to cut off federal funds from those school districts refusing to desegregate and also placed the power of the U.S. Attorney General's office at the disposal of private citizens faced with racial discrimination in public schooling. President Lyndon Johnson issued an executive order in September 1965 requiring the Attorney General to coordinate federal enforcement. With these two actions, the three branches of the federal government were aligned in their opposition to continued de jure segregation, and the pace of integration quickened.

In response, Southern school districts devised other ways to avoid desegregation. The school board of Prince Edward County, one of the counties involved in the original *Brown* case, simply closed its public schools and gave tuition grants to white students to attend segregated private schools. The Court declared the action unconstitutional in 1964.[23] The school district in New Kent County, Virginia, abandoned its previous dual school system and implemented a "freedom of choice" plan that allowed students to choose the school they wished to attend, thereby basing school admissions on choice rather than race. New Kent County was thus able to avoid engaging in de jure segregation. In practice, however, the schools of the district remained segregated. The so-called "Southern strategy" later embraced by the Nixon administration involved overt opposition to all forms of mandated desegregation remedies in favor of voluntary efforts such as freedom of choice and majority-to-minority transfer plans, as well as state subsidies to families for private school attendance.[24] The stigma associated with tuition grants and school choice from this period continues to tarnish their image, especially among minority group leaders who recall the bitter fights waged to challenge them. This continuing deep suspicion about the motives of those who propose school choice policies accounts for much of the discord between the leaders of minority groups, who view choice as a threat, and their grassroots members who view it as an opportunity. The state National Association for the Advancement of Colored People (NAACP), for example, was among those challenging the Milwaukee Public School Choice Program.

In 1968, the Court examined the freedom of choice practice in *Green v. New Kent County.*[25] In the process, the Court moved away from the

rhetoric of desegregation to focus on the remedies necessary to further integration. School officials could not satisfy the *Brown* mandate simply by ending separate schooling for blacks and whites. Rather, officials had to employ measures to assure that blacks and whites would go to school together. Justice Brennan, writing for a unanimous Court, noted that New Kent County's choice plan failed to substantively address segregation and ruled that school districts must eliminate past segregation "root and branch." *Green* further held that choice programs cannot be a district's first plan to remedy past discrimination, though the Court did not hold that "a 'freedom-of-choice' plan might of itself be unconstitutional." If choice plans were effective at creating integration in a previously segregated district, they would be considered acceptable. The New Kent school board was directed to develop a new plan to effectuate a system where there would be no black school and no white school, "but just schools." The thrust of *Green* was to end the years of delay that followed the *Brown* decisions in integrating black and white schools.

The high tide for integration is the Court's unanimous 1971 *Swann v. Charlotte-Mecklenburg Board of Education* decision.[26] In *Swann,* the Court approved a variety of remedial tools including busing, affirmative action plans utilizing flexible mathematical ratios, and the redrawing of school district boundaries to bring about an integrated schooling system. The Justices recognized the symbiotic relationship between residential segregation and school location by noting the common school board practice of building schools specifically intended for black or white students, of closing schools which appeared likely to become racially mixed, and of building new schools in the areas of white suburban expansion. At the same time, the Court backed away from outlawing one-race schools altogether. In some circumstances, Chief Justice Warren Burger noted, a "small number of one-race, or virtually one-race, schools within a district is not in and of itself the mark of a system that still practices segregation by law." What those circumstances might be was not altogether clear. Additionally, *Swann,* like *Green,* focused only on remedies for past de jure segregation, implying that desegregation remedies are only necessary when authorities "deliberately attempted" to segregate students. Further, once a district complies with *Brown I,* continued court-ordered year-by-year adjustments of the racial composition of the student body are not required.[27]

While state action to segregate students by race was impermissible, state action to integrate them in the interest of bringing about a diverse student body was not. In a key passage from *Swann* that carries implications for today's efforts to maintain integrated schools, Burger suggested

that the law would not limit a school district that sought on its own initiative to balance student enrollment by race.

> School authorities are traditionally charged with broad power to formulate and implement educational policy and might well conclude, for example, that in order to prepare students to live in a pluralistic society each school should have a prescribed ratio of Negro to white students reflecting the proportion for the district as a whole. To do this as an educational policy is within the broad discretionary powers of school authorities; absent a finding of a constitutional violation, however, that would not be within the authority of a federal court. (p. 16)

While the Court was deliberating over *Green* and *Swann,* some desegregation proponents argued that all segregation is de jure due to discrimination on the part of government officials in the establishment of neighborhood zones, the location of public housing, and the drawing of school district boundaries.[28] According to this argument, the courts have legal justification for intervening in Northern school segregation. In 1971, a federal district court followed this rationale in ruling that the Detroit public school system was illegally segregated.[29] The court also found that the State of Michigan had acted to reinforce the segregation by providing less transportation money for Detroit schools, by delaying a school board plan for developing high-quality magnet schools in segregated areas, and by generally concurring in the past actions of the Detroit school board. The district court went so far as to suggest a conspiracy by federal, state, and local officials in reinforcing segregation in the Detroit schools. The court fashioned a metropolitan desegregation order encompassing not only the city of Detroit but also fifty-three outlying, mostly white suburban school districts. Without such a remedy, Detroit would be mostly black, ringed by white suburban districts. When *Milliken v. Bradley* reached the U.S. Supreme Court, it would become a watershed decision.

Between 1968, when *Green* was decided, and 1974, when *Milliken* came before the high court, public opinion shifted. The initial controversy stirred by *Brown* centered primarily on Southern resistance. But over time, negative reaction came to focus on the activism of the judiciary in bringing about integration. After *Green,* criticism mounted that nonelected federal judges were usurping the powers of elected officials.[30] Concern over judicial activism reached its zenith when federal judges, realizing that many localities were unable or unwilling to comply with federal court decisions, started appointing court masters to oversee local change. In effect, the result was a transfer of power from traditional legislative representatives to

judicial appointees. Nothing attracted the criticism as much as forced busing. Polls showed high percentages of the American public opposed it as a desegregation remedy. The Nixon and Ford administrations were successful in introducing measures to curtail its use. After taking office in 1969, Richard Nixon made good on his promise to lessen the federal government's role in school desegregation by appointing more conservative Justices to the U.S. Supreme Court. First came Warren Burger in 1969, followed by Harry Blackmun in 1970, and Lewis Powell and William Rehnquist in 1972. Though both Burger and Blackmun joined in the 1971 *Swann* decision, these appointments would affect the course of desegregation law in subsequent decisions.

The 1973 case *Keyes v. School District No. 1* contains the first clue that the Justices were not of one mind in dealing with desegregation cases, though the decision did not part significantly from the reasoning of *Brown I*.[31] It was also the first time the Court examined public school segregation outside the South. The case involved the Denver school district, where petitioners had convincingly shown that school officials had engaged in deliberate racial segregation in one section of the system. They requested a district-wide desegregation order. In *Keyes,* the Supreme Court concluded that a district policy that produced intentional segregation "in a meaningful or significant segment" of a school system made all other instances of segregation in the system suspect.[32] The Court sent the case back to the trial judge to determine whether school officials could establish that other segregated schools in the district were not the result of intentional segregation. At the same time, the Court clarified the distinction between de jure and de facto discrimination. "The differentiating factor between *de jure* segregation and so-called *de facto* segregation," Justice Brennan wrote, "is *purpose* or *intent* to segregate."[33] Only actions that have segregative intent are unconstitutional and merit court-ordered desegregation plans. The changed definition served to open up to judicial scrutiny the North, where there had never been state-maintained segregation, yet individual school districts may have taken action to maintain racial segregation in part or all of their schools.

Several Justices expressed concern about trying to fit Northern school segregation into the de jure context through the "segregative intent" approach. Justice Rehnquist dissented, maintaining that the affirmative duty to integrate envisioned in cases like *Green* applied only to dual school systems in the South and should not be extended to the North. In his concurring and dissenting opinion, Justice Powell urged the Court to abandon the de jure/de facto dichotomy in favor of focusing on a national standard of "integration." This standard would require that whenever segregated

schools exist in a school district to a substantial degree, school officials have a responsibility of demonstrating that they nevertheless are operating an integrated school system. *Keyes* is important not only because of its application to Northern school districts, but also because for the first time, the Court included Mexican Americans with blacks as a protected class in the educational setting under the Fourteenth Amendment Equal Protection Clause.

The Court's 1974 *Milliken v. Bradley* decision signaled the beginning of a judicial retreat from aggressively pursuing school integration. By a 5-4 vote the Justices held that a desegregation remedy could cross school district boundaries *only* if all the involved districts had engaged in past de jure discrimination. Noting that the district court had not found the suburban districts to have been involved in the illegal segregation of the Detroit district, they were beyond the trial court's control. By precluding the use of metropolitan desegregation plans, the Court effectively prevented Northern schools from integrating because inner-city minority districts could not merge with wealthier and generally white suburban districts. *Milliken* implied that district lines were sacrosanct and that local control should be respected.

The dissenters bitterly attacked the decision. Justice Byron White pointed out that the Fourteenth Amendment Equal Protection Clause is worded in terms of the "state" and education is a state enterprise. The state should not be allowed to hide behind the talisman of local control. Justice Thurgood Marshall noted that a Detroit-only remedy would not bring about an effective remedy for de jure segregation in the city's schools. The limited remedy would result in whites fleeing to the suburbs, leaving the Detroit schools increasingly minority. Marshall argued that the majority's decision allowed the state to profit from its own wrong by enabling it to perpetuate the separation of the races. He observed that the majority was responding more to the mood of the country than to the command of the Equal Protection Clause. "In the short run," he concluded, "it may seem to be the easier course to allow our great metropolitan areas to be divided up each into two cities—one white, the other black—but it is a course, I predict, our people will ultimately regret."

Three recent Supreme Court decisions clearly demonstrate the judicial retreat from court-ordered integration. In 1991, the Court held that once a district operating under court-ordered desegregation is declared unitary, it can return to a neighborhood school policy even if one-race schools emerge so long as its motives are not to resegregate *(Board of Education of Oklahoma City Public Schools v. Dowell)*.[34] A year later, the Court ruled that a district court could allow partial withdrawal of a

court-ordered desegregation plan even if some areas of school operation are not unitary *(Freeman v. Pitts)*.[35] It also allowed a district to develop remedial policies designed to equalize the education of students in de facto segregated schools, thus implicitly condoning segregation due to private choices. In 1995, the Court ruled that a federal district court had exceeded its authority in ordering the Kansas City school district to develop magnet schools and to undertake other efforts for what the majority saw as a strategy to entice white students from the suburbs as a means of increasing minority achievement test scores in Kansas City *(Missouri v. Jenkins)*.[36] The majority asserted that the relationship between low test scores and prior segregative acts is too tenuous to permit such a judicial intrusion in school district affairs.

It is clear from this brief review of desegregation case law that after a brief flirtation with school integration, the federal judiciary has returned to its stance in the *Brown* cases. When de jure segregative acts can be proven in either the South or the North, the judiciary will mandate extensive remedies. But proving de jure segregation is extremely difficult in the absence of a state law or school district policy. The confluence of zoning laws, choice of residence, school building construction programs, and unstated motives is simply too complex. The question remains, however, whether racial balancing in the interest of promoting an integrated schooling environment, endorsed by former Chief Justice Burger, remains within the discretion of state and school officials. That the state at the least will be required to advance ample justification for such a policy is clear from a 1995 employment decision. In *Adarand Constructors, Inc. v. Peña,* a non-education employment case involving racial classifications, the Justices backed away from giving deference to so-called "benign" racial classifications designed to remedy racial imbalance. Instead, the Court held that "all governmental action based on race . . . should be subjected to detailed judicial inquiry to ensure that the *personal* right to equal protection of the laws has not been infringed."[37] This statement clearly casts doubt on the use of racial set-asides, as envisioned by Chief Justice Burger in *Swann,* to maintain integrated schooling systems. We return to this issue later in the chapter in the context of state efforts to assure diversity in school choice programs.

Economic Segregation

In 1973, the Supreme Court was faced with deciding whether substantial disparities in school funding violate the Equal Protection Clause of the Fourteenth Amendment. In a 5-4 ruling, with all four Nixon appointees

joining Justice Potter Stewart in the majority, the Court declared that it had no authority to order a remedy. The case involved the Texas system of school finance, which placed substantial funding for public schools in the hands of local school districts. The state had enacted a minimum foundation program that attempted to ameliorate some of the imbalance in per pupil expenditures. Eighty percent of the funding came from the state. The rest came from local districts. Thus, each district had to levy a property tax to support its contribution to the fund, known as the local fund assignment. In 1967–1968 Edgewood Independent School District, serving a predominantly Mexican American community in the core-city sector of San Antonio, paid $25 per student in local enrichment funding above its fund assignment at a property tax rate of $1.05 per $100 of valuation. The state's minimum foundation program added $222 per student, and with an additional $108 in federal funds, Edgewood had a total expenditure of $356 per student to spend. By contrast, Alamo Heights Independent School District, serving an affluent white residential community in San Antonio, paid $333 per pupil in local enrichment funding above its fund assignment at a property tax rate of 85¢ per $100 of valuation. The foundation program added $225 per student, with an additional $36 from federal funds, for a total of $594 per student, nearly twice as much as the Edgewood district. Similar interdistrict expenditure differences occurred elsewhere in Texas and throughout the nation.

The plaintiffs in the *San Antonio Independent School District v. Rodriguez* lawsuit argued that this system of educational finance violated the Equal Protection Clause by discriminating against the poor. In order to make their case, the plaintiffs tried to show that the poor, like racial minorities, are a protected class under the Fourteenth Amendment and that education is a fundamental constitutional right, thus requiring the state to demonstrate a compelling purpose in maintaining a finance system that denied equal educational opportunity because of substantial interdistrict disparities. Texas acknowledged that, required to do so, it could not show a compelling purpose. But the state argued that the poor are not a protected class and education is not a fundamental constitutional right. This being the case, all that was required of the state was to show that its finance program was rational. And this it could do because, while not perfect, the plan did reduce the disparities significantly. For example, Alamo Heights derived almost thirteen times as much money from local taxes as Edgewood did; the foundation program reduced the ratio to approximately 2:1.

The Supreme Court sided with the state.[38] The poor cannot be a protected class because, unlike racial groups, they cannot readily be identified

in the context of school finance. There was reason to believe, the majority noted, that the poorest families are not necessarily clustered in the poorest districts. And whether poor or not, no student was being absolutely deprived of education. Nor did the Court find education to be a fundamental right. Backing away from its statement in the *Brown* case that "today, education is perhaps the most important function of state and local governments," the majority noted that education is not among the enumerated rights in the Constitution and declined to find it there implicitly. Even if a certain "identifiable quantum of education" is a constitutionally protected prerequisite to meaningful exercise of freedom of speech or the right to vote, the state was providing it through the foundation program.

Four Justices dissented, the most outspoken being Justice Marshall, the architect of the *Brown* case.[39] Marshall condemned the Court for ignoring the plight of poor people locked into property-poor school districts. Finding the poor to be a readily discernible class—they live in property-poor districts—and education to be every bit as fundamental as the other rights to which the Court had given constitutional protection, such as the right to procreate, vote in state elections, and appeal a criminal conviction, Marshall demanded more of the state. He argued that the state was responsible for creating school districts and for tying school funding to the local property tax. Government-imposed land-use controls had influenced the location of businesses and residences, and hence determined each district's taxable property wealth. He characterized the Texas school finance system as a sham.

> If Texas had a system truly dedicated to local fiscal control, one would expect the quality of the educational opportunity provided in each district to vary with the decision of the voters in that district as to the level of sacrifice they wish to make for public education. In fact, the Texas scheme produces precisely the opposite result. Local school districts cannot choose to have the best education in the State by imposing the highest tax rate. Instead, the quality of the educational opportunity offered by any particular district is largely determined by the amount of taxable property located in the district—a factor over which local voters can exercise no control. (pp. 127–128)

The *San Antonio* decision ended all effort to seek equality of educational expenditures based on the federal Constitution. After 1973, litigation proceeded in state courts, with limited success. As of 1998, the supreme courts in nineteen states had found their educational systems to violate state constitutional requirements and had mandated equalization.[40]

Texas was one of those states. In *Edgewood I.S.D. v. Kirby*, the Texas Supreme Court adopted Marshall's approach to equalization.[41] In the other states, there either had been no litigation or the courts had upheld the state's program. The Committee on Educational Finance of the National Research Council's Commission on Behavioral and Social Sciences and Education recently observed that while state finance systems are more equitable than they used to be, "Looking at the nation as a whole, however, it is not clear that significant progress has been made in the last three decades in reducing spending disparities among states and districts."[42]

The *San Antonio* decision also is important to the contemporary debate over assuring equality of opportunity in choice schools because it includes a discussion of social science evidence. In contrast to the *Brown* decision, where the Court embraced social science evidence showing that segregation has a detrimental impact on minority children, the majority in *San Antonio* was reluctant to rely on social science research regarding the impact of financial inequity on student learning. The Justices were well aware of disagreement at the time among educational researchers about the relationship between student achievement and educational funding. James Coleman issued his provocative report on equality of educational opportunity in 1966.[43] The report showed little relationship between school resources and student achievement. By the time the case came before the U.S. Supreme Court, the social science community was consumed with debate about the validity of what came to be called the Coleman Report.[44] Writing for the Court in *San Antonio,* Justice Powell, himself a former president of the Richmond, Virginia, school board, cited the division among scholars in concluding that "the judiciary is well advised to refrain from imposing on the States inflexible constitutional restraints that could circumscribe or handicap the continued research and experimentation so vital to finding even partial solutions to educational problems and to keeping abreast of ever-changing conditions." In dissent, Justice Marshall replied that, if the relationship between expenditure and achievement was so tenuous, "it is difficult to understand why a number of our country's wealthiest school districts, which have no legal obligation to argue in support of the constitutionality of the Texas legislation, have nevertheless zealously pursued its cause before this Court."

Continuing Inequalities in Public Schools

There is no question that once all three branches of the federal government joined to enforce the *Brown* ruling, integration proceeded rapidly in the Southern states. When the 1964 Civil Rights Act was enacted, only

2 percent of black students in the South were in majority white schools. By 1988, the figure had reached 44 percent.[45] However, under the restraints of the *Milliken* decision, integration was much less successful in other regions of the country. For example, the percentage of black students attending virtually all-minority schools in the Northeast was nearly twice that of black students in the South in 1991–1992 (50.1 percent compared with 26.6 percent).[46]

The high water mark for school integration occurred in the mid-1980s. By the end of the 1990s, segregation of both blacks and Latinos was increasing across all regions of the country as school desegregation plans ended, busing fell out of favor, and school districts reverted to neighborhood attendance policies. Thirty-five percent of black students were attending 90–100 percent minority schools in 1996–1997, an increase of nearly 3 percent since the mid-1980s. Over a third of Latino students were attending such schools, a steady increase from 23 percent when figures were first collected in 1968–1969. Most students attended racially concentrated schools. Thus, in 1996–1997, the average white student attended a school that was 81.2 percent white, the average black student attended a school that was 54.5 percent black, and the average Latino student attended a school that was 52.5 percent Latino.[47]

The poverty rate among American children in 1995 was 21.5 percent, the highest rate by far of any industrialized country. Increasingly, income is concentrated in fewer and fewer families.[48] The result may be an increasing percentage of families at or below the poverty level. Somewhere between a fifth and a fourth of all American children are likely to be members of single-parent families or families where both parents work, live in substandard housing, have an inadequate diet, have no health insurance, and suffer the myriad other problems associated with poverty. These children also are most likely to be members of nonwhite families and attend schools that are racially concentrated. Table 4.1 illustrates that schools with high concentrations of black and Latino children also are schools where the poverty rate is high.

As we discuss in Chapter 6, economic inequalities resulting from the local funding of public schools are pervasive across the United States. Not only are there differences at the state level in per pupil expenditures, there also are disparities among districts within a single state and even among schools within a single school district. While the research on the relationship between school funding and student achievement remains conflicting, there is no dispute that students in poor schools with high concentrations of poor students do not do as well as students in other schools. In part this reflects the absence of spillover effects of students from higher socioeco-

Table 4.1. Overlap between Segregation and Poverty* in Public Schools, 1995–1996

% Poor in School	White School**	Black & Latino School**
50–100	7.7%	86.2%
0–10	31.0	3.2

* As measured by students applying for free lunches. Actual percentages of poverty may be underestimated in urban high schools, since many poor children in these schools refuse to sign up for free lunches.
** Percentage of racial concentration is 90–100 percent.
Source: data in Table 14 in Orfield and Yun, *Resegregation in American Schools,* Civil Rights Project, Harvard University, 1999.

nomic status (SES) families and in part the inadequacies of the schools—inferior teachers, larger classes, poorer equipment, poorly maintained buildings, and so on. Poor children in poorly funded schools lag far behind their peers in schools with average or above-average funding and below-average child poverty rates.[49]

It is in our urban school systems that racial segregation, poverty, and funding inadequacies come together to create the most serious problem for American education.[50] Nationwide, after adjusting for regional differences and the added expenses of educating children with special needs, urban districts lag behind nonurban districts in per pupil expenditures.[51] In selected states, there are often great disparities. Most fourth graders who live in U.S. cities can't read and most eighth graders can't do arithmetic.[52] At the high school level, more than half of inner-city students drop out before graduation. Those who do graduate are often poorly prepared for either advanced education or the workplace. Researchers in one study placed performance of students in poorly funded urban schools on a par with that of students in Nigeria and Swaziland.[53] Of course, wealthy families have known this for years and endeavor to seek a strong suburban public school for their children or pay tuition to send them to private schools. A look at one metropolitan region, Chicago, provides an apt illustration of how race, poverty, spending per pupil, and low test score performance come together in an urban district (Table 4.2). As is evident from the table, over 90 percent of the high school student population in the City of Chicago is nonwhite, compared with slightly over one quarter for the suburbs. Low-income students are clustered in the city schools. The suburban schools are better funded. Given this profile, it should not be surprising that test score performance by students in the Chicago schools pales in comparison to that of students in suburban schools.

Table 4.2. Urban and Suburban Public High Schools in the Chicago
Metropolitan Area, 1995

	City of Chicago N = 63	Suburbs N = 95
White (%)	10	74
Black (%)	63	13
Latino (%)	24	8
Asian (%)	3	6
Low income (%)	69	11
Spending per student	$6,596	$9,052
Math scores*	167	278

Source: Dennis Epple, "Stratification by Income, Race, and Outcomes in Chicago
Public High Schools," unpublished paper developed for the National Science Academy,
1999, and reproduced here with permission. The figures in the table are unweighted
averages of percentages in each group of schools.
* Math scores as reflected on the Illinois Goals Assessment Program.

The pattern of mostly nonwhite high-poverty urban districts that
are resource-poor ringed by mostly white low-poverty suburban school
districts that are resource-rich is reflective of American metropolitan environments as the new century begins. One offsetting factor is growth
in the nonwhite middle class. Like their white counterparts, these families
also seek to escape inner-city school districts. Another factor is the decline
in the percentage of white students in American education in general coupled with the rapid increase of nonwhite students. By 1996, the nonwhite
enrollment was 36 percent and is projected to reach 58 percent by 2050.
As time goes on, more and more nonwhite families will live in the suburbs.
There is no question that suburban and rural school districts are much
more integrated than central cities.[54] The fact that white and nonwhite
students are assigned to attend the same school, of course, does not necessarily mean that their learning and social environments are integrated.
Substantial within-school ability-grouping keeps students separated for
much of the school day. And this impacts student achievement. In the
Shaker Heights, Ohio, school district, where poor students are less than
8 percent of the enrollment, black students lag behind their white classmates on college admissions tests by more than 200 points.[55] Enrollment in high school honors and advanced placement classes is predominantly white. To combat the imbalance, the district eliminated admissions
criteria for academic classes two years ago, but few minority students
enroll.

Whether the increasing numbers of nonwhites outside central cities
will push the remaining whites into enclaves farther and farther from cen-

tral cities or into private schools remains to be seen. Equally important is whether the growing nonwhite middle class will become more closely affiliated with the white community or will maintain a separate cultural identity. The presence of middle-class whites in suburban school districts is especially important to continued enriched funding of these schools, since white voters in predominantly minority school districts are more likely to vote against tax levies. As one commentator notes with regard to the inner city, "*De facto* segregation creates a class of 'minority schools' in whose quality the white majority in society has no economic or personal stake." [56] With no stake, the white majority can demur, leaving it to someone else to fix the problems of these schools. Lacking political power, the minority community has resorted to the courts. That is one reason why minority plaintiffs in *Missouri v. Jenkins* fought hard to secure the funds to build magnet schools in the Kansas City district. Attracting a large white contingent back into the district would leverage the political influence that whites enjoy to the advantage of the minority community. The U.S. Supreme Court, however, found such efforts unwarranted and the district court's action supporting the funding of magnet schools an abuse of judicial authority. [57]

In a 1998 poll, 80 percent of black parents said academic achievement should be the primary focus of the school, compared with only 9 percent who opted for diversity and integration. [58] Sixty percent said they would switch to private schools if they had the money. In the same poll, 80 percent of blacks and 66 percent of whites said it was very important or somewhat important that their own child's school be racially integrated. School choice programs are designed to give parents greater opportunity to seek a quality education for their children. Do they also provide the opportunity for an integrated learning environment?

RACIAL AND ECONOMIC INEQUALITIES IN CHOICE SCHOOLS

Choice Schools and Ethnic Sorting

A consistent theme among the opponents of increased choice is that a key reason that families choose to leave their attendance-zone schools is to avoid other racial, ethnic, or religious groups. In particular, choice appeals to whites who want to avoid sending their children to school with blacks. Opponents maintain that if choice were expanded to include private schools, then schools would become more segregated and inequitable. [59]

To what degree do racism and the desire for isolation from other groups drive the choice decision?

Terry Moe's recent book, *Schools, Vouchers, and the American Public*, attempts to look at the role of racism in school choice using a large national survey that included 2,200 parents of school-age children, of whom 1,000 were parents in the inner city. Moe examined to what degree parents supported integration to achieve a common culture and busing to achieve racial and ethnic diversity. He found no evidence that attitudes on either of these questions were related to a family's decision to send its children to a private school or to its desire to have them leave their attendance-zone school.[60] Moe's results are consistent with other survey research on this issue and our own focus groups in San Antonio. However, attitudes, at least as expressed to a pollster, may not be valid measures of racism and the desire to send one's child to predominantly white schools. Most people know what the "correct answer" is when asked questions designed to uncover racism. When we look at actual choosing behavior, do we find greater evidence of racism?

Two recent papers on school choice suggest that parents do choose schools that have lower percentages of African Americans. Hamilton Lankford and James Wyckoff use 1990 Census data for eight metropolitan areas in the state of New York to estimate the impact of minority enrollment in public schools on a family's decision to send its children to private schools. They found that increased minority enrollment was an important predictor of whether a white family would take its children out of the public schools.[61] A second paper addressing the impact of minority enrollment on school choice uses the data from the National Educational Longitudinal Study and the National Center for Education Statistics. This paper, written by economist Robert Fairlie, found that not only do non-Hispanic whites flee schools with high concentrations of African Americans, so do Hispanic families.[62] However, as was the case with the research by Moe, the likelihood of parents choosing a private school for their children was unrelated to overtly expressed racist attitudes.

The above-described research provides policymakers with seemingly contradictory data. Whites and Hispanics tend to flee schools with large percentages of African American students, but the probability of flight appears unrelated to racism. Why, then, does increasing black enrollment lead other racial and ethnic groups to leave? One way of making sense of these seemingly contradictory findings is that whites and Hispanics use the percentage of blacks in a school as an indicator of academic quality. Given

the history in the United States of providing fewer resources and less-experienced teachers to schools that are predominantly African American, it makes sense that parents will expect a predominantly black school to be inferior. In addition, most parents believe that classmates who create positive academic spillovers are an important attribute of good schools. They also expect that low-income African American children are less likely to create such spillovers. Given these beliefs and expectations, it is rational for parents to expect that schools with higher black enrollments will provide a lower-quality educational environment. Such expectations among whites were a major reason that more affluent families left the inner cities and moved to the suburbs.

Regardless of the reasons that whites and Hispanics avoid predominantly African American schools, the above research has substantial implications for school choice policies. The first of these is that unless the historic pattern of underfunding inner-city public schools is reversed, whites and Latinos will continue to avoid schools with higher percentages of black students. The research of Lankford and Wyckoff as well as that of Fairlie found that schools with greater resources were less likely to experience white flight to private schools. The second implication is that unless a choice policy has strong regulations to prevent segregation or incentives to promote integration, increasing school choice will increase racial sorting.

One way of testing whether existing choice policies lead to increased segregation is to examine how well or how poorly charter schools around the country are integrated. Research consistently has shown that the racial and economic demographics of students attending charter schools are similar to those of traditional public schools. Table 4.3 shows the racial percentages for charter and public schools in twenty-seven states with charter schools in 1998–1999. For comparison purposes, the racial composition of American private schools in 1997–1998 is included.

The percentage of low-income students on free or reduced-price lunch attending charter schools is similar to that of public schools in the twenty-seven states with charter schools in 1998–1999: 39 percent for charter schools and 37 percent for public schools. Because they charge tuition, private schools enroll a much larger percentage of upper-income children, most of whom are white.

When viewed as a whole, the data show that traditional and public choice schools serve a sizable percentage of students of color and students from low-income families. But when viewed by the percentage of student body racial composition at the school level, a different pattern emerges.

Table 4.3. Racial Characteristics of Charter versus Public Schools in 27 States and All Private Schools

Racial/Ethnic Category	Charter Schools (%)	Public Schools (%)	Private Schools (%)
White	48	59	78
Black	24	17	9
Hispanic	21	18	8
Asian or Pacific Islander	3	4	0.5
American Indian or Alaskan Native	3	1	5
Other	1	NA	NA

Sources: State of Charter Schools: Fourth Year Report (U.S. Department of Education, 2000), p. 30. Data encompass 27 states with charter schools in 1998–1999. Charter school data are derived from surveys sent to the directors of these schools. Public school data are from 1997–1998. Numbers do not add up to 100 due to rounding. Private school data show racial composition of American private schools in 1997–1998. *Private School Universe Survey, 1997–98* (U.S. Department of Education, 1999).

Table 4.4 reveals that public choice schools are as segregated by race as traditional public schools. While there is considerable variation among states, charter schools serve slightly fewer children with disabilities than do traditional public schools (8 percent for charter schools and 11 percent for public schools).

Viewing the data at the school level is particularly important because factors that otherwise might be left out emerge. For example, in 1998–1999, the forty-three Texas charter schools serving at-risk students had much higher concentrations of minority students and lower concentrations of white students than traditional Texas public schools, while charter schools serving a not-at-risk student population had lower percentages of Hispanic and higher percentages of African American students than traditional Texas public schools. Most charter schools in Texas have racially and ethnically distinctive enrollments.[63] According to one study, Arizona charter schools enrolled a higher percentage of black students in 1997–1998 than regular public schools (7 percent versus 4 percent), but over half of the black students were attending just three schools. Extensive racial clustering has been found among Arizona charter schools, with charter schools typically twenty percentage points higher in white enrollment than regular public schools serving the same geographic area.[64] Arizona charter schools enrolling a majority of ethnic minority students tend to be either vocational-educational secondary schools or schools of last resort for students being expelled from traditional public schools. The racial clustering apparent in choice schools largely is the result of their mission and location. If a

Table 4.4. Minority Concentration in Public Schools and in Selected
School Choice Programs

School or Program	0–20% (mostly whites; few minorities) (%)	>80–100% (mostly minorities; few white) (%)	Total, racially distinctive schools (%)
U.S. public schools	61	9	70
U.S. charter schools*	38	27	65
Calif. public schools	17	23	40
Calif. charter schools	37	17	54
Tex. public schools	22	27	49
Tex. charter schools	8	55	63
Minn. public schools	83	2	85
Minn. charter schools	51	23	74

*These data encompass 552 charter schools operating in 26 states in 1997–1998. This study was conducted by the Institute for Education and Social Policy at New York University. In a study of charter schools operating in 10 states two years earlier, the U.S. Department of Education reported 44 percent were in the mostly white and 21 percent were in the mostly minority categories, respectively. The total of racially distinctive schools remains the same in both studies—65 percent. Both surveys were conducted primarily by telephone.

Sources: U.S. Department of Education, National Center for Education Statistics, Common Core of Data Survey, 1997–98; Institute for Education and Social Policy, New York University, 2000; Office of Research and Improvement, A Study of Charter Schools: First-Year Report (U.S. Department of Education, 1997); Texas Open-Enrollment Charter Schools: Third Year Evaluation (Texas Education Agency, 2000); Minnesota State Department of Education Data Center, 2000 (http://cfl.state.mn.us/datactr/datactr2.htm).

charter school is for at-risk students or has a curriculum designed to accentuate the contributions of a minority ethnic group, then we would expect it to enroll a higher percentage of minority children.[65]

The most appropriate measure of how well integrated a choice school is should not be the ethnic makeup of nearby attendance-zone public schools, but how well the ethnic composition of the choice school reflects the ethnic makeup of the metropolitan area.[66] When metropolitan areas divide into school districts that are ethnically or economically homogeneous, the result is highly segregated public schools. If a charter school (or any other form of choice school) draws students from across attendance zones and school districts, then the school's success at integrating students should be measured by how well the school's ethnic makeup reflects the metropolitan district. Indeed, Greene found this to be true when he rean-

alyzed a portion of the study by Cobb and Glass showing extensive racial clustering among Arizona charter schools in comparison with neighboring public schools. Contrary to Cobb and Glass, Greene found charter schools in Phoenix to be slightly more integrated than nearby public schools when the standard of comparison was the racial composition of metropolitan Phoenix.[67]

Racial Balance Measures

State efforts to require choice schools to have racially diverse student bodies are not likely to survive judicial scrutiny in many jurisdictions. This is clear from the pattern of case law that has developed since a legal challenge was mounted against the Akron city school district's prohibiting white students from transferring out of the school district in 1993, taking with them their state funds under Ohio's newly enacted open-enrollment statute. The policy also restricted nonwhites from transferring into the district. The policy was struck down as lacking a compelling purpose under the Fourteenth Amendment's Equal Protection Clause since the district had never been under a desegregation court order.[68]

Advocates for maintaining diversity in choice schools had greater hopes for a more artfully designed admissions policy to assure a racially diverse enrollment at the Boston Latin School (BLS), an academically oriented high school of choice within the Boston school district. When the policy was implemented in 1997, the Boston school district was three-quarters African American and Hispanic. The district had been under court-ordered desegregation during an earlier period, and BLS had maintained a 35 percent set-aside for nonwhites until faced with a lawsuit in 1995. Fearing that the nonwhite percentage of students at BLS would plummet unless steps were taken, the Boston School Committee had developed the policy to assure diversity in the BLS student body and to compensate for past discrimination. The committee contended that the low expectations veteran district elementary teachers held for nonwhite students were a manifestation of the lingering effects of past de jure segregation.

The newly devised admissions policy provided that the first half of the ninety spaces in the entering ninth-grade BLS class would be filled from the applicant pool strictly on the basis of rank-ordering student standardized test scores and grades. The second half also would be admitted on a rank-ordered basis, but within racial categories as determined by the racial breakdown of the students remaining in the applicant pool. For

Table 4.5. Percentages and Corresponding Numbers of Students for Second Half of
Boston Latin School Entering Class

Percentages of Racial / Ethnic Categories	Number of Students Admitted
40.4 White	18
27.8 Black	13
19.2 Asian	9
11.6 Hispanic	5
0 Native American	0

1997, Table 4.5 shows the percentages and numbers of admitted students for the remaining half of the entering class.

One white student sued when she was not admitted despite having higher scores and grades than nonwhite students who were admitted. Since half the class was to be admitted without regard to race or ethnicity, since anyone from across the district could apply for admissions, and since the racial/ethnic percentages for students in the remaining applicant pool would change from year to year, school officials believed the admissions policy effectively balanced the interests at stake. The U.S. Court of Appeals for the First Circuit disagreed. Applying the strict scrutiny test used by the U.S. Supreme Court to determine the constitutionality of race-based programs following the *Adarand* decision, the appellate court concluded in a 2-1 decision in 1998 that the admissions policy "is, at bottom, a mechanism for racial balancing—and placing our imprimatur on racial balancing risks setting a precedent that is both dangerous to our democratic ideals and almost always constitutionally forbidden."[69] The majority refused to accept the School Committee's proffered social science evidence regarding a legacy of discrimination against nonwhite students, pointing out that "When scientists (including social scientists) testify in court, they must bring the same intellectual vigor to the task that is required of them in other professional settings." Since the findings of the expert witness were not scientifically derived but based on observation and on experience in other districts, "It follows inexorably that, with no methodological support, [the expert witness] could not produce a meaningful analysis of causation and, accordingly, his conclusions cannot bear the weight of the School Committee's thesis." Other federal appellate courts have issued inconsistent rulings regarding what have become known as "controlled choice" measures, casting doubt on the constitutionality of both school-based racial set-asides and more broadly based requirements

that choice schools reflect the racial mix of the school district in which they are located.[70]

ACHIEVING DIVERSITY WITHOUT UNCONSTITUTIONAL DISCRIMINATION AGAINST PARENTS

Concern about segregating students by race and income in school choice programs forces school officials, educational scholars, and parents to reexamine current thinking about integrated learning environments and democratic education. Some believe that racial and economic stratification in choice schools is incongruent with democratic education because an integrated environment is a fundamental aspect of a publicly funded education in a diverse and democratic nation. Others argue that a democratic education entitles all students to a high-quality education, and racial demographics should be irrelevant to the state's responsibility to provide it. For the state to prevent parents from fully exercising freedom of choice in the interest of racial balancing not only conflicts with the vision of letting each parent select the preferred school for her children but also is unconstitutional.

The Case for Diversity

Supreme Court Justice Clarence Thomas begins his concurring opinion in *Missouri v. Jenkins,* the Kansas City school desegregation case, by stating, "It never ceases to amaze me that the courts are so willing to assume that anything that is predominantly black must be inferior."[71] Later in the opinion, he observes that if proponents of integration assert that black children only can learn in the company of whites, they must be saying that blacks are inherently inferior. "Under this theory," he writes, "segregation injures blacks because blacks, when left on their own, cannot achieve." Pointing to the nation's historically black colleges, Thomas labels such conclusions false and degrading.[72] Black colleges and high schools, he points out, can function "as the center and symbol of black communities, and provide examples of independent black leadership, success, and achievement."

There certainly is merit to the assertion that schools with a culturally centered curriculum can provide benefits to those who attend them. But Thomas, who was educated in Catholic schools, has an unrealistic perception of public schools in America. Most nonwhites do not attend the kind of school he envisions. Rather, they are assigned to resource-deprived

inner-city schools that more affluent white and minority families have long since abandoned and where learning and positive socialization experiences are minimal. Lacking funding to go anywhere else, these students have no choice but to remain where they are until they graduate or drop out. Over 50 percent of urban high school students in America drop out before graduation, with rates as high as 75 percent in some districts (Columbus, St. Louis, and Indianapolis).[73]

Even if racially concentrated schools are not resource-deprived, we do not believe it is good public policy for students living in an increasingly diverse and interdependent society to attend schools that are racially segregated. In their seminal book on affirmative action in higher education, William Bowen and Derek Bok offer this revealing statement from a young black male professional:

> I grew up in Detroit, and I really had no contact with any white people at all. My first roommate as a freshman was a white guy and we became very good friends, which was a surprise to me. . . . He was just a decent guy. Now, I'm the only black guy in this office, and I don't have any problem with that. But that goes back to my having had this guy as a roommate. A lot of [black] people wouldn't be able to function in this situation, just like a lot of white people wouldn't be able to function in an all black company. But if you get exposed to [people of different races] at a younger age, then I think a lot of the problems could be alleviated. I don't want my children to be constantly worried about race. I think they've got better things to do.[74]

Since values and beliefs are formulated at an early age, the cause of social awareness and respect for others probably is enhanced by having students learn in a racially diverse schooling environment. Common sense suggests as much. This, of course, is the underlying premise of the U.S. Supreme Court's school integration decisions, most notably *Green* and *Swann*.

But experience with forced school integration has dimmed enthusiasm for it except from die-hard integrationists. Research since the 1970s has been inconsistent on the relationship between school desegregation and student achievement.[75] Standardized test scores continue to show a wide gap between nonwhite and white student achievement. While the gap narrowed for a time in recent years, the typical black student still scores below 75 percent of American whites on most standardized tests.[76] Equally disturbing, when black and white students from similar socioeconomic backgrounds are assigned to the same school, black children at every class level do less well than white students.[77] Forced mixing of the races, coupled with parental and peer group unease about interracial re-

lationships, often balkanizes the public school environment along racial and socioeconomic lines, as a trip to the typical high school cafeteria will illustrate.[78]

While many factors contribute to nonwhite student underperformance and social isolation, three seem particularly noteworthy. First, the higher the aggregate SES of a school, the smaller the percentage of a student's achievement score that is explained by the student's own SES background. This means that a student's background matters less when positive spillovers from classmates are large.[79] The absence of higher SES students in inner-city schools denies enrolled students the positive spillovers associated with higher SES students. In combination with all the other deficiencies that characterize these schools, the absence of a motivated peer group contributes to lower student achievement. Lower SES students do better in schools with higher SES students.

Second, in many public schools, a counterculture contrary to the norms of the school may exist among nonwhites. In their study of school districts in two states, sociologist Laurence Steinberg and his associates discovered that many black and Hispanic high school students devalued academic accomplishment. The researchers note that "peer pressure among Black and Latino students *not* to excel in school is so strong in many communities—even among middle-class adolescents—that many positive steps that Black and Latino parents have taken to facilitate their children's school success are undermined."[80] Many black students may equate school norms, the school curriculum, and classroom teaching methodology with white American culture and language.[81]

Sociologists Claude Steele and Joshua Aronson observe from their research among undergraduates that even when nonwhites value learning, subtle cues from teachers and others around them regarding underperformance among nonwhites become a self-fulfilling prophecy. They term this "stereotype threat."[82] The experience of Dr. Benjamin Solomon Carson, a celebrated professor of neurosurgery and director of pediatric neurosurgery at the Johns Hopkins Hospital who specializes in the separation of Siamese twins, provides apt testimony to the Steele and Aronson contention. An African American, Carson admits to being an underachiever as a troubled child growing up fatherless in Detroit. His mother worked as a domestic. "When I thought I was stupid, I acted like a stupid person. And when I thought I was smart, I acted like a smart person and achieved like a smart person. I was fortunate, in that I had a mother who believed in me and kept telling me I was smart. You know, even as late as my first year of medical school, my faculty adviser advised me to drop out. He said I wasn't medical-school material."[83]

Acting contrary to the expectations of one's peers can be an isolating experience. At Proviso West High School in the near western suburbs of Chicago a few years back, only a handful of nonwhite students were enrolled with forty-one white students in American Studies, an honors course for high school juniors. The high school itself was nearly 80 percent nonwhite, a reversal of the percentages twenty years before. The black students in the honors class told a reporter that they were accused by other blacks of being "nerds" and sellouts to whites because they were honors students. Said one of the students, "We're not accepted by the white people because they think we're not smart enough. We're not accepted by black people because they think we're too smart. So we just hang with each other." [84] Steinberg and associates found the same alienation in segregated inner-city schools. Students who tried to do well in school were ostracized by their peers for "acting white." To excel academically, students had to hide their success from their peers. Other studies, however, question these findings, noting that black students who succeed are frequently elected to student body offices and are members of academic honor societies. [85]

Third, most low-income parents and students do not have the luxury of choosing their schools by choice of residence or by paying tuition at a private school. This means that their children are assigned to schools, thus undercutting a sense of ownership and commitment that would be the case if parents and students made an affirmative choice. Forced assignment helps explain why there often is little mixing of students of different races and backgrounds in integrated suburban schools. Thrown together, students find identity and support in groups of students like themselves. At private schools the mixing is more natural and more common.

By definition, choice schools entail a decision by parents to enroll their children. This instantly creates a common denominator among parents and students alike—the desire to attend the school and to study the curriculum that is offered. Having choosing parents is a major factor in the relative success of private schools with low-income students. As we have noted in Chapter 2, among the major school-level effects on achievement at Catholic schools are the socioeconomic and ethnic composition of the student body. Catholic schools improve the performance of high-risk and nonwhite students by having high percentages of minority children whose parents value education. As Steinberg and associates observe, "When parents are choosing a school, they are not only choosing a principal, a school facility, and a faculty. They are also choosing classmates— and potential friends—for their child." [86] This aspect of school choice— the choice of the peer group—is important to educational outcomes.

But if school choice results in schools that are as segregated by race and income as traditional public schools, how can this help foster equality of opportunity for all students to learn in an integrated school environment? Even more disturbing are the consequences for students left behind. Educational economist Henry M. Levin hypothesizes that "As higher SES students leave lower SES school environments for higher SES schools, their achievement will rise; however, their departure reduces the aggregate SES of the schools that they leave with a resulting decline in the achievement of the remaining students in those schools." [87]

Critics assert that choice schools are more highly segregated than are regular public schools. Therefore, choice increases segregation. But when the evidence shows that many choice schools actually are more integrated than public schools, critics argue that the integration occurred because the children of relatively advantaged low-income parents left their neighborhood schools and that this process left behind the most disadvantaged children. This process further injures society's least fortunate children because choosing families are more educated, more efficacious, and more involved in their children's education than are nonchoosing families. [88]

There are two problems with these assertions. First, almost any government program directed at low-income individuals or families has this outcome. Comparisons of those families who receive food stamps and enroll their children in government-supported medical care programs with those families who are eligible but do not enroll in the programs find that those who enroll have relatively higher levels of education, decisionmaking skills, and efficacy than those who do not. [89] Most opponents of school choice certainly would not argue that we should terminate the food stamp and children's medical programs because the most disadvantaged do not benefit from them. Rather, they would argue that the programs must expand their efforts to inform and recruit the least advantaged families.

Second, the level of integration is an outcome of families choosing where to send their children. Many public school districts in the United States adopted public choice programs in the expectation that if predominantly minority schools received special programs and additional resources, then white parents would enroll their children. Clearly, the public school officials expected the choosing families to have higher educations and greater parental involvement in education than the nonchoosing families. The success of the programs depended on this difference. When evaluating choice programs, the important issue is not who chooses, but what are the impacts of those choices. If choice increases integration and equalizes spillovers in a metropolitan area, then choice

has improved the school system. This is true whether or not choosing students have parents who are more involved in education and have higher socioeconomic status.[90]

Critics of increased choice are correct that, at least initially, public and private school choice *may* harm children in the most disadvantaged families. These children will lose classmates who create positive spillovers for them as the children of the slightly better off move to other schools. This outcome is a cost of increasing the choices available to low-income families. But the solution is not to abandon school choice policies. Rather, we must ensure that school choice policies include substantial incentives for choice schools to recruit the children of the most disadvantaged as well as for educating parents about choice options and helping them choose.

Proxies for Race

A provision in the North Carolina charter school law requires each charter school within one year after beginning operation to have a student population that "shall reasonably reflect the racial and ethnic composition of the general population residing within the local school administrative unit in which the school is located or the racial and ethnic composition of the special population that the school seeks to serve residing within the local school administrative unit in which the school is located."[91] As noted earlier, recent federal appellate court rulings indicate that such race-balancing measures are constitutional only in the context of court-ordered school desegregation. Controlled choice cases are also beginning to be heard at the state court level. In the spring of 2000, a South Carolina judge struck down that state's fledgling charter school law because of its racial quota provision.[92] The provision provided that a charter school's racial composition cannot differ from that of its host school by more than 10 percent. The trial judge ruled that the provision violates the U.S. Constitution because it constitutes racial discrimination in student admissions.

While racial set-asides are constitutionally suspect, such is not the case for other forms of set-asides that may overlap to some extent with race. As the U.S. Court of Appeals for the Fifth Circuit noted in its 1996 decision striking down an affirmative action admissions policy at the University of Texas School of Law, "We recognize that the use of some factors such as economic or educational background of one's parents may be somewhat correlated with race. This correlation, however, will not render the use of the factor unconstitutional if it is not adopted for the purpose of discrimination on the basis of race."[93] As we have noted, there

are distinct benefits to assuring that students from lower socioeconomic backgrounds are educated alongside students from higher socioeconomic backgrounds. In 1999 San Francisco replaced a long-running school desegregation plan that involved racial quotas with one that emphasized achieving diversity by other means, chiefly socioeconomic, that do not use race as the primary or predominant admissions criterion. The plan ended years of divisiveness associated with race-based student assignment and was upheld by the federal trial judge.[94] In the fall of 2000, the Wake County, North Carolina, school system became the largest school system to replace its policy of balancing elementary and secondary schools along racial lines with one that focuses on family income and student academic performance. Under the plan, none of the district's 110 schools will have a student population of more than 40 percent eligible for free or reduced-price lunches or more than 25 percent reading below grade level.[95]

In the context of a school choice program, the benefits of diversity are likely to be high, since all parents and students have subscribed to the school program and thus are more likely to form friendships across racial and economic lines. By according low-income families an opportunity to select the best schools for their children, equality of opportunity is advanced. The tradeoff is a diminution of the rights of some parents. A choice program that requires schools to serve all income levels undercuts the ability of parents to choose a school that mirrors their race and class but increases the rights of other parents to pursue an integrated education. We believe that the benefit in the form of social mobility for those heretofore disadvantaged by the current public educational system, together with the valuable socialization experience for all students, outweighs the cost to parent rights. A school choice system that fosters equality of opportunity by integrating students across racial and economic lines comes much closer than the current educational system to the ideal of the "common school." In Chapter 8 we provide the details of a plan that accomplishes these objectives.

SUMMARY

In principle, American jurisprudence has recognized the concept of parent rights. However, in the context of education, the right essentially is limited to choosing a private school in lieu of an assigned public school to satisfy the terms of the compulsory school law. Even home schooling is not a constitutional right but is dependent upon state legislation. This has the effect of giving states and school districts considerable authority over the

education of children. In response to the growing demand for school improvement, especially in inner-city school districts, where parents lack the means to move their children to better suburban public schools or to pay private school tuition, the majority of states have begun to embrace school choice policies. School choice has the potential to enfranchise parents with greater control over the education of their children as well as engender competition in the American educational system.

Despite nearly forty years of school desegregation efforts, American public schooling remains highly segregated by race and income. School choice programs for the most part reflect the same pattern. The evils of such a system are felt most directly by low-income students. Given the juxtaposition of parent choice with the value of an integrated education to both the student and society at large, a difficult tradeoff faces public policymakers. Should a publicly funded school choice program allow parents to choose the student population with which their children are to be educated, or should the state impose controls on the racial and economic makeup of the chosen school?

The use of racial balancing measures in school choice programs as a means of promoting diversity in learning environments has not yet been examined by the Supreme Court. But state and lower federal courts have cast doubt on whether racial diversity is significantly compelling to withstand constitutional challenge. An alternate means to the same end is to use proxies for race. So long as factors such as geography, parents' education, and family background are not used for the intent of racial discrimination, they are likely to be upheld. We believe that equality of opportunity is best served by using income as a means to assure that school choices are reflective of the broader makeup of society. By assuring a measure of racial and economic integration in all school choice programs, the state seeks the Archimedean point in balancing the parental right to choose with society's interest in fostering a learning environment that enhances positive student spillovers, equalizes educational opportunities for low-income and nonwhite students, and serves the interests of a pluralistic democratic society. We discuss how to construct such a policy in the final chapter.

FIVE

Vouchers and Tax Benefits: Tradeoffs between Religious Freedom and Separation of Church and State

IN CHAPTER 3, we explored contrasting positions between theorists who view education as a matter for parental determination and theorists who consider education too important to the maintenance of a democracy to leave to parent idiosyncrasies and prejudices. We observed that the former argue that by inculcating a set of values some parents abhor, a state-controlled education system takes sides and, by so doing, runs counter to the diversity and individual autonomy that are at the core of liberal democracy. Thus, if the state is to be value-neutral, a publicly funded educational system should treat religious and nonreligious schools equally. This would mean that a voucher or tax benefit system should encompass both. We noted, however, that we were discussing the philosophical dimensions of the issue, not its constitutionality. We address constitutional concerns in this chapter.

The rapid development of litigation over vouchers demonstrates that, immediately upon legislative enactment, a publicly funded voucher program runs headlong into the wall of separation between church and state evident in the anti-establishment provisions of both federal and state constitutions. This is so because 78 percent of the nation's private schools are religiously affiliated.[1] If voucher systems encompassing religious private schools cannot withstand constitutional challenge, they have substantially less value as a school reform measure. This chapter explores whether school vouchers that channel public funding to sectarian private schools are constitutional under both federal and state constitutions. In the process we analyze relevant state constitutional provisions and interpretive law in all fifty states. In a final section we focus on tax credits as a means of expanding school choice, since some view them as having advantages over vouchers.

The legality of school vouchers and tax benefits is complex because

it forces judges to determine the proper relationship between constitutional restraints on establishment of religion and protection for individual free exercise of religion, an area of the law where there is profound disagreement. Complicating the matter further is concern for the relationship between state and federal law inherent in the concept of federalism. Lack of consensus on these issues, together with the controversial nature of school vouchers and tax benefits, serves to highlight the political character of the judiciary and the role that judges' values play in judicial decision-making. Perceptions to the contrary, the judicial process is significantly political. This is especially true at the state level, where thirty-eight states use elections to choose or retain judges.[2] Political factors also are important at the federal level, where the president appoints judges with the advice and consent of the Senate. Differences in constitutional provisions among the states add to the complexity. This chapter addresses these concerns.

A TALE OF TWO JUDGES

Assume that your state constitution contains provisions specifying that no person shall be compelled to support any form of worship against his consent, that the state shall give no preference to any religious society, and that no public monies or portion thereof shall be drawn from the treasury for the support of any religious organization. Would school vouchers encompassing sectarian private schools violate these provisions? The conflicting decisions on the constitutionality of school vouchers handed down by two state trial judges in different states with constitutional provisions similar to these clearly demonstrate the complexities inherent in making this decision.

Judge Higginbotham and the Milwaukee Parental Choice Program

For five years after its enactment in 1990, the Milwaukee Parental Choice Program (MPCP) was undersubscribed, slow to reach its cap of 1 percent of the Milwaukee Public School enrollment.[3] The primary reason is that the program included only nonsectarian private schools, thus restricting the number of schools that could participate and the number of parents who would choose. In 1994–1995, there were only twenty-three nonsectarian private schools within the boundaries of the Milwaukee public school system. Of these, twelve chose to participate in the program. Under pressure from Republican Governor Tommy Thompson to expand the

range of choices available to parents and to expand the number of parents who could participate, the legislature in 1995 eliminated the provision barring participation by sectarian private schools. The legislature also raised the cap on the number of eligible participants to 7 percent of the Milwaukee Public School enrollment in 1995–1996 and 15 percent in 1996. The latter encompassed some fifteen thousand students. The schools were to receive the lesser of the schools' per pupil costs or the amount of per pupil state aid provided to students in the Milwaukee Public Schools—$4,400 in 1996–1997. The tuition then charged by a majority of the private schools was less than either of these amounts. The legislature placed no restrictions on how the schools spent the money they received. In addition, the legislature eliminated most of the reporting and accountability measures required by the earlier law.

The state supreme court upheld the original MPCP in 1992 by a 4-3 vote.[4] The decision, however, had no bearing on the matter of aiding religion since only nonsectarian private schools could receive state vouchers. Inclusion of sectarian private schools in the amended Milwaukee Parental Choice Program sparked a resumption of litigation, this time focused on Article I, Section 18, of the Wisconsin Constitution, which is explicit on erecting a wall of separation between church and state. The provision states in part: "nor shall any person be compelled to attend, erect or support any place of worship, or to maintain any ministry, without consent; nor shall . . . any preference be given by law to any religious establishments or modes of worship; nor shall any money be drawn from the treasury for the benefit of religious societies, or religious or theological seminaries." In 1995 the justices on the Wisconsin Supreme Court divided equally on the constitutionality of the 1995 amendments and sent the case back to the trial court for a hearing before Dane County Circuit Judge Paul Higginbotham.

In 1997, Judge Higginbotham ruled that the expansion of the program violated Article I, Section 18.[5] Judge Higginbotham pointed out that the Wisconsin Supreme Court previously had ruled that this provision imposes greater restrictions on state authority to aid private religious schools than the Establishment Clause of the First Amendment to the U.S. Constitution, which, together with the Fourteenth Amendment, prevents states from making laws "respecting an establishment of religion." While recognizing that the Wisconsin high court later opted to follow the U.S. Supreme Court's Establishment Clause precedents with regard to interpreting Article I, Section 18, Judge Higginbotham maintained that the Wisconsin high court never explicitly rejected its early pronouncement

that the Wisconsin constitutional provision is more restrictive than the First Amendment Establishment Clause.

Following a strict interpretation of Article I, Section 18, the judge then proceeded to apply it to the amended MPCP. He noted that the primary beneficiaries would be sectarian private schools, since 89 of the 122 eligible private schools in Milwaukee are sectarian. Further, he observed that religion is pervasively intertwined with the instructional program at these schools, citing the mission statements at a number of them. The judge noted no restrictions on how the private schools could use the funds, and he argued that because the schools receive more than they charge in tuition, "every dollar paid by the government exceeding the actual tuition provides a direct and substantial benefit to the religious schools." Higginbotham was particularly offended by what he considered religious coercion of taxpayers. "Perhaps the most offensive part of the amended MPCP," he wrote, "is it compels Wisconsin citizens of varying religious faiths to support schools with their tax dollars that proselytize students and attempt to inculcate them with beliefs contrary to their own." The judge also ruled that the amended MPCP constituted a private bill in violation of another constitutional provision and violated the judicially developed public purpose doctrine that legislation must serve the public interest. Rather than serve the public interest, Higginbotham found that the program served the interests of the sectarian private schools.

Judge Sadler and the Cleveland Scholarship Program

The Cleveland public scholarship program began on a pilot basis in the fall of 1996 following heavy promotion from Republican Governor George V. Voinovich. The program allowed parents with children in grades kindergarten through three to select private schools within the Cleveland City School District and public schools located in adjacent school districts. Unlike the original Milwaukee program, families in Cleveland could use their scholarships at sectarian private schools. By the summer of 1996, over fifty private schools had registered to participate, most of them sectarian. No adjacent school district had done so. During its first year, the program awarded 1,996 scholarships, up to a maximum of $2,250 each, to recipients chosen by lottery from a large applicant pool. Students who received a scholarship could renew it through the eighth grade. If a child attended a private school, the scholarship check was payable to the parent but transmitted directly to the school, where the parent then endorsed it over to the school. If the child attended an out-of-district public school, the

money went directly to the school. A companion program provided tutorial assistance grants up to $500 for parents whose children attended the Cleveland school system.

In Ohio, litigation began in the Court of Common Pleas of Ohio, Franklin County. Judge Lisa L. Sadler handed down a decision in July 1996 upholding the program.[6] In addressing the state constitutional claims, she noted that Article I, Section 7, and Article VI, Section 2, of the state constitution are coextensive with the First Amendment, despite their more restrictive wording. Article I, Section 7, provides in part that "No person shall be compelled to attend, erect, or support any place of worship, or maintain any form of worship, against his consent; and no preference shall be given, by law, to any religious society." Article VI, Section 2, requires an adequately financed public school system and provides that "no religious or other sect, or sects, shall ever have any exclusive right to, or control of, any part of the school funds of this state." Since the Cleveland program awards scholarships to parents without regard to the public or nonpublic nature of the schools they choose, Judge Sadler noted that any benefit to sectarian private schools was indirect. For this reason, there was no violation of either the First Amendment Establishment Clause or the anti-establishment provisions of the Ohio Constitution. The judge also ruled the program met the requirement of the state constitution's uniformity clause and its thorough and efficient clause. The latter requires the General Assembly to "secure a thorough and efficient system of common schools throughout the state." Plaintiffs argued that the program would impair the education of students in the Cleveland City School District by funneling high-achieving students and economic resources to private schools. But they did not convince Sadler. "Regardless of the merits of these arguments it is clear that any effect on those students remaining in the public school system is purely speculative," she wrote.

Differing Perspectives[7]

Note that despite virtually the same quite specific and restrictive constitutional provisions on state support for religious establishments, the judges reach opposite conclusions. Differences in the design of the two choice programs played some role in the decisions, but more important to the outcomes are differences between the judges in the way they interpret their respective constitutions. Long ago the legal community rejected the classical legal view that the law is a system of neutral rules that judges apply to reach one legally correct result. Judges cannot simply lay the

constitutional provision invoked beside the challenged statute and decide whether the latter squares with the former.[8] This is impossible because many constitutional provisions are open-ended and/or ambiguous. For example, how should the prohibition against "unreasonable" searches and seizures in the Fourth Amendment to the U.S. Constitution be interpreted? What is "due process of law" in the Fifth and Fourteenth Amendments? What does the First Amendment's prohibition of laws "respecting an establishment of religion" mean? Does the word "religion" mean a deity-bound faith, or can it encompass a philosophy of life as well? State constitutional provisions raise similar concerns.

In contrast to the classical view, legal realists maintain that since law is socially constructed, it is often indeterminate and subject to judicial idiosyncrasy. Research on court decisions shows clearly that the political orientation, background, and values of judges are important factors in judicial decisionmaking. Since the 1960s, many scholars have argued that all legal decisionmaking is simply politics disguised to legitimate configurations of power. Viewed from this perspective "lawyers, judges and scholars make highly controversial political choices, but use the ideology of legal reasoning to make our institutions appear neutral and our rules appear neutral."[9] U.S. Supreme Court Justice Abe Fortas is said to have written draft opinions without citations and then advised his law clerks to go out and find some supportive law. According to one of his biographers, "That did not mean that Fortas knew the supporting law was there. It meant that he considered law indeterminate and did not care about it much at all."[10]

Judges Higginbotham and Sadler clearly have different perspectives on the proper relationship between state establishment of religion and individual free exercise of religion. Despite a line of decisions by the Wisconsin Supreme Court suggesting otherwise, Higginbotham maintained that the state constitution is more restrictive of aid to religious institutions than the federal constitution. He bluntly acknowledged his disagreement with members of the U.S. Supreme Court about what constitutes a direct benefit to sectarian institutions. Addressing the procedure of having the state superintendent send a check directly to the school upon request by the parent, Higginbotham wrote:

> It can hardly be said that this does not constitute direct aid to the sectarian schools. Although the U.S. Supreme Court has chosen to turn its head and ignore the real impact of such aid, this court refused to accept that myth. Millions of dollars would be directed to religious institutions that are perva-

sively sectarian with a clear mission to indoctrinate Wisconsin students with their religious beliefs. Whether sent directly to the schools or sent directly to the schools with a mandate of restrictive endorsement by the parents, is irrelevant. . . . [T]he state cannot do indirectly what it cannot do directly. And that is provide money from the state treasury to pervasively sectarian religious schools for the purpose of educating Wisconsin students.[11]

In contrast, Ohio Circuit Judge Sadler quoted with approval from a U.S. Supreme Court decision upholding the provision of aid to a blind student to study religion at a sectarian college in observing that "the nonpublic sectarian schools participating in the scholarship program are benefitted only indirectly, and purely as a result of the 'genuinely independent and private choices of aid recipients.'"[12]

Clearly, judges' backgrounds and values affect their judicial perspective. At the time of the decision, Judge Higginbotham was the only African American on the Dane County bench. A liberal, Higginbotham previously served as minority affairs coordinator for Dane County and had been a member of the NAACP executive committee. One of the plaintiffs in the litigation was the NAACP. Governor Tommy Thompson sought to remove Higginbotham from the case by transferring it to another court but was unsuccessful. Thompson accused Higginbotham of being biased against the program.[13] Judge Sadler, a Republican, served as deputy legal counsel to Governor Voinovich. Voinovich appointed her to the Common Pleas Court in March 1996 when a vacancy occurred.[14] Four months later, Judge Sadler upheld the voucher plan.

In sum, different approaches to constitutional interpretation, coupled with ambiguous constitutional provisions involving government aid to religion and protection of religious freedom, suggest that the Higginbotham-Sadler dichotomy could be repeated many times with regard to school voucher and tax benefit programs if not precluded by the U.S. Supreme Court.

VOUCHERS, TAX BENEFITS, AND THE FEDERAL CONSTITUTION

Justice Higginbotham's decision striking down the amended Milwaukee voucher program was upheld in August 1997 by the Wisconsin Court of Appeals. Six months later, the Wisconsin Supreme Court overturned that decision and, in the process, became the first state supreme court to up-

hold vouchers for sectarian private school attendance. The Wisconsin high court's action had been anticipated by many, since the court had become more conservative following its upholding the original Milwaukee voucher program in 1992.[15] Unlike Judge Higginbotham and the appellate court, the Wisconsin justices viewed the state constitution to be coextensive with the federal constitution. Thus, they rested their decision on U.S. Supreme Court precedents, not on provisions of the state constitution, and in the process tilted in favor of free exercise of religion over separation of church and state.

Unlike Judge Higginbotham, the Wisconsin Supreme Court majority was not troubled either by the size of the voucher or by the fact that there are no controls on how private schools can spend the money. Rather, the majority focused on the attenuation of the connection between the state and religion by routing money through parents. The fact that the state actually sends the check directly to the private school where parents then endorse it over to the school was not a concern either. "The importance of our inquiry here," the majority wrote, "is not to ascertain the path upon which public funds travel under the amended program, but rather to determine who ultimately chooses that path."[16] The court also noted the presence of an opt-out provision for students who do not want to participate in religious activity at school. In September 1998 opponents of the expanded Milwaukee voucher program filed an appeal with the U.S. Supreme Court. A few months later, the Court announced that it was not taking the case.

Judge Sadler's position in her upholding the Cleveland voucher program prevailed before the Ohio Supreme Court in 1999 when the latter upheld the Cleveland voucher school program.[17] While the Ohio high court read the state constitution in conformity with the Establishment Clause of the First Amendment for purposes of this case and found no violation of either, the court did hold that the law's passage violated a state constitutional provision prohibiting the enactment of bills addressing more than one subject. Within weeks of the ruling, the Ohio Legislature reenacted the measure through a budget package geared specifically to education. Thereafter, opponents filed a lawsuit in federal court. The federal judge created a firestorm of opposition when, just before the opening of school in the fall of 1999, he suspended the voucher program pending a ruling on its constitutionality. Later, he modified the order so that students already enrolled in the program could continue. Emergency motions were filed with the U.S. Court of Appeals for the Sixth Circuit asking that the entire order be set aside so that eight hundred new voucher re-

cipients could enroll. Before the Sixth Circuit could rule, the U.S. Supreme Court took the unusual action of granting the Ohio attorney general's request that the trial judge's preliminary injunction be set aside entirely. What is particularly interesting about the Court's intervention is the lineup of Justices in the 5-4 ruling. Those in the majority were Chief Justice William H. Rehnquist and Justices Sandra Day O'Connor, Antonin Scalia, Anthony M. Kennedy, and Clarence Thomas. The dissenters were Justices John Paul Stevens, David H. Souter, Ruth Bader Ginsburg, and Stephen G. Breyer. While neither side issued an opinion, the inclination of five Justices to intervene at such a preliminary stage of litigation suggested special interest in the Cleveland voucher program. In December 1999 the federal district court struck the Ohio voucher program down as a violation of the Establishment Clause, a decision later affirmed in a 2-1 vote by the U.S. Court of Appeals for the Sixth Circuit.[18] In September 2001, the U.S. Supreme Court Justices announced that they would take the case.

Did the Wisconsin and Ohio supreme courts misread the rulings of the U.S. Supreme Court in upholding their respective voucher programs against charges of establishing religion? There has been considerable commentary in the legal community about what exactly the implications of these rulings are.[19] In a long line of decisions, the U.S. Supreme Court has construed the clause to prevent government from establishing a state church and from directly aiding any one religion—the Jeffersonian principle of separation of church and state. Yet there is considerable reason to believe the Supreme Court Justices will uphold a voucher program, if it is designed to avoid direct aid to religion, because the Justices have been inclined of late to reconsider the balance between the Establishment and the Free Exercise Clauses. In the next section, we briefly review the relevant precedents.

Channeling Money to Sectarian Private Schools

A voucher system designed essentially to channel public funds to sectarian private schools will not pass muster in federal court. This is clear from the Supreme Court's 1973 decision in *Committee for Public Education v. Nyquist* invalidating 6-3 a New York statute that provided financial assistance to private schools and to low-income parents.[20] In addition to maintenance and repair grants paid directly to private schools, the New York plan encompassed a tuition grant program for low-income families and a tax deduction program that varied by income level for other families so that their children could attend private schools. The Court ruled that both the New York tuition grant and tax deduction programs violated the Es-

tablishment Clause. Writing for the majority, Justice Powell noted that "if the grants are offered as an incentive to parents to send their children to sectarian schools by making unrestricted cash payments to them, the Establishment Clause is violated whether or not the actual dollars given eventually find their way into the sectarian institutions. Whether the grant is labeled a reimbursement, a reward, or a subsidy, its substantive impact is still the same." [21]

Other courts have followed the Court's *Nyquist* precedent in ruling on vouchers. For example, in 1995 a U.S. district court in Wisconsin relied on the *Nyquist* decision to reject a suit brought by five Milwaukee parents who contended that the original Milwaukee publicly funded voucher program denied them religious freedom and equal protection of the laws by not allowing them to select sectarian private schools. [22] Since tuition payments went directly to participating private schools, Judge John Reynolds noted that including religious schools would violate the Establishment Clause. "No case has overruled *Nyquist*'s prohibition on tuition grants and unrestricted direct subsidies to religious schools," he noted. Reynolds also pointed out that the Milwaukee program encompassed only private schools. Parents could not choose out-of-district public schools. The plaintiffs argued that the "present state of Establishment Clause jurisprudence is in flux" and that the current Supreme Court might uphold such a direct tuition reimbursement scheme to private sectarian schools, but the judge refused to speculate on the future of constitutional law.

Channeling Money to Parents and Students

While the Supreme Court majority in *Nyquist* found inconsequential the fact that the money first went to parents rather than directly to schools, they included a telling footnote. "Because of the manner in which we have resolved the tuition grant issue, we need not decide whether the significantly religious character of the statute's beneficiaries might differentiate the present case from a case involving some form of public assistance (e.g., scholarships) made available *without regard to the sectarian-nonsectarian, or public-nonpublic nature of the institution benefitted*" [emphasis added]. [23] In other words, if tuition vouchers could be redeemable at either public or private schools, the constitutional outcome might be different. For this reason, the Court observed that its decision did not compel a conclusion that the GI Bill impermissibly advances religion. This commentary foreshadowed the Court's seminal ruling in *Mueller v. Allen* a decade later. In *Mueller* the Supreme Court upheld 5-4 a Minnesota law that allows parents an income tax deduction for expenses incurred in providing tuition,

textbooks, and transportation for children in public or private schools. In a key passage, Justice Rehnquist observed in his opinion for the majority that "The historic purposes of the [Establishment] Clause simply do not encompass the sort of attenuated financial benefit, ultimately controlled by the private choice of individual parents, that eventually flows to parochial schools from the neutrally available tax benefit at issue in this case."[24] It did not trouble the majority that most of the benefits flow to parents of children in parochial schools. The dissenters viewed the indirect character of the aid plan as immaterial to its constitutionality. Writing for the four, Justice Marshall argued that "The statute is little more than a subsidy of tuition [at religious schools] masquerading as a subsidy of general educational expenses."

Four more recent cases have built on the *Mueller* reasoning. In 1986, the Court unanimously held that the Establishment Clause does not prevent the provision of vocational rehabilitation services to aid a blind student to pursue studies for the ministry at a Christian college. In *Witters v. Washington Department of Services,* the Court emphasized that aid is given to the student who then transmits it to the public or private educational institution of the student's choice.[25] Thus the money is not in the form of an impermissible direct state subsidy of religion. The Court was not troubled by the fact that the religious institution might use the assistance provided through the student for any purpose. The Court noted there was no incentive for the student to use the money at religious institutions and no significant part of the total funding for rehabilitation services would end up flowing there. Thus, the program does not "confer any message of state endorsement of religion." It is uncertain whether the fact that this case involved higher education undercuts its significance for elementary and secondary education. In the past, the Court has distinguished between these sectors of education in Establishment Clause cases.

In *Zobrest v. Catalina Foothills School District* (1993), the Court addressed whether the Establishment Clause bars a school district from providing a sign-language interpreter under the federal Individuals with Disabilities Education Act (IDEA) to a deaf student attending classes at a Catholic high school. The majority in the 5-4 ruling noted that "When the government offers a neutral service on the premises of a sectarian school as part of a general program that 'is no way skewed towards religion,' . . . it follows that under our previous decisions the provision of that service does not offend the Establishment Clause."[26] Handicapped children, not sectarian schools, are the primary beneficiaries of the sign-language interpreter. The majority observed that "respondent readily admits, as it must, that there would be no problem under the Establishment Clause

if the IDEA funds instead went directly to James' parents, who, in turn, hired the interpreter themselves." In dissent, Justices Blackmun and Souter sought to distinguish between the indirect aid upheld in *Mueller* and the provision of the sign-language interpreter. For the government to provide the sign-language interpreter, they maintained, offends the Establishment Clause because a government employee is serving as a conduit for religious messages conveyed to the student. They acknowledged, however, that "When government dispenses public funds to individuals who employ them to finance private choices, it is difficult to argue that government is actually endorsing religion."

In 1995 the Court ruled 5-4 in *Rosenberger v. Rector & Visitors of the University of Virginia* that a public university violates the Free Speech Clause of the First Amendment when it refuses to allow student activity fees to be paid to third-party printers of a student religious newspaper. While much of the focus of the majority's attention was on viewpoint discrimination, the Justices also noted that providing such assistance does not violate the Establishment Clause because the institution remains neutral toward religion. Drawing upon its earlier precedents, including *Mueller, Witters,* and *Zobrest,* the Court majority observed, "We have held that the guarantee of neutrality is respected, not offended, when the government, following neutral criteria and evenhanded policies, extends benefits to recipients whose ideologies and viewpoints, including religious ones, are broad and diverse." [27]

In its 1997 *Agostini v. Felton* decision, the Court relied on *Witters* and *Zobrest* to overturn an earlier ruling disallowing public school teachers to deliver compensatory education on sectarian private school campuses under a congressionally mandated program. Writing for the five-person majority, Justice O'Connor noted that since its original decision twelve years before, "we have departed from the rule relied on in *Ball* [one of the two earlier companion cases] that all government aid that directly aids the educational function of religious schools is invalid." [28] Citing *Witters,* she noted that a neutral government program that provides benefits without regard to the sectarian-nonsectarian or public-nonpublic nature of the institution benefited does not violate the Establishment Clause.

Finally, in 2000 the Court upheld the use of Chapter 2 federal funds to underwrite the costs of computers, computer software, and other instructional materials in religious nonprofit private schools.[29] Speaking for himself and three other Justices in *Mitchell v. Helms,* Justice Clarence Thomas was particularly expansive in allowing the channeling of governmental aid to religious institutions, even if used for religious purposes, so long as the government program is neutral. The plurality all but declared

vouchers constitutional. "If numerous private choices, rather than the single choice of a government, determine the distribution of aid pursuant to neutral eligibility criteria," Thomas wrote, "then a government cannot, or at least cannot easily, grant special favors that might lead to a religious establishment." He added, "Private choice also helps guarantee neutrality by mitigating the preference for pre-existing recipients that is arguably inherent in any governmental aid program and that could lead to a program inadvertently favoring one religion or favoring religious private schools in general over nonreligious ones."[30] Justices O'Connor and Breyer concurred in the decision but were more cautious in their reasoning. Justice O'Connor pointed out that the plurality's approval of the diversion of government aid for use in religious indoctrination was in tension with prior precedents and unnecessary to decide the case. However, she did acknowledge the difference between direct government aid and a private choice program where government funding is channeled to religious purposes via the decision of the aid recipient.

Based on these decisions, it appears likely that a majority of the present Justices on the U.S. Supreme Court will uphold against an Establishment Clause challenge a publicly funded voucher program that channels money to parents, allows parents to choose among a wide variety of public and private sectarian and nonsectarian schools, and does not provide a windfall for private religious schools that can be used for sectarian purposes. If the Supreme Court rules favorably on the Cleveland voucher program under the federal constitution, will the Justices allow state courts to apply their own state constitutional provisions to the issue? We now turn to that question.

THE SIGNIFICANCE OF FEDERALISM

Governmental power in our federal system is divided between a central government and fifty separate state governments. When there is conflict between federal and state law, federal law takes precedent by virtue of Article VI, Section 2, of the U.S. Constitution.[31]

To date, the U.S. Supreme Court has observed that the Establishment Clause of the First Amendment does not trump more restrictive state constitutional provisions. For example, while the Court ruled unanimously in *Witters v. Washington Department of Services* that the Establishment Clause does not prevent the provision of vocational rehabilitation services to aid a blind student to pursue studies at a Christian college to become a minister, the Justices noted that the Court was considering only the First

Amendment issue and that, on remand, the Washington State Supreme Court was free to consider the "far stricter" dictates of the Washington state constitution.[32] As discussed later in the chapter, the Washington high court struck down the aid plan. Further, there often are other provisions in state constitutions that may affect the outcome of litigation over state-funded voucher programs. These include provisions restricting expenditures of public monies to public schools only or requiring that public appropriations serve a public purpose.

A ruling by the U.S. Supreme Court that exclusion of sectarian private schools from a state voucher program violates the Free Exercise Clause and/or the Equal Protection Clause[33] of the federal constitution would reverse a trend by the present Court to give greater deference to state authority.[34] Proponents of state-funded voucher programs encompassing sectarian schools argue that such a strong assertion of federal authority is necessary to accord parents their full First Amendment rights, especially free exercise of religion. Opponents counter that such a ruling would emasculate the long-established wall of separation between church and state inherent in the Establishment Clause and run roughshod over state constitutional authority in the process.

As discussed later in the chapter, one-third of the states have antiestablishment constitutional provisions that are more strictly worded than the Establishment Clause of the First Amendment and consequently make the constitutionality of a voucher system encompassing sectarian private schools highly problematic unless a future U.S. Supreme Court decision moots them. Many of these provisions resulted from the ill-fated movement instituted by Rep. James Blaine of Maine in 1875 to add a constitutional amendment to the U.S. Constitution to halt public funding of Catholic education. While the Blaine Amendment failed, it sparked similar efforts at the state level as alarm grew over efforts by religious interests to secure state funding for their schools. By 1890, twenty-nine states had constitutional provisions limiting the transfer of public funds for sectarian purposes.[35]

At the same time, a number of state supreme courts have taken the position that their constitutional provisions pertaining to religion mean the same as the Establishment Clause of the First Amendment. This is true even though state constitutional provisions often have considerably different wording. For example, Illinois has a seemingly strict antiestablishment provision that prohibits the General Assembly and all political subdivisions from ever making any appropriation or paying from any public fund whatever "anything in aid of any church or sectarian purpose, or to help or sustain any school, academy, seminary, college, university, or

other literary or scientific institution, controlled by any church or sectarian denomination whatever. . . ."[36] However, the Supreme Court of
Illinois ruled in 1973 that the restrictions of this clause are identical to
those of the First Amendment.[37] Thus, how the U.S. Supreme Court decides the voucher question in the Cleveland case with regard to the federal
constitution will have great bearing on the meaning of constitutional provisions in Illinois and other states that have tied the meaning of their anti-
establishment constitutional provision to the First Amendment.

VOUCHERS AND STATE CONSTITUTIONS[38]

To determine how a state voucher program might fare under state constitutions, we reviewed the constitutions and interpretive case law of all fifty
states. Based on this review, we placed each of the fifty states into one
of three categories—restrictive, permissive, uncertain—with regard to
its likely orientation toward the constitutionality of state-funded school
vouchers encompassing sectarian private schools (see Table 5.1). Because
of the complexity of this task and the subjectivity inherent in making these
determinations, the classifications made here should be viewed as approxi-
mations. It will be useful to review Table 5.1 periodically in reading the
following discussion.

Restrictive States

Prohibition on Vouchers. The most restrictive constitutional provision,
of course, specifically would proscribe a publicly funded voucher program
involving any private school, whether sectarian or nonsectarian. Only the
Michigan Constitution falls into this category. Article 8, Section 2, of that
document prohibits the use of public monies by the state or its political subdivisions for the support of denominational or other nonpublic schools,
adding that "No payment, credit, *tax benefit, exemption or deductions,
tuition voucher,* subsidy, grant or loan of public monies or property shall
be provided, directly or indirectly, to support the attendance of any student or the employment of any person at any such nonpublic school or at
any location or institution where instruction is offered in whole or in part
to such nonpublic school students" [emphasis added]. The only exception
in that section is transportation of students to and from any school. Thus,
vouchers are not likely in Michigan absent amending the state constitution. A constitutional amendment on the November 2000 ballot to modify

Table 5.1. State Constitutional Orientation toward Voucher Programs*

State	Restrictive	Permissive	Uncertain	State	Restrictive	Permissive	Uncertain
AL				MT			X
AK	X	X		NE		X	
AZ		X		NV			X
AR		X		NH			X
CA	X			NJ			X
CO			X	NM			X
CT			X	NY		X	
DE	X			NC			X
FL			X**	ND	X		
GA			X	OH		X***	
HI	X			OK	X		
ID	X			OR			X
IL			X	PA		X	
IN			X	RI		X	
IA			X	SC		X	
KS	X			SD	X		
KY	X			TN			X
LA			X	TX			X
ME		X		UT		X	
MD		X		VT		X	
MA	X			VA	X		
MI	X			WA	X		
MN			X	WV		X	
MS		X		WI		X	
MO	X			WY	X		

* For purposes of this table, it is assumed that a state voucher program would encompass sectarian private schools.

** Litigation pending.

*** Litigation now under way in the U.S. Supreme Court.

§2 and permit a tuition voucher program for attendance at a private elementary or secondary school failed by a wide margin.

No Direct or Indirect Aid to Sectarian Private Schools. Other than the specific prohibition on tuition vouchers in the Michigan Constitution, the most restrictive state constitutional provision prohibits both direct and indirect aid to sectarian private schools. States in this category include Florida, Georgia, Montana, New York, and Oklahoma. As already noted, the Michigan Constitution also has a prohibition on direct and indirect aid. A variation of this wording can be found in state constitutions that prohibit expenditure of public monies that "support or benefit," "support or sustain," "support or assist," or "are used by or in aid of" any sectarian private school. For example, Article IX, Section 5, of the Idaho Constitution restricts the state legislature and any county, city, town, township, school district, or other public corporation from making any payment of public monies "to help support or sustain any school, academy, seminary, college, university, controlled by any church, sectarian or religious denomination whatsoever." Note that these provisions go beyond simply restricting direct aid to sectarian private schools. By including assistance that supports, benefits, or aids them, these provisions appear to have the same character as the prohibition on "indirect" aid in other state constitutions, an interpretation reflected in some of the case law. States with constitutional provisions like these include California, Colorado, Delaware, Illinois, Minnesota, Missouri, North Dakota, South Dakota, and Wyoming. The states of Hawaii and Kansas have constitutional provisions that restrict expenditure of public monies for the support or benefit of *any* private educational institution. Thus, if taken literally, these provisions would restrict aid benefiting nonsectarian private schools as well as those which are religiously affiliated.

In other states, constitutional provisions are restrictive regarding sectarian private schools but are silent with regard to those that are nonsectarian. However, as noted below, other constitutional provisions restricting use of public monies only for public schools appear to undercut the significance of the exclusion. Virginia is unique in specifically *allowing* assistance to nonsectarian private schools. Until the mid-1950s the Virginia Constitution restricted appropriations to schools owned or exclusively controlled by the state or its political subdivisions. Following a Virginia Supreme Court decision declaring tuition reimbursement to parents of children attending sectarian schools unconstitutional, the constitution was amended to allow such assistance at nonsectarian private schools and institutions of learning.[39]

What Is "Indirect Aid"? Despite the apparent strict separationist character of direct/indirect and support/benefit constitutional language, considerable room remains for judicial interpretation, and a sampling of the case law illustrates a divergence of opinion. One of the first and most often cited definitions of "indirect aid" comes from a 1938 New York ruling. In *Judd v. Board of Education* the Court of Appeals of New York, the state's highest court, struck down school busing for parochial students by a 4-3 vote because it was a form of indirect aid prohibited by Article XI, Section 3, of the state constitution.[40] That provision states in part, "Neither the state nor any subdivision thereof shall use its property or credit or any public money, or authorize or permit either to be used, directly or indirectly, in aid or maintenance, other than for examination or inspection, of any school or institution of learning wholly or in part under the control or direction of any religious denomination, or in which any denominational tenet or doctrine is taught." In deciding the case, the majority differentiated "direct" from "indirect" assistance: "Aid furnished 'directly' would be that furnished in a straight line, both literally and figuratively, to the school itself, unmistakably earmarked, and without circumlocution or ambiguity. Aid furnished 'indirectly' clearly embraces any contribution, to whomsoever made, circuitously, collaterally, disguised, or otherwise not in a straight, open and direct course for the open and avowed aid of the school, that may be to the benefit of the institution or promotional of its interests and purposes." School busing assistance, the court ruled, fell into the latter category. By implication, so would school vouchers.

In 1967 the Court of Appeals of New York had a change of view. By another 4-3 ruling, the court upheld the state's textbook loan program in *Board of Education v. Allen,* a decision later affirmed by the U.S. Supreme Court by a 6-3 margin.[41] Writing for the majority on the New York court, Judge Scileppi said of *Judd:* "We cannot agree with the reasoning of the majority in the *Judd* case and accordingly hold that it should not be followed. . . . The architecture reflected in *Judd* would impede every form of legislation, the benefits of which, in some remote way, might inure to parochial schools. It is our view that the words 'direct' and 'indirect' relate solely to the means of attaining the prohibited end of aiding religion as such." Subsequently, Article XI was amended to allow the legislature to "provide for the transportation of children to and from any school or institution of learning." The reasoning expressed by the Court of Appeals of New York in *Allen* suggests that a state voucher program whose primary purpose is aiding the education of children and which only indirectly benefits sectarian private schools has a good chance of being upheld in

that state. While the *Judd* decision has been discredited by its own judiciary, it has been cited elsewhere with approval by judges who adhere to a strict separationist viewpoint.[42]

The interpretive power of the state judiciary is well illustrated by the South Carolina Supreme Court, which simply ignored the prohibition on indirect aid to church-controlled educational institutions in the state's constitution when it upheld, in 1972, a tuition assistance program for students attending private colleges. The court noted in *Durham v. McLeod* that the student could choose any public or private institution in or out of the state.[43] Distinguishing its ruling the year before striking down funds made available for financial aid to students attending private colleges only,[44] the court observed, "In this case, the emphasis is on aid to the student rather than to any institution or class of institutions. All which provide higher education, whether public or private, sectarian or secular, are eligible. The loan is to the student, and all eligible institutions are as free to compete for his attendance as though it had been made by a commercial bank." The court noted that if sectarian schools had been excluded from the grant program, they would have been materially disadvantaged. In 1973, South Carolina changed its constitution so that it restricts only aid constituting a "direct benefit of any religious or other private educational institution." Thus, the constitution now conforms more closely to the South Carolina Supreme Court's ruling in *Durham*. Because of these developments, we place South Carolina in the permissive column of Table 5.1.

The South Carolina Supreme Court decision is important for two additional reasons. First, the channeling of funding to the family or to the student who then has a wide selection of public and private institutions from which to choose is an important design feature in school voucher programs because it attenuates the relationship between sectarian private schools and the state. Second, the exclusion of sectarian private schools from a general voucher program raises questions of religious discrimination and denial of free exercise rights under state constitutions. We have already noted that religious discrimination is an issue under the federal constitution.

As the majority of the New York judges recognized in *Board of Education v. Allen*, if taken literally, the *Judd* approach would make any state assistance that indirectly aids a sectarian school unconstitutional. In *Sheldon Jackson College v. State,* a 1979 decision, the Alaska Supreme Court noted that the Alaska Constitutional Convention rejected inclusion of the "direct or indirect" terminology because it did not want "to prevent the state from providing for the health and welfare of private school stu-

dents or from focusing on the special needs of individual residents."[45] The Alaska Constitution only restricts the expenditure of public funds "for the direct benefit of any religious or other private educational institution." The court noted that the state constitution "was designed to commit Alaska to the pursuit of public, not private education, without requiring absolute governmental indifference to any student choosing to be educated outside the public school system." Having said that, however, the Alaska Supreme Court unanimously struck down a state program providing grants to students in private colleges. The court noted that "merely channeling the funds through an intermediary will not save an otherwise improper expenditure of public monies. . . . Simply interposing an intermediary 'does not have a cleansing effect and somehow cause the funds to lose their identity as public funds. While the ingenuity of man is apparently limitless, the Court has held with unvarying regularity that one may not do by indirection what is forbidden directly.'" The justices observed in a telling sentence, "The courts have expressly noted that the *superficial form* of a benefit will not suffice to define its *substantive character*" [emphasis added]. Thus, despite the absence of an "indirect" component in the Alaska Constitution, the Alaska Supreme Court has come to the same conclusion as the *Judd* court with respect to educational benefits conferred indirectly on private educational institutions. For this reason, we list Alaska in the restrictive column of Table 5.1.

In summary, the presence of restrictive language in a state constitution is not definitive as to whether a state voucher program would be upheld. State judges often take an independent mind to interpreting state constitutional provisions, and what appears to be restrictive (New York) may turn out to be permissive and what appears to be permissive (Alaska) may turn out to be restrictive.

Funding for Public Schools Only. Several states have constitutional provisions restricting the expenditure of all public money to public schools, thus preventing the flow of public money to all private schools. Typical is the provision in the Massachusetts Constitution that "No grant, appropriation or use of public money or property or loan of public credit shall be made or authorized by the commonwealth or any political subdivision thereof for the purpose of founding, maintaining or aiding any . . . primary or secondary school . . . which is not publicly owned and under the exclusive control, order and supervision of public officers or public agents authorized by the commonwealth or federal authority or both. . . ." In 1970 the Supreme Judicial Court of Massachusetts, the state's highest court, unanimously issued an advisory opinion that channeling money to

students to help defray part of the cost of education at a private school would violate this provision.[46] In 1987 the court unanimously advised the state senate that a tax deduction bill for private school expenses would violate the same provision. The court noted that the form of payment is immaterial: "If aid has been channeled to the student rather than to the private school, the focus still is on the effect of the aid, not on the recipient."[47] Other states with similar provisions include California, Colorado, Nebraska, New Mexico, Virginia, and Wyoming. The states of Alabama and Pennsylvania have such a provision as well, but it can be overridden by a vote of two-thirds of the members elected to each house of the legislature. In part for this reason, these two states are listed in Table 5.1 as permissive toward a state voucher program. In some states, such as Connecticut, Delaware, and Texas, constitutional provisions restricting funding to public school purposes are limited to certain sources of funding, e.g., the public school fund. This leaves open the possibility of using other sources of funding for a state voucher program.

The wording of constitutional provisions can have a major impact on how they are interpreted. For example, prior to changing the restriction in the Nebraska Constitution from "in aid of" to "to" any school or institution not exclusively controlled by the state or its political subdivisions, the Nebraska Supreme Court ruled that a textbook loan program for private schools was unconstitutional as being "in aid of" institutions not publicly controlled. The court noted that it made no difference that the textbooks were loaned to students. "[T]he fact that the benefit of the secular textbooks goes originally to the student rather than directly to the school is a mere conduit and does not have the cleansing effect of removing the identity of the ultimate benefit to the school as being public funds."[48] But with the change in constitutional wording, the court in 1981 upheld a scholarship program enabling eligible Nebraska undergraduate students to attend postsecondary institutions including sectarian colleges provided the student is not pursuing a sectarian course of study.[49] The court noted that the money was not going to the institution, but rather to the student. Employing the same reasoning, the court a year later upheld a statute providing bus transportation to private school students and in 1989 upheld a statute authorizing public schools to loan textbooks to private school students.[50] Given the change, Nebraska is listed in the permissive category in Table 5.1.

Public Purpose Doctrine. Most states have a constitutional provision providing that public monies must be spent for a public purpose. Typical

is Kentucky constitutional provision §171, stipulating that "Taxes shall be levied and collected for public purposes only. . . ." By and large, courts defer to legislative judgment regarding what serves a public purpose. The prevailing view is well expressed by the Nebraska Supreme Court: "It is for the legislature to decide in the first instance what is and what is not a public purpose, but its determination is not conclusive on the courts."[51]

However, on rare occasions, a public purpose constitutional provision could prove fatal to a state voucher program. A case in point is the Kentucky Supreme Court decision striking down a textbook loan program for students in private schools.[52] Employing a form of strict constructionism, the court concluded that the public purpose envisioned in a provision of the state constitution was not being served, noting that "Nonpublic schools are open to selected people in the state, as contrasted with public schools which are open to 'all people in the state.'" The court held that the program also violated another constitutional provision prohibiting expenditures for sectarian schooling. Money spent on education must be spent exclusively in the public school system "except where the question of taxation for an educational purpose has been submitted to voters and the majority of the votes cast at the election on the question shall be in favor of such taxation," in accord with the state constitution. The court ruled the textbook loan program to be unconstitutional. "We cannot sell the people of Kentucky a mule and call it a horse," the justices wrote, "even if we believe the public needs a mule."

Closely related to the public purpose requirement is the nondelegation of legislative authority doctrine, which, as we shall see in Chapter 7 with regard to charter schools, restricts the ability of a legislature to turn its responsibilities over to private entities. A case in point is a 1976 Rhode Island Supreme Court decision striking down a statute requiring public school districts to bus children residing within their boundaries to private schools.[53] The court found the statute an unconstitutional delegation of legislative authority to private entities because it did not limit the ability of the private school to pass its transportation costs on to public officials. For delegation to be valid, the court set forth two conditions. First, the public policy of the legislation must be clearly spelled out. And second, there must be sufficient regulation to prevent private actors from exercising power in their own self-interest. Thereafter, the Rhode Island statute was amended to conform to these requirements and later upheld by the state supreme court. In the context of school choice, the nondelegation doctrine may restrict a legislature from turning over to private entities its constitutional responsibility to provide public schooling altogether or un-

less accompanied by sufficient accountability measures. Much will depend upon the wording of constitutional schooling provisions and upon judicial perspective.

Judicial Precedent. Even if state constitutional anti-establishment restrictions are relatively weak or ambiguous, a state supreme court may interpret them otherwise. Perhaps the best example is Washington State. In 1973 the Washington State Supreme Court unanimously struck down a state voucher program providing individual grants to needy and disadvantaged students seeking to attend the public or private school of their choice.[54] In unusually trenchant language, the court ruled that the program violated a provision of the Washington State Constitution that "All schools maintained or supported wholly or in part by the public funds shall be forever free from sectarian control or influence." Noting that the provision is more stringent than the Establishment Clause of the First Amendment, the court stated that there is "no such thing as a 'de minimis' violation of article IX, section 4 . . . the prohibition is absolute." The court was not persuaded that the free exercise rights of students were violated, that channeling money through parents attenuates state benefit to private schools, or that allowing students to attend either out-of-district public schools or private schools makes a difference.

In 1989, the Washington high court had a second opportunity to revisit the question when the U.S. Supreme Court remanded the *Witters* case involving state aid to a blind student studying religion at a sectarian private college. But this time the court was not of one mind. The justices struck down the aid program by a 5-4 margin, this time as a violation of Article I, Section 11, of the state constitution.[55] That provision states in part, "No public money or property shall be appropriated for or applied to any religious worship, exercise or instruction, or the support of any religious establishment." As before, the majority found no violation of the student's free exercise rights and no violation of equal protection of the laws. "We hold that when a person *'is getting a religious education'* (italics ours), to use the words of his attorney, that person comes squarely within the express prohibition contained in the Constitution of the State of Washington that *'no public money . . . shall be appropriated for or applied to any religious . . . instruction'.* (italics ours.) Const. art. I, §11 (part)." The dissenters focused on the flow of money to the individual, not the institution, arguing that it was in error to interpret the state constitutional provision as constraining individual decisions. Since the *Witters* ruling is relatively recent, the 5-4 split may well signal a repositioning of the court on the issue of indirect aid to religion and the proper balance between anti-

establishment provisions and free exercise rights. In particular, the views of the dissenters may be indicative of future trends on the Washington court—and elsewhere. Until that happens, however, the state is listed in the restricted column of Table 5.1.

In sum, there are sixteen states where there is an unfavorable legal climate for state voucher programs encompassing sectarian private schools. This may occur because the state constitution confines public funding to public schools only or because the state constitution and state judges prevent the flow of public money directly or indirectly to sectarian private schools. In many of these states, a constitutional amendment may be the only way for proponents of such programs to be successful.

Permissive States

No Anti-Establishment Provision. At the opposite end of the spectrum from the antivoucher stance of the Michigan Constitution are state constitutions that have no specific anti-establishment provisions. Maine, Maryland, Rhode Island, and Vermont fall into this category. In 1979 the Rhode Island Supreme Court upheld a student bus transportation program against a challenge under a section of the state constitution that requires the general assembly to promote public schools and "to adopt all means which may be necessary and proper to secure to the people the advantages and opportunities of education." Citing the U.S. Supreme Court's *Pierce v. Society of Sisters* decision in support of the right of parents to send their children to private schools, the high court noted, "We would . . . be fostering an anomaly if we held that the state is only obligated under article XII to assist those parents who choose public over private schools."[56] The Court of Appeals of Maryland, the state's highest court, has ruled that appropriations of public monies to sectarian private colleges and bus transportation for parochial students are constitutional as serving a public purpose as required by article 43 of the state constitution's Declaration of Rights.[57]

In 1999 the Supreme Judicial Court of Maine ruled against families who sent their children to a Catholic high school and sought to have the tuition paid by the state under the state's tuition payment program.[58] Failure to do so, the parents contended, denied them their free exercise of religion and equal protection of the laws. The tuition payment program was applicable in school districts that have no high schools and encompassed out-of-district public schools and nonsectarian private schools, but not religious private schools. Noting that the state and federal constitutions are coextensive, the Maine high court based its decision on the fed-

eral constitution. The justices first rejected the parents' free exercise of religion claims, pointing out that the state was not preventing parents from sending their children to religious private schools. Then the Maine high court concluded that if the tuition program were to encompass religious private schools, it would violate the Establishment Clause of the First Amendment. This is so because, as the program is designed, state monies flow directly to the schools parents choose, the tuition payment covers the bulk of the cost of educating the student, and there is no restriction on how the money is spent. The Maine justices did note that it might be possible for the legislature to redesign the program to give parents greater flexibility in choosing private schools, but advised that this is a function for legislators, not judges. Given the fact that the Maine Supreme Court did not indicate that the state constitution poses a greater bar than the federal constitution to a voucher program and given the justices' comments about how modifications in the design of the tuition payment program might change the outcome, we list Maine in the permissive category, despite the decision.

In 1999 the Supreme Court of Vermont ruled that a school district's payment of student tuition to a Catholic high school violates the state constitution's "Compelled Support Clause," which provides that no person "ought to, or of right can be compelled to" support any place of worship.[59] Noting the similarity between religious worship and religious education, the court found the absence of any restrictions on funding religious education through the tuition reimbursement plan a fatal flaw. However, like the Maine high court, the Supreme Court of Vermont explicitly left it to the legislature to correct the deficiency. It added that whatever the U.S. Supreme Court might decide in the future about a voucher program would not affect its interpretation of the state constitution. In the past, the Vermont Supreme Court has observed that as long as the general public benefit is the dominant interest served by state educational aid programs, the constitution is not offended when private institutions are recipients of the assistance.[60] Given the propensity for the Supreme Court of Vermont to look with favor on a carefully designed program, despite the 1999 decision, we list the state in the permissive column as well.

Supportive Legal Climate. There are eleven other states where some combination of weak anti-establishment constitutional provisions, strong free exercise provisions, the presence of a constitutional override provision on restricting appropriations to public education only, or supportive state supreme court precedent suggests a permissive climate for state

vouchers. The eleven states are Alabama, Arizona, Mississippi, Nebraska, New York, Ohio, Pennsylvania, South Carolina, Utah, West Virginia, and Wisconsin. We have discussed previously the constitutional provisions and interpretive law of Nebraska, New York, and South Carolina. And as already noted, the Wisconsin and Ohio supreme courts upheld the Milwaukee and Cleveland voucher programs, respectively.

With regard to the other states, none has a strict anti-establishment provision that prohibits indirect assistance to sectarian private schools. Most either prohibit direct assistance or restrict taxation and appropriations for sectarian purposes. State supreme courts in these states do not view prohibitions on direct aid as barring all assistance to sectarian private schools. In upholding a textbook loan program against a challenge under a constitutional provision prohibiting public funding "toward the support of any sectarian schools," the Mississippi Supreme Court noted that "If the pupil may fulfill its duty to the state by attending a parochial school it is difficult to see why the state may not fulfill its duty to the pupil by encouraging it 'by all suitable means.'"[61] To deny pupils textbooks when they transfer to parochial schools, the justices observed, "would constitute a denial of equal privileges on sectarian grounds."

In summary, vouchers encompassing sectarian private schools are permissible under Wisconsin and Ohio state constitutional law, and the constitutional climate appears favorable in at least a dozen other states. Whether a voucher program encompassing sectarian private schools will pass constitutional muster in these and other states depends in large measure upon how the program is designed, a topic addressed in the last section of the chapter.

Uncertain States

There is insufficient information for eighteen states to warrant placing them in either the restrictive or permissive columns of Table 5.1. They have been listed in the uncertain column because of ambiguous constitutional terminology, the absence of authoritative case law, or pending litigation.

Ambiguous Constitutional Terminology. Many states have provisions that restrict the direct advancement or support of religion but are silent on indirect advancement. In the absence of interpretive case law, the significance of these provisions for a state voucher program is not clear. For example, Article 12, Section 3, of New Mexico's constitution specifies that

"no part of the proceeds arising from the sale or disposal of any lands granted to the state by congress, or any other funds appropriated, levied, or collected for educational purposes, shall be used for the support of any sectarian, denominational or private school, college, or university." While direct support seems ruled out, the constitution does not address educational appropriations that may indirectly benefit denominational or private educational institutions. A 1976 attorney general opinion recognizes this fact in noting that a voucher system would aid children, not schools. The support of private schools, if any, opined the attorney general, would be only an indirect consequence, and therefore a voucher system for exceptional children would not be in violation of this section of the state constitution. The attorney general noted that the issue of advancement of religion could be addressed by limiting a voucher program to nonsectarian schools.[62]

In some states, the state supreme court has ruled that the state antiestablishment provision carries the same meaning as the First Amendment Establishment Clause despite often considerable variation in wording between the two. Thus, as noted earlier in the chapter, how the U.S. Supreme Court rules on the constitutionality of the Cleveland voucher program has great significance for litigation in these states.

Minnesota is one of the pioneering states in promoting school choice within the public sector, and by the mid-1990s, voucher proposals encompassing sectarian private schools were surfacing in the legislature under pressure from Republican Governor Arne Carlson. However, the Minnesota Supreme Court has issued ambiguous decisions involving the religion clauses in the state constitution. In 1970, the high court said that the limitations on state involvement with religion contained in the Minnesota Constitution are "substantially more restrictive" than the First Amendment to the U.S. Constitution.[63] But in 1990, the court noted that "Minnesotans are afforded greater protection for religious liberties against governmental action under the state constitution than under the first amendment of the federal constitution."[64] Indicative of possible shifting sands on the establishment versus free exercise issue in recent years in Minnesota is a 1993 appellate court decision involving the state's postsecondary choice program that enables high school students to attend college and obtain dual credit toward high school graduation and a college degree. At issue was whether students could choose to attend a sectarian private college. The appellate court answered in the affirmative, noting that the program is designed to benefit high school students, not the sectarian private college.[65] The court observed that participating colleges could be either public or private and that the state reimbursement is only 42 percent of the actual costs for tuition, materials,

and fees. Even if the college were pervasively sectarian, the appellate court noted, the constitutional provisions are not violated so long as the benefits are indirect and incidental.

Absence of Authoritative Case Law. In some states the absence of any relevant case law precludes a determination of how state constitutional provisions might apply to a state voucher program. A case in point is Texas, where the state constitution precludes appropriations "for the benefit of any sect, or religious society, theological or religious seminary" and prohibits use of the permanent and available school fund "for the support of any sectarian school." How these provisions would apply to a state voucher program that provides funding to parents who then select schools for their children is not known.

In a few states, the case law is so dated that its relevance to modern times is questionable. For example, the Iowa Supreme Court ruled in 1918 that direct payment of public monies to religious colleges would violate Article I, Section 3, of the state constitution, which prohibits enactment of any law "respecting an establishment of religion" and any law requiring persons to "pay tithes, taxes, or other rates for building or repairing places of worship, or the maintenance of any minister, or ministry." [66] Over fifty years later, the attorney general relied on this precedent to advise that the provision of tuition grants to Iowa students to attend accredited sectarian private colleges in the state would violate the state constitution, since the students would merely be conduits through whom the grants would flow to the colleges. [67] However, if only nonsectarian colleges were involved, there would be no violation of the provision.

Pending State Litigation. Litigation continues in Florida over its nascent voucher program, which encompassed only a handful of students and four Catholic schools in 2000. That year, a court of appeals reversed the trial court's ruling that the program violated the state constitution's uniformity clause. [68] Just because the provision does not specifically provide for a voucher program, the appeals court observed, does not mean that such a system is not a public means of providing adequate provision for educating children who are not being well served in public schools. Rather, the state had relied on vouchers to fulfill its constitutional mandate of assuring a uniform system of schooling. The case was sent back to the trial court for consideration of other state constitutional claims, chiefly whether the program violates article I, §3, prohibiting public monies from flowing directly or indirectly to religious organizations.

IMPLICATIONS FOR VOUCHER PROGRAM DESIGN

Might a voucher or tuition reimbursement program be most likely to withstand constitutional challenge in all but the most restrictive states if it is modeled after the original Milwaukee Parental Choice Program and excludes sectarian private schools? As in the case of refusing to fund abortions for low-income families,[69] it can be argued that the government has a right to confine funding to educational programs that are in accord with its mission. Since it would be constitutionally impermissible for the state to underwrite religious education, it can limit vouchers to public schools and secular private schools.

On the other hand, confining a voucher program to all but religious private schools seriously limits the supply of available schools and undercuts parental choice. Indeed, this was a major problem in the initial Milwaukee voucher program. Only a handful of nonreligious private schools participated, with four schools enrolling over 80 percent of the students. More significantly, exclusion of religious schools amounts to discrimination against the free exercise of religion. Both the U.S. Supreme Court and several state supreme courts have expressed particular sensitivity to this issue.[70] Writing for himself and three other Justices in a 2000 U.S. Supreme Court ruling, Justice Clarence Thomas spoke heatedly of continuing bias against pervasively religious institutions. "Nothing in the Establishment Clause," he wrote, "requires the exclusion of pervasively sectarian schools from otherwise permissible aid programs, and other doctrines of this Court bar it. This doctrine, born of bigotry, should be buried now."[71] It also can be argued that by excluding religion, the government engages in unconstitutional viewpoint censorship under the Free Speech Clause of the First Amendment.[72]

A voucher program encompassing religious private schools has the best chance of surviving constitutional challenge on anti-establishment grounds if it meets certain design requirements. To survive constitutional challenge in federal court based on the U.S. Supreme Court's precedents, a publicly funded voucher program should provide payments in the form of scholarships to parents of school-age children, should allow parents to choose among a wide variety of public and private nonsectarian and sectarian schools, and should give no preference to sectarian private schools. Whether the Cleveland voucher program measures up to these criteria will soon be known.

Given the fact that a state voucher program could be challenged on more than just anti-establishment grounds in most states, legislators must pay greater attention to design issues. First, the voucher must flow to par-

ents and not to institutions. Most states have a constitutional provision that prohibits direct expenditure of public money for sectarian purposes. The simplest way to circumvent this prohibition is to provide parents with certificates redeemable for educational services at approved schools and have the schools return the certificates to the state for payment. To avoid the problems experienced in litigation in Wisconsin, Ohio, and Maine, the legislature should tailor the amount of the voucher to the cost of instruction. This avoids the appearance of giving sectarian private schools a windfall which then can be diverted for sectarian purposes.

Second, the legislature should give parents a wide choice of public and private schools. Expansion of the Milwaukee voucher program to include sectarian private schools but not public schools foundered on this point in litigation at the lower court level in 1997. The Wisconsin Supreme Court, however, was not bothered by the exclusion, citing various options available to parents through other state laws. The lack of participation of out-of-district public schools in the Cleveland voucher program also constituted a stumbling block at the Ohio appellate court level. But, like the Wisconsin high court, the Ohio Supreme Court was not troubled, noting that the primary beneficiaries of the program were children, not sectarian schools. Whether the U.S. Supreme Court will view it the same way remains to be seen. Still, giving parents wide choice of public and private schools eliminates the potential for constitutional derailment.

Third, the legislature must state clearly the public purpose of the state voucher program. This will help it survive a challenge under the public purpose provision that is common in state constitutions. The most convincing purpose is to enfranchise middle- and low-income families with the means to seek improved educational opportunities for their children, so that the legislature clearly advances the state's interest in an educated citizenry. From an equity perspective, the present educational system accords the wealthy greater opportunities to control their children's education through choice of residence or payment of private school tuition. Legislatures effectively can demonstrate such a public purpose by varying the amount of the voucher with income level: The lower the income, the greater the voucher.

Fourth, legislators must include sufficient accountability measures to demonstrate that the voucher program will achieve the public purpose. These might include prohibiting discrimination in admissions, promoting toleration, requiring compliance with financial audits, and requiring students to participate in state-level testing programs. More will be said about this in the last chapter.

Even with design features like these, there is no assurance that a court

would uphold a voucher program encompassing sectarian private schools. Much will depend upon the wording of state constitutional provisions, the views of judges about the proper relationship between church and state, and the judges' partisan affiliation.

TAX BENEFITS

As noted earlier in the chapter, the U.S. Supreme Court upheld the Minnesota tax deduction program that permits parental deductions for tuition, textbook, and transportation expenses of children attending public or private schools. The decision prompted new interest in using tax deductions and tax credits as a way to promote school choice. Unlike a tax deduction, which reduces taxable income, a tax credit provides a dollar-for-dollar offset against the tax due. Educational tax credit programs have been enacted in several states, including Arizona, Iowa, Illinois, and Minnesota. In 1997, the Arizona Supreme Court followed the *Mueller* precedent to uphold its state's tax credit program against claims it violated the anti-establishment of religion provisions of both the state and federal constitutions.

Enacted in 1997, the Arizona statute permits any taxpayer—not just parents—to donate up to $500 to a school tuition organization (STO) and receive a dollar-for-dollar tax credit against the state income tax.[73] STOs are nonprofit, tax-exempt organizations that function as a kind of clearinghouse. They are required to allocate at least 90 percent of the revenue they obtain from the donations to scholarships and grants which parents can use to send their children to the school of their choice. In order to qualify for the money, the schools cannot discriminate on the basis of race, color, sex, handicap, family status, or national origin. However, to accommodate religious private schools, discrimination on religious grounds is permitted.

The Arizona tax credit program imposes two insulating layers between the government and religious private schools: the STOs and parents. While the STOs are accountable to some extent to the state, they serve to siphon off regulation that might otherwise be imposed on private schools. Funneling the scholarships from these organizations through parents to the schools further removes the state from the schools. This scheme also minimizes the relationship between the government and religion, an important consideration in that the Arizona Constitution has several strict constitutional provisions that separate church and state. Article II, Section 12, provides that no public money or property shall be "appropriated

for or applied to" religious instruction or the support of any religious establishment. Article IX, Section 10, specifies in part that no tax "shall be laid or appropriation of public money made in aid of any church, or private or sectarian school, or any public service corporation." The design of the tax credit program was intended to circumvent these two provisions.

It succeeded. The Arizona Supreme Court upheld the tax credit program by a narrow 3-2 vote.[74] The majority found the tax credit scheme indistinguishable from the Minnesota tax deduction plan upheld by the U.S. Supreme Court in 1982 and ruled that it did not violate the federal constitution. Nor did it violate the Arizona Constitution. Because no money enters state control, the taxpayer donations and resulting credits are not public monies and thus cannot be within the meaning of the state constitutional prohibitions on appropriation of public money for religious institutions. The majority rejected the claim that tax benefits are simply another form of government expenditure and thus the equivalent of a direct governmental appropriation.[75] The majority also disputed the claim that the framers of the state constitution intended a stricter prohibition on aid to religion than did the framers of the federal constitution and, in any case, noted that "we must view constitutional provisions 'in light of contemporary assumptions.'"

The Arizona scheme has captured considerable interest among school choice advocates because it avoids some of the drawbacks of voucher and individual tax credit plans that make them more vulnerable to constitutional attack. Figure 5.1 compares the features of the three approaches to school choice. As noted, each involves tradeoffs. There is no question that government vouchers are public money. For this reason, their constitutionality remains in doubt, particularly at the state level, where restrictions on the expenditure of public monies for private schools, especially religious private schools, abound. For the same reason, increased government regulation appears inevitable, as we shall see in Chapter 7. This, in turn, reduces private school participation.

Individual tax credits are more likely to be considered private, not government, money and thus less vulnerable to constitutional attack at the state level. The *Mueller v. Allen* decision would appear to insulate them from a successful constitutional challenge at the federal level if they include expenditures for both private and public schools. Because they are not government funds in the same sense as vouchers, they are less likely to be accompanied by restrictive regulatory measures imposed on schools. But there are tradeoffs here, too. Individual tax credits generally involve limited amounts of money, aren't paid until long after the school year begins, discriminate against the poor, complicate the tax system, and dimin-

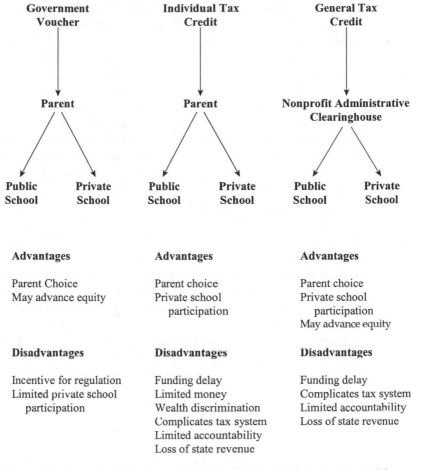

Figure 5.1. Comparing Vouchers and Tax Credits. Design features can modify or eliminate some of the advantages and disadvantages.

ish the incentive for government to impose accountability measures on private schools. On the other hand, the absence of regulatory creep likely will increase the number of participating private schools and will encourage efficiency.

The general tax credit has some distinct advantages over the individual tax credit. Because anyone, including corporations, can obtain a tax credit for making contributions to a scholarship pool, the amount of accumulated money could be greater than with either vouchers or individual tax credits. Greater amounts of money will enable more persons to

obtain scholarships, regardless of how much they themselves contribute to a scholarship clearinghouse. Thus general tax credits are more equitable. If the scholarship is large enough and available to many parents, new schools will spring up. This, of course, is the intent of those who argue for an expansive general tax credit program. As already noted with regard to Arizona, the intermediate nonprofit administrative clearinghouse, together with parent selection, diminishes the relationship between the government and religious schools, thus undercutting arguments about constitutionality under restrictive state constitutional provisions. The clearinghouse also has the potential to draw off increased regulation that would otherwise be imposed on participating schools.

However, some of the same drawbacks that accompany individual tax credits remain. Consider limited regulatory oversight. Would legislators be comfortable, for example, with private schools that reject scholarships from children with disabilities because the schools receive no public money, thus denying these children the opportunity to participate? Even more than individual tax credits, a general tax credit plan complicates the tax system. The most serious drawback is the potential for siphoning off substantial government revenue. For this reason, state legislatures are likely to limit the amount of contributions for which tax credits can be sought, thus reducing the amount of money available.

SUMMARY

Our discussion of the constitutionality of school voucher and tax benefit programs encompassing religious private schools demonstrates the complexity of the issue. Not only are two different judiciaries involved—federal and state—but also fifty-one constitutions (fifty-two, including the Commonwealth of Puerto Rico). Differences in state constitutions and the absence of relevant case law in many states make the outcome difficult to predict (see Table 5.1). We speculate that vouchers will have an uphill battle in about one-third of the states. The going should be relatively easy in another third, with the outcome in the remaining states uncertain. The wild card in such speculation is the U.S. Supreme Court's pending decision in the Cleveland voucher case. If the Court upholds the program, will it continue to allow the states to apply their own anti-establishment of religion provisions to the issue? If so, to what extent will state supreme court judges follow federal precedent? How will reliance on the more indirect approach of advancing school choice through tax deductions and credits affect the constitutionality question?

Differences among judges about the principles that will be used to guide constitutional interpretation, coupled with uncertainty about the proper role of religion in public life, tend to elevate the role of the judges' personal beliefs and political considerations. For this reason, the U.S. Supreme Court's decision on the constitutionality of the Cleveland voucher program will have significant influence on state judges struggling with the same issue. A case in point is the Arizona Supreme Court's reliance on the U.S. Supreme Court's tax deduction decision in *Mueller v. Allen* to uphold the general tax credit program in that state. As we have demonstrated, the supreme courts in some states have interpreted the religion clauses in their state constitutions to have the same meaning as the First Amendment religion clauses. It is important to note that since the judges in three-fourths of the states are elected, political fervor over vouchers and tax benefit plans likely will be influential as well.

The voucher program design features we advanced in this chapter stem from decisions already reached by the U.S. Supreme Court and state supreme courts regarding forms of assistance to religious organizations. While these features are essential to give voucher programs encompassing sectarian private schools the best chance for passing constitutional muster, they do not constitute the only features necessary for voucher programs to serve the public interest. In Chapter 8, we present additional features that we believe are essential for voucher, tuition reimbursements, and tax benefit programs to be effective as school reform measures in balancing the interests of liberty, diversity, equity, and efficiency.

The Economics of Choice

EDUCATION IS THE single largest government expenditure of state and local governments. For this reason, any education policy proposal must answer the questions: How much will it cost? How will the state raise the funds? and, What will be the long-term effects on expenditures and revenues? In this chapter we answer these questions for alternative school choice policies. We divide the chapter into four sections. The first looks at two ideas that underlie much of the current economic literature concerning school choice: Tiebout sorting and the median voter theorem. The second examines current patterns of public school funding and how increasing public choice options may change these patterns. The third studies the efficiency of public schools and how privatization might affect the costs of schooling. The final section analyzes the complex issues involved in the financing of vouchers, paying special attention to the tradeoffs between equity and efficiency.

TIEBOUT SORTING AND THE
MEDIAN VOTER THEOREM

In the introductory chapter we pretended to be consultants from a foreign country who studied America's system of public education to determine the degree to which it achieved equality of educational opportunity. We found extensive segregation of students by ethnicity and income, and we discovered that this segregation led to substantial inequality in educational opportunities and outcomes. Families with high incomes clustered together, and their schools had high per pupil expenditures. Families with moderate incomes tended to live together, and their schools had moderate per pupil expenditures. And, families with low incomes gathered in low-

income school districts with low per pupil expenditures. Why does this sorting occur?

The process by which people sort themselves into relatively homogeneous neighborhoods is known as "Tiebout sorting." Named for Charles Tiebout, the person who first modeled and explained the process, sorting into relatively homogeneous neighborhoods occurs because families have differing tastes for public services and differing abilities to pay for the services they desire. This leads a family to migrate to a neighborhood where the services provided by the local government and the tax rate charged by that government best suit the family's preferences. When families are choosing where to locate, the quality of the public schools available is typically the most important service they consider.[1] High-income families who value education move into neighborhoods occupied by other high-income families who value education. High-income individuals who do not place a high value on education seek out neighborhoods that have lower tax rates and less-well-endowed schools. For example, the wealthy elderly may move into areas with extremely low tax rates for education. Poor families, constrained by their income, locate in neighborhoods with low housing costs, low levels of educational expenditures, and low tax rates.

The Tiebout process leads to neighborhoods and schools that are homogeneous with respect to family income and the value families place on education. Carolyn Hoxby, a Harvard economist, argues that the Tiebout process is both efficient and equitable.[2] To see why, imagine that you live in a neighborhood in which every family has the same preferences for public services and an equal ability to pay. Elected public officials in such a community will attempt to provide exactly the quantity and quality of services everyone in the neighborhood desires. If they do not, then the neighborhood will elect a different set of officials.

What happens when a community becomes more heterogeneous? Assume for the moment that there is a neighborhood with only three families and that each family has a single voter. These three voters elect a local government. That government sets the service levels and levies the taxes needed to pay for them. Family L prefers low levels of services and taxes; Family M prefers moderate levels of services and taxes; and Family H prefers high levels of services and taxes. In this situation elected public officials will provide the level of services and taxes preferred by Family M. If the officials provide less than Family M desires, then M will join with Family H and vote for a set of officials who pledge to provide additional services. If officials provide more than Family M desires, then M will join with Family L to elect officials who pledge to provide fewer services than

are currently furnished. Although it may require several elections, ultimately the electoral process should lead to officials who provide exactly the level of services that Family M desires. The number of families and sets of preferences can be expanded to any size, and the outcome will be the same—the voter with the median preference will receive exactly the level of service that she desires. All voters who do not share the median voter's preferences will receive either a lower or a higher service level than they desire. Homogeneous neighborhoods lead to an efficient allocation of services because everyone's preferences are similar to those of the median voter.[3] By combining the Tiebout process with the median voter theorem, economists can develop sophisticated models to estimate the effects of various school choice policies.

FUNDING PUBLIC SCHOOLS

Currently more than 90 percent of public funding for elementary and secondary education comes from state and local governments, and these governments have decided to fund education at highly disparate levels. Two-thirds of the differences in per pupil expenditures occur at the state level.[4] Unequal funding occurs because states face different production costs, have dissimilar resources, and have voters who value education differently. For example, Massachusetts spends more on education than Alabama because the costs of producing education in Massachusetts are higher than in Alabama, Massachusetts has greater resources than Alabama, and the people of Massachusetts place a higher value on education than the people of Alabama. Variation in spending by school districts within a state occurs for the same reasons. School districts face different costs, have unequal tax bases, and tax themselves for education at disparate rates. Although the greatest differences in per pupil funding are differences between states, almost all efforts to equalize per pupil funding attempt to reduce inequalities among school districts within states. The reason for this is that Americans consider education to be a state and local function. This limits the role the national government can play in reducing funding inequalities among states.

Present Funding Patterns within States

Because of action by courts and legislatures, some states have reduced dramatically the spending inequalities across school districts. States generally have accomplished this reduction through foundation grants and district

power equalization (DPE). Table 6.1 provides a highly simplified example of how a typical state equalization system might work. Assume that there is a state with only two school districts, A and B. Using a foundation system, the state legislature sets a minimum tax rate for all districts at 3 percent of property values and guarantees that every district will have sufficient income to spend at least $6,000 per student. We will call this guaranteed-level expenditure the foundation level. The amount of aid the state will provide a district depends upon how much the district raises by taxing the assessed property in its district at 3 percent. If the 3 percent tax raises at least $6,000, then the district receives no state aid. If the 3 percent rate yields less than $6,000 per pupil, then the state makes up the difference between the amount raised and the $6,000 foundation level. To make the calculations easy we assume that District A has one hundred students, taxes its property at the required 3 percent, and has $100,000 assessed value per student. District B also has one hundred students, taxes its property at 3 percent, but it has an assessed value of $200,000 per student. Using the state formula, both District A and District B will spend $6,000 per student.

Table 6.1 shows how state assistance can equalize per pupil spending across districts. But in every state except Hawaii the amount of per pupil spending varies across districts.[5] These differences occur for many reasons. Districts populated by wealthier and more educated families generally demand more schooling than districts populated by less wealthy and less educated families; citizens in urban and suburban districts desire more schooling than citizens in rural districts; and the costs of educating students are higher in some districts than in others. These differences in preferences and costs lead to spending variations across districts. Table 6.2 provides an example of what happens to educational expenditures if the residents in District A choose to spend only the foundation level ($6,000) while residents in District B decide to spend $8,000 per pupil. The obvious problem with the funding system shown in Table 6.2 is that it provides unequal educational resources to students.

Would it be wise policy to force all school districts to have the same

Table 6.1. Foundation Level Spending with District Power Equalization

District	Taxable Property per Pupil	Tax Rate	Local Revenue per Pupil	State Aid per Pupil	Total Spending per Pupil
A	$100,000	0.03	$3,000	$3,000	$6,000
B	$200,000	0.03	$6,000	0	$6,000

Table 6.2. Foundation Level Spending with Add-on Spending Allowed

District	Taxable Property per Pupil	Tax Rate	Local Revenue per Pupil	State Aid per Pupil	Total Spending per Pupil
A	$100,000	0.03	$3,000	$3,000	$6,000
B	$200,000	0.04	$8,000	0	$8,000

per pupil expenditures? There are three key arguments against such a policy. The first is that producing education is more expensive for some students than for others. In their analysis of the differing costs of educating students, William Duncombe and John Yinger estimate that it costs about three and a half times as much to achieve similar student outcomes in the inner cities as in suburbs or small towns.[6] But in many states equalizing per pupil expenditures will reduce rather than increase the funds available to children in the inner cities. Cities typically have relatively large quantities of highly assessed commercial property. This allows inner-city school districts to generate greater income than districts without commercial property. If cities were required to have equal per pupil expenditures this would require many inner-city districts to reduce their per pupil funding for disadvantaged students.[7]

A second reason to reject a system that requires equal per pupil expenditures across districts is that it is undemocratic. If democracy means allowing the people to decide the public services they want and are willing to pay for, then allowing each school district to decide the amount and type of schooling it prefers is more democratic than forcing every district to consume the same type and level of schooling. Many democratic theorists would argue that so long as all students receive an education that develops people who are economically independent and can participate in the democratic process, democracy is best served by allowing *local* citizens to decide how much schooling they wish to provide to *local* students.[8]

A third reason for rejecting strict equality of expenditures is that it may reduce financial support for education. To see why this is so, imagine that you own a home but do not have children in the public schools. If a local school bond issue or tax increase is on the ballot and you believe that additional funds will improve educational outcomes *for students in your neighborhood,* then you may choose to vote for it despite the fact that you have no school-age children. The reason for your vote is not that you are altruistic toward the children in your neighborhood (though you may be), but that having good schools in *your* neighborhood increases the value of *your* house. If the state requires equal per pupil expenditures across all

districts, then any increase in taxes for education is no more likely to improve schools in your neighborhood than it is to improve schools elsewhere. This removes your economic incentive to vote for increased education spending.

Financing Public Choice Programs

Although decentralized funding has advantages, interdistrict variations in funding create problems for educational choice programs. The problems are particularly acute for those policies that allow students to attend public schools outside of their own school district. To see this, let's return to our hypothetical two-district state. Imagine that ten students from District A transfer to the better-funded District B schools. How much funding should District A transfer to District B? Should the amount be $3,000 (the aid District A receives from the state), $6,000 (the average per pupil spending in District A), $8,000 (the average per pupil spending in District B), or some other amount? What about the education taxes paid by the students' families? Should their tax rate be 3 percent (the tax rate in the district where they live) or 4 percent (the tax rate in the district where their children attend school)?

Assume for the moment that you live in District B and pay the taxes to support per pupil expenditures of $8,000. Would you be willing to accept students from District A if they bring less than $8,000 in funding with them? If your district receives less than $8,000, then every student who transfers from District A to District B will lower the *average* expenditure devoted to the children who live in your district. Even if the marginal cost of educating these students is less than $8,000, would you want to allow people who pay lower taxes than you to receive the level of educational quality that your higher taxes make possible? (The marginal cost is the cost to the district of educating an additional student.) We think it is reasonable to assume that taxpayers in District B will object to educating students who live in District A unless those students bring funding that is at least equal to the average per pupil cost in District B.[9]

Now assume that you live in District A. If the marginal cost of educating the students who transfer to District B is less than $6,000, but your district must send $6,000 to District B for each student who transfers there, then this will lower the educational quality for students who live in your district.[10] Certainly you and other parents in District A will object to giving District B more than $6,000 for each student who transfers. Teachers and school administrators in District A may oppose all transfers from

District A to District B, as past research shows that the students who transfer to higher-spending districts typically are students who produce above-average positive spillovers for other students in their school.

Charter schools present even more complex finance problems than those created by open enrollment. Currently, most charter schools are disadvantaged in the support they receive from state and local governments. For example, in some states, charter schools do not receive funding from the local school district and receive only the state's contribution. In addition, most states prohibit charter schools from issuing bonds to pay for capital expenses. This means that charter schools generally have difficulty getting started and begin with inferior facilities. Even if state governments ultimately allow charter schools to issue bonds for capital expenses, and the states fund the schools at a level equal to that of other schools in the district, finance problems remain. In our example of the two-school-district state, if there are charter schools located in both districts and the schools enroll out-of-district students, then all of the funding problems that occur with open enrollment also arise with charter schools.

The simplest way of handling the problems associated with open enrollment and charter schools is to equalize per pupil funding throughout the state and have the state government provide additional categorical funding for students with special needs. While this type of funding would resolve many problems, it would not eliminate the inequalities in educational funding that occur within school districts. Courts and state legislatures have spent considerable time and effort reducing spending disparities among school districts, but they have not addressed the spending inequalities that occur among schools within districts. Because teacher salaries constitute the largest expenditure category in education, differences in the average years of experience and the graduate education of teachers can lead to huge inequalities in the per pupil expenditures among schools within a district. If a school has predominantly senior teachers who have graduate degrees, the average teacher salary at that school might be $50,000. Another school in the district, one staffed by relatively new faculty, might have an average salary of only $30,000. If a state wanted to ensure that students receive equal funding, then it would require that each *school* receive the same per pupil funding.

Summary

The greatest inequalities in per pupil funding stem from differences among states rather than from differences among districts within the same state,

and no current or proposed school choice policy can rectify these inequalities. At the state level, there are important tradeoffs between centralized and decentralized control over educational expenditures. Centralized funding can reduce inequalities across districts, but centralizing control attenuates local democratic control, reduces allocative efficiency, and may lower the total financial support for public education by breaking the link between education taxes and property values. Most important, unless states provide substantial categorical assistance for the education of inner-city children, these children are likely to be harmed by policies that equalize per pupil expenditures across districts.

But centralizing control and equalizing funding has benefits as well as costs. Equal per pupil funding can reduce the inequalities of educational opportunity that perpetuate inherited socioeconomic differences. In Texas, for example, the court-ordered equalization of expenditures across districts has led to more equal academic outcomes between students from low- and high-income areas. Equal per pupil funding certainly would make the implementation of school choice programs substantially easier, as it would reduce the difficulties created when students choose schools outside their own district.

PROMOTING EFFICIENCY IN THE PRODUCTION OF EDUCATION

The Apparent Decline in the Efficiency of Public Schools

The economist who has made the longest sustained critical analysis of the productive efficiency of public schools is Eric Hanushek. He has examined the effects on efficiency of changes in class size, teacher training, teacher certification, noninstructional resources, and a host of other inputs into the production of schooling. Hanushek's examination of educational expenditures from 1890 to 1990 shows that, *after adjusting for inflation,* the annual growth rate in per pupil spending during this period was approximately 3.5 percent per year. In other words, real per pupil spending doubled every twenty years.[11] Figure 6.1 shows that the increase in expenditures was particularly steep during the period from 1970 to 1990. This growth has been approximately twice as great as the growth in the Gross Domestic Product. But while educational costs increased, educational outcomes did not. Figures 6.2 and 6.3 show that there was little improvement between 1973 and 1996 in the standardized test scores of students as measured by the National Assessment of Educational Progress (NAEP).

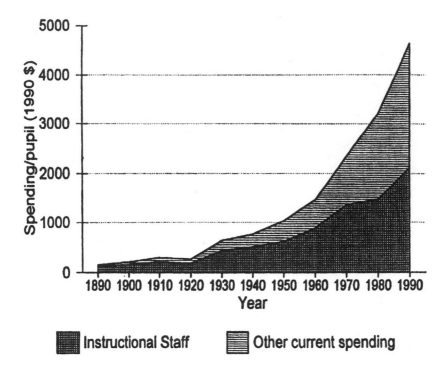

Figure 6.1. Increases in Instructional Staff and Other Expenditures per Student, 1890–1990. SOURCE: Eric A. Hanushek, *The Evidence on Class Size* (Rochester, N.Y.: Wallen Wallis Institute of Political Economy, University of Rochester, 1998), p. 4.

Possible Reasons for the Decline in Productive Efficiency

In this section we examine three frequently given reasons for the failure of school outcomes to keep up with school costs: (1) a changing student population, (2) teachers' unions, and (3) the Individuals with Disabilities Education Act (IDEA).[12]

Changes in the Student Population. Defenders of public schools suggest that schools have not become less efficient; rather, their tasks have been enlarged. No longer do schools simply provide academic instruction to students; they now must prevent teen pregnancy, reduce drug use, and supply after-school day care. In addition, as more children come from single-parent homes, live in poverty, and speak a language other than English, the average student has become more costly to educate.

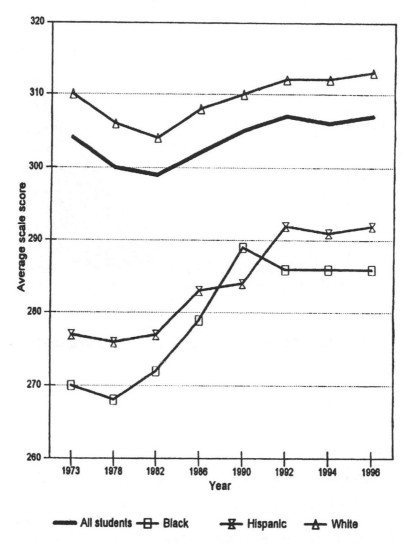

Figure 6.2. Mathematics Achievement (NAEP): Seventeen-year-olds by Race/
Ethnicity, 1973–1996. SOURCE: Hanushek, "The Evidence on Class Size," p. 7.

There are two difficulties with this explanation. First, if increases in
teen pregnancy, drug addiction, single-parent families, and English deficiencies are the causes of the decreases in efficiency, then we would expect
that the differences in test scores for minority and white students would
have widened. These social problems certainly have hit minority ethnic

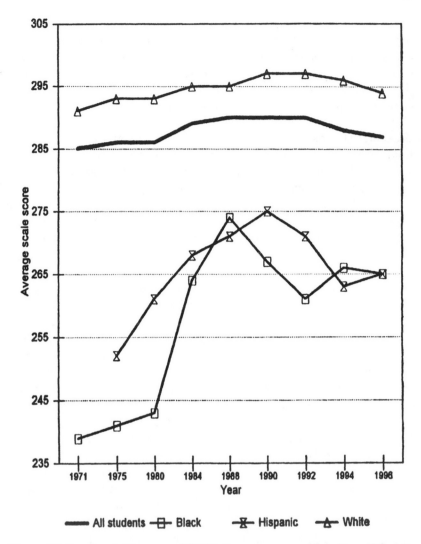

Figure 6.3. Reading Achievement (NAEP): Seventeen-year-olds by Race/Ethnicity, 1973–1996. SOURCE: Hanushek, "The Evidence on Class Size," p. 9.

groups much harder than they have hit whites. But the gap between minority and white students has declined, because educational outcomes for minorities have improved while the outcomes for the white population have remained stagnant.

A second problem with the explanation that the changes in the stu-

dent population have made education more difficult is that many changes in the American family should have improved educational outcomes.[13] For example, students have fewer siblings, more-educated parents, and more educational resources in the home. Research at the individual level shows that each of these factors improves student performance. But despite these changes, scores for white children have not improved.

Teachers' Unions. Many proponents of vouchers and privatization are fond of blaming teachers' unions for the declining efficiency of public schools. This literature describes unions as creating two obstacles to achieving greater efficiency. First, unions have gained unjustified salary increases. Second, unions are the source of many of the bureaucratic and regulatory inefficiencies that inhibit education reform.[14] Although there is little research concerning the impact of unions on educational costs, the available evidence indicates that the increased regulations and improved salaries brought about by unions increase educational costs by between 8 and 15 percent.[15] This is a significant impact, but it is not of the magnitude necessary to account for the observed declines in productivity.

The attention to teacher salaries does alert us to a major cause of the decline in educational productivity, increased personnel costs. Hanushek estimates that from 1890 to 1990, increases in the cost of classroom instruction have accounted for 43 percent of the increase in real per pupil spending in public schools. From 1970 to 1990, growth in instructional costs accounted for 50 percent of the increase in per pupil spending.[16] While some of this increase has been a result of real gains in teacher salaries, a significant portion of the increase comes from a reduction in pupil-teacher ratios. From 1950 to 1994, the average pupil-teacher ratio in U.S. public schools fell from 27.1 to 17.2, a decline of more than 35 percent.[17] This decreased ratio has been accompanied by an approximately equal increase in the number and cost of noninstructional personnel such as assistant principals, counselors, and custodians.

Although the real wages of teachers have increased in the past two decades, their position relative to other college graduates has declined. In 1980, 50.1 percent of female college graduates earned less than female schoolteachers. By 1990, that figure had fallen to 45.3 percent. And, although the relative position of male teachers improved slightly, only 36.5 percent of male college graduates earn less than male schoolteachers.[18] Because the earnings of teachers during the 1990s did not keep up with the earnings of other college graduates, the relative position of teachers has worsened. This pattern suggests that we are not paying teachers

too much, but too little. If the relative position of teachers continues to decline, schools cannot count on a supply of high-quality female teachers.

The Cost of Educating Students with Disabilities.   There is no doubt that the implementation of the Individuals with Disabilities Education Act (IDEA) has raised educational costs. Since the 1975 passage of IDEA, the percentage of elementary and secondary students classified as at least partially disabled has grown steadily and is now above 12 percent.[19] How much has IDEA increased costs? Hamilton Lankford and James Wyckoff analyzed spending in school districts in the state of New York to determine the extent to which IDEA accounted for increases in per pupil expenditures. For districts not in the state's five largest cities, they estimated that 19.9 percent of the increased spending was attributable to IDEA. The comparable figures for New York City and the next four largest cities were much larger, 60.5 percent and 24.3 percent, respectively.[20] The largest part of the costs of IDEA stems from an increase in instructional costs created by declines in pupil-teacher ratios. Hanushek estimates that nationwide as much as one-third of the decline in the pupil-teacher ratio since 1975 has been caused by increasing attention to students with disabilities.[21]

Demands of teachers' unions, rising numbers of students who are classified as disabled, and some changes in the student population have contributed to the growth in the per pupil costs of education. Some impacts of these changes have been indirect rather than direct. One effect of the changing student population in the inner cities has been an increase in the regulation of inner-city schools. When students come from home and neighborhood environments that lead to behavior problems in schools, those schools increasingly turn to external administrative control to deal with those behaviors. These controls always are regulatory in nature.[22] Similarly, IDEA has generated thousands of pages of federal, state, and local regulations governing how schools must treat children with disabilities. And as parents and their attorneys make additional demands on behalf of IDEA students, new rules are generated. Finally, teachers' unions have bargained successfully for regulations on what, when, how, and how much teachers can be required to do. All of this regulatory activity has reduced the autonomy of principals and teachers, and it has minimized school flexibility and instructional innovation. In short, many social forces have combined to increase bureaucracy, regulation, and political control of schools. These forces have, in turn, created an incentive structure that emphasizes following rules rather than finding efficient ways to educate students.

Privatization and Vouchers

Proponents of privatization and vouchers believe that such policies would lower the costs of producing education and improve educational outputs. Not surprisingly, opponents of a market approach to education argue the opposite. It is to this debate that we now turn.

Arguments That Vouchers Will Increase the Cost of Education. Proponents of vouchers often argue that because the tuition of most private schools is significantly lower than the average per pupil spending of public schools, private schools clearly are more efficient.[23] For example, our study of school choice in San Antonio found that the average tuition in private schools located within the boundaries of the San Antonio Independent School District was less than $1,500. The average per pupil expenditures on public school students in the San Antonio Independent School District was over $5,000. Henry Levin, an education economist at Columbia University's Teachers College, argues that such comparisons are inappropriate and misleading.[24] Levin points out that most sectarian private schools receive subsidies from the church with which they are affiliated, require students to pay fees for extracurricular activities, hold various fund-raising events, and often use as instructors clergy whose salaries understate the true market value of their services. In addition, most private schools keep their costs down by providing neither special education services nor vocational training programs.

Levin analyzed five areas where he believes voucher proponents have overlooked or underestimated the probable costs to the public treasury of implementing a voucher program.[25]

The first of these is the cost to the state of funding students who currently are in private schools. Levin estimates that if 75 percent of these students accept vouchers, and if the voucher is equal to 80 percent of public school per pupil funding, this would require a $20 billion increase in state and local government spending for education. If the voucher program included free transportation, the added cost of transportation would be $42 billion! Most of this enormous increase would be the result of three items: (1) transporting students who previously attended private schools, (2) the greater distance current public school students would travel if they could choose to attend any school they desired, and (3) the much larger catchment area that any given bus route would include. Levin estimates that other costs to the state of a voucher program would include $2.5 billion to monitor schools that accept vouchers, $1.8 billion to provide a minimal information program to educate parents concerning their

choices, and another $1.8 billion to adjudicate disputed claims between parents and schools.[26] Levin's estimates do not include the additional costs of monitoring the thousands of private schools that would accept vouchers. Such monitoring would also add substantially to the state's educational expenditures.

If Levin is correct in his estimates, then a nationwide voucher plan would add more than $73 billion per year to the states' cost of education, an amount equal to almost 25 percent of the public education budget nationally! Levin points out that while education reform might improve efficiency, even if it increased it by 10 percent (an unlikely increase in his estimation), this would save only $29.2 billion. One aspect of Levin's analysis deserves comment. He is not comparing the costs *to society* of education under the current system with the costs *to society* of education in a voucher system. He is comparing the costs *to the state* of the current system with the costs *to the state* of a voucher system.[27]

Twenty billion dollars of the increased state cost comes from shifting the costs of private education from parents of private school students to the state. Possibly as much as an additional $20 billion of the increased costs to the state of a voucher program comes from shifting the burden of transporting private school students from their parents to the state. Thus perhaps $40 billion of Levin's estimated $73 billion is not an increase in the total cost of education, and it should not be viewed as such. This $40 billion shifts costs currently paid by the private sector to the public sector.[28]

If privatizing education were to increase the efficiency of schooling by 10 percent, then, using Levin's figures concerning the expenses of various educational services, the additional cost *to society* of giving all children the opportunity to attend the school of their choice would be $5 billion plus the costs of additional monitoring of private schools. How likely is it that privatization will increase productive efficiency?

Arguments That Vouchers Will Decrease Educational Costs by Increasing Efficiency. The likelihood that privatization of schools will increase productive efficiency depends in large part on the willingness of states to fund private schools without regulating them to such a degree that they lose their competitive advantage. To illustrate the costs of regulation, we return to Levin's analysis of the expenses of a voucher program. Levin estimates that additional transportation expenses will constitute the largest single increase in the cost of education. He expects that if students can attend any school they wish, then they will be less likely to choose their neighborhood school. In addition, because the catchment areas will be

larger, more buses will be necessary and they will carry students much farther. For this reason, rather than 60 percent of current public school students being bused at an average cost of $415 per student, Levin expects that 80 percent of all students will be bused at an average cost of $1,500 per student.[29]

Why might Levin's expectations be too high? Because his figures are based on what transportation would cost if all current regulations concerning transportation to public schools would apply to private schools. Currently most local school districts make transportation available at no expense to all public school students who live more than a specified distance from their school. The districts use publicly owned buses driven by persons paid by the district. But in a less regulated school system the state might choose to implement a different transportation policy. For example, the state could give families a transportation voucher. If the transportation costs exceed the size of the voucher, the family would pay the difference. This would encourage families to include transportation costs in their school choice decision. Presumably if two schools were of approximately equal value to the parents, they would choose the school that would minimize their transportation cost.

To see how a transportation voucher might lower the costs of transporting students to choice schools let's compare a possible voucher system with Levin's expectations. Assume that there are 200 students. If we accept Levin's estimate that 80 percent of the students will require state busing at a cost of $1,500 per pupil, then transportation will cost $240,000 (160 students × $1,500). If the state gave all 200 students in the districts a $500 transportation voucher, however, then even if every student used the voucher the cost of transportation to the state would be only $100,000.

But what would happen to families who want their children to attend a school that is far from their home and for whom the transportation voucher does not cover their transportation expenses? While middle- and upper-income families might be able to afford these added expenses, low-income parents might not.

One way of handling this would be to make vouchers above $500 means-tested. If we assume that 20 percent of students in the two districts are eligible for free or reduced-price lunches and the state provides each such student with a $1,500 voucher, then even if every low-income student decided to attend a school far from home the total cost to the district of transportation would be $140,000 rather than $240,000. This is a savings of almost 42 percent over Levin's calculations for state-provided busing.[30]

Levin also estimates that the cost of a minimum information center would be $1.8 billion annually. This center would alert families to a school's educational philosophy, curriculum, test scores, student placement after graduation, and turnover rates. Although we favor an information program, we think that many states will choose not to provide it.[31] Does this mean that parents will be without information or assistance? No. If schools must compete for students, then it is likely that they will engage in recruiting. Just as there are published guides that help students choose colleges and find financial aid, it is likely that in large markets private enterprises will publish guides to local schools and will set up special counseling services to help families choose among schools. These services already exist in many cities. Certainly it is cheaper for a state to require that schools meet existing state regulations on truth in advertising than it is to establish a state information agency.[32]

In summary, whether a voucher policy will increase or decrease total costs depends, at least in part, on the degree of regulation that accompanies the policy. If private schools must abide by the same regulations concerning curriculum, pedagogy, transportation, and hiring that confront current public schools, then vouchers are unlikely to improve efficiency. On the other hand, to the extent that policymakers reduce regulation and encourage competition among schools, school choice is more likely to cut costs and improve outcomes. We now turn to the mechanisms that might bring about increases in efficiency.

Regulation versus Incentives

In the book *Making Schools Work: Improving Performance and Controlling Costs,* economists and education policy analysts, including both Eric Hanushek and Henry Levin, suggest that increasing the use of incentives would improve the efficiency of production. *Making Schools Work* argues that regulation and incentives are the two basic approaches to achieving educational accountability. Policymakers using the regulatory approach not only decide upon the desired outcomes, they also establish the procedures that those who are implementing the policy must follow. Those who implement the policies are rewarded and punished not by their success in achieving the desired policy outcomes, but by how well they document that they followed the regulatory rules. In contrast, the incentive approach allows those who implement the policy to determine how to achieve the outcomes that the policymakers identified. Evaluation is then based on the degree to which the desired outcomes are achieved.[33]

Proponents of the incentive approach maintain that regulation is an

inappropriate tool in education for a number of reasons. Regulations coming from state or district officials ignore differences among schools and assume that there is one best way of educating all children. Regulations also restrict flexibility, inhibit local initiatives, and create large monitoring costs as supervisors attempt to determine whether those charged with following the rules actually did so.[34] The monitoring costs are easily seen in the mountains of paperwork that the implementing officials must prepare to show that they did not violate the regulations.

Despite the problems of a regulatory approach, policymakers rarely use incentives to improve efficiency. Few principals receive a bonus for achieving equal or improved student outcomes at lower costs. Teachers rarely receive merit raises based on the improved achievement of their students. Schools do not receive additional resources because they have used their resources efficiently. States do not give additional funding to a district because student achievement in the district has improved. In fact, schools and districts may lose money if they improve the outcomes of high-risk students to such an extent that they are no longer eligible for categorical grants. On the other hand, almost everywhere the state regulates maximum class size; teacher certification, salaries, tenure requirements, and pay raises; the number and use of such support staff as vice-principals, secretaries, counselors, and medical personnel; the number of computers in a school (and, in some cases, in a classroom); which subjects will be taught with what pedagogical approach; what textbooks and other instructional materials will be used; and who is eligible for either gifted and talented or special education programs.

Regulating Class Size Reductions (CSR). Perhaps the best way to see how regulated service delivery reduces efficiency is to look at recent state efforts to mandate smaller class sizes. Class size reduction (CSR) is an almost ideal policy for politicians. Voters support CSR because they can understand its rationale. If classes have fewer students, then the teacher can give more attention to each one. Voters expect smaller classes to have fewer behavior problems and assume that this allows faculty and students to spend more time teaching and learning. Teachers like smaller classes because they find them less stressful; and teacher organizations like policies that reduce class size because they increase the demand for schoolteachers.

Mandating smaller classes became a particularly popular policy proposal in the 1990s. This popularity was a result of Project Star, an important and innovative educational experiment in Tennessee. Project Star randomly assigned kindergarten students to either smaller classes (ap-

proximately fifteen students) or larger classes (approximately twenty-three students). Students who initially were assigned to smaller classes remained in them for four years; students initially assigned to the larger classes continued in such classes for four years.[35] Test results showed that the students in the smaller kindergarten classes made significantly greater gains in math and reading than students in the larger classes. In addition, the students who remained in small classes through the third grade maintained the advantage created during kindergarten. Three years after returning to regular-size classes, most of the difference in test scores between the two groups of students remained.[36]

Project Star provides seemingly irrefutable evidence that common sense was right. Smaller classes improve educational outcomes. Based on the evidence from Project Star (and substantial lobbying by teacher organizations), the State of California provided funding for school districts to reduce the size of classes in grades K–3 from thirty to twenty students. Districts received $650 for each child in a reduced-size class during the first year, and that amount increased to $800 in the second year. The state also provided $400 million for the new facilities that the class size reduction required. The yearly cost of the CSR policy to California was over $1.8 billion per year. Evaluation of the CSR program by a consortium of research institutions found that this enormous increase in educational expenditures resulted in an increase in math scores of between one-twentieth and one-tenth of a standard deviation. Reading scores were unchanged.[37] Despite the observed improvement in math scores, proponents of privatization would argue that the CSR policy substantially reduced productive efficiency. Efficiency declined because CSR dramatically increased educational costs but did not improve educational outcomes to a similar extent.[38]

The California class size reduction policy illustrates the regulatory approach to improving educational outcomes. Rather than allowing school officials to decide how to use additional funding and then rewarding them on the basis of their success, the state chose a single educational strategy. It then funded only that strategy and regulated its implementation. A district could receive additional funds if, and only if, it reduced class size in grades K–3 to twenty students or less.

How might an incentive system have led to better outcomes in California? Proponents of privatization argue that if principals receive bonuses based on improved performance or improved efficiency, then they are likely to look for ways to achieve those outcomes. The principals might have read the research on Project Star and realized that significant improvements in test scores occurred only in kindergarten. With that in-

formation they might have then reduced the size of kindergarten classes and used their additional funds in more productive ways. By reading the research concerning class size and academic outcomes, they might have discovered that CSR has a much stronger impact on African American students than on white students and allocated CSR funds to schools that had larger percentages of minority students.[39] Principals or teachers might have read the study by Henry Levin and his colleagues that showed CSR was the least cost effective way of improving educational outcomes.[40] Most important, they might have read the studies showing that the effects of increases in teacher quality dwarf the effects of class size reductions.[41]

Would a voucher system achieve greater efficiency? Opponents of privatization point out that private schools are not more innovative in their delivery of education. Studies comparing private and public schools find that most private schools use the same curriculum, materials, and instructional techniques as public schools.[42] When a private school's curricular materials differ from those of the public schools, the difference is likely to be caused by the religious goals of the school rather than the desire to improve academic outcomes.

Summary

The jury remains out concerning whether choice, particularly choice that includes vouchers, can improve educational efficiency. There is, however, wide agreement among both proponents and opponents of privatization on one issue: if a policy regulates private schools to the same extent that public schools currently are regulated, then improved efficiency is unlikely. In fact, as Levin's analysis of possible voucher costs shows, a combination of vouchers and the current regulatory approach may increase the cost of education. The potential of school choice to improve efficiency stems from the likelihood that privatization will reduce regulation and will lead to the market competition that gives school boards, principals, and teachers incentives to become more efficient.

EQUITY CONSIDERATIONS AND VOUCHER POLICIES

In the first section of this chapter we saw that when policymakers decide whether or not to equalize per pupil funding across school districts they are making a tradeoff between increasing equality of educational opportunity and maximizing total funding for education. Policymakers designing a voucher policy must make an analogous choice. They must choose

whether schools accepting vouchers may require families to pay additional tuition and fees. (We refer to these additional charges as "add-ons.") For example, if the size of the voucher is $5,000, can a private school charge parents an additional $1,000?

Economic theory suggests that both the current system of free public schools and a voucher policy that does not allow add-ons create inefficiencies and lower total educational funding. To see why this is so assume that the following simplifying conditions are true:

1. All schools are equally efficient, and differences in per pupil expenditures are directly related to the quality of education.
2. Education is available only in schools. (This avoids complications added by home schooling and tutoring services.)
3. The only issue for parents is what combination of cost and academic quality falls on their indifference curve. (In other words, parents are not concerned with a religious education and they do not object to the values taught in public schools.)
4. The state spends $5,000 on each student who attends public schools, and this amount provides a level of schooling that meets the basic educational goals discussed in Chapter 1.

Given these assumptions, what should a family that wants a $7,000 education for its children do? In a system of free public schools, the family can either accept the $5,000 education or it can spend $7,000 to receive an additional $2,000 worth of education. Both options are inefficient. The family either receives less education than it would choose in a market system, or it pays far more than the marginal cost for the marginal benefit that the private school adds. A voucher plan without add-ons creates the same problem. A family can take the voucher and use it at a school that accepts the voucher as full payment, or it can purchase an additional $2,000 of education by paying $7,000 to a school that does not accept vouchers. A policy that permits add-ons eliminates this inefficiency. Parents whose demand for education is $5,000 or less can choose either a public school or a private school for which the voucher constitutes full payment. A family that demands $7,000 worth of education can purchase the additional $2,000 of education by enrolling its child in a school that charges a $2,000 add-on.

Why might policymakers reject add-ons? Because they will exacerbate inequalities in educational opportunities and perpetuate existing class differences. A family's demand for education is highly correlated with its income. Thus an add-on policy would encourage the sorting of students

by family income. Poor families will choose schools that do not charge additional tuition and fees, middle-income families will pick schools with small to moderate add-ons, and rich families will select schools with large add-ons. As we have stressed throughout this book, policies that encourage sorting by either income or ethnicity deny low-income students equality of opportunity.

A second problem with a policy that allows schools to charge additional tuition and fees is that it may encourage families without school-age children to vote for policies that reduce the size of the voucher. Imagine for a moment a voter who does not have children under the age of eighteen. Also imagine that the individual believes that most poor people are lazy and their children do not deserve state assistance. If a voucher policy allows add-ons, this hypothetical voter might support a voucher that provides only enough schooling to train students to the level necessary to work in low-paying jobs. The voter may presume that the children of caring parents will not be harmed by a small voucher, as these parents will be willing and able to pay the add-ons. This voter may be less willing, however, to vote for a small voucher if no add-ons are allowed. Without add-ons, everyone's children (and grandchildren) will receive only the amount of schooling that a small voucher can purchase. Our hypothetical voter knows that a smaller voucher would reduce economic growth and would injure the children and grandchildren of people like herself.

Adults without school-age children are not the only voters who may support vouchers that allow add-ons. Some parents of school-age children may prefer such a policy. Currently thousands of parents pay for their children to attend private colleges and universities because they want to give their children an advantage over students who attend public universities. While these parents might prefer a partial voucher to help them pay their child's tuition to the private college, they do not want the government to pay the entire cost, as this would reduce their ability to give a competitive advantage to their child. These parents support educational sorting by socioeconomic status, and we expect many families support sorting for elementary and secondary schools as well as for colleges.

Are there policies that would both promote greater allocative efficiency and avoid the inequalities in educational opportunities that add-ons would create? One possibility is a sliding-scale voucher. The state might provide all students with a voucher sufficient to purchase the level of schooling necessary to meet basic educational objectives. For schools charging tuition above that level, the state might pay a portion of the extra cost. The state's share would decline as a family's economic situation improved. For example, if a school charged $2,000 above the value of the

voucher, the state might pay $1,800 of that fee for families with incomes less than 150 percent of the poverty level, $1,000 for families with incomes three times the poverty level, and nothing for families with incomes that are more than three times the poverty level. The drawbacks of such a policy would be increased monitoring and implementation costs and the invasion of privacy for families that apply for the additional funding.

THE IMPACT OF VOUCHERS ON PUBLIC SCHOOLS

A major political obstacle that any voucher proposal must face is the public's fear that vouchers will destroy the public school system. How realistic is this fear? The voucher programs for low-income students in Cleveland and Milwaukee have not ruined the public schools in those cities. A private scholarship program in the Edgewood Independent School District of Texas that offers full tuition to all low-income students has attracted less than 10 percent of the eligible students in the district. But generalizing from any of the existing voucher or scholarship programs is risky. They are relatively small and may be available for only a short time.

Current voucher policies in Milwaukee and Cleveland limit vouchers to low-income families. However, such vouchers neither increase income integration in schools nor do they prevent private schools from skimming the best available students from the public schools. An alternative to limiting vouchers to low-income families is to limit them to areas with low-performing public schools. Florida currently does this. Simulation results suggest that if vouchers are targeted to low-performing public schools, then high-income families will migrate to these areas.[43] While this may not integrate the schools, it may integrate neighborhoods. As we will explain in the final chapter, a better policy would be to require schools that accept vouchers to meet quotas of low-income students. If this were done, any school that accepts vouchers from middle- and high-income students must also enroll students from poor families.

CONCLUSIONS

Almost all writers who examine the efficiency of producing education conclude that policies should emphasize incentives rather than regulations. State policies should provide incentives for local school boards to allocate funds efficiently. School boards should provide incentives to administrators and principals to improve productive efficiency. Schools should pro-

vide incentives to teachers, parents, and students to work hard, to stay involved, and to care about learning. And choice policies must structure incentives in ways that encourage socioeconomic integration in schools and neighborhoods. Economic and political analysis can assist in determining the cost effectiveness of various educational changes and in structuring incentives to achieve the goals that policymakers desire.

Current economic, demographic, and political trends emphasize the importance of improving productive efficiency. The steady increase in real wages of college graduates, particularly those with strong cognitive skills, indicates that teacher salaries must increase if schools are to attract and retain good teachers. The competition for their skills is growing, and it probably is growing at an increasing rate. At the same time, the rapid expansion in the elderly population will force policymakers to reduce the rate at which funding for education increases. This will occur because of the expansion of programs for the elderly and because elderly voters tend to oppose increased educational expenditures.

School choice, particularly choice that includes market competition, may help policymakers meet the challenges that demography is creating for education. If school choice is to do this, however, the policymakers must resist calls for a regulatory approach to accountability. We hope, however, that policymakers will not be so influenced by efficiency concerns that they adopt policies that deepen current inequalities in educational opportunities. To do so would violate the basic American ideal of equality of opportunity.

Our review of the economic issues surrounding school choice shows once again that there is no perfect policy. If education policies include only public school choice, then policymakers must choose between maximizing funding for public education and greater equality of educational opportunities. Unequal funding across districts increases total educational expenditures, but it increases inequalities in educational opportunities and makes it difficult to implement choice programs. Policies that facilitate expanded school choice by equalizing funding across districts may have the unintended consequence of reducing funding for inner-city students and the total funding for education. Policies that increase productive efficiency (those that use incentives) will reduce regulatory accountability. Finally, voucher policies that maximize equality of opportunity are likely to increase the complexity of programs and their monitoring costs.

A review of the many tradeoffs involved in financing school choice leads us to conclude that the move toward greater equality of per pupil funding will continue, and that this will facilitate open enrollment, charter schools, and privatization. We believe that so long as such funding does

not reduce the funds available to inner-city students, equalizing funding across districts and schools has more benefits than costs. However, the existing simulation models indicate that coupling a voucher policy with equal per pupil funding will increase sorting by socioeconomic status. There are ways to design choice programs that prevent this sorting, and we would hope that policymakers will structure voucher programs in ways that encourage rather than discourage socioeconomic integration.

SEVEN

School Choice Regulation: Accountability versus Autonomy

SUPPOSE THAT THE STATE enacted a voucher program that enabled parents to receive tax money to send their children to a public or private school of their choice. Which of these accountability measures should the private schools be required to meet?

- They should be required to hire teachers who are certified by the state.
- They should be required to follow certain curriculum requirements about what courses to offer and what their content should be.
- They should be required to submit yearly financial statements and agree to public audits.
- They should be required to give their students standardized tests and publish the average results for the school as a whole.
- They should be required to set aside a certain percentage of their new spaces every year for low-income children.
- Religious private schools should be required to admit children of all faiths on an equal basis.

When Stanford political science professor Terry Moe asked parents and nonparents this question, there was a general consensus that the private schools should meet all of these requirements in the interest of being accountable to both parents and taxpayers.[1] Yet, when U.S. Department of Education researchers asked private school representatives about complying with such measures as a condition for participating in a public school transfer program, most said they would not want to participate.[2] Thus, by imposing a host of accountability measures, the state limits the supply of available schools and significantly curtails a competitive market. For some voucher advocates, no government regulation is necessary at all. The only form of accountability should be the market.

ARE MARKETS PREFERABLE TO DEMOCRATIC CONTROL?

The arguments of those who favor markets to ensure accountability come from two sources. First, there are the classical economic arguments for consumer control. Second, there are the claims made by a newer economic theory known as New Institutional Economics (NIE). This latter theory forms the basis of the critique of public schools put forth by John Chubb and Terry Moe in *Politics, Markets and America's Schools*.[3]

Classical Economic Theory

Classical economic theory maintains that consumers are the primary beneficiaries of the free market. Rather than government telling producers what to produce, how to produce it, and the price to charge, the market turns these decisions over to producers. But consumers will purchase only those goods that they want. And, so long as there are multiple producers, competition forces them to provide those goods at low prices.

How might such a system work in education? Suppose as a parent of a school-age child I have a tuition voucher that can be used at any school. I look for a school that is safe and will teach my child the skills he needs for the next grade. If I choose a school using these criteria and the school fails to provide the safety and skills, then I take my child and my voucher elsewhere. But what happens if only public schools in my district are available, and they fail to provide a safe and effective school? I can voice my complaint to the school board, but I can do little else unless I can afford to move to another school district or pay tuition and fees for private schools.

Now assume that I want a Christian education for my child and enroll him in a nearby Catholic school. Though I am not a Catholic, I choose this school because it is convenient and has a good reputation. After my child has started attending the school, I discover that the school's emphasis on Catholic doctrines is so forceful that I fear that my child will doubt the doctrines of his own faith. I have two options. First, I could ask the Catholic school to exempt my child from those classes that stress Catholic doctrines. Alternatively, I could seek out another school. If I choose the former approach, then the Catholic school may accede to my request lest they lose the income from my voucher. Compare this with the *Mozert* case, discussed in Chapter 3. When those parents requested that their children be exempted from reading certain materials because the readings conflicted with their faith, the school board said, "Our way or the highway."

The differences, of course, are that the public schools were not subject to the same financial pressures as the Catholic school, and the *Mozert* parents could not take the money that the state was spending to educate the *Mozert* children and use it to purchase education elsewhere.

Opponents of using the market to ensure accountability claim that the above scenarios are not realistic. One free market advocate acknowledges that the market works most effectively when the quality of a service is easily determined by the user, the service is purchased frequently enough for consumers to learn from past experience, and consumers have the necessary decisionmaking skills to make good choices.[4] In the real world, some parents are poorly informed about schools; many parents face language problems; others know little about what would constitute a "good education"; and still others have poor decisionmaking skills. Finally, most of the information parents would receive about their child's school would come from that school. It is hardly an unbiased source. Thus, opponents argue, while the market may be efficient for the production of toothpaste and cars, it is inappropriate for education.

New Institutional Economics

New Institutional Economics (NIE) accepts the traditional economic assumptions that individuals respond to the incentives that institutions create. It also recognizes that the market never functions perfectly. There always are information costs, some producers will attempt to mislead consumers, and markets are not purely competitive. But just as the market has imperfections, so too does the governmental provision of services. In the real world, not all citizens vote, and those who do are highly unrepresentative of those who do not. Organized groups have far more influence on policy than unorganized interests. And, in the absence of competition, it is nearly impossible for the public to know if the government is doing a reasonable job of providing the services people want and providing them efficiently. The question then is, will the imperfect market or the imperfect government perform better?

For most goods and services, NIE claims that the market is superior. Why? The answer lies in what NIE calls the principal-agent problem. Assume my car has a mechanical problem that requires repairing. Unless I am very knowledgeable about cars and have access to the necessary tools, I will take the car to a repair shop and pay the shop to make the necessary repairs. But there is a potential problem between me (the principal) and the repair shop (the agent). I am not fully informed about what is causing the problem or what it actually costs the shop to make the repair. The

mechanic may tell me that expensive repairs are needed when they are not, or he may overcharge me for the work he actually does. If I undertake the research to determine the mechanic's costs and then monitor his work, I will be expending a lot of time and effort. I must weigh the likelihood that the repair shop will cheat me against the costs of gaining the necessary information and monitoring the work. (These costs are called transaction costs.) How do we usually solve the principal-agent problem? We talk to friends and neighbors, check the records of the Better Business Bureau to see who are the mechanics with the most complaints, check the Web sites of trusted sources like Tom and Ray of the NPR radio program *Car Talk*, or get multiple bids. Once we have found an acceptable shop, we do not continue to pay all of the transaction costs. Rather, we become repeat customers of the repair shop that we believe treated us fairly and did good work. This continued relationship lowers our costs and gives the repair shop an incentive to treat us fairly.

It might seem that having government repair shops would solve the principal-agent problem. If mechanics have a set salary paid by the government, then they have no reason to overcharge us, to do unnecessary work, or to do the work poorly. Why, then, doesn't the state provide auto and truck repair? Because to do so would be inefficient and would lead to inferior service. If mechanics act as other government employees who provide services, they will form an interest group and lobby for higher wages, better working conditions, shorter hours, and so forth. Or they could seek to form a union and achieve these same advantages through a collective bargaining agreement with the state. In any case, the salary of mechanics will be based on how many years they have worked for the state, not on the quality and quantity of their work. If there is no penalty for shoddy work, the mechanics would have little incentive to be careful in their repairs. Because there would be no reward for it, mechanics would not look for ways to do their work more efficiently and cheaply. In fact, improving efficiency would endanger their jobs. In short, there would be a principal-agent problem where the principals are the citizens and the agents are the mechanics. But now the power rests almost entirely with the agents. They are organized and can lobby to achieve their goals. As consumers would not be organized, their interests would carry less weight.

What are the principal-agent problems in public education? The traditional method that citizens use to control those who provide government services is to set up an oversight institution such as a school board, a district superintendent, state education agency, or legislative committee. These institutions then issue rules and regulations that govern the activities of the service providers. Unfortunately, this does not solve the

principal-agent problem; it often makes the problem much worse. This occurs for two reasons. First, oversight institutions often are "captured"; they identify with the interests of those who provide the service rather than with the consumers or the general public. Second, oversight institutions may overregulate the service providers. This leads to enormous paperwork, stifles innovation and creativity, and reduces efficiency.

Why might the institutions that oversee public education become captured? One reason is that the personnel in the superintendent's office, on the local school board, and in state departments of education are former public educators or are closely allied with public education. It is a rare superintendent who previously was not a teacher and a principal. The typical school board includes teachers, ex-teachers, and the spouses of teachers. The state education agency is populated by individuals who previously were teachers, superintendents, and graduates of colleges of education. Even if these institutions were not populated by previous public school employees, capture tends to occur because teachers and principals are organized to present their demands, while citizens, parents, and students are not. On a typical education issue the only side that will be represented is that of the producers. If citizens elect the oversight institution, then that institution is likely to respond to the preferences of the most active voters. Public school teachers are the most active voters in school board elections, and teacher associations often are the most powerful organizations involved in political campaigns. These associations provide both campaign funding and campaign workers to candidates who are responsive to the teachers' interests.

The second difficulty with government provision of services is that the oversight institutions develop so many rules and regulations that the service providers spend as much time showing that they follow the rules as they do in providing the service. These rules and regulations also limit their autonomy and initiative. Chubb and Moe have argued persuasively that the problem of overregulation has been especially troublesome in education because the overseers are continually changing the regulations. Education is a controversial and important issue. When people who have a particular educational perspective gain a majority in the state legislature, on the state board of education, or on the school board, they want to ensure that their educational goals are those that govern not only current educational practices, but also future practices. The best way to accomplish this is to create new rules and regulations that tell schools and teachers what to teach and how to teach it. Chubb and Moe maintain that when an interest gains ascendancy, its proponents can "specify precisely what

they want the schools to do and build these specifications explicitly into legislative mandates and administrative regulations." They add,

> In this way they can formally enshrine not only the goals schools are required to pursue, but also the criteria and standards they are to employ, the procedures and methods they are to follow, the types of personnel they are to hire, and virtually anything else of relevance to the implementation of policy. The dangers of political subversion are therefore vastly reduced, because there is little or no discretion left to subvert.[5]

When a different interest gains control of the oversight institutions, its proponents have other educational goals and create further regulations to guarantee that their goals remain in place when they lose control. This process is repeated endlessly, and it creates thousands of pages of conflicting rules. For example, the Texas Education Code contains 322 double-column pages of statutes that apply to public schools, and the Texas Administrative Code contains 1,151 double-column pages of regulations required by the State Board of Education. This regulatory labyrinth limits the autonomy of public school principals and teachers to such an extent that they cannot produce efficiently or effectively.

We can summarize the argument for market accountability rather than regulatory accountability as follows. The information and monitoring costs to individual citizens are sufficiently large that citizens will attempt to solve the principal-agent problem by creating specialized institutions to oversee public schools. This creates two problems. First, service producers sometimes capture the oversight institutions. Second, in an effort to enshrine its educational goals and practices, each set of policymakers will formulate additional rules and regulations that govern what public educators provide and how they provide it. This produces schools with unclear missions, inconsistent goals, and conflicting classroom practices. It also destroys teacher creativity and innovation.

New Institutional Economics argues that when we compare imperfect markets and imperfect government services, markets generally have the advantage. The solution, therefore, is not only to privatize public education, but also to prevent oversight institutions from creating additional rules and regulations that the private schools must follow. Before we jump on the NIE bandwagon, it is important to remember that there are two fundamental differences between car repair and education. First, when we leave the repair shop we know rather quickly whether the desired outcome has occurred. The car either works better or it does not. This is not true

of education. It usually is not obvious to parents whether their child is gaining the skills and training necessary for success in school or in the job market. Second, those who pay for public education through their tax dollars may expect it to produce democratic citizens as well as individuals who are economically productive, and they will want proof that the schools are achieving those goals. These differences suggest that the argument for an accountability system based solely on the market may be legally and politically naïve. The central concern for policymakers is to locate the proper balance between accountability and autonomy within the realities of law and politics—no easy task. We address legal constraints in this chapter; political constraints are left to the final chapter.

LEGAL CONSTRAINTS ON INSTITUTIONAL AUTONOMY [6]

The combination of state constitutional law, state statutes, state administrative regulations, charters, and contract terms constitutes the legal framework within which school choice takes place. Each of these can be the source of regulation. Together and over time, they threaten the independence of choice schools. Here, we sketch how this is so, with particular attention to state constitutional law, which often is overlooked in discussions on the development of choice initiatives.

State Constitutions, State Regulation, and State Action

Thirteen state constitutions require the establishment of a system of "common schools." [7] The Washington State Constitution, for example, requires the legislature to establish a system of common schools and to dedicate revenue from the common school fund, and the state tax for common schools provides for their support. [8] In a 1909 decision, the Washington State Supreme Court defined a common school as "one that is common to all children of proper age and capacity, free, and subject to, and under the control of, the qualified voters of the school district." [9] One commentator has concluded that because charter schools are not "under the control" of the local community, the Washington State Constitution would have to be amended to accommodate them. [10] The state at present has no charter school statute. Fifteen states have a constitutional provision requiring a general and uniform system of education. [11] The combination of terms such as "general," "uniform," "thorough," "public," and "common" appearing in state constitutions can pose serious challenges to school choice programs unless the legislation is carefully crafted. Both the Milwaukee

and Cleveland publicly funded voucher programs initially foundered in the lower courts on these provisions.

Unconstitutional Delegation Law. When choice plans encompass private entities, they are subject to challenge under what is known as unconstitutional delegation, a judicially created doctrine concerning the ability of government to delegate its core governmental functions to private parties. That education is a core governmental function is beyond dispute. As the U.S. Supreme Court observed in the seminal *Brown v. Board of Education* decision, "Today, education is perhaps the most important function of state and local governments." [12]

The leading illustration of unconstitutional delegation law in the school choice context is litigation that greeted enactment of the Michigan charter school statute in 1993. The statute prohibited churches and religious organizations from operating charter schools, termed "public school academies," but permitted other private entities to do so. The lawsuit contended that these academies were in effect licensed private schools not under the control of the state, contrary to a provision of the Michigan Constitution stipulating that the state legislature "shall maintain and support a system of free public elementary and secondary schools as defined by law." [13] Virtually all state constitutions have similar provisions. [14] The Michigan lawsuit also contended that the charter school law violated a constitutional provision vesting the state board of education with "leadership and general supervision over public education." [15] Though the legislation had defined a public school academy in the charter school law as a public school, the trial court looked beyond the declaration and concluded that the thrust of the charter school legislation was actually to allow private organizations to operate schools and to do so without oversight by the state board of education. Therefore, the charter school law was unconstitutional. The decision was affirmed at the appellate court level in a 2-1 decision. That court, too, refused to accept the legislation at face value. "The Court must look through forms and behind labels into the substance of the law," wrote the judges. "The people have a right to have the limitations in a state constitution respected and given the fair and legitimate force which its terms required." [16]

By the time the case reached the Michigan Supreme Court, the legislature had revised the law to make it clear that the academies were under the control of the state board of education and subject to its regulations. Other new restrictions prohibited public school academies from levying taxes and required all teachers except college professors who teach in the academies to be certified in accordance with state board of education reg-

ulations. In its 1997 decision upholding the constitutionality of the charter school law, the Michigan Supreme Court cited these changes.[17] The majority noted that the state now decided the issuance and revocation of charters, controlled the money, and required academies to comply with school code provisions. Notice how concern about complying with the state constitution forced changes in the law. Yet, by making the changes, the legislature may have negated the very value of public school academies by making them subject to all the rules, regulations, and restrictions that are imposed on traditional public schools. One wonders whether the legislature may have done too much. Might there have been less intrusive accountability measures that would have satisfied constitutional requirements?

The key to permissible delegation is the presence of guidelines and regulations to limit the discretion of private entities to usurp governmental authority for their own interests. At the same time, the guidelines and regulations cannot be so controlling that they thwart the purpose of including private schools in choice plans in the first place. In a 1999 ruling permitting private entities to operate public charter schools, a New Jersey state court cited this guideline set forth by the New Jersey Supreme Court: "To be constitutionally sustainable, a delegation must be narrowly limited, reasonable, and surrounded with stringent safeguards to protect against the possibility of arbitrary or self-serving action detrimental to third parties or the public good generally."[18] In this case, the court ruled that since charter schools are not private, even if operated by a private entity, and are subject to the control of the commissioner of education, the legislature had not unconstitutionally delegated educational authority to them. The lower court ruling was affirmed by the Supreme Court of New Jersey a year later with two caveats.[19] First, noting that public policy as rooted in the state constitution requires an end to segregation in New Jersey public schools regardless of cause, the high court held that the commissioner of education must assess the impact of charter schools on racial balance in public schools generally and take whatever steps are necessary to prevent segregation. Second, because the state constitution requires a thorough and efficient system of public schools, the commissioner must consider the economic impact charter schools may have on districts of residence and either disapprove charter school applications or adjust the funding set forth in the charter school legislation to assure constitutional compliance.

Notice again how by making the privately operated charter schools subject to the authority of the state commissioner of education, the legislature avoided an unconstitutional delegation of a core governmental responsibility. But the tradeoff is clearly evident. Unless the commissioner is

circumspect in exercising authority, the imposition of the requirement has the effect of limiting institutional autonomy, thus undermining the potential for innovation and competition.

How the unconstitutional delegation doctrine applies to publicly funded voucher programs and tax benefit programs is an interesting question, because the delegation of educational responsibility is not directly to private schools but to parents, who have a constitutional interest in controlling the education of their children. Would the doctrine require the state to impose conditions on parents for the expenditure of the money in a way that does not undermine the public purpose in the state's providing for education? On participating private schools? On both parents and schools? We will have a chance to consider these questions later in this chapter with regard to the Milwaukee and Cleveland voucher programs.

State Action.   Another significant constitutional issue facing public choice schools operated by private organizations or private schools participating in publicly funded voucher programs is whether they have become sufficiently a part of the state that they must recognize the constitutional rights of their constituents. The Fourteenth Amendment to the U.S. Constitution and its enabling statute, 42 U.S.C. §1983, require states and their political subdivisions, including public schools, to do so. The relevant portion of the Fourteenth Amendment provides that no state shall "deprive any person of life, liberty, or property, without due process of law." Its enabling statute, §1983, provides that every person who "under color of any statute, ordinance, regulation, custom, or usage" deprives a person of his or her constitutional or federal statutory rights can be sued in federal court. The constitutional rights referred to include the freedoms of speech, religion, assembly, and association; the right to be free from unreasonable search and seizure; the right to due process of law; the right to equal protection of the laws; and other rights such as marriage and privacy that the U.S. Supreme Court has deemed fundamental. The matter is important, because other than in the case of slavery, the U.S. Constitution does not apply to wholly private action.

Note that the Fourteenth Amendment applies to "states" and its enabling statute applies to persons acting as governmental officials (the U.S. Supreme Court has interpreted the word "persons" to include political subdivisions of states such as public school districts). Thus, unlike public schools, private schools operating independently of the state are not required to comply with constitutional law. Because the relationship between a private school and its constituents is contractual in nature, the school has great authority to determine conditions of employment and

student enrollment, for example, through faith-based hiring and admissions policies. Is the same true of charter schools operated by private entities or of private voucher schools?

State charter laws routinely specify that schools operated pursuant to a charter are public. Thus, private entities seeking charters must agree to operate public schools. Still, when the state grants autonomy to private entities to operate schools—assuming, of course, that doing so does not run afoul of unconstitutional delegation law—it is not clear how much of the operation remains public. As one commentator notes, simply declaring that a charter school is a public entity does not necessarily make it so.[20] It is conceivable that courts may nullify such a declaration if it is not in keeping with the general thrust of other provisions in the legislation.

In some states, charter schools are organized as nonprofit corporations or exercise the same powers as business corporations. In ruling in 1995 that Amtrak must observe individual constitutional rights despite language in the federal statute stipulating that Amtrak is not an agency or part of the government, the Supreme Court noted, "It surely cannot be that government, state or federal, is able to evade the most solemn obligations imposed in the Constitution by simply resorting to the corporate form."[21] What was critical to the Court's decision in the Amtrak case was the fact that the government appoints a majority of the board of directors. Of course, states do not appoint the board of directors of private schools. But in the case of charter schools operated by private entities, the chartering agency does approve governing boards, oversees their operation, and, at the renewal point, often can remove board members.

Private schools that want to participate in publicly funded voucher programs can find some solace in a 1982 U.S. Supreme Court decision. In *Rendell-Baker v. Kohn,* the Court was confronted with claims by two teachers that their First Amendment free speech rights and Fourteenth Amendment due process rights were violated when they were terminated by a private school. The school served maladjusted high school students and received nearly all of its funding from the state.[22] While the school did have to comply with various state regulations as a result of the funding, personnel matters were left to the discretion of the school. The majority concluded that the school had not sacrificed its private status by becoming substantially publicly funded.

Rendell-Baker indicates that the threshold for finding private organizations subject to constitutional constraints is high. It must be established that the nexus between the state and the challenged action of the private entity is sufficiently close that the private entity's action may fairly be treated as that of the state. Thus, in another 1982 ruling on state action,

the Supreme Court rejected the contention that a private nursing home was a state actor in transferring Medicaid patients based on medical judgment to a lower level of care, noting that the decision was not prompted by the state or its officials.[23] By contrast, the Court decided a few years later that a private physician under contract to provide orthopedic services on a part-time basis at a state prison hospital was a state actor.[24] The critical factor was not that the physician was on the public payroll or paid by contract but rather that he was exercising power possessed by virtue of state law and made possible because he had been clothed with state authority to render medical services to prison inmates. Were it otherwise, the state could avoid its constitutional obligations simply by delegating governmental functions to private entities. In 2001 the Court ruled similarly in a case involving the Tennessee Secondary School Athletic Association.[25] The five in the majority found the association so closely entwined with the state that the association's regulatory activity amounted to state action. The Justices found no significant offsetting reason to rule to the contrary. With regard to private schools involved in voucher and tax credit programs, preserving institutional autonomy may be just such an offsetting reason, as indeed it was in the *Rendell-Baker* case.

The best example of where substantial state funding coupled with pervasive state regulation was sufficient to establish the nexus between a private school and the state is *Milonas v. Williams,* a 1982 decision of the U.S. Court of Appeals for the Tenth Circuit.[26] In that case, a private school for involuntarily confined youths which received substantial state funding and regulation was required to observe student Fourteenth Amendment due process rights. The involuntary educational character of the confinement, however, diminishes its significance to a voluntary educational choice program.

It is important to note that a state legislature or regulatory agency may require private schools to observe the constitutional rights of their employees and students as a condition of participation in a publicly funded voucher or tax credit program. In Milwaukee, the State Superintendent of Public Instruction developed an extensive list of regulations that impacted private schools participating in the original voucher program enacted in 1990.[27] Included among them was a provision that private schools had to serve children with disabilities under the Individuals with Disabilities Education Act (IDEA) and a provision requiring recognition of all state and federal guarantees protecting the rights and liberties of individuals. Specifically listed were freedom of religion, expression, and association; protection against unreasonable search and seizure; equal protection; and due process. When the program was challenged in state

court in 1991, the trial court terminated the regulations pertaining to special education but allowed those requiring private schools to observe the constitutional rights of students to remain in force. Significantly, the latter turned the private schools into the equivalent of public schools for purposes of constitutional law.

Yet it is apparent that this was not understood by private school operators or parents, and the provision was not enforced by the Wisconsin State Department of Public Education. John Witte, the official evaluator of the Milwaukee voucher program, observes that private school operators were unwilling to give up their independent powers to expel students. Expulsion procedures for choice students, he notes, "were no different than for non-choice students."[28] Imagine the tensions that would have surfaced in the schools if officials had to follow constitutional due process requirements before expelling choice students but not students whose parents paid tuition! The matter became moot in 1998 when the constitutional rights provision in the original state department regulations was made essentially advisory after a bitter dispute between legislators and state department officials.[29] At present, the only accountability measures remaining for the Milwaukee voucher program pertain essentially to fiscal matters. While this has generated political controversy, no litigation has surfaced.

In sum, state constitutional law clearly affects the development of school choice programs including the privatization of public education through the operation of public schools by private entities or through participation of private schools in publicly funded voucher programs. If regulation of private schools becomes significantly pervasive, it may be an important contributing factor in a court's determining that the schools have become sufficiently public that they are subject to state and federal constitutional constraints.

State Statutes, Administrative Regulations, Charters, and Contracts

State statutes are obviously central to school choice because they detail how the system is to be configured and operated. At present, charter school laws have been enacted in thirty-seven states and encompass some two thousand schools. Of these, about 12 percent are operated by private organizations, most of them for-profit. In addition, a few companies such as Edison Schools operate public schools under contract with school districts.

Statutory provisions for school choice vary from state to state, sometimes dramatically. Thus, there is a world of difference between the Rhode

Table 7.1. Comparison of Arizona, Massachusetts, and Michigan Charter School Statutes (Selected Provisions)

Provisions	Arizona	Massachusetts	Michigan*
Charter granting agency	Local sch. brds, state brd of ed., state brd for charter schools	Commonwealth brd of ed. (local districts must approve public school conversions)	Sch. dists, community colleges, state colleges & universities
Charter recipients	Public body, private person, private org.	Nonprofit orgs, teachers, parents	Partnership, nonprofit or business org., labor union, any association
For-profit EMO	Permitted to secure charter directly	Charter recipient may contract with EMO	Charter recipient may contract with EMO
Length of charter	15 years	5 years	10 years
Total number	No limit	120 (48 public conversions & 72 newly created)	No limit**
State regulations	Exempt from most	Subject to specific set of commonwealth brd of ed. rules	Subject to same state brd of ed. rules as public schools
Teacher credentials	Set forth in charter	State-certified (public conversion); state-certified unless pass state test (newly created)	State-certified except if college or univ. professor
Collective bargaining	No cb in state	Depends on charter	Subject to cb law; if sch. district grants charter, covered by district cb contract
Student assessment	State testing	Same as regular public school	State testing

Source: Ariz. Rev. Stat. §15.181 to §15.189; Mass. Gen. Laws ch. 71, §89; and Mich. Comp. Laws §§380.501–507.
  * Charter schools in Michigan are known as "public school academies."
  ** State universities are limited as to how many charters they grant in any one year.

Island restrictive charter school statute described earlier and the Arizona charter school statute, which is among the most permissive (see Table 7.1). Even when states are supportive of choice, the statutory framework reveals significant differences. Table 7.1 compares the charter statutes in Arizona, Massachusetts, and Michigan, the three states with the largest

number of charter schools operated by private organizations (often referred to as educational management organizations, or EMOs).

What is interesting about the table is that even with these relatively permissive choice statutes, charter schools in two of the states are subject to significant constraints. Thus, in Massachusetts the number of charter schools is capped, the schools are subject to a list of commonwealth board of education rules, most teachers have to be state-certified, and collective bargaining is possible. In Michigan, in addition to many of these same measures, the schools are subject to the same state board of education rules as apply to public schools. While these constraints are significant, they do not tell the whole story. As we shall describe below, the charters and subcontracts with educational management organizations can add additional restrictions.

In some cases, the legal framework is unclear. The experiences of the Wilkinsburg School District outside Pittsburgh provide a good example of the problems an unclear legal framework can engender. The district contracted with Alternative Public Schools, Inc., to operate one of its low-performing elementary schools. The Wilkinsburg teachers union bitterly opposed the move, eventually suing the district for violating state law. While Pennsylvania's school code allowed the contracting-out of various support services, it was silent on contracting-out the entire instructional program. In 1995 the Pennsylvania Supreme Court upheld the arrangement by a 4-2 vote in a surprising decision that saw contracting-out as a way for the local school district to meet its obligation under the state constitution to provide "a thorough and efficient system of public education." [30] However, the union was successful in challenging the district's decision to furlough twenty-four teachers to make way for the private company to hire its own employees. A Pennsylvania trial court later terminated the contract in light of the enactment of a charter school law that prohibits for-profit companies from directly operating public schools.

State administrative regulations also vary from state to state. This is particularly true with regard to holding choice schools accountable. There is no consensus on what accountability means for choice schools. [31] For example, as Table 7.1 reveals, charter schools in Arizona are minimally regulated. The Massachusetts charter law is augmented by a specific list of administrative regulations. [32] The Michigan practice is to hold state charter schools accountable to a host of state board rules that apply to public schools generally. As we described earlier, the latter was imposed to satisfy state unconstitutional delegation law. In addition to state board of education oversight, Michigan charter schools, called "public school

academies," are also subject to the administrative rules developed by their respective authorizing bodies. Charters in Michigan can be issued by local and intermediate school boards, community college boards, and governing boards of state public universities. The Michigan governor appoints board members at state universities. Republican Governor John Engler, a strong proponent of charter schools, apparently viewed the authorizing body as a way to end-run the elected state board of education.[33] Nearly 90 percent of the 173 public school academy charters operating in Michigan as of the fall of 2000 have been issued by state universities. Thus, not only are public school academies subject to the authority of the state board of education, they also are governed by the policies of their respective authorizing bodies.

Spurred by accusations that the Michigan academies are not being held sufficiently accountable and by criticism from academy boards that services do not justify the 3 percent fee authorizing bodies receive from public school academy allotments, authorizing bodies have begun to take their oversight role more seriously, though considerable confusion exists as to what their actual function is.[34] A case in point is Central Michigan University, which among the state universities has granted the most charters. Expressing increased concern that public school academy boards are being dominated by the educational management companies they hire to run the school, the university developed a comprehensive list of policies in 1999 delineating the role of the board and the company that must be included in all its charter agreements. The term "educational service provider" (ESP) is used in these regulations to clarify that the management function resides with the public school academy board, not its hired operator. Among other things, the policies require the academy board to provide detailed information about the ESP to the university charter school office prior to execution of the agreement, to assure that board members are completely independent of the ESP, to employ its own legal counsel to negotiate an arm's-length agreement, and to assure that the contract addresses a long list of provisions delineating the respective functions of the academy board and the ESP.[35] Nondelegable academy board functions include, among others, adopting curriculum and curriculum amendments; determining food service and transportation; expelling older students; and selecting, hiring, and terminating or contracting-out employees.

Yet another layer of legal requirements affects the tradeoff between institutional accountability and autonomy in the context of public charter schools—the negotiated charter and, where relevant, the subcontract

with a private educational management organization. The significance of these sources of law will be demonstrated by examining the operation of charter schools in Michigan.

School Choice Accountability: Michigan's Public School Academies

About 70 percent of the state's charter schools ("public school academies") are operated by private educational management organizations (EMOs). It would be erroneous to say that the academies are legally autonomous. Noting that his list is by no means exhaustive, one Michigan authority sets forth some fifty-nine provisions of the school code that apply to the academies, as well as thirty-nine other state statutes and twenty-five federal statutes.[36] Table 7.2 highlights key accountability provisions that emanate from the Michigan charter statute, state and authorizing body regulations, approved charters, and contracts negotiated by public school academy boards with educational management companies.

The accountability provisions in Table 7.2 are numerous. Under the statute, the authorizing body for a public school academy is responsible for oversight and monitoring regarding governance, the school's compliance with state and federal law, and teacher qualifications. The academies are subject to both state board and authorizing body regulations. In addition to serving as the fiscal agent for the academy, the authorizing body monitors the academy's compliance with the terms of the charter and has the nonappealable power to revoke it. Among other things, the charters between the authorizing bodies and the academies specify the relationship of the authorizing body to the academy board, the role of the academy board, the mission and curriculum of the school, and the goals against which the charter is to be assessed. Educational management contracts negotiated by academy boards with private companies delineate the relationship between the academy board and the management company. Some of the contracts convey other powers to the academy board, such as selecting an education auditor for reviewing academy management and removing the director hired by the educational management company. Though not all of these provisions are systematically or uniformly enforced, charter school administrators in the state decry the amount of paperwork that they must prepare. School administrators say they spend an average of 8.6 hours per month completing the reporting forms of their authorizing bodies, in addition to filing the nearly one hundred required state reporting forms a year.[37]

In sum, it is apparent that state constitutions, state statutes, state and intermediate-level regulations, charters, and contract terms can im-

pact significantly the autonomy of charter schools whether publicly or privately operated. The schools often are saddled with meeting the same criteria as regular public schools for such matters as teacher certification, collective bargaining, student assessment, student discipline, open meetings and records, fiscal accounting, and reporting. In addition, as public schools, they must recognize the constitutional rights of students and teachers. Rather than a lack of accountability, it appears that if all the various requirements were strictly enforced, the real problem would be excessive oversight and control. The fact that many of the overseers are closely aligned with the bureaucracy of traditional public education adds to the concern.

Because the legal framework for school choice programs is in its infancy, we turn now to look briefly at the greater experience with privatization in prisons and public housing, and with the delivery of special education services by specialized private schools, to learn what tradeoffs are apparent in these sectors when private organizations perform public services.

LESSONS FROM PRIVATIZATION OF PRISONS, PUBLIC HOUSING, AND SPECIAL EDUCATION

Privatization of Prisons

Like schooling, the operation of prisons was once the province of private entities. Even after the conversion to public prisons in the twentieth century following rampant abuses, contracting-out was common practice for things like laundry, food, and health services. Rising costs and overcrowding renewed interest in privatization. Privatization began first with nonsecurity and community-based facilities. During the 1980s, nine states adopted legislation permitting contracting-out prison operation. Currently, half the states and the federal government have enacted enabling legislation for the privatization of prisons, and more than one hundred private prison facilities are operating in the country, with an annual growth rate of 30 percent.[38] In 1996, 3 percent of the adult prisoner population was housed in private prisons. While as many as seventeen firms operate prisons, two—Corrections Corporation of America and Wackenhut—control almost 75 percent of all beds under contract.

The unconstitutional delegation doctrine surfaced early on in prison privatization, since the adjudication and confinement of felons are at the apex of governmental responsibilities. A decade ago, the Criminal

Table 7.2. Key Accountability Provisions for Michigan's Privatized Public School Academies (Charter Schools)

Source	Governance & Reporting	Curriculum & Assessment	Personnel	Fiscal
Statute	Subject to state brd of ed leadership and supervision Subject to authorizing body oversight & monitoring; revocation of charter by authorizer nonappealable Subject to fed. and state law applicable to school districts, e.g., civil rights, spec ed Must meet authorizing body's requirements for governance structure Compliance with state open meetings, freedom of information, coll. barg. laws, among others	Charter must specify educ goals and methods Subject to state student assessment	Teacher certification (unless college professor) & background checks required Subject to terms of coll. barg. contract if authorized by local district (right to coll. barg. generally)	At least annual audit by CPA Authorizing body is fiscal agent and forwards payment to school
State ed. regs	Same as traditional public school	Same as traditional public school	Same as traditional public school	Same as traditional public school
Authorizer regs* for charter schools	Brd mtngs at least monthly; copy of agenda & minutes Nondiscrim. policies Annual rpt Submit EMO contract	Technology plan Report student assessment measures & results	Teacher certification and background check data Submit contracts and job descriptions with employee groups	Submit budget info including previous year audit Insurance policies & various compliance forms Submit correspondence from various entities, e.g., dept. of ed, legal action

Charter	Authorizer appoints academy brd; governance details set forth Oversight activities by authorizer detailed Specifies grds & procedures for charter revocation	Details curriculum and student assessment Academic reports specified	Authorizes academy brd to contract with personnel Authorizes academy brd to contract with EMO Specifies that coll. barg. is responsibility of academy brd	Details financial activities of authorizer body and academy brd
EMO** contracts	EMO accountable to academy brd; periodic rpts and annual review required Financial, education, student records are property of academy and available for inspection and audit	Substantial changes to educational goals or programs require academy brd approval Accountable to academy brd for student performance	Must inform academy brd of compensation and fringe benefit schedules Delineates who are employees of academy and of EMO	Terms of compensation for EMO specified Academy brd selects indep. auditor EMO provides academy brd with projected budget for approval, monthly financial statements, quarterly financial and student performance rpts, annual audit

* The authorizer regulations set forth here reflect those developed by the state universities that have granted a large number of public school academy charters in the state. The regulations differ slightly among the universities. Central Michigan University developed a detailed list of policies in 1999 for clarifying the role of the academy board and the educational management company, termed "educational service provider." The policies have been incorporated into the charters granted to the public school academies by the university and must be reflected in the terms of the contracts the academy boards negotiate with service providers.

** EMO = educational management organization (now termed "educational service provider" in many contracts) that operates the charter school under contract with a public school academy board. The accountability provisions listed here are among those included in a majority of the ten sample EMO contracts examined. Given the small sample and variability from contract to contract, they are not definitive on accountability contract terms but do convey some idea of what the contracts typically say regarding accountability.

Sources: Mich. Comp. Laws §§380.501–507 and various sections (2000); Mich. Admin. Code, various sections (2000); charter documents from state universities; and ten sample charters and EMO contracts.

Justice Section of the American Bar Association commissioned a comprehensive study of constitutional, statutory, and contractual issues involved in prison privatization. The resulting Model Statute and Model Contract were designed to guide the development of privatization policies that would not unconstitutionally contract away government's responsibility and control.[39] Professor Ira P. Robbins, who conducted the study, stressed the importance of accountability and designed the Model Statute and Model Contract to provide it. It has been reported that half the states have enacted enabling legislation requiring that private facilities comply with local and state regulations and also meet standards set by the American Corrections Association (ACA).[40] To help protect against incompetent private-party operation of facilities, most states that allow prison privatization specify the qualifications that contractors must exhibit in order to be eligible for subcontracting. The contracts themselves are detailed regarding the conditions contractors must meet and provide incentives for achieving and sanctions for failing to achieve specified goals. Theoretically, contracts are carefully monitored.

Prison privatization remains controversial. Abuses are often reported, with critics pointing out that corporate concern for profits takes precedence over humane treatment and service delivery for people whose civil rights have been suspended as a result of their convictions.[41] A widely reported example of abuse in the spring of 2000 focused on the management of a juvenile prison in Jena, Louisiana, by the Wackenhut Corporation, the world's largest private prison operator. After extensive media attention to physical abuse and inmate neglect found by the Justice Department and a New Orleans judge, Wackenhut announced that it was abandoning its contract to run the facility. The Justice Department found a quarter of the inmates "traumatically injured" in a two-month period. According to investigators, guards reportedly routinely threw the inmates against walls, twisted their arms, or shoved them to the ground because the guards had not been taught other methods of control. Classes were rarely offered and no special education provided, despite the fact that a quarter of the inmates had IQs less than 70. Racism was pervasive, with inmates mostly black and guards mostly white. Low pay and poor management led to high turnover, even among wardens. Though it said it had made extensive improvements, the corporation found itself overwhelmed with investigations and lawsuits. The director of the Juvenile Justice Project of Louisiana, which had sued both Wackenhut and the state, called privatization a failure in Louisiana. "The sooner we end that experiment the better," he said.[42]

But correctional privatization is certainly not without its supporters,

including those federal and state policymakers who have welcomed its development amidst concern about overcrowding and the resultant cost. Supporters also are quick to point out that the greatest abuses of prisoners have taken place in government-operated prisons, triggering large-scale class action lawsuits resulting in extensive reform orders and judicial oversight.[43] Operating a prison is no picnic, regardless of whether a prison is operated by government or private organizations.[44] The central concern for prison privatization continues to be reaching a balance between legitimate government oversight and the autonomy of private operators to employ innovative and cost-effective ways to deal with incarcerated offenders.[45]

Though the U.S. Supreme Court has yet to rule on the matter, there is a general consensus among lower federal courts and in legal commentary that private corporations operating prisons on a contracting-out basis act under color of state law and are subject to constitutional law regarding inmate rights.[46] Furthermore, the government cannot avoid liability by contracting-out. As one commentator who has had extensive experience in negotiating prison privatization contracts notes,

> Once the contract is signed, it is essential to understand that the government will remain liable for violations of the constitutional rights of the prisoners, even if the private company is responsible for the acts or omissions. Under 42 U.S.C. §1983, the operator is an extension of the government, and its actions remain "state actions." The government cannot hide behind its private operator. An inmate can sue either party.[47]

Case law also is clear on this point. In a 1997 ruling, a Florida federal judge observed that when a governmental entity delegates public functions to a private entity, the private entity becomes sufficiently public that it may be held accountable as though it were public. Here, the court noted that Florida had enacted a statute permitting counties to contract with private entities to run their jails and prisons. Thus, the private operator of a county jail could be held liable for unconstitutionally detaining an arrestee over a three-day period.[48]

Three lessons from the prison privatization experience emerge that are relevant to the operation of public schools by private entities under charters and contracting-out agreements. First, constitutional constraints prevent the government from contracting-out its core correctional responsibilities without maintaining oversight and some means of outcomes assessment. Second, without appropriate incentives, private prison operators cannot be expected to provide expensive services. In effect, there is

a tradeoff between the profit motive of private organizations and governmental inefficiency in providing the service itself. Third, because corrections is a core governmental responsibility, both the government and its private agent must recognize the limited constitutional rights due inmates—a particular problem in prisons where inmates have no legitimacy and neither economic nor political power. The government cannot avoid its obligation to do so via contracting-out.

Privatization of Public Housing

To help low-income families obtain decent housing and to promote economically mixed housing, Congress established a housing certificate program in 1974 and expanded the program to include housing vouchers in 1983.[49] Now merged, the two programs give low-income families wide choice among housing vendors in the private market. Some million and a half households participate in the program nationwide. Eligible low-income families first obtain a voucher from the public housing authority and then seek out an apartment and an owner willing to execute a lease. Generally, the tenant pays no more than 30 percent of household income toward the monthly rent, with the housing authority picking up the balance in relation to local fair market rent levels established by the Department of Housing and Urban Development (HUD).

Though the statute leaves considerable discretion to the private housing provider in selecting tenants, it spells out the conditions for termination of leases, the amount of assistance, housing quality standards, and types of housing. Implementing federal regulations are more detailed. For example, the regulations specify criteria for such areas as sanitary facilities, food preparation and refuse disposal, space and security, thermal environment, illumination and electricity, structure and materials, interior air quality, water supply, lead-based paint, access, site and neighborhood, and smoke detectors.[50] The extensive regulation of the landlord-tenant relationship and the housing quality standards deter many private housing vendors from participating in the program.[51] This results in an undersupply of housing and, together with discrimination in tenant selection, serves to concentrate Section 8 housing opportunities in poor, minority neighborhoods with high crime rates.

Landlords face stringent barriers to removing a problem tenant under the Section 8 program. The owner may terminate a lease only for grounds specified in HUD regulations.[52] When the term of the lease is over, the landlord may choose not to renew it, but only if there is good cause or other sufficient reason. These restrictions limit the discretion of landlords

to evict unruly tenants whose behavior falls short of the good cause provisions listed in the regulations. And they have constitutional implications. In an instructive 1986 decision, a federal district court in California found sufficient government involvement in the Section 8 program to give the tenant a constitutionally protected property right in his lease. The court acknowledged that the flow of public money alone to the private landlord is insufficient to constitute governmental action. "When, however, the relevant statutes and regulations are viewed in their entirety this court concludes that 'state action' exists." [53]

Other federal courts have held that tenants faced with eviction also are entitled to a due process hearing. In 1992 an Ohio court went so far as to observe that unless good cause for eviction is demonstrated, a Section 8 tenant "may remain in the housing for life, and his right to do so is a constitutionally protected property interest." [54] In this case, the landlord had secured an eviction against the tenant in state court over a dispute involving graffiti allegedly painted on the building by the tenant's son. The tenant argued that the eviction action had not comported with her right to due process of law. The appellate court agreed, noting that federal regulations and the lease agreement require a meeting with the landlord to discuss the proposed termination. This had not happened. Nor had the final amount of damages owed by the tenant been determined. Further, the trial court had not adequately considered the tenant's mitigating circumstances. The appellate court overturned the eviction notice. The Supreme Court of New Jersey ruled in 1999 that though a private landlord may opt not to participate in the Section 8 voucher program, once an existing tenant becomes eligible for a Section 8 voucher, the landlord may not terminate the tenant's lease. [55]

That housing is considered an important interest deserving of federal court protection is evident in the 1997 decision of an Illinois federal court holding that a private landlord violated a tenant's due process rights in conjunction with her eviction. [56] The judge noted, "Plaintiff lost her subsidized housing unit, her housing subsidy, her personal possessions, and was rendered homeless. The nature of plaintiff's interests sufficiently outweigh the government's administrative and fiscal interests in a summary disposition of this case." Citing U.S. Supreme Court precedents regarding private actors carrying out governmental responsibilities, the judge noted that the tenant had sufficiently described a symbiotic relationship between defendants and the government to satisfy the threshold requirement for state action for the protection of constitutional due process. The judge ordered the parties to discuss settling the case before making another appearance in court.

Two lessons relevant to school vouchers emerge from this cursory review of the Section 8 housing voucher program. First, substantial flow of public monies to private providers in combination with extensive regulation reduces vendor autonomy, which in turn deters private providers from participating in the program. Second, the flow of public money coupled with extensive regulation subjects private vendors to the same constitutional constraints that apply to government.

Contracting-Out Special Education to Private Schools

Provision of special education services by specialized private schools is the most well-known form of contracting-out in public education. Private organizations undertaking these responsibilities are subject to extensive accountability under the Individuals with Disabilities Education Act (IDEA). Under IDEA, the state and school district remain responsible for ensuring that a handicapped child placed by the state or school district in a private school obtains a free, appropriate education: "In all cases . . . the State educational agency shall determine whether such schools and facilities meet standards that apply to State and local educational agencies and that children so served have all the rights they would have if served by such agencies." [57] Federal regulations give state education agencies the responsibility of ensuring that these requirements are met. [58] And opinions issued by the Office of Special Education Programs (OSEP), which is responsible for overseeing IDEA, make this clear. [59] In 2000, Florida hitched the voucher concept to the education of children with disabilities. Under the terms of the McKay Scholarship Program for Students with Disabilities, if the child is underperforming, the parent can seek a state scholarship to send the student to another district school or apply to a participating private school for special education services.

When private organizations agree to provide special education services to public agencies on a contracting-out basis, they surrender a significant degree of autonomy. A New Jersey appellate court refused to set aside the state's stringent bookkeeping and accounting practices for private schools serving students with disabilities, noting that "private schools that choose to receive handicapped public school pupils under Chapter 46 [state law] must therefore relinquish some of the privacy and control over their affairs that they otherwise would have under the general provisions of Chapter 6 [state law pertaining to private schools]." [60] A federal district court in New York found that since the city board of education retained primary responsibility for services to handicapped students the board placed in private school and the school was subject to considerable

monitoring and regulation, the plaintiff had a good chance of proving at trial that the actions of the school were the equivalent of state action. The motion by the school to dismiss the lawsuit was denied. The case involved a private school psychologist who alleged that her dismissal was in retaliation for her complaining to the city board of education about the suspension of a student.[61]

Somewhere in between the private organization that specializes in contracting with public agencies to provide special education services and the private school operated independently of the state is the private organization operating a public school pursuant to a contracting-out agreement or charter. What services must it offer children with disabilities? The 1997 amendments to IDEA make it clear that the local education agency that issues the contract or charter is responsible for assuring that special education services and funding for them occur in the same manner as in its other public school programs.[62] Where charters are issued by state-level agencies, the entity receiving the charter is responsible for providing special education services as though it were a newly created school district, subject to the provisions of state law.[63] However, funding can be a problem in these instances, since charter schools normally do not have the authority to tax, thus limiting their sources of funding to what they can get from the state.[64] Aware of this problem, plaintiffs' attorneys usually file suit against both the charter school and its state chartering entity.

The status of voucher and tax credit programs encompassing religious and nonreligious private schools with regard to provision of special education services remains unclear. As previously noted, schools participating in the Milwaukee voucher program were exempted by the trial court from providing special education services. In Cleveland, the schools are exempted by state law from educating "separately educated handicapped students," meaning those who have an individualized education program providing for the student to spend at least half of each school day in a class or school setting separated from nonhandicapped students.[65] How federal disability law may affect these state-level determinations awaits further developments. However, it is important to note that the Individuals with Disabilities Education Act is a uniquely human law that cuts across racial and income groups. Any dramatic expansion of school choice is likely to be accompanied by a demand from the advocates of special education that children with disabilities be assured a full opportunity to participate. As congressional reauthorization of IDEA in 1997 demonstrated, few politicians are likely to lend overt support to an effort to exclude these children. At the same time, efforts are likely to be made to place greater emphasis on outcomes assessment than on procedural

compliance and to give parents a choice of settings within which their children can be educated. This, in turn, will foster greater experimentation in both public and private schools on how to educate effectively children with disabilities.

VOUCHERS AND PRIVATE SCHOOL REGULATION

Publicly funded voucher programs encompassing private religious and nonreligious schools are ongoing in Milwaukee, Cleveland, and the state of Florida. In the fall of 2000, ninety-one private schools in Milwaukee and fifty-six private schools in Cleveland enrolled a total of twelve thousand voucher students. The Florida voucher program implemented in 1999 initially encompassed four Catholic schools and fifty-six students. But the number of failing public schools that were to supply students for vouchers declined so rapidly the following year that only a handful of students received vouchers. A number of states have voucher-like programs pending before their legislatures. To what extent has the flow of public money to private schools in Milwaukee and Cleveland increased state regulation? Before responding to this question, we must examine the extent to which the state can permissibly regulate private schools in the absence of such funding.

In 1925 the U.S. Supreme Court struck down an Oregon statute requiring all children to attend public schools.[66] The Court unanimously ruled that the law denied the property rights of the private school operators and interfered with the right of parents to control the education of their children. As described in Chapter 4, this is an important ruling for both private schools and parents. At the same time, the Court recognized that the state has the right to impose reasonable regulations on private schools. "No question is raised," wrote Justice James McReynolds, "concerning the power of the State reasonably to regulate all schools, to inspect, supervise and examine them, their teachers and pupils; to require that all children of proper age attend some school, that teachers shall be of good moral character and patriotic disposition, that certain studies plainly essential to good citizenship must be taught, and that nothing be taught which is manifestly inimical to the public welfare."[67]

While the Supreme Court did not clarify what is reasonable, two years later in *Farrington v. Tokushige* it declared that a Hawaiian statute had gone too far in regulating private foreign-language schools—chiefly Japanese—by giving the department of public instruction virtual control

over them.[68] The regulations specified the payment of a per-student fee; the reporting of the names, sex, parents or guardians, place of birth, and residence of each student; teaching permits and pledges; times when the schools could operate; courses to be taught; and textbooks to be used. The statute required English equivalents to be incorporated in the foreign-language textbooks, and gave the department of public instruction the right to appoint inspectors to enforce the law. The government's purpose in promoting Americanism was insufficient to justify the restrictions. Wrote Justice McReynolds for the Court, "Enforcement of the act probably would destroy most, if not all, of [the schools]; and, certainly, it would deprive parents of fair opportunity to procure for their children instruction which they think is important and we cannot say is harmful."

Over the years, states have relied on *Pierce* to set standards of varying comprehensiveness for private schools. In practice, these accountability measures have been for the most part modest, encompassing such matters as health and safety codes, length of the school year, enrollment reporting, and, less frequently, minimal curricular specifications and teacher qualifications. Legal challenges for the most part have been decided in favor of states, even when the free exercise of religion supplies the cause of action.[69] The relationship between private religious schools and accountability is an important consideration, since 78 percent of private schools are religiously affiliated. The U.S. Supreme Court ruled in 1990 that religion cannot provide the basis for an exemption from otherwise neutral state laws of general applicability.[70] The case, *Employment Division, Department of Human Resources of Oregon v. Smith,* involved the denial of unemployment benefits to a worker who was terminated for using peyote in a Native American religious ceremony. The Court ruled that the denial did not interfere with the worker's free exercise of religion because the law was applied to anyone who used illegal drugs.

Thus, unless the state singles out religion for some particular form of regulation, no exemption is required from accountability measures applied to a broad class of subjects. But the Justices did recognize a "hybrid situation" where religious rights in combination with other constitutional rights might justify an exemption. Writing for the majority, Justice Antonin Scalia cited *Wisconsin v. Yoder* as an example. In *Yoder,* the Court granted Old Order Amish parents the right to have their children exempted from compulsory schooling beyond the eighth grade.[71] That case, he observed, involved not only free exercise of religion but also the fundamental right of parents to control the upbringing of their children. The extent to which the combination of free exercise of religion and parental

rights in the context of school vouchers will justify an exemption for religious private schools from state regulation remains to be seen, though, as noted in Chapter 4, recent decisions have not been supportive.

As noted in that chapter, Congress tried to overturn the *Smith* ruling in 1993 by enacting a statute known as the Religious Freedom Restoration Act that required government to establish a compelling purpose whenever its action substantially burdened the free exercise of religion. In 1997 the Supreme Court struck down the law as an intrusion on the prerogative of the Court to decide the dimensions of constitutional rights.[72] However, there is growing effort in some states to enact laws that give special protection to religious freedom. For example, Texas enacted a law in 1999 known as the Texas Religious Freedom Restoration Act that prohibits government from substantially burdening a person's free exercise of religion unless it can establish a compelling governmental interest and show that it is using the least restrictive means of furthering that interest.[73] Free exercise of religion means an act or refusal to act that is substantially motivated by sincere religious desire. Such a law could affect efforts by a state to regulate religious private schools. There is the possibility, of course, that state laws like these will meet the same fate as the earlier congressional effort. The issue is not likely to arise in Texas because the state does not regulate private schools other than to require that they have a course in good citizenship, and it has no publicly funded voucher program.

Private schools also are subject in varying degrees to selected federal civil rights laws such as Title VII of the 1964 Civil Rights Act, which prohibits discrimination in employment on the basis of race, color, religion, sex, or national origin, though there often are exemptions in these laws for very small schools and for those that are religiously affiliated. However, most private schools are not subject to a number of federal laws that require receipt of federal funds to be applicable. These include the Individuals with Disabilities Education Act, Section 504 of the Rehabilitation Act of 1973, prohibiting discrimination based on handicap, and Title IX of the 1972 Education Amendments, prohibiting sex discrimination.

In sum, it is worth emphasizing that, contrary to common perception, the state has considerable authority under federal constitutional law and recent Supreme Court decisions to regulate both nonreligious and religious private schools. This authority exists even in the absence of any flow of public money to them directly or indirectly. Currently many states do not exercise the authority for essentially political reasons.

One would assume that when private schools, including those that are religiously affiliated, participate in publicly funded voucher programs,

the amount of regulation is likely to increase. This has not happened to any great extent with either the Milwaukee or Cleveland voucher programs, both of which have been upheld by their respective state supreme courts, as we noted in Chapter 5. Two-thirds of the private schools in Milwaukee and four-fifths of the private schools in Cleveland are religious. In the case of Milwaukee, participating private schools are subject to the underwhelming regulations for Wisconsin private schools generally, e.g., have a primary purpose of providing education, offer instruction for a minimum number of hours annually, and offer a sequential curriculum.[74] The voucher law requires each choice school to meet only one of the following: at least 70 percent of the students in the program are to advance one grade level each year, the private school's average attendance rate for students in the program is to be at least 90 percent, at least 80 percent of the students in the program are to demonstrate significant academic progress, or at least 70 percent of the families of pupils in the program are to meet parental involvement criteria established by the private school.[75]

The Milwaukee private schools also are required to adhere to federal antidiscrimination law (though, as noted earlier, they are not required, following a trial court ruling, to serve children with disabilities), observe all health and safety laws that apply to public schools, and submit an annual financial audit to the Wisconsin Department of Public Instruction (DPI). The schools are required to admit applicants randomly, except for siblings of enrolled students, and to exempt students who are not of the school's faith from religious activities. Controls like these on admissions do pose some intrusion on the autonomy of the school and undercut the ability of choice schools to be different from traditional public schools. Yet, notice that there are no requirements for teacher certification, curriculum content, student assessment, student discipline, enrollment diversity, or compliance with open meetings and open records acts. Many charter school programs are subject to these kinds of accountability measures.

Following early and bitter disputes between the DPI and legislative leaders, the Wisconsin Legislature eliminated most of the initial accountability measures when the program was expanded in 1995. Included among them was the requirement for an annual evaluation. The legislature directed the Legislative Audit Bureau to conduct a financial and performance evaluation in 2000. That report focused mostly on fiscal matters, noting that the lack of a uniform testing requirement precluded an assessment of academic achievement.[76] Critics lament the lack of regulatory accountability for the program.[77]

The Cleveland, Ohio, scholarship (voucher) program for low-income

families exerts only limited accountability measures on participating private schools, though the state does have an extensive set of regulations that private schools must follow to be considered state-accredited (called "chartered" in Ohio state law).[78] Included among them are requirements regarding length of the school day and year, specification of curricular contents, teacher certification, and participation in statewide student testing. However, religious private schools with "truly held religious beliefs" are exempt from state accrediting and are subject only to a few minimal state regulations, following a 1976 Ohio Supreme Court ruling.[79] These are limited to length of the school day and year; pupil attendance reporting; a bachelor's degree for professional staff; a general list of courses of study; and compliance with state and local health, fire, and safety laws. Both state-accredited and nonaccredited private schools may participate in the scholarship program—the latter by approval of the state superintendent of instruction.

The Cleveland scholarship law prohibits participating schools from discriminating on the basis of race, religion, or ethnicity, and from teaching hatred; requires minimum enrollment per class and for the school as a whole; and prohibits dissemination of false or misleading information.[80] Voucher schools may not charge more than 10 percent of the voucher in additional tuition or fees. Except for enrolled students and siblings, admission is by lot in kindergarten through third grades. Scholarships for children already in private schools are limited to 50 percent of the total. After third grade, the students may continue at the school through the eighth grade. Schools are not required to be coeducational or to admit separately educated handicapped students.[81]

Despite the fairly limited regulations on religious private schools evident in the Milwaukee and Cleveland choice programs, the programs are too new and localized to tell us much about the extent of regulation in a larger program where substantial state resources flow to religious private schools. Policymakers face a dilemma in this respect. On the one hand, state constitutions require some accountability to avoid unconstitutionally delegating the core governmental responsibility for education to private organizations, and the *Pierce* ruling permits reasonable regulation of private schools. On the other hand, private authorities can challenge accountability regulations as unreasonable under both the *Pierce* and *Farrington* rulings. Parents may challenge encompassing regulation as a denial of their constitutional right to choose private schools and, in the case of religious private schools, as a violation of their free exercise of religion. Between the restrictions of the state constitution and those of the federal

constitution lies a narrow policymaking channel for wise accountability measures that strike a balance between institutional accountability and autonomy.

Tax credit plans, especially those that place several layers of insulating private action between the state and the private school as described in Chapter 5, are less likely to be accompanied by extensive new regulation of private schools, at least in the short run. However, the realities of politics suggest that any significant expansion of money via tax credits to private schools will trigger calls by public school advocates for increased monitoring and control. And, as noted at the beginning of the section, the state has considerable authority to regulate private schools if it chooses to do so. The use of tax credits, like school vouchers, is too new and too limited at this writing to offer insight into future patterns.

IMPLICATIONS FOR POLICYMAKING

The greatest fear of school choice proponents is that encroaching regulation in the interest of accountability will diminish institutional autonomy. This would deter new schools from forming and undercut the potential of school choice to improve education. They are justified in their fears. Evidence from the limited experience with school choice so far shows that, at least on paper, regulation is very much part of the legal framework. The same is true with regard to privatization in other sectors.

In part, regulation reflects a sincere concern on the part of policymakers that choice schools be accountable to parents and the state for providing a core governmental service. But it also reflects the stranglehold that bureaucratic agencies and controls have on education. Powerful interest groups, chiefly in the form of teachers' unions and lobbies for traditional public schools, use their political muscle to stifle the competition by tying it up in red tape.

The only sure way to prevent legislatures and administrative agencies from enacting restrictive accountability measures is to amend the state constitution, a difficult process.[82] At the same time, it is naïve for choice proponents to argue that all the accountability that is needed can be provided by the market. There are important parent and state interests that require state oversight. As one group of choice proponents note, "School founders, staff, and parents must, for example, recognize that things like state-wide tests are part of the deal."[83] The central concern for policymakers is to identify those things that "are part of the deal" and to avoid

others that, while embraced by many in the education community and the general public, serve only producer-interests or are weakly linked to student and institutional outcomes. In the final chapter, we present as part of our school voucher proposal the accountability measures that we believe will best serve parent and state interests without unduly undermining institutional autonomy.

The Politics of Choice and a
Proposed School Choice Policy

AMERICAN POLITICAL INSTITUTIONS make expanding school choice to the private sector extremely difficult. James Madison designed the Constitution to prevent changes that might harm existing interests, and his vision of limited government remains in place. We can see this clearly at the national level. Such changes as the passage of Social Security legislation, extending civil rights to minorities, and the first Clean Air Act required the concurrence of three political conditions—extraordinary popular support over a long period, media focus on a particular crisis, and impressive political leadership. Even when these three conditions occur simultaneously, organized interests may defeat legislation that the majority supports. For example, despite public support, high visibility events, and the willingness of President Clinton to place health care and gun control at the top of his political agenda, entrenched special interests defeated universal health care and effective control of handguns and automatic weapons. In both situations, well-organized interests overruled the preferences of a large majority of American citizens.

State governments, like the national government, generally give organized interests numerous opportunities to kill legislation. Proponents of new legislation must win numerous times with many different sets of legislators, while opponents often need to win only once. Table 8.1 shows the various obstacles that a bill must overcome to become law in many state capitals.[1] State legislatures often have additional rules to slow down legislation. In Texas, for example, if eleven of thirty-one state senators sign a petition to prevent a bill from coming to the floor for a vote, that effectively defeats the legislation. Therefore, even if legislation has the majority support of the population and a majority of legislators support it, organized opposition to the legislation is likely to defeat legislative proposals.

Table 8.1. The Legislative Process

Steps in the Legislative Process	Possible Ways to Defeat the Bill
1. Bill is introduced to the House.	The chamber leader sends the bill to an unfriendly committee chairperson or refuses to refer the bill to a committee.
2. Bill is scheduled for hearings in committee.	The committee chair schedules the bill late in the session or not at all.
3. Committee hearings.	The committee chair schedules only unfriendly witnesses.
4. Committee mark-up (where the committee makes changes in the bill).	The committee's changes make the bill ineffective.
5. Committee vote.	The committee votes to defeat the bill and gives it a negative recommendation.
6. The House Rules Committee places the bill on the calendar for debate and a vote.	The bill is placed on the calendar so late that there will be no vote; or the Rules Committee allows unlimited debate and floor amendments.
7. The floor debate and amendments.	The House amends the bill to make it ineffective.
8. The floor vote.	A majority of those voting vote No.
9. Steps 1–5 and 7 & 8 are repeated in the Senate.	Opponents repeat their efforts from the other chamber.
10. Conference Committee. The House and Senate versions are combined into one bill.	The committee rewrites the bill in such a way that it is no longer an effective reform.
11. Full House and Senate vote on the conference bill.	One or both chambers vote against the conference bill.
12. The bill is sent to the governor for his signature.	The governor vetoes the bill.

This is particularly true if the organized opposition has a strong positive image in society.[2]

POLITICAL FORCES THAT OPPOSE EXPANDING SCHOOL CHOICE

Perhaps the biggest obstacles to expanding school choice are inertia and fear. Most Americans are satisfied with the public schools their children attend and never consider alternatives to the current educational system.[3] Even inner-city parents whose children receive a demonstrably inferior education believe their children's schools are doing a good job. In the San

Antonio Independent School District, a district where students were losing an average of two percentiles per year in math and one in reading, 45 percent of parents assigned their children's schools a grade of A and another 36 percent assigned the schools a grade of B. Because most public school parents are satisfied with their children's schools, they view with suspicion proposals that would fundamentally alter primary and secondary education.

The children of the most politically active Americans—higher-status citizens who live in the suburbs—generally receive an education that allows them to gain entrance to quality colleges and universities. When the opponents of public funding for private schools argue that vouchers will destroy public schools, suburban families have good reasons to fear those results. Inertia and fear also affect middle-income families. Survey research shows that 65 percent of Americans say that they have not heard about vouchers. A much smaller percentage of adults have considered the implications of vouchers and are familiar with the arguments for them.[4]

An additional political problem faced by choice proponents is that the interests that choice will benefit most have not given it a high priority. Lobbyists for Catholics, Evangelicals, and inner-city minorities have not placed school choice at the top of their agenda.[5] This is not true of choice opponents. They have made preventing public funding for educational vouchers and tax credits their highest priority.

Producers of Public Education and Their Organizations

Proposals to expand school choice to include public funding for private schools, tax credits, or weakly regulated charter schools run directly against the interests of public school teachers and administrators. Unfortunately for choice proponents, teachers' organizations are the most politically powerful single interest in many state legislatures. The National Education Association (NEA), the American Federation of Teachers (AFT), and their state affiliates are a dominant presence in state and national Democratic Party organizations. For example, from January 1999 through June 2000, the AFT gave $279,000 in soft money to national Democratic organizations.[6] Its state affiliates gave thousands more to the Democratic Party's candidates for the U.S. Congress and for state legislative seats. Similarly, at its 2000 annual convention the NEA passed a dues increase so that it could spend an additional $7 million per year on its political action efforts.[7] Just as important as their monetary contributions are the thousands of volunteers that teacher organizations supply to po-

litical campaigns. In return for this campaign assistance, the leaders of the Democratic Party at the state and national levels vigorously oppose all proposals for vouchers or tax credits for private schools. Democratic presidential candidate Al Gore promised in his 2000 campaign that he would *never* support school vouchers.[8]

The political strategy of teacher organizations on the issue of expanding choice among public schools has changed slightly over the past decade. Early in the charter school debate the NEA opposed charters while the AFT supported them. The NEA feared that charter schools would hire uncertified teachers and that teachers at charter schools would not be union members. The AFT, in contrast, argued that charter schools can provide public school teachers with greater freedom and flexibility and are a way to defeat the more dangerous policy options of school vouchers and tax credits.[9] Today both the AFT and the NEA oppose charters schools unless they meet the following requirements: take no money from other public schools, are subject to the same union membership and collective bargaining rules as other public schools in the district, charge no tuition or fees, are nonprofit, accept students with special needs, meet or exceed the same academic standards and assessment requirements as other public schools, and hire only fully certified teachers.[10] No state's charter schools meet these conditions.

When unions have been unable to block charter school legislation, they often have been successful in imposing so many conditions that few charter schools can form. A case in point is Rhode Island, where no existing public school can be converted into a charter school unless two-thirds of the certified teaching personnel currently assigned to the proposed school approve. A more complex two-thirds requirement is necessary before a school district can approve the creation of a new charter school. That same two-thirds must approve any departure from state statutes and regulations, and from school district rules. The union must be given an opportunity to present its comments to the chartering entities and receive a written reply.[11] All charter schools, whether newly created or converted from an existing public school, are subject to the state's teacher certification, tenure, and collective bargaining laws; may not be operated by for-profit organizations; and are subject to rules developed both by the commissioner of elementary and secondary education and by the state board of education.[12] Rhode Island limits the number of charter schools to twenty, and they may serve no more than 4 percent of the Rhode Island school-age population. Not surprisingly, Rhode Island has few charter schools.

Liberal and Minority Interest Groups

Liberal interest groups have provided strong and effective opposition for any and all choice proposals that include private schools. The more active of these groups have been the PTA, associations of school administrators, labor unions, the American Civil Liberties Union (ACLU), People for the American Way, the League of Women Voters, the Anti-Defamation League (ADL), the American Association of University Women (AAUW), Americans United for the Separation of Church and State (AU), and the National Association for the Advancement of Colored People (NAACP).[13]

The opposition of the PTA, school administrators, and organized labor is expected. The interests of the PTA are closely aligned with those of teachers' organizations. As John Coons and Stephen Sugarman have pointed out, the "P" in PTA is largely ornamental.[14] Similarly, associations of public school administrators oppose school choice because they are likely to be its first casualties. Such unions as the AFL-CIO have solidarity as well as ideological reasons for siding with the teachers' organizations, and public employee unions oppose all privatization and outsourcing efforts that might threaten public employee jobs.

The ACLU, ADL, AU, and AAUW argue that allowing public funding for private schools would mean that public funds will be used for religious indoctrination. They are particularly concerned that the indoctrination would be that of religious fundamentalists, a worldview that these four groups find alien and unacceptable. The League of Women Voters and People for the American Way claim multiple reasons for opposing school choice. First, the groups are concerned that vouchers will take funds away from public schools (which the groups believe are currently underfunded). Second, they fear that schools which attract fundamentalist parents will instill intolerance, racism, and sexism in students. Third, these groups maintain that vouchers violate the Establishment Clause of the U.S. Constitution. Finally, they claim that vouchers are inherently unfair to those students who are left behind.

In 1997, the NAACP joined People for the American Way to form Partners for Public Education.[15] The sole purpose of this organization is to defeat all proposals that would use public funds for private school education. The participation of People for the American Way is logical given the statist and secular ideology of its members. However, more than three-quarters of inner-city parents favor vouchers, and many would like the option of moving their children out of attendance-zone public schools.[16] Therefore, the NAACP's stand against vouchers places the organization in

opposition to the wishes of the people it claims to represent. Why might the NAACP do this? One reason is that the public schools traditionally have been the best route for African Americans to move into the middle class. Second, because of the tremendous campaign assistance that teachers' unions give black candidates for office, the NAACP does not wish to offend those unions.[17] Third, African Americans and other minorities have no reason to trust either the Republican Party or the conservative and libertarian interest groups that are spearheading the drive for vouchers and tax credits. Republicans, libertarians, and conservatives generally have opposed the government programs that the NAACP and other minority-based interest groups support. Even African Americans who are strongly pro-voucher fear that middle- and upper-income whites are simply using the voucher issue to gain funding for their children to attend private schools. Once vouchers are in place, African Americans fear that conservatives and libertarians will abandon all equity aspects of voucher policies.[18]

POLITICAL FORCES SUPPORTING INCREASED SCHOOL CHOICE

A tremendous advantage of the antivoucher groups is that they need not agree on what the best choice policy would be, they need only agree that policies which include public funds for private schools are inferior to the status quo. Proponents of vouchers, however, must offer a concrete alternative that can obtain a legislative majority. Hubert Morken and Jo Renée Formicola have shown that the *potential* pro-voucher forces stretch well beyond current private school parents, existing private schools, and churches with direct ties to parochial schools. Business interests may see vouchers as a matter of market competition and efficiency. Racial activists, some liberals, and many religious leaders believe that government should take the lead in providing equal freedom and equal educational opportunity. Conservatives assert that school choice is about empowering parents as well as restricting the domain of government activity. Libertarians often oppose any government role in education.[19] Obviously, no single voucher proposal can please all of these interests.

The Republican Party generally has led the legislative efforts for charter schools, tax credits, and vouchers. But to achieve greater public funding for private schools the GOP needs to build a coalition that includes some minority leaders and some Democrats as well as the GOP's basic constituencies—the Christian Right, libertarians, and upper- and upper-

middle-income suburbanites. To obtain the support of suburban legislators most voucher proposals must require accountability provisions such
as statewide tests and not include home schooling. To obtain support from
representatives of minority districts, policy proposals must include limitations on the ability of schools to reject applicants. But these provisions
often are unacceptable to the Christian Right and libertarians. The Christian Right has been particularly opposed to any provision that limits a
school's rights to decide which students to admit or expel as well as proposals that would not allow sectarian schools to require that all of its students attend such religious services as morning chapel.

Because of the many difficulties that face a bill in a state legislature
and the difficulty of achieving a coalition that includes both minorities and
members of the Christian Right, Coons and Sugarman have suggested that
a voucher proposal is more likely to be successful if it is presented as a
referendum to the voters than as a bill to the state legislature.[20] To attract
minorities and sympathetic liberals, the measure can include equity and
accountability provisions. Presumably, when confronted with a choice
of a proposal with these provisions or the status quo, more libertarian-
oriented voters as well as those from the Christian Right would choose to
support the voucher initiative.

We believe it is unlikely that any statewide voucher proposal will win
a referendum. Political science research shows that to defeat initiatives,
opponents need only scare or confuse voters.[21] The voucher referenda in
California, Oregon, Michigan, and Colorado have shown that opponents
will spend the funds to create the necessary levels of fear and confusion.
And many states do not have a referendum process.

How might a large-scale voucher proposal ultimately win approval?
We believe several things must happen. First, there must be political entrepreneurs to lead the fight to legitimize the policy and to shepherd it
through the legislature.[22] Second, a leading elected politician with substantial political clout must agree to head the fight. The most likely candidate for this role is a Republican governor. Third, some Democrats and
minorities must sign on early in the development of policy proposals. Unless individuals who are advocates for the disadvantaged sign on at the
beginning, proposals will lack the necessary equity provisions to increase
equality of educational opportunity. Finally, it will be helpful if there is an
event that increases public awareness of the problems that low-income
and minority families have in obtaining an adequate education.

The national government provides an alternative way to introduce a
broadly based voucher plan. During periods that the Republican Party
controls all three branches of government it is possible that the federal

government could finance a large-scale voucher program. The Department of Education could fund an experiment that guarantees that existing public schools would not suffer funding declines for several years. This could alleviate the fears of a sufficient number of legislators at the state level to allow a state to participate in the federal experiment. As an alternative, the federal government could increase choice with a substantial tax credit program to families with school-age children. To encourage participation by low-income families, the policy could provide a negative credit and no-interest loans to low-income families who signed the loan over to a private or out-of-district public school.

ATTRIBUTES OF AN EQUITABLE AND EFFICIENT POLICY PROPOSAL

We began this book with the argument that *in a liberal democracy* education should provide every able student the economic skills necessary to become economically independent, the political knowledge and skills to participate in democratic government, and the moral reasoning essential to understand and practice ethical behavior. We also claimed that education policies should encourage greater equality of educational opportunity among people of different ethnic groups, social classes, and genders. While there are many other worthy objectives for education, we maintain that these four provide the most essential criteria for judging the success or failure of a choice policy.

How should we operationalize the above goals so that we can measure policy effectiveness? We would argue that if a policy is effective, then the average student score on standardized tests will increase and the difference in student scores between the top and bottom quintiles will decrease. To the extent that the moral reasoning of students improves, violence by students on and off school grounds and the rate of juvenile delinquency should decrease. In addition, more students will participate in voluntary activities that improve their community and the lives of other people. In the long run, effective education policies will lead to less unemployment, less crime, less violence, and greater participation in democratic government and civic activities.

An effective school choice policy will address all four sets of variables that influence academic outcomes—the skills and interests of students, the involvement of parents, the quality of the classmates, and the practices of schools. The policy can do this if it: (1) assists parents and students in

matching students' talents and interests with appropriate curricula and pedagogies, (2) allows parents to choose the values their children will learn, (3) treats low-income and minority families as *clients* of schools rather than as *targets* of educational experts, (4) encourages greater equality in the positive spillovers students receive from their classmates, (5) allocates greater resources to disadvantaged students, (6) improves the incentive structures that face schools, administrators, and teachers, and (7) reduces the number of regulations on schools. A good policy also will encourage accountability. In the section below we present the basic outline of a proposal that we believe provides the best set of tradeoffs among the competing goals and objectives of educational policy.

A PROPOSAL TO EXPAND SCHOOL CHOICE [23]

We propose legislation that would include private schools and would encompass an entire state.[24] The legislation would read as follows.

1. There will be two new categories of schools—Public Scholarship Schools and Private Scholarship Schools.
   a. Thematic, magnet, and charter public schools for which attendance zones do not determine the majority of student admissions will be public scholarship schools. Each will be a nonprofit corporation governed by rules fixed by its authorizing agency. Public scholarship schools will be exempt from all state regulations and regulations issued by authorizing agencies except those specifically designated in this legislation. These schools will be funded through vouchers awarded to students.
   b. Private scholarship schools are schools owned and controlled by nongovernmental individuals and organizations. A private scholarship school may be either a for-profit or a not-for-profit entity. Private scholarship schools will be authorized by the state board of education or a separately designated state agency. An existing private school that meets current state licensing requirements shall be automatically authorized upon a petition to the state authorizing agency from the school. Private scholarship schools will be eligible to redeem vouchers awarded to students.
2. The state will designate no more than 20 percent of the state's school-age children as low-income. If a school redeems vouchers by students not designated as low-income, at least 20 percent of a school's student body must be designated as low-income.

3. Additional requirements for school eligibility include:
   a. A scholarship school cannot charge low-income students additional tuition or fees except for transportation beyond a two-mile radius.
   b. A school may not advocate unlawful behavior, teach hatred, or provide deliberately misleading information about the school.
   c. A school cannot choose applicants based on their race, ethnicity, or national origin. Public scholarship schools cannot discriminate against students based on a student's disability.
   d. A school cannot compel a student to profess ideological or religious beliefs.
   e. No *public* scholarship school may discriminate among applicants based on religion, nor may it advocate any religious doctrine.
   f. Nonprofit schools that redeem vouchers must use all income from them for educational goods, services, or facilities.
   g. A school must enroll at least twenty students.
4. The size of the basic voucher will range in size from 70 percent to 90 percent of the average per pupil cost in the state necessary to educate a student at that grade level. The average per pupil cost will include all state and local expenditures for education except those for students with special needs and students with disabilities. Students who are designated as low-income students will receive the maximum basic voucher. The size of the voucher would fall as a student's family income rises until the voucher reaches 70 percent of the average per pupil cost. During the five years following the passage of this legislation, the minimum voucher to students will increase to 80 percent of the state's average per pupil cost to educate a student at that grade level.
5. State and federal funds for students with special needs and for students with disabilities will be added directly to a qualifying student's basic voucher. Vouchers for students with disabilities will equal 100 percent of the current costs of educating a similarly disabled child in the public schools.
6. The 20 percent quota of students who qualify for free or reduced-cost lunches will be phased in over a three-year period. Schools that maintain their quota for a minimum of two years will be eligible for a one-year grace period if they fail to meet their quota.
7. Upon petition by the teacher and the private scholarship school, teachers who move from public to private schools may remain in the state's pension plan. The teacher and school contributions to the plan must be equal to the teacher and state contributions of a teacher making the same salary in the public schools.

Accountability Provisions[25]

As noted in the previous chapter, holding choice schools accountable for the expenditure of public monies is both controversial and fraught with legal implications. To our knowledge, there are no studies identifying those accountability measures that balance the interests of the state and parents, are legally sound, and do not undermine organizational autonomy. We opt for a minimally restrictive accountability system. We do so because we believe that choice schools should be given the maximum opportunity to develop their own missions and academic programs, particularly when educational research identifying so-called "best practices" is thin and disputatious. Thus, we do not believe it is necessary for the legislation to specify teacher and administrative credentials, employment contracting, employee evaluation and retention, textbooks or the content of the instructional program, student discipline procedures, subject matter testing, site-based decisionmaking, and the myriad other provisions that commonly bind traditional public schools and sometimes public charter schools as well. Accordingly, the legislation we propose would have only the accountability features that we think are most compatible with a choice system that emphasizes parental decisionmaking and school autonomy:

1. Public and private scholarship schools are exempt from all state and regulatory measures pertaining to education except those specified in this legislation and those contained in federal law. Private scholarship schools are exempt from all laws currently governing private schools.

2. Scholarship schools are subject to state and local health and safety laws.

3. Public scholarship schools must recognize all federal constitutional rights of their teachers and students just as regular public schools. Private scholarship schools are exempt from these requirements.

4. Private scholarship schools are exempt from the state's public sector collective bargaining law. Public scholarship schools are exempt from the state's public sector collective bargaining law unless a majority of the teachers within the school choose to unionize.

5. A scholarship school must have a formal governance structure, including a board of directors that has a fiduciary responsibility for the financial affairs of the school. The process for selecting board members, the length of their terms, and the frequency of board meetings must be specified. A member of the board shall be designated as the school's pri-

mary contact person to outside persons and agencies. Board meetings of public scholarship schools must be held in accordance with the state open-meetings law. The board of directors shall develop a set of bylaws and institutional policies that are clearly communicated to parents, students, staff members, and the authorizing agency.

6. Each scholarship school shall develop an informational brochure to include a description of the school and its mission, its governance structure, its curriculum, the qualifications of its administrators and teachers, students' responsibilities, discipline procedures, admissions requirements and procedures, transportation arrangements, and graduation requirements. Following its first year of operation as a scholarship school, each school shall incorporate in its brochure student outcomes information, including dropout rates, achievement results on national and/or state literacy and numeracy assessment tests, and (if applicable) graduation, college attendance, and employment rates. The brochure shall be made available in the prevailing languages spoken in the metropolitan area within which the school is located.

7. Each scholarship school shall establish a grievance procedure under which the board shall address grievances it receives from a parent concerning the alleged denial of admission of the parent's child to the school or, if the child is in attendance at the school, concerning the education of the child at the school or the suspension or dismissal of the child from the school.

   a. The decision of the board of directors shall be final and nonappealable unless the parent or student files an exception to the decision with the board as constituting a denial of any right of the parent or child under the United States Constitution or federal laws. If the board does not act on the exception within thirty days or overrules the exception, the parent may appeal the board's decision to the school's authorizing agency.

   b. An adverse decision by the authorizing agency may be appealed by either party into state district court. This section does not deprive a parent of any legal remedy.

8. Scholarship schools must report their enrollment on a monthly basis to the authorizing agency and the state department of education.

9. Scholarship schools must undergo an annual fiscal audit by an independent auditing entity, with the audit filed with the authorizing agency and the state audit bureau. The state audit bureau may conduct a site visit if it determines one to be necessary. Mismanagement of funds shall be grounds for revocation of the scholarship school's status as determined by the authorizing agency.

10. A violation of any of these accountability provisions may result in the revocation of the scholarship school's status under this program as determined by the authorizing agency. The authorizing agency's revocation decision is appealable to state district court.

Additional Measures to Assist Low-Income Students and New Scholarship Schools

Our proposal may create a financial hardship for choosing families whose incomes are above the low-income designation but are below the median family income. For these families the costs of transportation or school add-ons may effectively limit their choices. To assist these families, we propose a privately funded scholarship program modeled on the Arizona measure that survived a court test in 1999.[26] The fund would allow a state tax credit of up to $500 for taxpayers who donate to a school scholarship organization (SSO). The scholarship organizations would be defined as charitable organizations that allocate at least 90 percent of their annual revenue for educational scholarships or tuition grants to children to allow them to attend a public or private scholarship school. The scholarships or grants could not be limited to a single school and must be awarded on the basis of demonstrated need. The fund would work this way. A parent who enrolls her child in a scholarship school and experiences financial hardship would apply to an SSO. The SSO, in turn, would determine the basis for the financial hardship and provide the parent with a grant it deems appropriate.

The lack of start-up funds surfaces repeatedly in state and national studies as the most serious concern of choice school operators. To address this concern and to stimulate the development of new schools, we suggest that the state establish a Choice School Incentive Fund. Modeled after a measure developed by the Arizona Board of Education,[27] this fund would make grants available to public and private scholarship schools for start-up costs associated with leasing, renovating, or remodeling existing structures. It also would be available for start-up costs involving hiring staff members, leasing or purchasing computers and technology, equipping classrooms, obtaining insurance, developing an accounting system, and any other cost reasonably related to establishing a school. Because existing state education agencies are not always supportive of school choice programs, we propose that a separate state agency administer the incentive fund.

The legislature should set a reasonable limit on the amount a choice school could obtain. Choice school operators would submit an appli-

cation that included an itemized accounting of how the money would be spent. In determining whether a grant should be made, the state agency could seek information about the financial status of the school and its board of directors, as well as consult with the authorizing agency. If the school fails to begin operating within eighteen months of receiving the grant, the school must reimburse the state agency for the amount of the grant plus interest. Once a school is operating, it may file an application for one additional grant. Ownership of any tangible properties secured through the grant remains with the choice school. However, if a choice school fails, title to the property automatically transfers to the authorizing agency.

DISCUSSION OF THE TRADEOFFS WE MADE

The name of this book makes clear that all policy proposals must make difficult tradeoffs among desirable goals. In this section we provide the justifications for the choices we made and suggest some policy alternatives the reader might wish to consider.

Vouchers for All Income Levels and a Quota for Low-Income Students

Among the more important choices we made were to include all children, to award low-income children a larger voucher than that received by other children, and to require that all schools redeeming vouchers from students not classified as "low-income" enroll a minimum of 20 percent of low-income children. Because we believe segregating students by socio-economic status and by ethnicity creates inequalities in educational opportunities, we provided parents and schools with incentives to integrate schools across income groups. We reward schools by providing larger vouchers for low-income students. Many of these students may bring very large vouchers with them because the state has determined that they are at-risk, because they are eligible for Title I funding, or because they have qualifying disabilities. Although the integration of students across socio-economic status will not solve completely the problem of racial segregation, we believe that it certainly would help.

The above proposal gives a substantial incentive to parents whose children currently attend private schools or who have a strong desire to move their child from a public to a private school. Assume for the moment that you are a middle-income parent who currently spends $4,000 per year to send your child to a private school. Also assume that the average

state expenditure for children of your child's age is $5,500 and that your voucher will equal 70 percent of that amount ($3,850). The policy proposal gives you a $3,850 incentive to seek out a choice school that currently enrolls at least 20 percent of its students from low-income families or to demand that your child's current private school enroll low-income students. We believe the combination of incentives will lead existing choice schools to increase their capacity and it will encourage the formation of private schools in low-income neighborhoods.

The decision to base the size of the voucher on family income is not without its costs. The greatest of these are the intrusion of the state into the financial affairs of its citizens and the monitoring costs of checking the incomes that the families report. For the forty-three states with an individual income tax, the costs of implementing and monitoring the sliding-scale voucher should not be too great, as these states already collect the information necessary to set the size of a child's voucher. However, the number of people who would have access to that information would rise, as school personnel would know the approximate family income of all of its enrollees. Individual families would decide whether this reduction in their privacy is worth the value of the voucher.

Allowing Schools to Charge Families Additional Tuition and Fees

Our proposal differs from many other voucher proposals, as well as from the existing publicly funded voucher programs, by allowing schools to charge additional fees to families who are not classified as low-income. There are advantages and disadvantages to this decision. The most obvious disadvantage is that schools that charge such fees may not enroll families whose income is just above the level designated as low-income. A second disadvantage is that low-income students who reside more than two miles from the school may face significant transportation costs. Our research in San Antonio found that if a school fails to provide free transportation to low-income families, this reduces the probability of their children attending. A third disadvantage of allowing schools to charge fees is that it reduces equality of educational opportunity because wealthier families can purchase additional education more easily than can low- and middle-income families. Related to that problem is the possibility that over time the state may choose to force families to pay an increasingly larger share of the costs of education and this will place a substantial burden on families who are not classified as low-income. One way of addressing these problems is to have privately funded scholarship programs subsidize low- and middle-income families.

Allowing private scholarship schools to charge   nal fees may place public scholarship schools at a disadvantag   rently, many magnet and thematic schools are more expensive   an are regular attendance-zone schools, and reducing the cu   ome of these schools is likely to reduce the quantity and quality   programs. In the short term, the state might provide these scho   uchers equal to 100 percent of the per pupil cost of students who attended the school in the previous year. In the long term, however, we believe that public schools of choice will become more efficient if they are treated in exactly the same way as private voucher schools. This would mean that these schools could charge parents additional fees if the cost of their education warrants it, and they could turn to private donors to supplement their income. Many charter schools already do this. In addition, for most charter schools the income they would receive from vouchers will be greater than the funding they currently receive from the state.

What are the advantages of allowing schools to charge tuition and fees above the size of their voucher? One of the biggest advantages will be that it will encourage private schools to recruit students with disabilities. Although the Individuals with Disabilities Education Act (IDEA) and its regulations require the state to provide "proportionate" funding for students who have special education needs and attend private schools, such funding does not always cover the total costs of such an education. Many parents currently choose private schools and pay the additional costs.[29] If parents are not allowed to pay these additional costs, then it is highly unlikely that private schools will permit such students to enroll. They certainly will not actively recruit students with special needs when educating the students will cost far more than the payment the school will receive.

A second advantage of allowing additional fees is that asking families to make a financial commitment may increase their interest and involvement in their child's education. Although we are not aware of research that addresses this specific question, it is reasonable to assume that parents who allocate their own funds to the education of their children will become more involved in the choice process and in their children's education. Allowing schools to charge tuition and fees beyond the level of the voucher also increases efficiency, because it enables schools to charge parents the marginal costs of the educational benefits that a school provides. As we saw in Chapter 6, allowing additional fees should increase the total expenditures that a society allocates to education.

Transportation

We chose not to require voucher schools to provide transportation to students. We did this to encourage productive efficiency and to lower the total costs of introducing a voucher program. Henry Levin has estimated that the transportation costs of a voucher program that provides free busing to all students would be more than $1,500 per pupil.[30] This is more than three times the current transportation costs. Providing free transportation would remove transportation costs from a family's decision concerning which school to attend. But efficient public policy encourages people to consider all the costs of their decisions.[31]

Allowing schools to refuse free transportation to students does not compel them to make this choice. It is likely that many schools will subsidize transportation to low-income students to meet the 20 percent quota. In fact, to attract students from all income levels a school may choose to subsidize transportation for all of its students. However, the school has a strong incentive to provide transportation in an efficient manner. The school might subsidize private transportation, or it might reduce costs by recruiting students in specific geographic areas. The key is to provide schools with flexibility and parents with appropriate incentives.[32]

Student Admission

Many voucher proposals as well as current voucher policies require schools to select new students using a lottery. This requirement prevents choice schools from skimming the best students from among the applicants. We believe that a lottery requirement infringes too much on the special character of choice schools. For example, when parents choose a sectarian school they may do so with the expectation that the school will teach certain values. Requiring sectarian schools to admit students who may not subscribe to the school's basic tenets could deprive the school of the very characteristics that make it special. Similarly, if a public choice school is a math and science thematic school, it seems reasonable to admit students based on their interest in math and science.

Our proposal prohibits all scholarship schools from choosing applicants based on their race, ethnicity, or national origin. However, we prohibit only public schools from denying an applicant on the basis of disability or handicap. We prefer that private scholarship schools enroll students with disabilities. Nevertheless, we recognize that the voucher the state provides for some students with disabilities may fall substantially

short of the funding necessary to educate these students in private schools. In such a situation, requiring a school to accept a severely disabled student might effectively shut down the school.

We believe that our proposal will improve education for students with disabilities. If the state provides vouchers equal to the full cost of educating these students, many scholarship schools may develop special programs for students with disabilities. Many of these programs may provide educational experiences superior to those the students with disabilities receive in public schools. For example, we might expect nonprofit organizations such as the March of Dimes to develop their own schools to assist students with birth defects. This already has occurred with charter schools in some areas. A good example is the Metro Deaf School in St. Paul, Minnesota, one of the original charter schools approved in that state. The school's mission is to promote excellence in deaf education based on a bicultural/bilingual (Bi-Bi) educational philosophy centered on the deaf child's ability and tendency to interact with the world through visual means. American sign language is the primary language, with English taught as a second language through reading and writing.

Home Schooling

One of the most difficult decisions in designing our proposal concerned home schooling. As we discussed in Chapter 3, John Locke presents a strong case for parental provision of education. Nevertheless, we chose to require that voucher schools have at least twenty students. The rationales for this policy are to discourage parents from choosing to home school their children solely for the purpose of gaining additional family income, and to encourage all students who receive state funds for their education to provide positive spillovers to other students. Not funding home schooling also makes sense in terms of political feasibility. School choice opponents certainly would argue that allowing parents to home school their children and to collect substantial funding for so doing would encourage some parents to exploit their children. An alternative to our proposal would be to require that children educated at home participate in an outcomes-based evaluation that would include whatever standardized tests the state government determines are necessary.[33]

Additional Benefits and Costs of the Proposed Policy

We believe that the proposed equity-based voucher system has advantages other than improving the educational opportunities for low-income chil-

dren. The first of these is greater ethnic and socioeconomic integration. *Brown v. Board of Education* was decided almost fifty years ago, yet our schools are becoming increasingly segregated. Our proposal encourages parents and schools to work toward greater integration. Our proposal also offers religious groups the opportunity to increase their efforts to develop moral reasoning in children and to encourage children to continue their religious traditions. Many parents fear that their children will leave their religious traditions and become assimilated into a more secular culture. Our proposal allows religious groups to start new sectarian schools that instruct children in the core values and practices of their religion. Of course, the opportunity to establish schools that teach a particular worldview is not limited to religious organizations. Like-minded parents who are secular humanists or postmoderns also may establish schools that inculcate the core values of those belief systems so long as those core beliefs do not include teaching hatred or racism.

Opponents of vouchers worry that vouchers will increase the number of cults that harm students and threaten civil order. Will not our proposal encourage David Duke Academies, Jonestown Institutes, and David Koresh Conservatories? Presumably David Duke Academies would not be eligible for vouchers because they teach hatred and racism. More important, we do not believe that vouchers will encourage cults. Fringe groups arise, even in highly authoritarian regimes, and there is no evidence that countries which currently use vouchers have more cults or more ritual suicides.

Our proposal also offers teachers and administrators substantial incentives, though the incentives probably are not sufficient to make them voucher advocates. Teachers who share a similar vision of what constitutes an appropriate curriculum and pedagogy can start their own school, one not overwhelmed by regulation and bureaucracy. If the teachers can attract a sufficiently large clientele, then they can pay themselves more than they currently receive and have greater freedom and autonomy. Our proposal also allows public school teachers to move to a private choice school while remaining in the state's pension plan. This may encourage teachers who find their working conditions in the public schools unacceptable to transfer to private schools rather than leaving the teaching profession.

The above-described benefits would not come without costs. To achieve our goals we are asking everyone who selects a public or a private choice school to take part in equalizing educational opportunities for the most disadvantaged in our society. A second cost is that citizens who currently live in areas with good public schools take the risk that a voucher

system could leave them worse off. In the short term we doubt that our proposed legislation would affect attendance-zone schools in wealthy suburbs. In the long run, however, suburban support for education taxes might decline. As was discussed in Chapter 6, a system that includes vouchers and open enrollment encourages states to move to a centralized tax system that prevents property owners from directing their taxes to schools in their own neighborhood.

The cost most cited by opponents of choice is that the most disadvantaged children in society—those who live in poor areas, have parents who either cannot or will not participate in choice programs, are more likely to have learning disabilities, and have underdeveloped educational skills—will be clustered with similar children in attendance-zone schools. This, of course, has been our greatest concern throughout the book, and our proposal includes extensive measures to prevent such an outcome. Our proposal gives low-income children and children with disabilities the largest vouchers so that choice schools have a large incentive to recruit them and develop programs that improve their performance. We have removed the informational burden from parents and have placed it on schools. We have made it possible for churches and not-for-profit, community-based organizations to develop schools. These agencies have been successful in starting and operating day-care programs for disadvantaged children. A voucher program would encourage these organizations to extend their programs to kindergarten and beyond. Most important, by forcing current attendance-zone schools to compete for students we have provided a large incentive to teachers and administrators to improve their schools. When Florida identified the lowest-performing schools and informed them that the following year their students would be eligible for $4,000 vouchers, all of these schools increased their performance dramatically.[34]

A final potential cost of our proposal is that allowing different groups in society to have their own schools will lead to greater fragmentation of American society and reduce the common bonds that we obtain through common schools. We believe that our proposal will have the opposite effect. As we showed in Chapter 2, current public schools neither create a common core of democratic values nor do they outperform private schools in the teaching of tolerance and other democratic values. A society that forces the beliefs of the majority on the minority teaches intolerance. Just as the Founders reached an agreement in 1789 that the government should not dictate the religious practices of its citizens, the adoption of our proposal would demonstrate that Americans understand that a core democratic belief is that education should foster freedom of conscience.

Such a belief is more likely to bring us together than struggles over whose beliefs will be force-fed to everyone's children.

The Political Feasibility of the Proposed Policy

What is the likelihood that a voucher proposal such as ours could obtain sufficient political support to become law? Any one of three events could make our proposal politically feasible. First, the Supreme Court could decide that to deny public funds to sectarian schools participating in a school choice program violates the equal protection requirement. If this were to occur, then we would expect that most of the current opponents of vouchers will line up behind a proposal such as ours in order to avoid a policy of unrestricted vouchers. Second, if it became clear that a state legislature was going to pass a voucher proposal that had few equity provisions, then current voucher opponents might choose to support a voucher proposal with strong equity features. The most likely scenario for the passage of an equity-based voucher proposal is for minority leaders and legislators who represent minority districts to develop the legislative proposal and then lead the struggle for its passage. Minority group leadership would destroy the current coalition between minority interest groups and other groups opposed to vouchers. It also would reduce the credibility of statements by teachers' unions that they are protecting the most disadvantaged in society.

Charter Schools and Alternative Choice Proposals

Supporters of limiting school choice to public schools might argue that the public sector can provide all the choice that is necessary through the continued growth of relatively unregulated charter schools. Certainly charter schools represent a step in the direction of deregulating schooling and giving more options to parents for educating their children. But, charter schools are not sufficiently autonomous. As public schools, they are still subject to many of the legal and bureaucratic constraints that bind traditional public schools. Private schools participating in publicly funded voucher programs remain private. Historically, private schools have been viewed from a different legal perspective than public schools. Therefore, they are better positioned than charter schools to escape the tight coils of regulation. More significantly, public choice schools never can fulfill the quest of parents who seek a religiously based education for their children. The fact that nearly four-fifths of the nation's private schools are religious testifies to this fact.

The most popular alternatives to our proposal would limit vouchers to only low-income families, to students in low-income neighborhoods, or to students in low-performing schools. Such policies lower the costs to the state of voucher programs by reducing the number of eligible students. These alternatives suffer two major shortcomings. First, limiting vouchers to low-income families, low-income neighborhoods, or students in low-performing schools reduces the policy's potential to integrate schools across socioeconomic groups. Second, such limitations reduce the political support for vouchers. If only students whose public attendance-zone schools are classified as *low-performing* can receive vouchers, then the supply of private schools will not increase substantially. It is unlikely that individuals and organizations will wish to start a private school if the size and location of their potential clientele changes with each year's classification of schools.

To lower the cost of vouchers to the state, some proposals deny vouchers to students who currently attend private schools. We see such a limitation as unjust, particularly if the children excluded are from low- and middle-income families. Excluding students who previously were in private schools would encourage families to move their children from private to public schools for one year and then to move them back after they qualified for the voucher. This is disruptive to the child's education and to planning by public and private schools. An alternative to immediately providing vouchers to private school students would be to provide vouchers only to private school students from low-income families. The remaining private school students could be included in the second or third year of the program.

A final alternative to our voucher proposal is to use tax credits. A tax credit could be at the federal or state level. Families that send their child to a private school can reduce their tax bill by that amount. Supporters of tax credits argue that voucher proposals suffer from two important weaknesses. First, any direct transfer of state funds to sectarian schools encounters immediate opposition from individuals who believe this violates the separation of church and state. Second, vouchers are much more likely to lead to government regulation than are tax credits.[35]

But tax credits have their own drawbacks. One critical concern is that they do not assist low-income families. Nor do they encourage integration across socioeconomic strata; therefore they fail to equalize the positive spillovers students receive from their classmates. However, as we noted in the last chapter, the drawbacks of tax credit programs can be modified through design. Thus, individual tax credits in combination with tuition

scholarships produced by a general tax credit program promote equality of opportunity. And the addition of a low-income set-aside for schools seeking to admit scholarship recipients promotes integration across race and class.

CONCLUDING REMARKS

Diane Ravitch recently made a compelling argument for an equity-based voucher bill.[36] In that argument she cited a 1994 speech by Secretary of Education Richard Riley in which he made two statements that help to frame the choice debate. First, Riley stated that "Some schools are excellent, some are improving, some have the remarkable capacity to change for the better, and some should never be called schools at all."[37] Second, he quoted John Dewey's famous statement, "What the best and wisest parent wants for his child, that must be what the community wants for all of its children. Any other ideal for our schools is narrow and unlovely; it destroys our democracy."[38] Ravitch argued that these quotes force us to consider two questions, "Who has to attend those schools that never should be called schools?" and "What would the best and wisest parents do if their children were assigned to one of those schools?"

Of course we know the answers to these questions. "Who has to attend the worst schools?" They are not the children of either public policymakers or of school teachers and administrators. They are minority students from poor families who lack the means to escape the schools to which they are assigned. "What would the best and wisest parents do if their children were assigned to one of those schools?" They would move to a different neighborhood, put their children into private schools, or home school them.[39]

After answering the above questions, Ravitch then addressed the most common responses that voucher opponents make to failing public schools: vouchers will remove the few families in the poorly performing schools who have the skills necessary to effectively complain to public officials. This will ensure that these schools do not improve and will further harm those students who remain behind. Ravitch's response is worth quoting at length.

> What should we do about those children and those schools? Many people say, "We must reform those schools." Of course, they are right. For policy makers and academics this is the appropriate response to clearly inadequate

schools. But for parents, this is an outrageous proposition, for our own children live this day, in the here and now, and they cannot wait around to see whether the school will get better in five or ten years. I suggest that we project our passion for our own children's welfare—as Dewey suggested—onto those parents who lack our money, power, and education; they love their children as much as we love ours. Their desperation about their children's future is greater than ours because they know that the odds are stacked against them. They should not be expected to wait patiently for the transformation of the failing institutions where their children are required to go each day, the places where the secretary of education says do not deserve to be called schools at all. We surely would not be willing to make the same sacrifice of our own children. Why should they?[40]

We believe that the only acceptable answer to Ravitch's question is that public policy should not force any parents to sacrifice their children to the *possibility* that future children will face a better situation. We can do something today to avoid that sacrifice. We can adopt a school choice policy that gives all parents the opportunity to search out a better education for their children.

Notes

1. SCHOOL CHOICE OPTIONS AND ISSUES

1. Lawrence Kohlberg, "Moral Reasoning," in *Educating the Democratic Mind*, ed. Walter C. Parker.

2. Throughout this book we use "liberalism" in its classic meaning—limited constitutional government built on individual rights. This doctrine began with Thomas Hobbes and John Locke and provided the philosophic basis of the United States Constitution and Bill of Rights. Contemporary liberals and conservatives are both "liberals" when liberalism is used in this sense.

3. Department of Education, Public Affairs, "State of American Education," remarks prepared for Richard W. Riley, secretary of education, speech delivered at Georgetown University, February 15, 1994.

4. Throughout this book we will concentrate on factors that public policy can influence. For example, it may be that parent education and income have more influence on academic learning than characteristics of schools. The former two variables, however, are unlikely to be changed by education policy, at least in the short term. It makes sense, therefore, for policy analysis to focus on the characteristics of schools.

5. Jonathan Kozol, *Savage Inequalities: Children in America's Schools;* Paul T. Hill, Lawrence C. Pierce, and James W. Guthrie, *Reinventing Public Education: How Contracting Can Transform America's Schools,* 41–44.

6. Douglas S. Massey and Nancy A. Denton, *American Apartheid: Segregation and the Making of the Underclass.*

7. Of course, these are not the only reasons school choice has stayed on the agenda. Advocates of using the free market to allocate government-funded services and those who object to the values that currently are being taught in the public schools also desire a change in choice policies.

8. For data on student learning in cities see Kenneth Godwin, Frank Kemerer, and Valerie Martinez, "Comparing Public Choice and Private Voucher Programs in San Antonio," in *Learning from School Choice,* ed. Paul E. Peterson and Bryan C. Hassel, 275–306; and Cecilia E. Rouse, "Making Sense of the Achieve-

ment Effects from the Milwaukee Parental Choice Program," *Quarterly Journal of Economics* (Cambridge, Mass.: National Bureau of Economic Research, December 1997), 584, Figure II.

9. Gary Orfield et al., *The Growth of Segregation in American Schools: Changing Patterns of Separation and Poverty since 1968;* Gary Orfield et al., *Deepening Segregation in American Public Schools.*

10. Marilyn J. Gittell, ed., *Strategies for School Equity: Strategies for Creating Productive Schools in a Just Society.*

11. William Evans, Sheila Murray, and Robert Schwab, "Schoolhouses, Courthouses, and Statehouses after Serrano," *Journal of Policy Analysis and Management* 16 (1): 10–31.

12. Eric Hanushek et al., "Summary," in *Making Schools Work: Improving Performance and Controlling Costs,* 151–176.

13. Jeffrey R. Henig, "The Local Dynamics of Choice: Ethnic Preferences and Institutional Responses," in *Who Chooses? Who Loses? Culture, Institutions, and the Unequal Effects of School Choice,* ed. Bruce Fuller and Richard F. Elmore, 95–117.

14. Ibid., 106; David L. Armour and Brett M. Peiser, "Interdistrict Choice in Massachusetts," in *Learning from School Choice,* ed. Paul E. Peterson and Bryan C. Hassel, 157–186.

15. Steven Glazerman, "A Conditional Logit Model of Elementary School Choice: What Do Parents Value?" (unpublished paper, University of Chicago, Harris School of Public Policy, November 1997).

16. Henry M. Levin, "The Economics of Educational Choice," *Economics of Education Review* 10 (1990): 137–158.

17. Valerie Martinez, Kenneth Godwin, Frank Kemerer, and Laura Perna, "The Consequences of School Choice: Who Leaves and Who Stays in the Inner City," *Social Science Quarterly* (September 1995): 485–501; Greg Vanourek, Bruno V. Manno, Chester E. Finn, Jr., and Louann A. Bierlein, "Charter Schools as Seen by Students, Teachers, and Parents," in *Learning from School Choice,* ed. Paul E. Peterson and Bryan C. Hassel, 187–212.

18. John E. Chubb and Terry Moe, *Politics, Markets and America's Schools.*

19. "Education Flexibility Bill Passes," *Dallas Morning News,* April 22, 1999.

20. Eric A. Hanushek, "The Evidence on Class Size," Occasional Paper Number 98-1, W. Allen Wallis Institute of Political Economy (Rochester, N.Y.: University of Rochester, 1998).

21. Myron Lieberman, *The Teacher Unions: How the NEA and AFT Sabotage Reform and Hold Students, Parents, Teachers, and Taxpayers Hostage to Bureaucracy,* 76–86, 89–108.

22. See ibid., 30.

23. See John Dewey, *Democracy and Education,* 84–87.

24. Michael Walzer, *Spheres of Justice: A Defense of Pluralism and Equality,* Chapter 8.

25. Ibid.

26. Amy Gutmann, *Democratic Education,* 45.

27. Thomas A. Downes, "Evaluating the Impact of School Finance Reform on the Provision of Public Education: The California Case," *National Tax Journal* 45 (1992): 405–420; W. A. Fischel, "Did Serrano Cause Proposition 13?" *National Tax Journal* 42 (1989): 465–473.

28. Milton Friedman, *Capitalism and Freedom.*

29. David Boaz and R. Morris Barrett, *What Would a School Voucher Buy? The Real Cost of Private Schools.*

30. Henry M. Levin, "Educational Vouchers: Effectiveness, Choice and Costs," *Journal of Policy Analysis and Management* 17, no. 3 (1998): 373–392; Henry M. Levin and Cyrus E. Driver, "Costs of an Educational Voucher System," *Economics of Education Review* 16 (1997): 303–311. Notice that it is possible that vouchers could prove more efficient and lower the total costs of education but, despite this, the costs to taxpayers would increase. This could occur because the taxpayers would pay the tuition and fees now paid by those who currently pay the costs of private schools.

31. For an alternative analysis of how different goals can be used to evaluate choice policies, see Henry M. Levin, "A Comprehensive Framework for Evaluating Educational Vouchers," Occasional Paper 5 (New York: National Center for the Study of Privatization in Education, Teachers College, Columbia University, n.d. [http://www.ncspe.org]).

2. THE OUTCOMES OF SCHOOL CHOICE POLICIES

1. Political scientist Michael Mintrom argues in his book *Policy Entrepreneurs and School Choice,* Chapter 9, that the analogy of cars to education is inappropriate because the consumers of education (students) also are part of the production process. Mintrom does not present his argument in detail, but assumes that the most informed consumers of education will be families with children who create positive spillovers for their classmates. The parents of these children will seek out similar families and cluster in a few schools. This clustering will make other schools worse rather than better. Notice, however, that the clustering process does not eliminate the benefits of competition. If poorly performing schools lose revenues, they will improve or go out of business. Mintrom assumes that the cost of peers who leave is greater than the benefit derived from forcing all schools to improve, but he offers no evidence to support his conclusion.

2. Ellen B. Goldring and Rina Shapira, "Choice, Empowerment, and Involvement: What Satisfies Parents?" *Educational Forum* 58 (1993): 276–281.

3. Mark Schneider et al., "Institutional Arrangements and the Creation of Social Capital: The Effects of School Choice," *American Political Science Review* 91 (1997): 82–93.

4. John E. Chubb and Terry M. Moe, *Politics, Markets and America's Schools.*

5. Ibid., 11 (emphasis in the original).

6. Ibid., 99.

7. For a discussion of school-based management and rule making in Texas

see Frank R. Kemerer and Jim Walsh, *The Educator's Guide to Texas School Law,* 5th ed., Chapter 1.

8. Howard L. Fuller, George A. Mitchell, and Michael E. Harmann, "The Educational Impact of Teacher Collective Bargaining in Milwaukee" (paper presented at the conference Teacher Unions and Education Change, Kennedy School of Government, Harvard University, Cambridge, Mass., September 24–25, 1998).

9. Ibid.

10. Ibid., Table 1.

11. Chubb and Moe, *Politics, Markets,* 64.

12. Ibid., 65.

13. Ibid.

14. Richard F. Elmore and Bruce Fuller, "Empirical Research on Educational Choice: What Are the Implications for Policy-Makers?" in *Who Chooses? Who Loses? Culture, Institutions, and the Unequal Effects of School Choice,* ed. Bruce Fuller and Richard F. Elmore, 187–201.

15. Ibid., 189–198.

16. We examine the validity of this assertion in Chapter 5.

17. Throughout this book we use "liberalism" in its classic meaning—limited constitutional government built on individual rights. This doctrine began with Thomas Hobbes and John Locke and provided the philosophic basis of the United States Constitution and Bill of Rights. Contemporary liberals and conservatives are both "liberals" when liberalism is used in this sense.

18. For a review of this literature see Kenneth Godwin, Carrie Ausbrooks, and Valerie Martinez, "Are Public Schools More Effective than Private Schools in Teaching Political Tolerance?" *Phi Delta Kappa* 82 (March 2001): 542–546.

19. National Center for Education Statistics (NCES), *The Condition of Education, 1997.*

20. We use "demand" in its economic sense. People not only value a good at a certain level, but they are willing and able to pay for that level.

21. Gary Orfield and John T. Yun, *Resegregation in American Schools,* 13–16.

22. Ibid., 21.

23. Hamilton Lankford and James Wyckoff, "Primary and Secondary School Choice among Public and Religious Alternatives," in *Market Approaches to Education: Vouchers and School Choice,* ed. Elchanan Cohn; Hamilton Lankford and James Wyckoff, "Why Are Schools Racially Segregated? Implications for School Choice Policies" (paper presented at the School Choice and Racial Diversity Conference, Teachers College, Columbia University, May 22, 2000).

24. Orfield and Yun, *Resegregation,* 19–20.

25. Caroline Minter Hoxby, "Does Competition among Public Schools Benefit Students and Taxpayers?" Working Paper 4978 (Cambridge, Mass.: National Bureau of Economic Research, 1994).

26. Stephen Plank et al., "Effects of Choice in Education," in *Redesigning American Education,* ed. Edith Rasell and Richard Rothstein, 115–118.

27. Claire Smrekar and Ellen Goldring, "Social Class Isolation and Racial Diversity in Magnet Schools" (paper presented at the School Choice and

Racial Diversity Conference, Teachers College, Columbia University, May 22, 2000).

28. Frank R. Kemerer, "School Choice Accountability," in *School Choice and Social Controversy: Politics, Policy, and Law,* ed. Stephen D. Sugarman and Frank R. Kemerer, 190.

29. David J. Armor and Brett M. Peiser, "Interdistrict Choice in Massachusetts," in *Learning from School Choice,* ed. Paul E. Peterson and Bryan C. Hassel, 165–170.

30. Eric Ambler, "Who Benefits from Educational Choice: Some Evidence from Europe," *Journal of Policy Analysis and Management* 13 (1994): 454–476; Stephen J. Ball, Richard Bowe, and Sharon Gewirtz, "School Choice, Social Class and Distinction: The Realization of Social Advantage in Education," *Journal of Education Policy* 11 (1996): 89–112; Edward B. Fiske and Helen F. Ladd, *When Schools Compete: A Cautionary Tale;* Sabrina Lutz, "The Impact of School Choice," *Equity and Excellence in Education* 29 (1996): 48–54; Taryn R. Parry, "Will Pursuit of Higher Quality Sacrifice Equal Opportunity in Education? An Analysis of the Education Voucher System in Chile," *Social Science Quarterly* 77 (1996): 821–841.

31. For a discussion of these programs see Terry Moe, "Introduction," in *Private Vouchers,* ed. Terry Moe, 1–40.

32. For reviews of the various studies on who chooses and who does not, see Valerie Martinez et al., "The Consequences of School Choice: Who Leaves and Who Stays in Inner-City Schools," *Social Science Quarterly* 76 (September 1995): 485–501; and Terry Moe, ed., *Private Vouchers.* For information on charter schools see Nina Shokraii Rees, *School Choice 2000: What's Happening in the States.*

33. Jeffrey Henig, "The Local Dynamics of Choice: Ethnic Preferences and Institutional Responses," in *Who Chooses? Who Loses? Culture, Institutions, and the Unequal Effects of School Choice,* ed. Bruce Fuller and Richard F. Elmore, 98.

34. Amy Stuart Wells, "African-American Students' View of School Choice," in *Who Chooses? Who Loses? Culture, Institutions, and the Unequal Effects of School Choice,* ed. Bruce Fuller and Richard F. Elmore, 25–49; Robert Bulman, "Money Is Not Everything: Habitus, Cultural Capital and School Choice" (mimeo, Department of Political Science, University of California, Berkeley, 1998).

35. Bulman, "Money Is Not Everything," 11.

36. Ibid., 12.

37. Wells, "African-American Students," 35.

38. Frank R. Kemerer and Carrie Y. Ausbrooks, *Comparing Public and Private Schools: Student Survey Report.*

39. Wells, "African-American Students," 39.

40. Writings of theorists who argue that private schools will fail to teach tolerance and respect for the cultural traditions and religious understandings of others include John Dewey, *Democracy and Education,* Amy Gutmann, *Democratic Education,* and Eamonn Callan, *Creating Citizens: Political Education and Liberal Democracy.*

41. Herbert McClosky and Anthony Brill, *Dimensions of Tolerance,* 13.

42. Patricia Avery et al., "Exploring Political Tolerance with Adolescents," *Theory and Research in Social Education* 20 (1992): 386–420.

43. Horace Mann, "The Necessity of Education in a Republican Government," in *Lectures on Education,* 123–126; John Dewey, *Democracy and Education;* James A. Banks, *An Introduction to Multicultural Education;* Sonia Neito, "Moving beyond Tolerance in Multicultural Education," *Multicultural Education* 1 (1994): 9–38; R. Freeman Butts, "Antidote for Anti-politics: A New Text of Civic Instruction," *Education Week* 48, no. 38 (1995); Melinda Fine, *Habits of Mind: Struggling over Values in America's Classrooms;* Eamonn Callan, "Virtue, Dialogue, and the Common School," *American Journal of Education* 104 (1995): 1–33.

44. For an excellent academic statement of this argument see Callan, "Virtue, Dialogue." For a political account of the argument see Richard W. Riley, "What Really Matters in American Education," U.S. Department of Education; published on the Web at http://ed.gov/Speeches/09-1997/index.html (September 23). Cited in Jay Greene, Joseph Giammo, and Nicole Mellow, "The Effect of Private Education on Political Participation, Social Capital and Tolerance: An Examination of the Latino National Political Survey," *Georgetown Public Policy Review* 5 (Fall 1999): 54.

45. Alan Peshkin, *God's Choice: The Total World of a Fundamentalist Christian School.*

46. David Blacker, "Fanaticism and Schooling," *American Journal of Education* 106 (1998): 241–272.

47. An exception is Greene et al., "The Effect of Private Education," which examines the effects of public and private schools on political tolerance and political participation. Greene and his colleagues find that Latinos who attended private schools are more likely to vote and that they have slightly higher scores on political tolerance than Latinos who attended public schools. The study, however, did not control for selection bias.

48. Using descriptions provided by the Fort Worth Independent School District and the Texas Association of Independent Schools, all Fort Worth schools were evaluated and assigned to one of six categories: (1) public with balanced proportions of white, African American, and Latino students; (2) public where the majority of students were African American, (3) public where the majority of students were Latino, (4) private secular, (5) private Catholic, and (6) private evangelical. A similar procedure was used in New York City.

49. John Sullivan, James Pierson, and George Marcus, *Political Tolerance and American Democracy;* Marcus et al., *With Malice;* Avery et al., "Exploring Political Tolerance."

50. This is a subset of the groups used in Marcus et al., *With Malice,* Appendix B.

51. Readers who wish to examine the questions asked as well as the reliability of the scales for tolerance, threat, and democratic norms can find these data at the Web site of the Center for the Study of Education Reform (http://www.coe.unt.edu/cser), or they can write for copies of the paper, "Comparing Tolerance in Public, Private, and Evangelical Schools," by Kenneth Godwin et al., 1999.

52. William Sander and Anthony C. Krautmann, "Catholic Schools, Dropout Rates and Educational Attainment," *Economic Inquiry* 33 (1995): 217–233; Arthur R. Goldberger and Glen G. Cain, "The Causal Analysis of Cognitive Outcomes in the Coleman, Hoffer and Kilgore Report," *Sociology of Education* 55 (April–July 1982): 103–122.

53. This was done with a two-equation model where the first stage employed probit regression to estimate the selection bias correction. Then, that correction was included in the second equation, which used ordinary least squares regression to estimate the dependent variable of interest. For details of the model as well as the probit results see Godwin et al., "Comparing Tolerance."

54. Ibid.

55. Robert Crain, "Private Schools and Black-White Segregation: Evidence from Two Big Cities" (Stanford, Calif.: Stanford University, Institute for Research on Educational Finance and Government, ERIC document #259 430); Jay P. Greene and Nicole Mellow, "Integration Where It Counts: A Study of Racial Integration in Public and Private School Lunchrooms" (mimeo, University of Texas, Department of Government, 1998).

56. Jonathan Kozol, "I Dislike the Idea of Choice and I Want to Tell You Why," *Educational Leadership* 50 (1992): 92; cited in Jay P. Greene, "Civic Values in Public and Private Schools," in *Learning from School Choice,* ed. Paul E. Peterson and Bryan C. Hassel.

57. Greene, "Civic Values," Table 4-4.

58. Ibid. A small part of the private-public school difference on volunteering is the result of the greater likelihood that private schools will require volunteer activity from their students; 15.5 percent of private school students indicated that they volunteered because it was required, while only 13.4 percent of public school students reported volunteering because it was required.

59. These data were first analyzed by James Coleman, Thomas Hoffer, and Sally Kilgore, *High School Achievement;* James Coleman and Thomas Hoffer, *Public and Private High Schools;* Thomas Hoffer, Andrew M. Greeley, and James S. Coleman, "Achievement Growth in Public and Catholic Schools," *Sociology of Education* 58 (April 1985): 74–97.

60. Chubb and Moe, *Politics, Markets,* 22.

61. Ibid., 82–90.

62. Jane Hannaway, "The Organization and Management of Public and Catholic Schools: Looking Inside the 'Black Box,'" *International Journal of Education* 15 (1991): 463–481.

63. Ibid., 477.

64. Ibid., 471.

65. Ibid., 474.

66. Anthony S. Bryk, Valerie E. Lee, and Peter B. Holland, *Catholic Schools and the Common Good.*

67. Valerie E. Lee, Julia B. Smith, and Robert Croninger, "How High School Organization Influences the Equitable Distribution of Learning in Mathematics and Science," *Sociology of Education* 70 (1997): 128–150.

68. Interestingly, Lee never indicates that these findings are highly consistent

with those of Chubb and Moe or that they support the claims made for private schools. In fact, she attempts to cover this up by never breaking down the data in a way that would allow the reader to make direct comparisons between public and private schools. Fortunately, it is possible to calculate these differences from the numbers in her tables.

69. We used a stratified random sample for grades 6–8 of public schools where the sample was stratified on the basis of the seven voting sectors for school board members. Within each sector we chose one attendance-zone middle school and a nearby private school. Both of the multilingual schools were included in the sample. For details on the survey procedures see Frank Kemerer, Valerie Martinez, and Kenneth Godwin, *Comparing Public and Private Schools: Teacher Survey Results.*

70. National Center for Education Statistics (http://nces.ed.gov/pubs/ps/459t3120.html).

71. Ibid.

72. Goldring and Shapira, "Choice, Empowerment"; John F. Witte, "Who Benefits from the Milwaukee Choice Program?" in *Who Chooses? Who Loses?* ed. Bruce Fuller and Richard F. Elmore, 118–137; Valerie Martinez et al., "The Consequences of School Choice"; Terry Moe introduction to *Private Vouchers,* ed. Terry Moe, 74–99; Jay P. Greene, William G. Howell, and Paul E. Peterson, "Lessons from the Cleveland Scholarship Program," in *Learning from School Choice,* ed. Paul E. Peterson and Bryan C. Hassel, 357–392.

73. Goldring and Shapira, "Choice, Empowerment," Table 4.

74. Anne Henderson, *Parent Participation and Student Achievement: The Evidence Grows.*

75. Analysis of the demographic and family characteristics of those admitted to the multilingual program indicates that although students' test scores were the best predictor of admission to the program, African American students and students from intact families also were slightly more likely to be admitted.

76. Kenneth Godwin, Frank Kemerer, and Valerie Martinez, "Comparing Public Choice and Private Voucher Programs in San Antonio," in *Learning from School Choice,* ed. Paul E. Peterson and Bryan C. Hassel, 281.

77. Hoxby, "Does Competition among Public Schools Benefit Students and Taxpayers?"

78. Ibid.; also, Hoxby, "Analyzing School Choice Reforms That Use America's Traditional Forms of Parental Choice," in *Learning from School Choice,* ed. Paul Peterson and Bryan Hassel, 133–155.

79. Kevin B. Smith and Kenneth J. Meier, *The Case against School Choice: Politics, Markets, and Fools,* Table A.7.

80. John Witte, "Private School versus Public School Achievement: Are There Findings That Should Affect the Educational Choice Debate," *Economics of Education Review* 11 (1995): 371–394.

81. Coleman, Hoffer, and Kilgore, *High School Achievement;* Coleman and Hoffer, *Public and Private High Schools;* Hoffer, Greeley, and Coleman, "Achievement Growth."

82. Goldberger and Cain, "The Causal Analysis."

83. Witte, "Private School," 373.

84. K. L. Alexander and A. M. Pallas, "Private Schools and Public Policy: New Evidence on Public and Private High Schools," *Sociology of Education* 56 (1983): 170–182.

85. Witte, "Private School," 383.

86. Ibid., 385.

87. Sander and Krautmann, "Catholic Schools."

88. William N. Evans and Robert M. Schwab, "Finishing High School and Starting College: Do Catholic Schools Make a Difference?" *Quarterly Journal of Economics* 100 (1995): 966–991.

89. Derek Neal, "The Effects of Catholic Secondary Schooling on Educational Achievement," *Journal of Labor Economics* 15 (1997): 98–123.

90. Ibid., 117.

91. Ibid., 118.

92. Adam Gamoran, "Student Achievement in Public Magnet, Public Comprehensive, and Private City High Schools," *Educational Evaluation and Policy Analysis* 18 (1996): 1–18.

93. Plank et al., "Effects of Choice in Education."

94. Godwin et al., "Comparing Public Choice," 286.

95. Milwaukee later allowed sectarian schools to participate in the program, but the evaluation results discussed here refer only to students in secular private schools.

96. John F. Witte et al., "Fourth-Year Report on the Milwaukee Parental Choice Program" (photocopy, Department of Political Science, University of Wisconsin, Madison, December 1994).

97. Ibid., 28.

98. The most frequent reason that students remained in public schools after applying for a voucher was that the private school they wished to attend was fully enrolled.

99. Jay P. Greene, Paul E. Peterson, and Jiangtao Du, "The Effectiveness of School Choice: The Milwaukee Experiment" (paper presented at the annual meeting of the American Political Science Association, San Francisco, September 1996).

100. Cecilia Elena Rouse, "Private School Vouchers and Student Achievement: An Evaluation of the Milwaukee Parental Choice Program," *Quarterly Journal of Economics* 113 (1998): 553–602.

101. Ibid., 593.

102. Sam Schulhoffer-Wohl, "MPS Gains Are Linked to Vouchers," *Milwaukee Journal Sentinel,* online edition, April 23, 2001 (http://www.jsonline.com/news/metro/apr01/study240423o1a.asp).

103. For two different evaluations of the Cleveland program see Kim Metcalf et al., "A Comparative Evaluation of the Cleveland Scholarship and Tutoring Grant Program: Year Two," available on the Web at http://www.aft.org/research/vouchers/clev/metcalf98.htm. For an alternative evaluation see Greene, Howell, and Peterson, "Lessons from the Cleveland Scholarship Program."

104. Jay P. Greene, *An Evaluation of the Florida A-Plus Accountability and School Choice Program.*

105. Gregory Camilli and Katrina Bulkley, "Critique of 'An Evaluation of the Florida A-Plus Accountability and School Choice Program,'" *Educational Policy Analysis Archives* 9 (March 4, 2001). Available on the Web at http://eppa.asu.edu/epaa/v9n7.

106. Godwin et al., "Comparing Public Choice."

107. The reports on the Cleveland, Washington, Dayton, and New York programs are available on the Web at http://data.fas.harvard.edu/PEPG.

108. William Howell and Paul E. Peterson, "School Choice in Dayton, Ohio: An Evaluation after One Year," Working Paper PEPG/00-07 (Cambridge, Mass.: Taubman Center for State and Local Government, Harvard University, February 2000).

109. Records supplied to the authors by the San Antonio Independent School District.

110. Jeffrey R. Henig and Stephen D. Sugarman, "The Nature and Extent of School Choice," in *School Choice and Social Controversy: Politics, Policy, and Law,* ed. Stephen D. Sugarman and Frank R. Kemerer, 29.

3. POLITICAL THEORY AND SCHOOL CHOICE

1. Stephen Gilles, "On Educating Children: A Parentalist Manifesto," *University of Chicago Law Review* 63 (1996): 937–1034.

2. We use "state" to refer to all parts of government. It includes national, regional, and local governments and their agents. For example, a local school board and its members are part of the state.

3. John Rawls, *A Theory of Justice,* 136–141.

4. For a description of these school wars see Charles L. Glenn, *The Myth of the Common School,* Chapter 7.

5. Diane Ravitch, *Left Back: A Century of Failed School Reforms.*

6. Stephen L. Carter, *The Culture of Disbelief: How American Law and Politics Trivialize Religious Devotion.*

7. Brian S. Crittenden, *Parents, the State, and the Right to Educate.*

8. Christopher Lasch, *Haven in a Heartless World: The Family Besieged,* 3.

9. John Locke, *First Treatise,* §§56–57.

10. John Stuart Mill, *On Liberty,* 54.

11. John Locke, *A Letter Concerning Toleration,* 26.

12. Nathan Tarcov, *Locke's Education for Liberty,* 72.

13. Mill, *On Liberty,* 104.

14. Ibid., 106.

15. Ibid.

16. Locke, *Some Thoughts Concerning Education,* §§135, 189. Nathan Tarcov argues that the general orientation and contours of Locke's educational ideas remain applicable to our liberal democratic polity. See Tarcov, *Locke's Education for Liberty,* 207–211.

17. Mill, *On Liberty,* 105.

18. Crittenden, *Parents, the State,* 62.

19. John Dewey, *Democracy and Education*, 122.

20. Richard Rorty, *Contingency, Irony, and Solidarity*, 177.

21. Dewey, *Democracy and Education*, 97, 119–120.

22. Steven C. Rockefeller, "Comment on Charles Taylor's Essay," in *Multiculturalism: Examining the Politics of Recognition*, ed. Amy Gutmann, 89–91.

23. Dewey, *Democracy and Education*, 87.

24. Locke, *Some Thoughts*, §70.

25. Dewey, *Democracy and Education*, 85.

26. Richard Rorty, "Habermas and Lyotard on Postmodernity," in *Habermas and Modernity*, ed. Richard J. Bernstein, 174.

27. Amy Gutmann, *Democratic Education*, 39.

28. When focusing on the likelihood that neutrality cannot cultivate moral character, Gutmann concedes the legitimacy of "*partially* prejudicing" the choices of children. Gutmann, *Democratic Education*, 43, emphasis in original.

29. Ibid., 31–32.

30. Amy Gutmann, "Undemocratic Education," in *Liberalism and the Moral Way of Life*, ed. Nancy L. Rosenbaum, 74.

31. Ibid., 75.

32. Ibid., xi (emphasis in the original).

33. Gutmann, *Democratic Education*, 14, 118. Gutmann recognizes that democratic institutions such as local school boards or state boards of education often encourage certain teachings that lead to illiberal policy outcomes.

34. John Rawls, *Political Liberalism*, 56–65.

35. William Galston, *Liberal Purposes*, 251; see also his "Two Concepts of Liberalism," *Ethics* 105 (April 1995): 516–534.

36. Gutmann, *Democratic Education*, 45. Gutmann writes that the "religious freedom [of parents] does not extend to exercising power over their children so as to deny them the education necessary for exercising full citizenship or for choosing among diverse ways of life that lie outside the Amish community." "Civic Education for Diversity," *Ethics* 105 (1995): 570.

37. See Gutmann, "Civic Education," 561, 576–577.

38. Gutmann describes "conscious social reproduction" as "the ways in which citizens are or should be empowered to influence the education that in turn shapes the political values, attitudes, and modes of behavior of future citizens." It is the commitment "to collectively re-create the society we share." Gutmann, *Democratic Education*, 14, 39.

39. Gutmann somewhat illogically claims three things about conscious social reproduction: (1) There is a social consensus that the goal of education is the conscious social reproduction of democratic values, (2) Local governments cannot use democratic means to violate the principles that Gutmann includes in the meaning of conscious social reproduction, and (3) Those who disagree with conscious social reproduction as the fundamental goal of education have no right to complain because they were part of the democratic process that chose that goal. Clearly, if there were a consensus that conscious social reproduction is the primary educational goal, it would not be possible to have a majority choose another goal. Also, if Gutmann argues that there is a need to prohibit local or state governments

from changing what social reproduction means, then she can hardly argue that there exists a consensus concerning her definition. And, if citizens cannot change her definition, then she cannot argue that those who disagree necessarily participated in a majoritarian democratic process for choosing it. See Gutmann, *Democratic Education,* p. 14 for points 1 and 2, and p. 39 for points 2 and 3.

40. Gutmann, *Democratic Education,* 122.

41. Gutmann, "Undemocratic Education," 78.

42. Ibid., 79.

43. Rawls, *Political Liberalism,* x–xi.

44. Ibid., 196–197. An example of this would be when a religion attempts to gain government power to prevent free speech or, in the case of education, to prevent the teaching of evolution.

45. *Wisconsin v. Yoder,* 406 U.S. 205 (1972). *Mozert v. Hawkins County Board of Education,* 827 F.2d 1058 (6th Cir. 1987), *cert. denied,* 484 U.S. 1066 (1988).

46. Gutmann, "Civic Education," 571.

47. *Mozert v. Hawkins,* 827 F.2d 1058 (6th Cir. 1987).

48. Eamonn Callan, *Creating Citizens: Political Education and Liberal Democracy,* 36–37.

49. Peter P. Nicholson, "Toleration as a Moral Ideal," in *Aspects of Toleration,* ed. John Horton and Susan Mendus, 165.

50. Galston, "Two Concepts of Liberalism," 521.

51. Ibid., 523.

52. Callan, *Creating Citizens,* 35.

53. Ibid., 152.

54. Jeff Spinner-Halev, *Surviving Diversity: Religion and Democratic Citizenship,* 5.

55. Ibid., 55.

56. Lorraine Smith Pangle and Thomas L. Pangle, "What the American Founders Have to Teach Us about Schooling for Democratic Citizenship," in *Rediscovering the Democratic Purposes of Education,* ed. Lorraine M. McDonnell, P. Michael Timpane, and Roger Benjamin, 23.

57. Anthony S. Bryk, Valerie Lee, and Peter Holland, *Catholic Schools and the Common Good.*

58. James P. Comer, Norris Haynes, Edward T. Joyner, and Michael Ben-Avie, eds., *Rallying the Whole Village: The Comer Process for Reforming Education.* See also James P. Comer, *Waiting for a Miracle: Why Schools Can't Solve Our Problems and How We Can.*

59. Comer, *Waiting for a Miracle,* 99.

60. The diversity of communitarian writers makes it necessary to limit our analysis of the implications of communitarian theory for education to those theorists who address explicitly the issue of school choice.

61. Stephen Mulhall and Adam Swift, *Liberals and Communitarians,* 42–51.

62. Derek L. Phillips, *Looking Backward: A Critical Appraisal of Communitarian Thought,* 185.

63. Alasdair MacIntyre, *After Virtue: A Study in Moral Theory,* 204.

64. Ibid., 204–205.

65. Charles Taylor, "The Politics of Recognition," in *Multiculturalism: Examining the Politics of Recognition,* ed. Amy Gutmann, 43.

66. Ibid., 59.

67. Ibid., 58–60.

68. Benjamin Barber, *Strong Democracy: Participatory Politics for a New Age,* and *An Aristocracy of Everyone: The Politics of Education and the Future of America;* Michael Walzer, *Spheres of Justice: A Defense of Pluralism and Equality,* Chapter 8.

69. Barber, *Strong Democracy,* xv.

70. Ibid., 297.

71. Ibid., 296–297.

72. Walzer, *Spheres of Justice,* 218.

73. Ibid., 219.

74. Ibid., 225.

75. Stephen L. Carter, *The Dissent of the Governed: A Meditation on Law, Religion, and Loyalty,* 27.

76. Barber, *Strong Democracy,* 296.

77. Ibid.

78. Lorraine M. McDonnell, "Defining Democratic Purposes," in *Rediscovering the Democratic Purposes of Education,* ed. Lorraine M. McDonnell, P. Michael Timpane, and Roger Benjamin, 9.

79. This reasoning leads Walzer to reject not only private schools, but also tracking and special programs for academically gifted students. See Walzer, *Spheres of Justice,* 220–221.

80. Gutmann, "Undemocratic Education," 117–118. Although Gutmann allows exit, she does not permit the state to pay for the education of children who exit, as this would eliminate the link between public funding and democratic accountability. This places Gutmann in an awkward position. She has argued in *Democratic Education* that the right of exit is a basic liberal right. But the ability of families to exercise this right depends on income, and the poor probably will not be able to prevent their children from being forced to listen to the teachings decided by the majority. In perhaps her most interesting statement concerning education, Gutmann admits that the poor may not have the exit option. She argues, however, that "the unfairness inherent in their inability to opt out of the public school system is the unfairness of poverty, not the unfairness of not subsidizing private schools with public tax money." Amy Gutmann, "Why Should Schools Care about Civic Education?" in *Rediscovering the Democratic Purposes of Education,* ed. Lorraine M. McDonnell, P. Michael Timpane, and Roger Benjamin, 83–84. This passage indicates how little Gutmann values parent rights. She surely would not make the same argument concerning the unfairness of poverty if the right in question were access to legal counsel, medical care, or basic literacy and numeracy.

81. K. Anthony Appiah, "Identity, Authenticity, Survival," in *Multiculturalism: Examining the Politics of Recognition,* ed. Amy Gutmann, 162–163.

82. Nancy Rosenbaum, "Pluralism and Self-Defense," in *Liberalism and the Moral Life,* ed. Nancy Rosenbaum, 71–88.

83. Rawls, *A Theory of Justice,* 205–216.

84. Spinner-Halev, *Surviving Diversity,* 48–54.
85. Callan, *Creating Citizens,* 147–148.
86. Spinner-Halev, *Surviving Diversity,* 25.
87. Ibid., 112.
88. Mulhall and Swift, *Liberals and Communitarians,* 251. Note that for classical and political liberals it is not necessary that all students receive a liberal education. Whether or not a student participates in an education that encourages autonomy is the decision of the family.
89. For a discussion of how such a system might work see James W. Skillen, *Recharging the American Experiment: Principled Pluralism for Genuine Civic Community.*

4. PARENT RIGHTS, SCHOOL CHOICE, AND EQUALITY OF OPPORTUNITY

1. *Meyer v. Nebraska,* 262 U.S. 390 (1923).
2. *Pierce v. Society of Sisters,* 268 U.S. 510 (1925).
3. Barbara Bennett Woodhouse, "'Who Owns the Child?': *Meyer* and *Pierce* and the Child as Property," *William and Mary Law Review* 33 (1992): 995–1122. Woodhouse offers a fascinating examination of these cases in the context of viewing the child as property subject to parental control. Included is a review of the history of the American family and of family law, as well as the evolution of the children's rights movement. The latter was well under way at the time of the *Meyer* and *Pierce* decisions. Woodhouse maintains that Justice James G. McReynolds, who wrote the decisions for the Court, was heavily influenced by a property-rights-oriented Columbia Law School professor, William Dameron Guthrie. Guthrie filed a short but persuasive amicus brief with the Court in the *Meyer* case, arguing against state efforts to curtail the authority of parents and alerting the Justices to the even more sweeping assertion of state authority over the education of children in the Oregon statute. Later, Guthrie headed one of two teams of lawyers for the Society of Sisters in oral argument before the Court in the *Pierce* case. Woodhouse asserts that McReynolds, whom she labels "the most bigoted, vitriolic, and intolerant individual ever to have sat on the Supreme Court" based on his own writings, was heavily influenced by Guthrie's brief and incorporated most of the latter's ideas into his opinion.
4. *Wisconsin v. Yoder,* 406 U.S. 205 (1972), p. 239.
5. *Norwood v. Harrison,* 413 U.S. 455 (1973).
6. *Runyan v. McCrary,* 427 U.S. 160 (1976).
7. *Planned Parenthood v. Danforth,* 428 U.S. 52 (1976), p. 74. Nine years before, the Supreme Court ruled that juveniles are entitled to basic due process protections in delinquency hearings, including notice of the charges, legal counsel, the privilege against self-incrimination, and the right to confront witnesses *(In re Gault,* 387 U.S. 1 [1967]). The case involved a fifteen-year-old boy who was committed to a state institution as a juvenile delinquent until he reached twenty-one for allegedly making indecent statements in a phone call to a neighbor. No notice of the arrest had been given to Gault's parents, nor were they informed of the

specific charges filed with the court. The accuser was not present at Gault's first hearing, and no record was made. At the second hearing, conflicting testimony was given and a probation officer's referral report was filed with the court, but no copy was made available to the parents or to the youth. Again, the accuser was not present and no record was made. The decision of the court was not appealable under Arizona law.

8. *Troxel v. Granville,* 120 S.Ct. 2054 (2000).

9. *Prince v. Commonwealth of Massachusetts,* 321 U.S. 158 (1944).

10. *Wisconsin v. Yoder,* 406 U.S. 205 (1972).

11. In his partial dissent, Justice William O. Douglas objected to letting the religious beliefs of the parents control the wishes of the child. He wrote, "Where the child is mature enough to express potentially conflicting desires, it would be an invasion of the child's rights to permit such an imposition without canvassing his views. . . . As the child has no other effective forum, it is in this litigation that his rights should be considered." Douglas added that it was the future of the child, and not the future of the parents, that was at stake. *Yoder,* p. 242.

12. *Employment Division, Department of Human Resources of Oregon v. Smith,* 494 U.S. 872 (1990).

13. *Scoma v. Chicago Board of Education,* 391 F.Supp. 452 (N.D. Ill. 1974). See also *State v. DeLaBruere,* 577 A.2d 254 (Vt. 1990) (criminal conviction of parents for refusing to send their child to a school meeting state law requirements did not violate parents' free exercise of religion nor their right to control the education of their children).

14. *Herndon v. Chapel Hill–Carrboro City Board of Education,* 89 F.3d 174 (4th Cir. 1996), *cert. denied,* 519 U.S. 1111 (1997).

15. *Mozert v. Hawkins County Board of Education,* 827 F.2d 1058 (6th Cir. 1987).

16. *Brown v. Hot, Sexy and Safer Productions, Inc.,* 68 F.3d 525 (1st Cir. 1995).

17. *Swanson v. Guthrie Independent School District No. I-L,* 135 F.3d 694 (10th Cir. 1998), p. 700.

18. David Fisher, "Note, Parental Rights and the Right to Intimate Association," *Hastings Law Journal* 48 (1997): 399–433. For a discussion of the defeat of a parent rights constitutional amendment in Colorado, see Linda L. Lane, "Comment, The Parental Rights Movement," *University of Colorado Law Review* 69 (1998): 825–849.

19. *City of Boerne v. Flores,* 117 S.Ct. 2157 (1997).

20. *Brown v. Board of Education,* 347 U.S. 483 (1954). For a new and penetrating analysis of the legacy of the *Brown* decision, see James T. Patterson, *Brown v. Board of Education: A Civil Rights Milestone and Its Troubled Legacy.*

21. *Brown v. Board of Education,* 349 U.S. 294 (1955).

22. For an engrossing account of how Southern communities sought to thwart desegregation, see J. W. Peltason, *Fifty-eight Lonely Men: Southern Federal Judges and School Desegregation.*

23. *Griffin v. County School Board of Prince Edward County,* 377 U.S. 218 (1964).

24. See Betsy Levin, "Race and School Choice," in *School Choice and Social Controversy*, ed. Stephen D. Sugarman and Frank R. Kemerer. See also M. O'Brien, "Private School Tuition Vouchers and the Realities of Racial Politics," *Tennessee Law Review* 64 (1997): 359–407, and "Note, Segregation Academies and State Action," *Yale Law Journal* 82 (1973): 1436–1461.

25. *Green v. New Kent County*, 391 U.S. 430 (1968).

26. *Swann v. Charlotte-Mecklenburg Board of Education*, 402 U.S. 1 (1971).

27. This was the basis of the Court's ruling five years later in *Pasadena City Board of Education v. Spangler*, 427 U.S. 424 (1976).

28. Eleanor Wolf, "Northern School Desegregation and Residential Choice," in *The Supreme Court Review*, ed. Philip Kurland and Gerhard Casper, 64.

29. *Bradley v. Milliken*, 338 F.Supp. 582 (E.D. Mich. 1971).

30. See Jack Bass, *Unlikely Heroes*, for a description of the tribulations four judges on the U.S. Court of Appeals for the Fifth Circuit and their families experienced in desegregating the South in the late 1950s and the 1960s. The four were Elbert Tuttle, John Minor Wisdom, Richard Rives, and John R. Brown—all Republicans except Rives. Along with the four, the Bass book also includes as unlikely heroes Federal District Court Judges Frank M. Johnson, Jr., and J. Skelly Wright. Both Johnson and Wright were later elevated to court of appeals judgeships. See also Frank Kemerer, *William Wayne Justice: A Judicial Biography*. Not only did Judge Justice desegregate the school district of Tyler, Texas, where his courtroom was located, he also presided over the most extensive school desegregation order on record, encompassing the entire state. Denunciations against the ruling and its author quickly spread from Tyler to every school community in Texas.

31. *Keyes v. School Dist. No. 1*, 413 U.S. 189 (1973).

32. Ibid., p. 209.

33. Ibid., p. 208.

34. *Board of Education of Oklahoma City v. Dowell*, 498 U.S. 237 (1991).

35. *Freeman v. Pitts*, 503 U.S. 467 (1992).

36. *Missouri v. Jenkins*, 515 U.S. 70 (1995). In an opinion written by Justice David Souter, the four dissenters noted that the federal district court judge had used test scores as a means of ascertaining whether the Kansas City school district's remedial programs were curing continuing deficiencies in student achievement within the district, not as indicators of continuing discrimination. Likewise, the primary purpose of requiring teacher salary increases was to retain strong teachers in the district, not attract students from the suburbs. The dissenters accused the majority of undercutting the district court's ability to remedy the legacy of discrimination within the Kansas City district by phrasing the issue in terms of an impermissible interdistrict remedy.

37. *Adarand Constructors, Inc. v. Peña*, 515 U.S. 200 (1995), p. 227.

38. *San Antonio Independent School District v. Rodriguez*, 411 U.S. 1 (1973).

39. For an enriching discussion of Marshall's role in bringing about the *Brown* litigation, see Richard Kluger, *Simple Justice*. For a detailed account from the legal perspective, see Mark Tushnet, *Making Civil Rights Law*.

40. Committee on Education Finance, National Research Council, *Making Money Matter: Financing America's Schools*, ed. Helen F. Ladd and Janet S. Hansen, 73.

41. Writing for the court in the original decision, Justice Oscar Mauzy pointed out that to achieve an "efficient system of public free schools" under Article VII, Section 7, of the Texas Constitution, "There must be a direct and close relationship between a district's tax effort and the education resources available to it; in other words, districts must have substantially equal access to similar revenues per pupil at similar levels of tax effort." *Edgewood I.S.D. v. Kirby,* 777 S.W.2d 391 (Tex. 1989), p. 397.

42. Committee on Education Finance, NRC, *Making Money Matter,* 89.

43. James Coleman et al., *Equality of Educational Opportunity.*

44. See, for example, *Racial Isolation in the Public Schools;* Samuel Bowles and Henry M. Levin, "The Determinants of Scholastic Achievement," *Journal of Human Resources* 3 (1): 3–24; James S. Coleman, *The Evaluation of Equality of Educational Opportunity;* and Frederick Mosteller and Daniel P. Moynihan, eds., *On Equality of Educational Opportunity.* The *San Antonio* decision only served to accelerate the debate, which rages to this day.

45. Gary Orfield and John T. Yun, *Resegregation in American Schools,* p. 13, Table 8.

46. Ibid., p. 21, Table 15.

47. Ibid., p. 17, Table 11.

48. According to Congressional Budget Office information released in 1999, the top one-fifth of American households with the highest incomes now earn half of all income in the country. Their share has risen since 1977, while the share of the one-fifth with the lowest incomes has fallen. According to a published report, the wealthiest 2.7 million have as much to spend as the poorest 100 million. David Cay Johnston, "Gap between Rich and Poor Found Substantially Wider," *New York Times,* September 5, 1999.

49. Kevin J. Payne and Bruce J. Biddle, "Poor School Funding, Child Poverty, and Mathematics Achievement," *Educational Researcher* 28, no. 6 (August–September 1999): 4–13.

50. For a penetrating look at the limits of school reform in the urban school district, given the disadvantages of children in this setting, see James Traub, "What No School Can Do," *New York Times Magazine,* January 16, 2000.

51. In 1994, urban districts spent about $4,500 per student, compared with $5,066 in nonurban districts. As noted in the text, these figures are adjusted for regional differences in the cost of education and the added expense of educating children with special needs. "Quality Counts," *Education Week,* January 8, 1998, pp. 20–21. This special 270-page report provides a wealth of statistics, often on a state-by-state basis, on the condition of America's urban school systems.

52. Ibid., 10.

53. Payne and Biddle, "Poor School Funding," 11.

54. John F. Witte, "Is America Avoiding Race?" (paper presented at the annual meeting of the American Political Science Association, September 25, 2000, San Francisco).

55. Debra Viadero, "Even in Well-Off Suburbs, Minority Achievement Lags," *Education Week,* March 15, 2000.

56. Stephen Eisdorfer, "Public School Choice and Racial Integration," *Seton Hall Law Review* 24 (1993): 937–952.

57. *Missouri v. Jenkins,* 515 U.S. 70 (1995). The Chicago school district is pursuing a somewhat similar strategy in spending lavishly on schools for the academically gifted as a means of stemming the flow of talented students to the suburbs. However, the strategy is not without criticism, especially since the academic schools enroll a disproportionate percentage of white students (57 percent white compared with 10 percent of the Chicago public school system as a whole). Dirk Johnson, "Chicago Schools' Answer to Tug of the Suburbs," *New York Times,* June 2, 2000.

58. Ann Bradley, "Black Parents Want Focus on Academics," *Education Week,* August 5, 1998.

59. Terry Moe, *Schools, Vouchers, and the American Public,* Chapter 5.

60. Ibid.

61. Hamilton Lankford and James Wyckoff, "Why Are Schools Racially Segregated? Implications for School Choice Policies" (paper presented at the School Choice and Racial Diversity Conference, Teachers College, Columbia University, New York, May 7, 2000).

62. Robert W. Fairlie, "Racial Segregation and the Private/Public School Choice" (paper presented at the School Choice and Racial Diversity Conference, Teachers College, Columbia University, New York, May 7, 2000).

63. *Texas Open Enrollment Charter Schools: Third Year Report,* Part II, pp. 29–31. A multivariate analysis confirmed the effect of race on parents' charter school decision. Despite controlling for family characteristics, choice of at-risk or not-at-risk charter school, distance from the old school to the new school, transportation problems, and the like, Anglo parents are still likely to send their child to a school that is more Anglo than the public school the child left. Similarly, African American parents are likely to send their children to schools that are more African American, and Hispanic parents are likely to send their children to schools that are more Hispanic. While almost no parents were willing to say that race is important in choosing a Texas charter school, race remains a good predictor of the schools that parents ultimately choose. *Third Year Report,* Part II, p. 13.

64. Casey D. Cobb and Gene V. Glass, "Ethnic Segregation in Arizona Charter Schools," *Education Policy Analysis Archives* 7, no. 1 (1999) (http://epaa.asu.edu/epaa/v7n1/).

65. In states like Minnesota, which is overwhelmingly white, many charter schools are located in Minneapolis and St. Paul, where minority students are clustered. The growing number of charter schools serving at-risk students in response to charter school legislation explains why many of these schools enroll large numbers of students of color. Carol Ascher and Nathalis Wamba, "An Emerging Market for a New Model of Equity?" (paper presented at the School Choice and Racial Diversity Conference, Teachers College, Columbia University, New York, May 7, 2000).

66. Jay P. Greene makes this argument in "Choosing Integration" (paper presented at the School Choice and Racial Diversity Conference, Teachers College, Columbia University, New York, May 7, 2000).

67. Ibid.

68. *Equal Open Enrollment Association v. Board of Education of Akron City School District,* 937 F.Supp. 700 (N.D. Ohio 1996).

69. *Wessmann v. Gittens,* 160 F.3d 790 (lst Cir. 1998), p. 799.

70. *Tuttle v. Arlington County School Board,* 195 F.3d 698 (4th Cir. 1999) (oversubscribed public school's use of race/ethnicity factor in admissions to achieve racial and ethnic diversity violates the Fourteenth Amendment Equal Protection Clause), and *Eisenberg v. Montgomery County Public Schools,* 197 F.3d 123 (4th Cir. 1999), *cert. denied,* 120 S.Ct. 1420 (2000) (denial of a white student's transfer to a magnet school in order to maintain racial diversity in district schools violates the Fourteenth Amendment Equal Protection Clause). For a scathing attack on these Fourth Circuit rulings, see John C. Boger, "Willful Colorblindness: The New Racial Piety and the Resegregation of Public Schools," *North Carolina Law Review* 78 (2000): 1719–1786. Included in Boger's critique is the federal district court judge's decision declaring the Charlotte-Mecklenburg School District unitary in student assignment despite the school board's own contention otherwise and preventing the board from using racial criteria in making student assignments to magnet schools in the interest of fostering diversity. The judge based his ruling on the Fourth Circuit's *Tuttle* and *Eisenberg* precedents. *Cappacchione v. Charlotte-Mecklenburg School Board,* 57 F.Supp.2d 228 (W.D.N.C. 1999). The decision was affirmed by the Fourth Circuit in September 2001. Other federal appellate courts have upheld the use of racial criteria in making student assignments. See *Hunter v. Regents of the University of California,* 190 F.3d 1061 (9th Cir. 1999), *cert. denied,* 121 S.Ct. 186 (2000) (university interest in operating a laboratory elementary school is sufficiently compelling to permit use of race-based admissions criteria), and *Brewer v. West Irondequoit Central School District,* 212 F.3d 738 (2nd Cir. 2000) (case remanded to trial court to determine whether school district's interest in reducing racial isolation is sufficiently compelling and narrowly tailored to justify prohibiting white student from transferring out of a mostly minority urban school district). Similar judicial inconsistency exists in higher education despite a murky 1979 U.S. Supreme Court precedent permitting race to be considered as one of many factors in student admissions to public colleges and universities. *Regents of the University of California v. Bakke,* 438 U.S. 265 (1979). In December 2000, the U.S. Court of Appeals for the Ninth Circuit upheld a race-conscious admissions policy at the University of Washington Law School despite the enactment of a 1998 state initiative prohibiting preferential treatment in public education and employment. *Smith v. University of Washington Law School,* 233 F.3d 1188 (9th Cir. 2000), *cert. denied,* 121 S.Ct. 2192 (2001). That same month, a federal district court ruled similarly with regard to the University of Michigan admissions policy for its literature, arts, and science college. *Gratz v. Bollinger,* 122 F.Supp.2d 811 (E.D. Mich. 2000). Both courts based their decisions on the *Bakke* decision. However, in 1996 the U.S. Court of Appeals for the Fifth Circuit struck down a race-conscious admissions policy at the University of Texas School of Law, concluding that *Bakke* is no longer good law. *Hopwood v. State of Texas,* 78 F.3d 932 (5th Cir.), *cert. denied,* 518 U.S. 1033 (1996). In 2000, a federal district court ruled similarly with regard to student admissions at the University of Georgia. *Johnson v. Board of Regents of the University System of Georgia,* 106 F.Supp.2d 1362 (S.D. Ga. 2000). In 2001, a different federal judge from the one presiding in *Gratz v. Bollinger* ruled against a race-conscious admissions policy at the University of Michigan Law School. *Grutter v. Bollinger,* 137 F.Supp.2d

821 (E.D. Mich. 2001). Both cases are being appealed to the U.S. Court of Appeals for the Sixth Circuit and may end up before the U.S. Supreme Court. If so, the high court will have an opportunity to reconsider its *Bakke* decision.

71. *Missouri v. Jenkins,* 515 U.S. 70 (1995), p. 114.

72. While an integrated school is neither a necessary nor a sufficient condition for African Americans to succeed in schools, a large body of research shows that black students who attend predominantly white schools have significantly better educational outcomes than African American students who attend schools where the majority of students are people of color. For a review of the literature on the benefits of integration for African Americans, see Roslyn Arlin Mickelson, "Subverting *Swann:* First- and Second-Generation Segregation in the Charlotte-Mecklenburg Schools," *American Educational Research Journal* 38, no.2 (2001).

73. *Quality Counts '98: The Urban Challenge,* special report, *Education Week,* January 8, 1998, pp. 66–67.

74. As quoted in William G. Bowen and Derek Bok, *The Shape of the River,* p. 239.

75. Compare, for example, the discussion in Gary Orfield, "Unexpected Costs and Uncertain Gains of Dismantling Desegregation," in *Dismantling Desegregation,* ed. Gary Orfield and Susan Eaton, 104–106, with the discussion in David J. Armor, *Forced Justice,* Chapter 2. For a dispassionate discussion, see Christopher Jencks and Meredith Phillips, "The Black-White Test Score Gap: An Introduction," in *The Black-White Test Score Gap,* ed. Christopher Jencks and Meredith Phillips, and David Grissmer et al., "Why Did the Black-White Score Gap Narrow in the 1970s and 1980s?" in the same source, pp. 206–211.

76. Jencks and Phillips, "The Black-White Test Score Gap," 1.

77. John U. Ogbu, "Class Stratification, Racial Stratification and Schooling," in *Class, Race and Gender in American Education,* ed. L. Weis. The underperformance of black students persists into college and beyond. See Bowen and Bok, *The Shape of the River,* 72–78.

78. For a comprehensive look at the stress introduced into a suburban Chicago school district that experienced a rapid influx of black students, see H. G. Bissinger, "'We're All Racist Now,'" *New York Times Magazine,* May 29, 1994.

79. For a summary of the research, see Henry M. Levin, "Educational Vouchers: Effectiveness, Choice, and Costs," *Journal of Policy Analysis and Management* 17, no. 3 (1998): 381–382.

80. Laurence Steinberg, with B. Bradford Brown and Sanford Dornbusch, *Beyond the Classroom,* 158–159.

81. See John H. Ogbu, "Racial Stratification and Education in the United States: Why Inequality Persists," *Teachers College Record* 96, no. 2 (Winter 1994): 264–298, and Signithia Fordham and John Ogbu, "Black Students' School Success: Coping with the Burden of 'Acting White,'" *Urban Review* 18, no. 3 (1986): 176–206.

82. Claude Steele and Joshua Aronson, "Stereotype Threat and the Test Performance of Academically Successful African-Americans," in *The Black-White Test Score Gap,* ed. Christopher Jencks and Meredith Phillips.

83. Claudia Dreifus, "A Conversation With: Benjamin S. Carson," *New York Times,* January 4, 2000.

84. Bissinger, "'We're All Racist Now,'" 53.

85. Philip J. Cook and Jens Ludwig, "The Burden of 'Acting White': Do Black Adolescents Disparage Academic Achievement?" in *The Black-White Test Score Gap,* ed. Christopher Jencks and Meredith Phillips. Cook and Ludwig attribute the problem of black underachievement more to poor schools and the burdens of poverty. For a critique of the chapter by Ronald E. Ferguson and the authors' response, see pp. 394–398.

86. Steinberg, *Beyond the Classroom,* 155.

87. Levin, "Educational Vouchers," 382.

88. J. Douglas Willms and Frank Echols, "The Scottish Experience of Parental School Choice," in *School Choice: Examining the Evidence,* ed. Edith Rasell and Richard Rothstein.

89. Greene, "Choosing Integration."

90. Ibid.

91. N.C. Gen. Stat. 115C-238.29F(g)(5) (1997). Despite the provision, about half of the state's fifty-seven charter schools were in violation in 1999 by enrolling a disproportionately high percentage of black students. The chairman of the State Charter School Advisory Committee recognized that the schools faced closure but asserted that the law would be changed before that would occur. Tim Simmons, "Charter Schools Still Tilt Racially," *News and Observer,* January 3, 1999.

92. Darcia Bowman, "Judge Overturns South Carolina's Charter School Law," *Education Week,* May 24, 2000, p. 25. The previous June, the Supreme Court of South Carolina upheld the denial of a charter to the Lighthouse Charter School because it failed to satisfy the Charter School Act's health, safety, civil rights, and racial composition requirements. However, the court sent the case back to the trial court for a determination whether the 10 percent racial variance provision was a denial of equal protection of the laws. *Beaufort County Board of Education v. Lighthouse Charter School,* 516 S.E.2d 655 (S.C. 1999).

93. *Hopwood v. State of Texas,* 78 F.3d 932 (5th Cir. 1996), p. 947, n. 31. For an in-depth discussion of the perils of race-based admissions policies, see Erica J. Rinas, "Note: A Constitutional Analysis of Race-Based Limitations on Open Enrollment in Public Schools," *Iowa Law Review* 82 (1997): 1501–1534. For a discussion of the arguments that might support a Fourteenth Amendment compelling state interest test for a race-based admissions policy, see "The Constitutionality of Race-Conscious Admissions Programs in Elementary and Secondary Schools," *Harvard Law Review* 112 (1999): 940–957. The University of Michigan at Ann Arbor presently is embroiled in litigation over its admissions policy that encompasses racial preferences. Rather than modify the policy, the university has launched a major effort to establish empirically the benefits of the policy to its student body. Whether the effort will provide the compelling state interest that is required to survive challenges under the Fourteenth Amendment remains to be seen. Steven A. Holmes, "A Most Diverse University's New Legal Tack," *New York Times,* May 11, 1999.

94. *San Francisco NAACP v. San Francisco Unified School District,* 59 F.Supp.2d 1021 (N.D. Cal. 1999). Dr. Gary Orfield, who chaired the court's Consent Decree Advisory Committee, opposed the settlement, claiming that the schools of the district likely would become resegregated, to the detriment of non-

white students, if it were adopted. While appearing sympathetic to the concern, the federal judge noted that precedent, including the U.S. Supreme Court's *Adarand v. Peña* decision, prevented further use of racial quotas. For a period after the decision, Orfield's prediction came true, as the school district dawdled in implementing a new assignment policy based on the court-approved settlement. By the fall of 2000, incoming classes in 20 of the district's 116 schools were more than 60 percent of one race or ethnic group. Under the old race-based assignment policy, no one race or ethnic group's proportion of a school's enrollment could exceed 45 percent. The district's incoming superintendent, Arlene Ackerman, greeted the news by saying she hoped to implement an attendance plan that permitted consideration of student economic background to assure diversity. Robert C. Johnston, "San Francisco Schools Becoming More Segregated," *Education Week,* September 6, 2000. For a penetrating discussion of the San Francisco court decision and its implication for affirmative action policies generally, see David L. Levine, "The Chinese American Challenge to Court-Mandated Quotas in San Francisco's Public Schools: Notes from a (Partisan) Participant-Observer," *Harvard Blackletter Law Journal* 16 (2000): 39–145.

95. Patrick Jonsson, "Poverty, Not Race, as Test for Diversity," *Christian Science Monitor,* May 23, 2000. For a legal analysis of the Wake County school district's policy, see Elizabeth J. Bower, "Note, Answering the Call: Wake County's Commitment to Diversity in Education," *North Carolina Law Review* 78 (2000): 2026–2052.

5. VOUCHERS AND TAX BENEFITS

1. National Center for Education Statistics, *Private School Universe, 1997–98.* Thirty percent of American private schools are Catholic, 48 percent are affiliated with other religions, and 22 percent are nonsectarian. Slightly over 11 percent of American students are educated in private schools. U.S. Department of Education, National Center for Education Statistics, *The Condition of Education 1998* (http://www.nces.ed.gov/pubs98/condition98/c9842a01.html).

2. Stephen P. Croley, "The Majoritarian Difficulty: Elective Judiciaries and the Rule of Law," *University of Chicago Law Review* 62 (1995): 725–726. Croley notes that only in twelve states are judges chosen by legislative or executive appointment.

3. John F. Witte et al., *Fourth Year Report: Milwaukee Parental Choice Program.*

4. *Davis v. Grover,* 480 N.W.2d 460 (Wis.), *reconsideration denied,* 490 N.W.2d 26 (Wis. 1992). The court upheld the program against charges that it violated the judicially developed public purpose doctrine, was enacted as a private bill in violation of Article IV, Section 18, of the Wisconsin Constitution, and did not satisfy the uniform school provision of Article X, Section 3. The uniformity provision states that "The legislature shall provide by law for the establishment of district schools, which shall be as nearly uniform as practicable." Because the private schools are not district schools and because children participating in the

choice program can always return to the public schools, the court determined that the program met this constitutional requirement.

5. *Jackson v. Benson*, No. 95 CV 1982 (Wis. Cir. Ct., Dane Cnty. 1997).

6. *Gatton v. Goff*, Nos. 96 CVH-1-198, 96 CVH-01-721, 1996 WL 466499 (Ohio Com. Pl., Franklin Cnty. July 31, 1996).

7. For a detailed analysis, see Frank R. Kemerer, "The Constitutional Dimension of School Vouchers," *Texas Forum on Civil Liberties & Civil Rights* 3 (1998): 142–151.

8. U.S. Supreme Court Justice Owen Roberts is often cited for this so-called "T-square" rule of mechanical judicial decisionmaking. See *U.S. v. Butler*, 297 U.S. 1 (1936), p. 62.

9. Joseph Singer, "The Player and the Cards: Nihilism and Legal Theory," *Yale Law Journal* 94 (1984): 5–6, as quoted in Laura Kalman, *The Strange Career of Legal Liberalism*. Kalman's book explores in great detail the paradigmatic shifts in approaches to constitutional decisionmaking during the past fifty years from the perspective of liberal scholars in the legal community. These scholars embrace the rights-oriented decisionmaking evident in the decisions of the Warren Court, beginning with the momentous 1954 *Brown v. Board of Education* decision striking down de jure school segregation.

10. Kalman, *The Strange Career*, 46.

11. *Jackson v. Benson*, No. 95 CV 1982 (Wis. Cir. Ct., Dane Cnty, 1997), p. 28.

12. The U.S. Supreme Court ruling referenced in Judge Sadler's commentary is *Witters v. Washington Department of Services*, 474 U.S. 481 (1986).

13. Mike Miller, "Judge Won't Step Aside on School Choice," *Capital Times*, April 9, 1996.

14. Bruce Cadwallader, "Candidates for Common Pleas Judgeship Part of Youthful Push; Candidate Profiles," *Columbus Dispatch*, October 28, 1996.

15. Two important changes had occurred in the court's makeup. First, Jon Wilcox was elected to the Wisconsin Supreme Court in April 1997. A Republican and former state representative strongly supportive of vouchers, Wilcox had been appointed to the high court by Governor Thompson in 1992 and had participated in the Milwaukee voucher decision. Later, accusations surfaced that voucher proponents had engaged in "dirty tricks" in financing Wilcox's campaign. Mark Walsh, "Campaign Cash from Voucher Backers at Issue in Wisconsin," *Education Week*, May 24, 2000. Second, conservative Pat Crooks was elected to the court in 1996, replacing Justice Rollie Day, who had voted against expansion of the Milwaukee choice program to include sectarian private schools in the tie vote resulting in return of the case to the trial court. The election of Crooks was viewed as tipping the balance on the seven-member court in favor of vouchers to sectarian schools.

16. *Jackson v. Benson*, 578 N.W.2d 602 (Wis.), *cert. denied*, 119 S.Ct. 466 (1998).

17. *Simmons-Harris v. Goff*, 711 N.E.2d 203 (Ohio 1999).

18. *Simmons-Harris v. Zelman*, 72 F.Supp.2d 834 (N.D. Ohio 1999), *aff'd*, 234 F.3d 945 (6th Cir. 2000). In splitting 2-1, the appeals court judges portrayed polar positions on the application of the Establishment Clause to the voucher ques-

tion. The strong rhetoric that characterized both the majority and the dissenting opinion, especially the latter, underscored the divisiveness of the matter.

19. See, for example, David Futterman, "Note, School Choice and the Religion Clauses," *Georgetown Law Journal* 81 (1993): 711–740; "Comment, School Choice Vouchers and the Establishment Clause," *Alabama Law Review* 58 (1994): 543–573; Michael Stick, "Educational Vouchers: A Constitutional Analysis," *Columbia Journal of Law and Social Problems* 28 (1995): 423–473; Kathleen Sullivan, "Parades, Public Squares and Voucher Payments: Problems of Government Neutrality," *Connecticut Law Review* 28 (1996): 243–260. The most thorough analysis to date will be found in Jesse Choper, "School Choice: Federal Constitutional Issues under the Religion and Speech Clauses of the First Amendment," in *School Choice and Social Controversy: Politics, Policy, and Law,* ed. Steve Sugarman and Frank Kemerer.

20. *Committee for Public Education v. Nyquist,* 413 U.S. 756 (1973).

21. Ibid., p. 786.

22. *Miller v. Benson,* 878 F.Supp. 1209 (E.D. Wis. 1995). The decision was later vacated and the case declared moot by the U.S. Court of Appeals for the Seventh Circuit in light of legislation extending the program to sectarian private schools and in light of litigation begun in state court. The appeals court noted that the plaintiffs in the case ought not to "play off one court system against the other. The state legislature gave plaintiffs what they sought, and this case is therefore moot." 68 F.3d 163 (7th Cir. 1995), p. 165.

23. *Nyquist,* p. 782, n. 38.

24. *Mueller v. Allen,* 463 U.S. 388 (1983), p. 400.

25. *Witters v. Washington Department of Services,* 474 U.S. 481, reh'd denied, 475 U.S. 1091 (1986).

26. *Zobrest v. Catalina Foothills School District,* 509 U.S. 1 (1993), p. 10.

27. *Rosenberger v. Rector & Visitors of the University of Virginia,* 515 U.S. 819 (1995), p. 839.

28. *Agostini v. Felton,* 521 U.S. 203 (1997), p. 225.

29. *Mitchell v. Helms,* 120 S.Ct. 2530 (2000).

30. Ibid., pp. 2541–2542.

31. Article VI, Section 2, provides, "This Constitution, and the Laws of the United States which shall be made in Pursuance thereof; and all Treaties made, or which shall be made, under the Authority of the United States, shall be the supreme Law of the Land; and the Judges in every State shall be bound thereby, any Thing in the Constitution or Laws of any State to the Contrary notwithstanding."

32. *Witters,* 474 U.S., p. 489. Justice Harry Blackmun made the same point in his dissent in *Zobrest v. Catalina Foothills Sch. Dist.,* 509 U.S. 1 (1993) (Establishment Clause does not bar a school district from providing a sign-language interpreter under the Individuals with Disabilities Education Act to a deaf student attending classes at a Roman Catholic high school). He cited an Arizona Attorney General opinion to the effect that under Article II, Section 12, of the state constitution, interpreter services could not be furnished to petitioner. That provision provides that "No public money or property shall be appropriated for or applied to any religious worship, exercise, or instruction, or to the support of any religious

establishment." No litigation, however, commenced at the state level following the U.S. Supreme Court's decision.

33. The Equal Protection Clause of the Fourteenth Amendment reads, "[N]or shall any State . . . deny to any person within its jurisdiction the equal protection of the laws."

34. It may be that the Supreme Court will find deference to anti-establishment of religion provisions in state constitutions serves a compelling purpose for limiting free exercise of religion while at the same time serving the principle of federalism. For a comprehensive discussion of issues of federalism, see "Symposium: Constructing a New Federalism," *Yale Law and Policy Review* 14 (1996).

35. Joseph P. Viteritti, "Choosing Equality: Religious Freedom and Educational Opportunity under Constitutional Federalism," *Yale Law and Policy Review* 15 (1996): 146–147. See also Stephen K. Green, "The Blaine Amendment Reconsidered," *American Journal of Legal History* 36 (1992): 38–69.

36. Ill. Const., art. 10, §3.

37. *People ex rel. Klinger v. Howlett,* 305 N.E.2d 129 (Ill. 1973). Much earlier precedents also addressed the aid issue. In *Cook County v. Chicago Industrial School for Girls,* 18 N.E. 183 (Ill. 1888), the high court held that tuition reimbursement paid by Cook County to Catholic organizations functioning as the Chicago Industrial School for Girls violated the state constitution's mandate against use of public monies to support any sectarian institution. But several decades later the same court ruled that reimbursement of less than actual cost was not a constitutional violation. *Dunn v. Chicago Industrial School for Girls,* 117 N.E. 735 (Ill. 1917).

38. For an earlier, more detailed discussion with complete citations, see Frank R. Kemerer, "State Constitutions and School Vouchers," *West's Education Law Reporter* 120 (1997): 1–42, and Kemerer, "The Constitutional Dimensions," 161–180.

39. *Almond v. Day,* 89 S.E.2d 851 (Va. 1955). In *Almond* the court ruled that tuition payments to parents of children attending sectarian private schools pursuant to vouchers approved by the Superintendent of Public Instruction violated Article 8, Section 10, of the state constitution, requiring no expenditure of public funds to any school not owned or exclusively controlled by the state or its political subdivisions. However, following a 1956 amendment to this section authorizing assistance to students attending nonsectarian private institutions, the court distinguished the *Almond* ruling in *Miller v. Ayres,* 191 S.E.2d 261 (Va. 1972), regarding assistance to students in nonsectarian schools.

40. *Judd v. Board of Education,* 15 N.E.2d 576, *reh'g denied,* 17 N.E.2d 134 (New York 1938).

41. *Board of Education of Central School District No. 1 v. Allen,* 228 N.E.2d 791 (New York 1967), *aff'd,* 392 U.S. 236 (1968).

42. A good example is the Hawaii Supreme Court, which cited *Judd* with approval in its 1969 ruling rejecting use of public funds to provide bus transportation to parochial students. *Spears v. Honda,* 449 P.2d 130 (Haw. 1969).

43. *Durham v. McLeod,* 192 S.E.2d 202 (S.C. 1972) *(per curiam), appeal dismissed,* 413 U.S. 902 (1973).

44. *Hartness v. Patterson,* 197 S.E.2d 907 (S.C. 1971) (state financial aid for students attending private colleges violates the direct/indirect prohibitions of Article IX, Section 9, of the South Carolina Constitution).

45. *Sheldon Jackson College v. State,* 599 P.2d 127 (Alaska 1979).

46. *Opinion of the Justices to the House of Representatives,* 259 N.E.2d 564 (Mass. 1970).

47. *Opinion of the Justices to the Senate,* 514 N.E.2d 353 (Mass. 1987). In a footnote the court noted that the "language of our anti-aid amendment is 'much more specific' than the First Amendment to the U.S. Constitution."

48. *Gaffney v. State Department of Education,* 220 N.W.2d 550 (Neb. 1974).

49. *Lenstrom v. Thone,* 311 N.W.2d 884 (Neb. 1981).

50. *State ex rel. Bouc v. School District,* 320 N.W.2d 472 (Neb. 1982); *Cunningham v. Lutjeharms,* 437 N.W.2d 806 (Neb. 1989).

51. *Lenstrom,* 311 N.W.2d, p. 888.

52. *Fannin v. Williams,* 655 S.W.2d 480 (Ky. 1983).

53. *Jennings v. Exeter–West Greenwich Regional School District Committee,* 352 A.2d 634 (R.I. 1976).

54. *Weiss v. Bruno,* 509 P.2d 973 (Wash. 1973), *modified,* 523 P.2d 915 (Wash. 1974) (allowance of attorney fees).

55. *Witters v. State Commission for the Blind,* 771 P.2d 1119 (Wash.) *(en banc), cert. denied,* 493 U.S. 850 (1989).

56. *Members of Jamestown School Committee v. Schmidt,* 405 A.2d 16 (R.I. 1979).

57. *Horace Mann League of America, Inc. v. Board of Public Works,* 220 A.2d 51 (Md.), *appeal dismissed and cert. denied,* 385 U.S. 97 (1966) (construction grants to sectarian private colleges are constitutional so long as they serve a public purpose); *Board of Education of Baltimore County v. Wheat,* 199 A. 628 (Md. 1938) (bus transportation to parochial students constitutional as serving a public purpose).

58. *Bagley v. Raymond School Department,* 728 A.2d 127 (Me.), *cert. denied,* 528 U.S. 947 (1999).

59. *Chittenden Town School District v. Vermont Department of Education,* 738 A.2d 539 (Vt.), *cert. denied sub nom., Andrews v. Vermont Department of Education,* 528 U.S. 1066 (1999).

60. *Vermont Educational Buildings Financial Agency v. Mann,* 247 A.2d 68 (Vt.), *appeal dismissed,* 396 U.S. 801 (1969) (construction assistance to church-related institution through a state building finance program does not violate either the state or federal constitution). In 1994, the Supreme Court of Vermont did uphold a tuition reimbursement program for a parent who sent his son to an out-of-state religious private school. However, the decision was based on the federal constitution, since the state constitution has no specific anti-establishment clause. The court noted no violation of the First Amendment Establishment Clause because (1) the reimbursement went to the parent and not to the school, (2) the school board paid tuition for all high school students because it did not have its own high school, (3) sectarian reasons did not motivate the town's decision not to have a high

school, (4) no substantial numbers of students were sent to religious schools, (5) the extent of state regulation of private schools was minimal, and (6) the subsidy program did not promote sectarian education. *Campbell v. Manchester Board of School Directors,* 641 A.2d 352 (Vt. 1994). Interestingly, the same court struck down the practice in 1964 as a violation of the First Amendment Establishment Clause, but this was prior to the U.S. Supreme Court's rulings in *Mueller* and *Witters,* both of which were cited in support of the *Campbell* decision.

61. *Chance v. Mississippi State Textbook Rating and Purchasing Board,* 200 So. 706 (Miss. 1941).

62. *Op. Atty Gen.* No. 76-6 (1976). However, a later attorney general opinion raised grave doubts about the constitutionality of vouchers under the state constitution. *Op. Atty Gen.* No. 99-01 (1999).

63. *Americans United, Inc. v. Independent School District No. 622,* 179 N.W.2d 146 (Minn. 1970), *appeal dismissed,* 403 U.S. 945 (1971) (program providing for transportation of children to sectarian private schools does not violate the Minnesota Constitution). Article I, Section 16, provides that no money "be drawn from the treasury for the benefit of any religious societies or religious or theological seminaries." Article XIII, Section 2, restricts expenditures of public money "for the support of schools wherein the distinctive doctrines, creeds or tenets of any particular Christian or other religious sect are promulgated or taught." In 1974 the Minnesota Supreme Court struck down a state tax credit plan for parents who send their children to nonpublic schools. The decision was based solely on the First Amendment Establishment Clause; no consideration was given to the provisions of the Minnesota Constitution. *Minnesota Civil Liberties Union v. State,* 224 N.W.2d 344 (Minn. 1974), *cert. denied,* 421 U.S. 988 (1975). As noted in the chapter, the U.S. Supreme Court reached the opposite conclusion nearly ten years later in *Mueller v. Allen.*

64. *State v. Hershberger,* 462 N.W.2d 393 (Minn. 1990) (state requirement that slow-moving vehicles display a triangular reflective symbol violates the free exercise rights of the Amish under Article I, Section 16, since the state failed to demonstrate that its objective for public safety could not be achieved through the use of white reflective tape and a red lantern).

65. *Minnesota Federation of Teachers v. Mammenga,* 500 N.W.2d 136 (Minn. App. 1993).

66. *Knowlton v. Baumhover,* 166 N.W. 202 (Iowa 1918). In *Rudd v. Ray,* 248 N.W.2d 125 (Iowa 1976), the Iowa Supreme Court suggested that Article I, Section 3, which prohibits enactment of any law "respecting an establishment of religion" and any law requiring persons to "pay tithes, taxes, or other rates for building or repairing places of worship, or the maintenance of any minister, or ministry," is similar to the First Amendment of the U.S. Constitution, noting that "to the extent our provision differs from the First Amendment to the United States Constitution we think our framers were merely addressing the evils incident to the state church." In going on to uphold a provision of salaried chaplains and religious facilities at the state penitentiary, the court noted that it was striking a balance between anti-establishment and free exercise interests. The decision seems to undercut the strict anti-establishment character of *Knowlton.*

67. *Op. Atty. Gen.* (Hill), April 25, 1969.

68. *Bush v. Holmes*, 767 So.2d 668 (Fla. Dist. Ct. App. 2000).

69. *Rust v. Sullivan*, 500 U.S. 173 (1991).

70. *Church of the Lukumi Babalu Aye, Inc. v. City of Hialeah*, 508 U.S. 520 (1993) (violation of the free exercise of religion for a city to prohibit animal sacrifices for religious purposes when other forms of killing animals are permitted, e.g., meat slaughtering, eradication of insects). In the state education context, see, for example, *Chance v. Mississippi State Textbook Rating and Purchasing Board*, 200 So. 706 (Miss. 1941) (failing to include private school students in a textbook loan program amounts to denial of equal privileges on religious grounds), and *Durham v. McLeod*, 192 S.E.2d 202 (1972) *(per curiam), appeal dismissed,* 413 U.S. 902 (1973) (exclusion of religious schools from a student college tuition assistance program would materially disadvantage the schools).

71. *Mitchell v. Helms,* 120 S.Ct. 2530 (2000), p. 2552. In *Mitchell,* the Court ruled 6-3 that the use of Title I federal funding to provide instructional equipment including computers and computer programs at religious private schools does not violate the Establishment Clause.

72. *Rosenberger v. Rector & Visitors of the University of Virginia,* 515 U.S. 819 (1995) (university refusal to allow student activity fees to be paid to third-party printers of a student religious newspaper violates the Free Speech Clause of the First Amendment as unconstitutional viewpoint censorship).

73. Ariz. Rev. Stat. 43-1089 (1998). The Commonwealth of Puerto Rico has a similar plan. Enacted in 1995, the Educational Foundation for the Free Selection of Schools Act establishes a nonprofit corporation to receive donations from individuals and businesses for making tuition subsidies to low-income families for attending public and private schools. The donors may in return claim a tax credit of $250 for individuals and $500 for corporations. If the donation exceeds the maximum limit of the credit, the donor may claim the excess as a tax deduction. P.R. Laws Ann. tit. 18, §913; P.R. Laws Ann. tit. 13, §8440a (1996).

74. *Kotterman v. Killian,* 972 P.2d 606 (Ariz.), *cert. denied,* 528 U.S. 921 (1999). In 2001 an Illinois appellate court ruled similarly with regard to that state's tuition tax credit program. The statute provides a credit of up to $500 against the state income tax equal to 25 percent of tuition, book fees, and lab fees at a public or private school. The court noted that even if the tax credit were considered public money, the ruling would be the same since the state supreme court has ruled the Illinois Constitution's anti-establishment of religion provision to be coextensive with the Establishment Clause of the First Amendment. Based on the *Mueller v. Allen* precedent, the state measure is constitutional. *Toney v. Bower,* 744 N.E.2d 351 (Ill. App. 4 Dist., 2001).

75. Adele Robinson, "Risky Credit: Tuition Tax Credits and Issues of Accountability and Equity," *Stanford Law and Policy Review* 11 (2000): 257–258.

6. THE ECONOMICS OF CHOICE

1. U.S. Department of Education, Office of Educational Research and Improvement, *Parents and School Choice: A Household Survey.*

2. Caroline Hoxby, "Are Efficiency and Equity in School Finance Substitutes or Complements?" *Journal of Economic Perspectives* 10 (1996): 51–72.

3. This discussion assumes that taxes and services are the only issues in the election, that voters have consistent preferences, and that the preference curve has a single peak.

4. William N. Evans, Sheila E. Murray, and Robert M. Schwab, "School-houses, Courthouses, and Statehouses after Serrano," *Journal of Policy Analysis and Management* 16 (1997): Table 3.

5. Hawaii has a single school district that encompasses the entire state.

6. William Duncombe and John Yinger, "Why Is It So Hard to Help Central City Schools?" *Journal of Policy Analysis and Management* 16 (1997): 99.

7. Eric A. Hanushek, "When School Finance 'Reform' May Not Be Good Policy," *Harvard Journal on Legislation* 28 (1991): 423–455; Paul N. Courant and Susanna Loeb, "Centralization of School Finance in Michigan," *Journal of Policy Analysis and Management* 16 (1997): 114–136. It is not always the case that inner-city districts spend more than suburban districts. For example, some suburban districts in the Chicago metropolitan area spend more per pupil than the center city district. The critical issue for inner-city districts is that the cost of educating high risk and disadvantaged students is much greater than the cost of educating the average student in a middle-class suburban district.

8. Amy Gutmann, *Democratic Education.*

9. While school district officials may be willing to accept students so long as the funding they bring with them exceeds the marginal cost of their education, we believe that voters are unlikely to accept this arrangement for very long. This will be particularly true if the students who are transferring into the district are of a lower socioeconomic status than district residents.

10. If District A is spending more than the foundation level for education, then the loss of students whose parents demand more education than the median voter will reduce the demand for educational expenditures in District A because the families of the leaving students will now want the lowest possible education taxes. This will further lower educational expenditures in District A. See Kangoh Lee, "An Economic Analysis of Public School Choice Plans," *Journal of Urban Economics* 41 (1997): 1–22.

11. Eric A. Hanushek, "The Evidence on Class Size," Occasional Paper Number 98-1 (Rochester, N.Y.: W. Allen Wallis Institute of Political Economy, University of Rochester, 1998); Eric A. Hanushek and Steven G. Rivkin, "Aggregation and the Estimated Effects of School Resources," *Review of Economics and Statistics* 78 (1997): 611–627.

12. This act was originally titled Education for All Handicapped Children Act.

13. Hanushek, "The Evidence on Class Size."

14. Examples of this literature include Myron Lieberman, *The Teacher Unions: How the NEA and AFT Sabotage Reform and Hold Students, Parents, Teachers, and Taxpayers Hostage to Bureaucracy,* and Howard L. Fuller, George A. Mitchell, and Michael E. Hartmann, "The Educational Impact of Teacher Collective Bargaining in Milwaukee, Wisconsin" (paper prepared for Teacher Unions and Educational Change conference, Harvard, Kennedy School, September 24–25, 1998).

15. Caroline Minter Hoxby, "How Teachers' Unions Affect Education Production," *Quarterly Journal of Economics* 111 (1996): 671–718.

16. Eric A. Hanushek, "Outcomes, Costs, and Incentives in Schools," in *Improving America's Schools: The Role of Incentives,* ed. Eric A. Hanushek and Dale W. Jorgenson, p. 47, Table 2-2.

17. Hanushek, "The Evidence on Class Size," 3.

18. Hanushek and Rivkin, "Aggregation and the Estimated Effects," 55–58.

19. Ibid.

20. Hamilton Lankford and James Wyckoff, "Where Has the Money Gone? An Analysis of School District Spending in New York," *Educational Evaluation and Policy Analysis* 17 (1995) 195–218.

21. Hanushek, "The Evidence on Class Size," 16.

22. Kenneth J. Meier, J. L. Polinard, and Robert D. Wrinkle, "Bureaucracy and Organizational Performance: Causality Arguments about Public Schools," *American Journal of Political Science* 44 (July 2000): 590–602.

23. David Boaz and R. Morris Barrett, "What Would a School Voucher Buy? The Real Cost of Private Schools," Cato Briefing Paper No. 25 (Washington, D.C.: Cato Institute, 1996).

24. See Henry M. Levin, "Educational Vouchers: Effectiveness, Choice, and Costs," *Journal of Policy Analysis and Management* 17 (1998): 373–392, and Henry M. Levin and Cyrus E. Driver, "Costs of an Educational Voucher System," *Educational Economics* 5 (1997): 265–293.

25. Ibid.

26. Ibid.

27. The total costs of education to society equal the sum of the costs to the state of public education plus the costs to the private sector of private education. If the state assumes the costs currently paid by the private sector, this is not an increase in the total cost *to society* of education. It simply shifts the burden of private education from parents and nongovernmental organizations to the state.

28. It should be noted that there are real additional costs in transportation, as more students will need transportation to more distant schools. It is for this reason that we have not included the entire $42 billion as a transfer cost. At least half of the additional costs will stem from additional transportation provided to students who currently attend public schools.

29. Levin, "Educational Vouchers," 386.

30. The savings would be substantially greater than this, as presumably many low-income children would attend neighborhood schools. On the other hand, as Levin pointed out in a personal communication to the authors, we have included neither the information and transaction costs that parents would incur in a privatized, decentralized system nor losses in economic efficiency that economies of a centralized transportation system might create. In addition, a $500 voucher would only provide $2.75 per day to families who are not low-income. As the real cost of safe and reliable transportation is greater than that for most families, our transportation voucher would require middle-class parents to shoulder additional educational costs.

31. We discuss the merits of an information agency as part of a voucher plan in Chapter 8.

32. It should be noted that moving the information costs from a state expense to a school and parent expense does not eliminate the cost. Levin suggests that the total costs to society of our decentralized information system are likely to be greater than would occur in a public system which could take advantage of economies of scale.

33. Eric A. Hanushek et al., *Making Schools Work: Improving Performance and Controlling Costs,* 53.

34. Ibid., 54.

35. Some students did change from larger to smaller classes when spaces in the smaller classrooms opened up. Unfortunately, these transfers were not random. See Hanushek, "The Evidence on Class Size."

36. For discussions of the Project Star results see *Special Issue: Class Size Issues and New Findings, Educational Evaluation and Policy Analysis* 21 (1999).

37. CSR Research Consortium, *Class Size Reduction in California: Early Findings Signal Promise and Concern.*

38. The studies showing no significant educational gains after kindergarten in Tennessee and the small gains observed in California fit well with other studies on the effects of class size. Hanushek analyzed ninety studies that included 277 estimates of the effects of class size on student achievement. He found that only 15 percent of the estimates showed that smaller pupil-teacher ratios statistically improved performance, while 13 percent showed a statistically significant decline in performance. In the twenty-three studies that were methodologically most sophisticated, one found that smaller classes improved student performance, three found that smaller classes had a statistically negative impact on student performance, and nineteen showed no statistically significant difference between smaller and larger classes. Hanushek, "The Evidence on Class Size," 21, 24. Research by Steven Rivkin, Eric A. Hanushek, and J. F. Kain, "Teachers, Schools and Academic Achievement" (Working Paper no. 669, National Bureau of Economic Research, Cambridge, Mass., 1998), shows that it takes extremely large reductions in class size (about ten students) to obtain a small improvement in test scores (a 0.19 standard deviation).

39. Julian R. Betts and Jamie L. Shkolnik, "The Behavioral Effects of Variations in Class Size: The Case of Math Teachers," *Educational Evaluation and Policy Analysis* 21 (1999): 193–213; Alex Molnar et al., "Evaluating the SAGE Program: A Pilot Program in Targeted Pupil-Teacher Reduction in Wisconsin," *Educational Evaluation and Policy Analysis* 21 (1999): 165–177.

40. Henry Levin, Harold Glass, and Greg Meister, *Cost Effectiveness of Four Educational Interventions.*

41. Dominic J. Brewer et al., "Estimating the Cost of National Class Size Reductions under Different Policy Alternatives," *Educational Evaluation and Policy Analysis* 21 (1999): 179–192; Eric A. Hanushek, "Some Findings from an Independent Investigation of the Tennessee STAR Experiment and from Other Investigations of Class Size Effects," *Educational Evaluation and Policy Analysis* 21 (1999): 143–163.

42. Janet Weiss, "Policy Theories and School Choice," *Social Science Quarterly* 79 (1998): 523–532.

43. See Charles F. Manski, "Educational Choice (Vouchers) and Social Mo-

bility," *Economics of Education Review* 11 (1992): 351–369; Hamilton Lankford and James Wycoff, "Primary and Secondary School Choice among Public and Religious Alternatives," *Economics of Education Review* 11 (1992): 317–337; Thomas J. Nechyba, "Public School Finance in a General Equilibrium Tiebout World: Equalization Programs, Peer Effects, and Private School Vouchers," Working Paper 5642 (Cambridge, Mass.: National Bureau of Economic Research, 1996); and Dennis Epple and R. Romano, "Competition between Private and Public Schools: Vouchers and Peer Effects," *American Economic Review* 88 (1998): 33–62.

7. SCHOOL CHOICE REGULATION

1. Terry Moe, *Schools, Vouchers, and the American Public.* In asking the questions, Moe found that more than three-quarters of parents and nonparents agree that private schools participating in a voucher program should meet these requirements. With regard to a set-aside for low-income families, more than 85 percent of inner-city respondents thought so.

2. Lana Muraskin and Stephanie Stullich, *Final Report: Barriers, Budgets, and Costs Using Private Schools to Alleviate Overcrowding in Public Schools.*

3. John Chubb and Terry Moe, *Politics, Markets and America's Schools.*

4. E. S. Savas, *Privatization and Public-Private Partnerships,* 83.

5. Chubb and Moe, *Politics, Markets,* 43.

6. Portions of the following sections appeared in Frank R. Kemerer and Catherine Maloney, "The Legal Framework for Educational Privatization and Accountability," *West's Education Law Reporter* 150 (2001): 589–627.

7. Ariz. Const. art. XI, §6; Calif. Const. art. IX, §5; Idaho Const. art. IX, §1; Ind. Const. art. VIII, §1; Ky. Const. §183; Miss. Const. art. 8, §206; Neb. Const. art. VII, §1; Nev. Const. art. XI, §2; N.Y. Const. art. XI, §1; Ohio Const. art. VI, §2; Or. Const. art. VIII, §3; S.D. Const. art. VIII, §15; Wash. Const. art. IX, §2. In some cases, case law uses the term "common school" in referring to state public schooling constitutional provisions which themselves do not employ the term. See, for example, *Wilson v. Stanford,* 66 S.E. 258 (Ga. 1909).

8. Wash. Const. art. IX, §2.

9. *School Dist. No. 20 v. Bryan,* 99 P. 28 (Wash. 1909), p. 30.

10. See L. K. Beale, "Note, Charter Schools, Common Schools, and the Washington State Constitution," *Washington Law Review* 72 (1997): 535–566.

11. Ariz. Const. art. XI, §1; Colo. Const. art. IX, §2; Fla. Const. art. IX, §1; Idaho Const. art. IX, §1; Ind. Const. art. VIII, §1; Minn. Const. art. XIII, §1; Nev. Const. art. XI, §2; N.M. Const. art. XII, §1; N.C. Const. art. IX, §2; N.D. Const. art. VIII, §2; Or. Const. art. VIII, §2; S.D. Const. art. VIII, §1; Wash. Const. art. IX, §2; Wis. Const. art. X, §3; Wyo. Const. art. VII, §1.

12. *Brown v. Board of Education,* 347 U.S. 483 (1954), p. 493.

13. Mich. Const. art. 8, §2.

14. Allen W. Hubsch, "The Emerging Right to Education under State Constitutional Law," *Temple Law Review* 65 (1992): 1325–1348. In an appendix, Hubsch lists the primary constitutional provision of each state that pertains to the establishment of an educational system.

15. Mich. Const. art. 8, §3.

16. *Council of Organizations and Others for Education about Parochiaid v. Governor of Michigan,* 548 N.W.2d 909 (Mich. App. 1996), pp. 912–913.

17. *Council of Organizations and Others for Education about Parochiaid, Inc. v. Governor,* 566 N.W.2d 208 (Mich. 1997).

18. *In re Charter School Application,* 727 A.2d 15 (N.J. Super. A.D. 1999), p. 44 (citing the New Jersey Supreme Court's decision in *Ridgefield Park Education Association v. Ridgefield Park Board of Education,* 393 A.2d 278 [N.J. 1978]).

19. *In re Charter School Application of Englewood on Palisades Charter School,* 753 A.2d 687 (N.J. 2000).

20. Jason L. Wren, "Note, Charter Schools: Public or Private? An Application of the Fourteenth Amendment's State Action Doctrine to These Innovative Schools," *Review of Litigation* 19 (Winter 2000): 137.

21. *Lebron v. National R.R. Passenger Corp.,* 513 U.S. 374 (1995), p. 397.

22. *Rendell-Baker v. Kohn,* 457 U.S. 830 (1982).

23. *Blum v. Yaretsky,* 457 U.S. 991 (1982).

24. *West v. Atkins,* 487 U.S. 42 (1988).

25. *Brentwood Academy v. Tennessee Secondary School Athletic Association,* 531 U.S. 288 (2001).

26. *Milonas v. Williams,* 691 F.2d 931 (10th Cir. 1982), *cert. denied,* 460 U.S. 1069 (1983).

27. For a discussion, see Frank R. Kemerer et al., "Vouchers and Private School Autonomy," *Journal of Law and Education* 21 (1992): 613–628.

28. John F. Witte, *The Market Approach to Education,* 88.

29. Interview with Charles Toulmin, Wisconsin Department of Public Instruction, September 27, 1999.

30. *School District of Wilkinsburg v. Education Association,* 667 A.2d 5 (Pa. 1995).

31. Jeff Archer, "Accountability Measures Vary Widely," *Education Week,* May 17, 2000.

32. Mass. Regs. Code, tit. 603, §§1.01–1.13 (2000).

33. Jerry Horn and Gary Miron, *Evaluation of the Michigan Public School Initiative,* 58.

34. Ibid., p. 61. See also Public Sector Consultants and Maximus, Inc., *Michigan's Charter School Initiative: From Theory to Practice,* 1999, p. 26 (http://www.mde.state.mi.us/reports).

35. *Educational Service Provider Policies,* Charter Schools Office, Central Michigan University, July 15, 1999.

36. Leonard C. Wolfe, *Public School Academy Authorizing Bodies: Chartering Authorities, Oversight Bodies and Fiscal Agents: A Framework for Oversight,* Dykema Gossett, P.L.L.C., August 1998 (document prepared for Central Michigan University, Eastern Michigan University, Ferris State University, and Grand Valley State University).

37. Horn and Miron, *Evaluation of the Michigan Public School Initiative,* 58.

38. Peter J. Duitsman, "Comment, The Private Prison Experiment: A Private Sector Solution to Prison Overcrowding," *North Carolina Law Review* 76 (1998): 2218 and 2265, n. 361.

39. The Model Statute and Model Contract are set forth with extensive legal commentary in Ira P. Robbins, "The Legal Dimensions of Private Incarceration," *American University Law Review* 38 (1989): 531–852.

40. See Ellen Simon, "Who's Minding the Rights of Inmates When Justice Goes to the Lowest Bidder?" *Human Rights* 19 (Spring 1992): 22.

41. See, for example, Warren Ratliff, "The Due Process Failure of America's Prison Privatization Statutes," *Seton Hall Legislative Journal* 21 (1997): 371–424; Nicole B. Casarez, "Furthering the Accountability Principle in Privatized Federal Corrections: The Need for Access to Private Prison Records," *University of Michigan Journal of Law Reform* 28 (Winter 1995): 249–303 (argues that Congress should enact legislation to subject private federal prison records to the Freedom of Information Act so that more thorough monitoring can take place); and Laura S. Farris, "Comment, Private Jails in Oklahoma: An Unconstitutional Delegation of Legislative Authority," *Tulsa Law Journal* 33 (Spring & Summer 1998): 959–977.

42. Fox Butterfield, "Private Company to Pull Out of Operating Troubled Prison," *New York Times,* April 27, 2000; Butterfield, "Privately Run Juvenile Prison in Louisiana Is Attacked for Abuse of Six Inmates," *New York Times,* March 27, 2000. A similar story of wider abuses involving Corrections Corporation of America's prison operations in Youngstown, Ohio, is chronicled in Barry Yeoman, "Steeltown Lockdown," *Mother Jones,* May/June 2000, 38–47. For an earlier critical look at CCA's operations, see Simon, "Who's Minding the Rights of Inmates?"

43. See, for example, *Ruiz v. Estelle,* 503 F.Supp. 1265 (S.D. Tex. 1980), *aff'd in part,* 679 F.2d 1115 (5th Cir. 1982). Regarded as the most extensive prison reform order entered by a federal court after what may have been the longest civil rights trial in legal history, it completely overhauled the Texas prison system amidst great public outcry and repeated denunciations against the trial judge. The story of this case from the perspective of the judge who issued the order is told in Frank R. Kemerer, *William Wayne Justice: A Judicial Biography.* See also Steve J. Martin and Sheldon Ekland-Olson, *Texas Prisons: The Walls Came Tumbling Down,* and Ben M. Crouch and James W. Marquart, *An Appeal to Justice: Litigated Reform of Texas Prisons.*

44. For a sobering account of what it's like being a correctional officer in a brutal penal system, see Ted Conover, *Newjack: Guarding Sing Sing.*

45. David Wecht, "Note, Breaking the Code of Deference: Judicial Review of Private Prisons," *Yale Law Journal* 96 (1987): 815–837 (maintaining that strict oversight standards are insufficient, Wecht argues that increased judicial scrutiny of the discretionary practices and decisions of private prison officials is necessary to ensure that concern for profits does not take precedence over the rights of prisoners under the Due Process Clause of the Fourteenth Amendment).

46. At this writing, a case is pending before the U.S. Supreme Court on whether companies that operate prisons under contract with the federal government may be sued for constitutional violations committed by their employees. The U.S. Court of Appeals for the Second Circuit had responded in the affirmative. Noting that private companies deemed to be acting under color of state law are considered state actors and subject to suit for the violation of federal constitutional

rights, the appeals court ruled that it should be no different for companies that are engaging in federal action under contract with the federal government. The case arose when an employee of Correctional Services Corporation (CSC) refused to allow an inmate with a heart condition to use the elevator to reach his room on the fifth floor of a halfway house. The inmate suffered a heart attack while walking up the stairs. He sued CSC for violating his constitutional rights. *Malesko v. Correctional Services Corporation,* 229 F.3d 374 (2nd Cir. 2000), *appeal granted,* 121 S.Ct. 1224 (2001).

47. Martin E. Gold, "The Privatization of Prisons," *Urban Lawyer* 28 (1986): 379–380.

48. *Blumel v. Mylander,* 954 F.Supp. 1547 (M.D. Fla. 1997).

49. 42 U.S.C. §1437f(o) (2000).

50. 24 C.F.R. §982.401 (2000).

51. See Mark A. Malaspina, "Note, Demanding the Best: How to Restructure the Section 8 Household-Based Rental Assistance Program," *Yale Law and Policy Review* 14 (1996): 287–351.

52. 24 C.F.R. §982.310(a)–(e) (2000).

53. *Gallman v. Pierce,* 639 F.Supp. 472 (N.D. Cal. 1986), p. 481.

54. *Gorsuch Homes, Inc. v. Wooten,* 597 N.E.2d 554 (Ohio App. 1992), p. 558. In this case, the court ruled in part that state eviction procedures did not satisfy the requirements of procedural due process under the Due Process Clause of the Fourteenth Amendment. Citing the U.S. Supreme Court's seminal decision in *Goldberg v. Kelly,* 397 U.S. 254 (1970), that state-conferred benefits cannot be taken away without complying with due process requirements, the Ohio appeals court concluded that before a tenant can be evicted from her apartment because of failure to pay a disputed repair bill, the tenant must be given an opportunity to confront and to cross-examine adverse witnesses before a neutral adjudicator.

55. *Franklin Tower One v. N.M.,* 725 A.2d 1104 (N.J. 1999). In the course of reaching its decision in favor of the tenant, the Supreme Court of New Jersey noted that while Congress did not require landlords to participate in the Section 8 program, states may do so in the interest of ending housing discrimination against low-income families. New Jersey has a statute that prohibits a private landlord from refusing to rent or lease a house or apartment because of the prospective tenant's source of income. The court suggested, but did not rule, that this law might prohibit a private landlord from refusing to participate in the Section 8 program.

56. *Anast v. Commonwealth Apartments,* 956 F.Supp. 792 (N.D. Ill. 1997).

57. 20 U.S.C. §1412 (a)(10)(B)(ii) (2000).

58. 34 C.F.R. §300.401(b) and (c) (2000).

59. See, for example, *Letter to Garvin,* 30 Indiv. with Disabilities Educ. Law Rep. 609 (May 14, 1998).

60. *Council of Children with Special Needs, Inc. v. Cooperman,* 501 A.2d 575 (N.J. Super. Ct. App. Div. 1985).

61. *Ross v. Allen,* 515 F.Supp. 972 (S.D.N.Y. 1981).

62. 20 U.S.C. §1413(a)(5) (2000). For a discussion, see Laura Rothstein, "School Choice and Children with Disabilities," *School Choice and Social Contro-*

versy: Politics, Policy, and Law, ed. Stephen D. Sugarman and Frank R. Kemerer, 334–341.

63. Jay P. Heubert, "Schools without Rules? Charter Schools, Federal Disability Law, and the Paradoxes of Deregulation," *Harvard Civil Rights–Civil Liberties Law Review* 32 (1997): 320. Heubert notes that state law may place responsibility for providing special education services on autonomous charter schools or on the school district in which the children with disabilities reside or, as in the case of Massachusetts, split the difference. In Massachusetts, autonomous charter schools are required to pay the costs of educating children who can be served in other public school settings, but the district of residence has responsibility for those who need private school placement. Mass. Gen. Laws Ann. ch. 71, §89(t) (West 2000).

64. Whether for-profit educational management organizations actually deliver is another question. Scathing reports have surfaced in recent years asserting that Edison Schools, Sabis International, and Beacon Management significantly shortchange children with severe disabilities in Massachusetts in the interest of profits and that conflict-of-interest considerations prevent local and state authorities from intervening on behalf of parents. Nancy J. Zollers and Arun K. Ramanathan, "For-Profit Charter Schools and Students with Disabilities: The Sordid Side of the Business of Schooling," *Phi Delta Kappan,* December 1998, 297–304. See also Peggy Farber, "The Edison Project Scores—and Stumbles—in Boston," *Phi Delta Kappan,* March 1998, 506–511. For a general discussion of the problems school choice may pose for children with disabilities, see Rothstein, "School Choice and Children with Disabilities."

65. Ohio Rev. Code Ann. §§3313.974(C) and 3313.977(B) (West 2000).

66. *Pierce v. Society of Sisters,* 268 U.S. 510 (1925).

67. Ibid., p. 534.

68. *Farrington v. Tokushige,* 273 U.S. 284 (1927).

69. For a list of decisions favoring the state, see *New Life Baptist Church Academy v. East Longmeadow,* 885 F.2d 940 (lst Cir. 1989), pp. 950–951. The most notable exception to general deference to the state is a 1976 Ohio Supreme Court ruling, *State v. Whisner,* 351 N.E.2d 750 (Ohio 1976) (state board's minimum regulations for private elementary schools were so intrusive as to violate the parents' right to freedom of religion and their right to control their children's upbringing).

70. *Employment Division, Department of Human Resources of Oregon v. Smith,* 494 U.S. 872 (1990).

71. *Wisconsin v. Yoder,* 406 U.S. 205 (1972).

72. *City of Boerne v. Flores,* 521 U.S. 507 (1997).

73. Tex. Civ. Prac. & Rem. Code §§110.001–012 (Vernon 2001).

74. Wis. Stat. §118.165 (2000).

75. Wis. Stat. §119.23(7)(a) (2000).

76. *An Evaluation: The Milwaukee Parental Choice Program,* Wisconsin Legislative Audit Bureau, February 2000 (http://www.legis.state.wi.us/lab/windex .htm).

77. Alex Molnar, "Unfinished Business in Milwaukee," *Education Week,* November 17, 1999.

78. Ohio Admin. Code Ann. §3301-35-04 (West 2000). The statewide testing requirement is found in Ohio Rev. Code Ann. §3301.16 (West 2000) and has been upheld as applied to private schools chartered by the state. *Ohio Association of Independent Schools v. Goff,* 92 F.3d 419 (6th Cir. 1996), *cert. denied,* 520 U.S. 1104 (1997).

79. Ohio Admin. Code Ann. §3301-35-08 (West 2000). The Ohio Supreme Court decision striking down extensive standards imposed on religious private schools is *State v. Whisner,* 351 N.E.2d 750 (Ohio 1976). The court agreed with a "born again" fundamentalist Christian sect that the standards imposed on their school violated both parent free exercise of religion and the right of parents to control their children's upbringing. The court noted that the standards allocated instructional time "almost to the minute" in a prescribed curriculum, required that "all activities" of the private school must conform with board of education policies, and required school-community interaction contrary to the school's desire to remain separate from the community. *Whisner* is generally regarded as the exception to general judicial deference to state regulation of religious and nonreligious private schools.

80. Ohio Rev. Code Ann. §3313.976(A) (West 2000).

81. Ohio Rev. Code Ann. §§3313.976–3313.977 (West 2000).

82. One way to amend state constitutions is through the constitutional initiative process, whereby voters in a general election can bypass the legislature. But the initiative process has not been successful to date in enacting voucher programs and constraining state bodies from regulating them. Such measures have been soundly defeated in Oregon (1990), Colorado (1992), California (1993 and 2000), Washington (1996), and Michigan (2000). Furthermore, only twenty-three states allow the state constitution to be amended through the initiative process.

83. Bruno V. Manno et al., "Charter School Accountability: Problems and Prospects," *Charter Schools in Action,* Final Report, Part IV, July 1997, p. 12.

8. THE POLITICS OF CHOICE AND A PROPOSED SCHOOL CHOICE POLICY

1. States differ in this process. Some states do not have subcommittees, and Nebraska has only a single legislative chamber.

2. Anne Schneider and Helen Ingram, "The Social Construction of Target Regulations: Implications for Politics and Policy," *American Political Science Review* 87 (June 1993): 334–347.

3. Terry Moe, *Schools, Vouchers, and the American Public,* Table 2.1.

4. Ibid., Chapter 6.

5. Hubert Morken and Jo Renée Formicola, *The Politics of School Choice,* 187.

6. http://www.opensecrets.org/parties/softsearch_2000.htm. An investigation of states that require reporting of contributions by groups to state candidates shows that in every state, teacher organizations along with trial lawyers are the largest donors to Democratic candidates for office. Teacher organizations are par-

ticularly important to black elected officials. See Morken and Formicola, *The Politics of School Choice,* 221.

7. "NEA Trains Political Guns on NRA," *Education Week,* July 12, 2000.

8. "AFT Backs Away from Charter School Support," *Education Week,* July 12, 2000.

9. Albert Shanker, "Restructuring Our Schools," *Peabody Journal of Education* 65 (1988): 1.

10. "AFT Backs Away."

11. R.I. Gen. Laws §§16-77-3(c), 16-77-4.1, 16-77-5(c) (2000).

12. R.I. Gen. Laws §§16-77-3(d) and (g); 16-77-4(b)(12); 16-77-11(4), (7), and (14) (2000).

13. All of these organizations have materials on their Web site indicating their reasons for rejecting vouchers. For example, see http://www.pta.org/Programs/bbvouchers.htm; http://www.aauw.org/1000/schlvouc.html; http://www.november2000.org/issues/education/; http://www.pfaw.org/issues/education/voucher.criteria.shtml.

14. John E. Coons and Stephen D. Sugarman, *Making School Choice Work for All Families,* 84.

15. http://www.pfaw.org/issues/education/

16. Moe, *Schools, Vouchers,* Table 7.2.

17. Morken and Formicola, *The Politics of School Choice,* 220–221.

18. Ibid., 224–225.

19. Ibid., 4.

20. Coons and Sugarman, *Making School Choice Work for All.*

21. Harlan Hahn and Sheldon Kamieniecki, *Referendum Voting: Social Status and Policy Preferences.*

22. For a discussion of the charter school success and the role of political entrepreneurs see Michael Mintrom, *Policy Entrepreneurs and School Choice.*

23. As we pointed out in the preface to this book, John Coons and Stephen Sugarman are among the writers who have influenced our thinking on school choice. This is particularly true when it comes to the development of a policy proposal that might meet the goals and objectives we believe to be most important. In their books, *Scholarships for Children* and *Making School Choice Work for All,* Coons and Sugarman provide and justify a policy that provides vouchers for all children and gives preferences to low-income children. Our proposal draws heavily from theirs, and we urge the reader to get their books for an extensive justification of their ideas.

24. An alternative to statewide legislation would be for the legislature to authorize an experiment that included a major metropolitan area. The advantage of an experiment is the greater likelihood the courts would accept it as constitutional.

25. For a detailed discussion of accountability issues, see Frank R. Kemerer, "School Choice Accountability," in *School Choice and Social Controversy: Politics, Policy, and Law,* ed. Stephen D. Sugarman and Frank R. Kemerer, 174–211.

26. Ariz. Rev. Stat. §43-1089 (2001). The Arizona Supreme Court held that the statute does not violate either the federal or state constitution's religion clauses. *Kotterman v. Killian,* 972 P.2d 606 (Ariz.), *cert. denied,* 528 U.S. 921 (1999).

27. Ariz. Admin. Code R7-2-316 (2000).

28. Coons and Sugarman, *Scholarships for Children,* 27.

29. Laura F. Rothstein, "School Choice and Students with Disabilities," in *School Choice and Social Controversy,* ed. Stephen D. Sugarman and Frank R. Kemerer, 347–348.

30. Henry M. Levin, "Educational Vouchers: Effectiveness, Choice, and Costs," *Journal of Policy Analysis and Management* 17 (1998): 386.

31. For example, assume that a family is choosing between School A and School B and that the family prefers School B to School A. However, School B is much farther from the family's residence than School A, and it would cost the state an additional $1,000 per year to bus the student to School B. If the difference in value between School B and School A is less than $1,000 to the family, then society is better off if the family sends its child to School A.

32. User charges have been shown to be an effective, efficient, and equitable tool to allocate services to low-income families. For example, the World Bank generally asks villages in less industrialized countries to pay a small portion of the costs of constructing a school, hospital, or irrigation system because even a small charge encourages the village to decide which construction project it values most. For discussions and examples of user charges for publicly funded services see R. Kenneth Godwin, "Charges for Merit Goods: Third World Family Planning," *Journal of Public Policy* 11 (1991): 415–429, and Richard Rose, "Charges as Contested Signals," *Journal of Public Policy* 9 (1989): 261–286.

33. Coons and Sugarman have proposed a different method for dealing with the home schooling issue. Their proposal allows the state to provide a smaller voucher to students for whom the majority of their instructors are their own relatives. *Scholarships for Children,* 10.

34. "Vouchers Stall as Florida Schools Up Their Scores," *Education Week,* July 12, 2000, pp. 1, 33, 34.

35. Morken and Formicola, *The Politics of School Choice,* 83.

36. Diane Ravitch, "Somebody's Children: Educational Opportunity for *All* American Children," in *New Schools for a New Century: The Redesign of Urban Education,* ed. Diane Ravitch and Joseph P. Viteritti, 252.

37. Department of Education, Public Affairs, "State of American Education," remarks prepared for Richard W. Riley, secretary of education, speech delivered at Georgetown University, February 15, 1994. Cited in Ravitch, "Somebody's Children," 252.

38. Ravitch, "Somebody's Children," 252.

39. Ibid., 253.

40. Ibid.

Selected References

Alexander, K. L., and A. M. Pallas. "Private Schools and Public Policy: New Evidence on Public and Private High Schools." *Sociology of Education* 56 (1983): 170–182.

Ambler, Eric. "Who Benefits from Educational Choice: Some Evidence from Europe." *Journal of Policy Analysis and Management* 13 (1994): 454–476.

Armor, David J. *Forced Justice.* New York: Oxford University Press, 1995.

Ascher, Carol, and Nathalis Wamba. "An Emerging Market for a New Model of Equity?" Paper presented at the School Choice and Racial Diversity Conference, Teachers College, Columbia University, New York, May 7, 2000.

Ball, Stephen, Richard Bowe, and Sharon Gewirtz. "School Choice, Social Class and Distinction: The Realization of Social Advantage in Education." *Journal of Education Policy* 11 (1996): 89–112.

Banks, James A. *An Introduction to Multicultural Education.* Boston: Allyn & Bacon, 1994.

Barber, Benjamin. *An Aristocracy of Everyone: The Politics of Education and the Future of America.* New York: Ballantine Books, 1992.

———. *Strong Democracy: Participatory Politics for a New Age.* Berkeley: University of California Press, 1984.

Bass, Jack. *Unlikely Heroes.* New York: Simon and Schuster, 1981.

Beale, L. K. "Note, Charter Schools, Common Schools, and the Washington State Constitution." *Washington Law Review* 72 (1997): 535–566.

Bernstein, Richard J., ed. *Habermas and Modernity.* Cambridge, Mass.: MIT Press, 1985.

Betts, Julian R., and Jamie L. Shkolnik. "The Behavioral Effects of Variations in Class Size: The Case of Math Teachers." *Educational Evaluation and Policy Analysis* 21 (1999): 193–213.

Blacker, David. "Fanaticism and Schooling." *American Journal of Education* 106 (1998): 241–272.

Boaz, David, and R. Morris Barrett. *What Would a School Voucher Buy? The Real Cost of Private Schools.* Washington, D.C.: Cato Institute, 1996.

Boger, John C. "Willful Colorblindness: The New Racial Piety and the Resegre-

gation of Public Schools." *North Carolina Law Review* 78 (2000): 1719–1796.

Bowen, William G., and Derek Bok. *The Shape of the River.* Princeton, N.J.: Princeton University Press, 1998.

Bower, Elizabeth J. "Note, Answering the Call: Wake County's Commitment to Diversity in Education." *North Carolina Law Review* 78 (2000): 2026–2052.

Bowles, Samuel, and Henry M. Levin. "The Determinants of Scholastic Achievement." *Journal of Human Resources* 3 (1968): 3–24.

Brewer, Dominic J., et al. "Estimating the Cost of National Class Size Reductions under Different Policy Alternatives." *Educational Evaluation and Policy Analysis* 21 (1999): 179–192.

Bryk, Anthony S., Valerie E. Lee, and Peter B. Holland. *Catholic Schools and the Common Good.* Cambridge, Mass.: Harvard University Press, 1993.

Callan, Eamonn. *Creating Citizens: Political Education and Liberal Democracy.* Oxford: Clarendon Press, 1997.

Carter, Stephen L. *The Culture of Disbelief: How American Law and Politics Trivialize Religious Devotion.* New York: HarperCollins, 1993.

———. *The Dissent of the Governed: A Meditation on Law, Religion, and Loyalty.* Cambridge, Mass.: Harvard University Press, 1998.

Casarez, Nicole B. "Furthering the Accountability Principle in Privatized Federal Corrections: The Need for Access to Private Prison Records." *University of Michigan Journal of Law Reform* 28 (1995): 249–303.

Choper, Jesse. "School Choice: Federal Constitutional Issues under the Religion and Speech Clauses of the First Amendment." In *School Choice and Social Controversy: Politics, Policy, and Law,* ed. Stephen D. Sugarman and Frank R. Kemerer, 235–265. Washington, D.C.: Brookings Institution Press, 1999.

Chubb, John, and Terry Moe. *Politics, Markets and America's Schools.* Washington, D.C.: Brookings Institution Press, 1990.

Cobb, Casey D., and Gene V. Glass. "Ethnic Segregation in Arizona Charter Schools." *Education Policy Analysis Archives* 7, no. 1 (1999) (http://epaa.asu.edu/epaa/v7n1/).

Coleman, James S. *The Evaluation of Equality of Educational Opportunity.* Santa Monica, Calif.: Rand Corporation, 1968.

Coleman, James S., et al. *Equality of Educational Opportunity.* Washington, D.C.: U.S. GPO, 1966.

———, eds. *Redesigning American Education.* Boulder, Colo.: Westview Press, 1997.

Coleman, James S., and Thomas Hoffer. *Public and Private High Schools.* New York: Basic Books, 1987.

Coleman, James S., Thomas Hoffer, and Sally Kilgore. *High School Achievement.* New York: Basic Books, 1982.

Comer, James P. *Waiting for a Miracle: Why Schools Can't Solve Our Problems and How We Can.* New York: Dutton, 1997.

Comer, James P., Norris Haynes, Edward T. Joyner, and Michael Ben-Avie, eds.

Rallying the Whole Village: The Comer Process for Reforming Education.
New York: Teachers College Press, 1996.

"Comment, School Choice Vouchers and the Establishment Clause." *Alabama Law Review* 58 (1994): 543–574.

Committee on Education Finance, National Research Council. *Making Money Matter: Financing America's Schools,* ed. Helen F. Ladd and Janet S. Hansen. Washington, D.C.: National Academy Press, 1999.

Conover, Ted. *Newjack: Guarding Sing Sing.* New York: Random House, 2000.

Cook, Philip J., and Jens Ludwig. "The Burden of 'Acting White': Do Black Adolescents Disparage Academic Achievement?" In *The Black-White Test Score Gap,* ed. Christopher Jencks and Meredith Phillips, 375–400. Washington, D.C.: Brookings Institution Press, 1998.

Coons, John E., and Stephen D. Sugarman. *Making School Choice Work for All Families.* San Francisco: Pacific Research Institute for Public Policy, 1999.

———. *Scholarships for Children.* Berkeley, Calif.: Institute for Governmental Policy Studies.

Courant, Paul N., and Susanna Loeb. "Centralization of School Finance in Michigan." *Journal of Policy Analysis and Management* 16 (1997): 114–136.

Crittenden, Brian. *Parents, the State, and the Right to Educate.* Carlton, Victoria: Melbourne University Press, 1988.

Croley, Stephen P. "The Majoritarian Difficulty: Elective Judiciaries and the Rule of Law." *University of Chicago Law Review* 62 (1995): 689–790.

Crouch, Ben M., and James W. Marquart. *An Appeal to Justice: Litigated Reform of Texas Prisons.* Austin: University of Texas Press, 1989.

CSR Research Consortium. *Class Size Reduction in California: Early Findings Signal Promise and Concern.* Santa Monica, Calif.: Rand Corporation, 1999.

Dewey, John. *Democracy and Education.* New York: MacMillan Company, 1916.

Downes, Thomas A. "Evaluating the Impact of School Finance Reform on the Provision of Public Education: The California Case." *National Tax Journal* 45 (1992): 405–420.

Duitsman, Peter J. "Comment, The Private Prison Experiment: A Private Sector Solution to Prison Overcrowding." *North Carolina Law Review* 76 (1998): 2209–2265.

Duncombe, William, and John Yinger. "Why Is It So Hard to Help Central City Schools?" *Journal of Policy Analysis and Management* 16 (1997): 85–113.

Eisdorfer, Stephen. "Public School Choice and Racial Integration." *Seton Hall Law Review* 24 (1993): 937–957.

Evans, William N., and Robert M. Schwab. "Finishing High School and Starting College: Do Catholic Schools Make a Difference?" *Quarterly Journal of Economics* 100 (1995): 966–991.

Fairlie, Robert W. "Racial Segregation and the Private/Public School Choice." Paper presented at the School Choice and Racial Diversity Conference, Teachers College, Columbia University, New York, May 7, 2000.

Farris, Laura S. "Comment, Private Jails in Oklahoma: An Unconstitutional Delegation of Legislative Authority." *Tulsa Law Journal* 33 (1998): 959–977.

Fine, Melinda. *Habits of Mind: Struggling over Values in America's Classrooms.* San Francisco: Jossey-Bass, 1995.

Fischel, W. A. "Did Serrano Cause Proposition 13?" *National Tax Journal* 42 (1989): 465–473.

Fisher, David. "Note, Parental Rights and the Right to Intimate Association." *Hastings Law Journal* 48 (1997): 399–433.

Fiske, Edward B., and Helen F. Ladd. *When Schools Compete: A Cautionary Tale.* Washington, D.C.: Brookings, 2000.

Fordham, Signithia, and John U. Ogbu. "Black Students' School Success: Coping with the Burden of 'Acting White.'" *Urban Review* 18 (1986): 176–206.

Friedman, Milton. *Capitalism and Freedom.* Chicago: University of Chicago Press, 1962.

Fuller, Bruce, and Richard F. Elmore, eds. *Who Chooses? Who Loses? Culture, Institutions, and the Unequal Effects of School Choice.* New York: Teachers College Press, 1996.

Futterman, David. "Note, School Choice and the Religion Clauses." *Georgetown Law Journal* 81 (1993): 711–740.

Galston, William. *Liberal Purposes.* Cambridge: Cambridge University Press, 1991.

———. "Two Concepts of Liberalism." *Ethics* 105 (April 1995): 516–534.

Gamoran, Adam. "Student Achievement in Public Magnet, Public Comprehensive, and Private City High Schools." *Educational Evaluation and Policy Analysis* 18 (1996): 1–18.

Gilles, Stephen. "On Educating Children: A Parentalist Manifesto." *University of Chicago Law Review* 63 (1966): 937–1034.

Gittell, Marilyn J., ed. *Strategies for School Equity: Strategies for Creating Productive Schools in a Just Society.* New Haven, Conn.: Yale University Press, 1998.

Glenn, Charles L. *The Myth of the Common School.* Amherst: University of Massachusetts Press, 1988.

Godwin, R. Kenneth. "Charges for Merit Goods: Third World Family Planning." *Journal of Public Policy* 11 (1991): 415–429.

Godwin, R. Kenneth, Carrie Ausbrooks, and Valerie Martinez. "Are Public Schools More Effective Than Private Schools in Teaching Political Tolerance?" *Phi Delta Kappan* 82 (2001): 542–546.

Gold, Martin E. "The Privatization of Prisons." *Urban Lawyer* 28 (1986): 359–399.

Goldberger, Arthur S., and Glen G. Cain. "The Causal Analysis of Cognitive Outcomes in the Coleman, Hoffer and Kilgore Report." *Sociology of Education* 55 (1982): 103–122.

Goldring, Ellen B., and Rina Shapira. "Choice, Empowerment, and Involvement: What Satisfies Parents?" *Educational Forum* 58 (1993): 276–281.

Green, Steven K. "The Blaine Amendment Reconsidered." *American Journal of Legal History* 36 (1992): 38–69.

Greene, Jay P. "Choosing Integration." Paper presented at the School Choice and

Racial Diversity Conference, Teachers College, Columbia University, New York, May 7, 2000.

———. *An Evaluation of the Florida A-Plus Accountability and School Choice Program.* New York: Manhattan Institute, 2001.

Gutmann, Amy. *Democratic Education.* Princeton, N.J.: Princeton University Press, 1987.

———. "Undemocratic Education." In *Liberalism and the Moral Way of Life,* ed. Nancy L. Rosenbaum, 71–88. Cambridge, Mass.: Harvard University Press, 1989.

———, ed. *Multiculturalism: Examining the Politics of Recognition.* Princeton, N.J.: Princeton University Press, 1994.

Hahn, Harlan, and Sheldon Kamieniecki. *Referendum Voting: Social Status and Policy Preferences.* Westport, Conn.: Greenwood, 1987.

Hannaway, Jane. "The Organization and Management of Public and Catholic Schools: Looking Inside the 'Black Box.'" *International Journal of Education* 15 (1991): 463–481.

Hanushek, Eric A. "The Evidence on Class Size." Occasional Paper Number 98-1, W. Allen Wallis Institute of Political Economy. Rochester, N.Y.: University of Rochester, 1998.

———. "Some Findings from an Independent Investigation of the Tennessee STAR Experiment and from Other Investigations of Class Size Effects." *Educational Evaluation and Policy Analysis* 21 (1999): 143–163.

———. "When School Finance 'Reform' May Not Be Good Policy." *Harvard Journal on Legislation* 28 (1991): 423–455.

———, et al. *Making Schools Work: Improving Performance and Controlling Costs.* Washington, D.C.: Brookings, 1994.

Hanushek, Eric A., and Dale W. Jorgenson, eds. *Improving America's Schools: The Role of Incentives.* Washington, D.C.: National Academy Press, 1996.

Henderson, Anne. *Parent Participation and Student Achievement: The Evidence Grows.* Columbia, Md.: National Committee for Citizens in Education, 1995.

Heubert, Jay P. "Schools without Rules? Charter Schools, Federal Disability Law, and the Paradoxes of Deregulation." *Harvard Civil Rights–Civil Liberties Law Review* 32 (1997): 301–353.

Hill, Paul T., Lawrence C. Pierce, and James W. Guthrie. *Reinventing Public Education: How Contracting Can Transform America's Schools.* Chicago: University of Chicago Press, 1997.

Hoffer, Thomas, Andrew M. Greeley, and James S. Coleman. "Achievement Growth in Public and Catholic Schools." *Sociology of Education* 58 (1985): 74–97.

Horn, Jerry, and Gary Miron. *Evaluation of the Michigan Public School Initiative.* Kalamazoo: Western Michigan University, January 1999.

Horton, John, and Susan Mendus, eds. *Aspects of Toleration.* London: Methuen, 1985.

Hoxby, Caroline Minter. "Are Efficiency and Equity in School Finance Substitutes or Complements?" *Journal of Economic Perspectives* 10 (1996): 51–72.

———. "Does Competition among Public Schools Benefit Students and Taxpay-

ers?" Working Paper 4978. Cambridge, Mass.: National Bureau of Economic Research, 1994.

———. "How Teachers' Unions Affect Education Production." *Quarterly Journal of Economics* 111 (1996): 671–718.

Hubsch, Allen W. "The Emerging Right to Education under State Constitutional Law." *Temple Law Review* 65 (1992): 1325–1348.

Jencks, Christopher, and Meredith Phillips. "The Black-White Test Score Gap: An Introduction." In *The Black-White Test Score Gap,* ed. Christopher Jencks and Meredith Phillips, 1–51. Washington, D.C.: Brookings Institution Press, 1998.

———, eds. *The Black-White Test Score Gap.* Washington, D.C.: Brookings Institution Press, 1998.

Kalman, Laura. *The Strange Career of Legal Liberalism.* New Haven, Conn.: Yale University Press, 1996.

Kemerer, Frank R. "The Constitutional Dimension of School Vouchers." *Texas Forum on Civil Liberties & Civil Rights* 3 (1998): 137–185.

———. "State Constitutions and School Vouchers." *West's Education Law Reporter* 120 (1997): 1–42.

———. *William Wayne Justice: A Judicial Biography.* Austin: University of Texas Press, 1991.

Kemerer, Frank R., and Carrie Y. Ausbrooks. *Comparing Public and Private Schools: Student Survey Report.* Denton, Tex.: Center for the Study of Educational Reform, November 1996.

Kemerer, Frank R., Joe B. Hairston, and Keith Lauerman. "Vouchers and Private School Autonomy." *Journal of Law and Education* 21 (1992): 601–627.

Kemerer, Frank R., Valerie Martinez, and Kenneth Godwin. *Comparing Public and Private Schools: Teacher Survey Results.* Denton, Tex.: Center for the Study of Educational Reform, January 1997.

Kemerer, Frank R., and Jim Walsh. *The Educator's Guide to Texas School Law,* 5th ed. Austin: University of Texas Press, 2000.

Kluger, Richard. *Simple Justice.* New York: Knopf, 1975.

Kohlberg, Lawrence. "Moral Reasoning." In *Educating the Democratic Mind,* ed. Walter C. Parker, 201–222. Albany: State University of New York Press, 1996.

Kozol, Jonathan. *Savage Inequalities: Children in America's Schools.* New York: Harper Perennial, 1992.

Lane, Linda L. "Comment, The Parental Rights Movement." *University of Colorado Law Review* 69 (1998): 825–849.

Lankford, Hamilton, and James Wyckoff. "Primary and Secondary School Choice among Public and Religious Alternatives." *Economics of Education Review* 11 (1992): 317–337.

———. "Primary and Secondary School Choice among Public and Religious Alternatives." In *Market Approaches to Education: Vouchers and School Choice,* ed. Elchanan Cohn, 393–423. New York: Pergamon, 1997.

———. "Why Are Schools Racially Segregated? Implications for School Choice Policies." Paper presented at the School Choice and Racial Diversity Conference, Teachers College, Columbia University, New York, May 7, 2000.

Lasch, Christopher. *Haven in a Heartless World: The Family Besieged*. New York: Basic Books, 1979.

Lee, Valerie E., Julia B. Smith, and Robert Croninger. "How High School Organization Influences the Equitable Distribution of Learning in Mathematics and Science." *Sociology of Education* 70 (1997): 128–150.

Levin, Betsy. "Race and School Choice." In *School Choice and Social Controversy,* ed. Stephen D. Sugarman and Frank R. Kemerer, 266–299. Washington, D.C.: Brookings Institution Press, 1999.

Levin, Henry M. "The Economics of Educational Choice." *Economics of Education Review* 10, no. 1 (1990): 137–158.

———. "Educational Vouchers: Effectiveness, Choice, and Costs." *Journal of Policy Analysis and Management* 17 (1998): 373–392.

———. "The Public-Private Nexus in Education." *American Behavioral Scientist* 43 (1999): 124–137.

Levin, Henry M., and Cyrus E. Driver. "Costs of an Educational Voucher System." *Educational Economics* 5, no. 3 (1997): 265–293.

Levin, Henry M., Harold Glass, and Greg Meister. *Cost Effectiveness of Four Educational Interventions*. Stanford, Calif.: Center for Educational Research at Stanford, 1984.

Lieberman, Myron. *The Teacher Unions: How the NEA and AFT Sabotage Reform and Hold Students, Parents, Teachers, and Taxpayers Hostage to Bureaucracy*. New York: Free Press, 1997.

Locke, John. *A Letter Concerning Toleration*. Indianapolis: Hackett Press, 1983.

———. *Some Thoughts Concerning Education,* ed., with introduction by, Ruth W. Grant and Nathan Tarcov. Indianapolis: Hackett Press, 1996.

———. *Two Treatises of Government with a Letter on Toleration,* ed. J. W. Gough. Oxford: Basil Blackwell, 1956.

Lutz, Sabrina. "The Impact of School Choice." *Equity and Excellence in Education* 29 (1996): 48–54.

McClosky, Herbert, and Anthony Brill. *Dimensions of Tolerance*. New York: Sage, 1983.

McDonnell, Lorraine M., P. Michael Timpane, and Roger Benjamin, eds. *Rediscovering the Democratic Purposes of Education*. Lawrence: University of Kansas Press, 2000.

MacIntyre, Alasdair. *After Virtue: A Study in Moral Theory*. London: Duckworth, 1981.

Malaspina, Mark A. "Note, Demanding the Best: How to Restructure the Section 8 Household-Based Rental Assistance Program." *Yale Law and Policy Review* 14 (1996): 287–351.

Mann, Horace. *Lectures on Education*. New York: Arno Press, 1969.

Manno, Bruno V., et al. "Charter School Accountability: Problems and Prospects." *Charter Schools in Action,* Final Report, Part IV. Hudson Institute, 1997.

Manski, Charles F. "Educational Choice (Vouchers) and Social Mobility." *Economics of Education Review* 11 (1992): 351–369.

Marcus, George, et al. *With Malice toward Some: How People Make Civil Liberties Judgments*. Cambridge and New York: Cambridge University Press, 1995.

Martin, Stephen J., and Sheldon Ekland-Olson. *Texas Prisons: The Walls Came Tumbling Down.* Austin: Texas Monthly Press, 1987.

Martinez, Valerie, et al. "The Consequences of School Choice: Who Leaves and Who Stays in the Inner City." *Social Science Quarterly* 76 (1995): 485–501.

Massey, Douglas S., and Nancy A. Denton. *American Apartheid: Segregation and the Making of the Underclass.* Cambridge, Mass.: Harvard University Press, 1993.

Meier, Kenneth J., J. L. Polinard, and Robert D. Wrinkle. "Bureaucracy and Organizational Performance: Causality Arguments about Public Schools." *American Journal of Political Science* 44 (2000): 590–602.

Mickelson, Roslyn Arlin. "Subverting *Swann*: First- and Second-Generation Segregation in the Charlotte-Mecklenburg Schools." *American Educational Research Journal* 38, no. 2 (2001): 1–38.

Mill, John Stuart. *On Liberty.* Indianapolis: Hackett Press, 1978.

Mintrom, Michael. *Policy Entrepreneurs and School Choice.* Washington, D.C.: Georgetown University Press, 2000.

Moe, Terry. *Schools, Vouchers, and the American Public.* Washington, D.C.: Brookings, 2001.

———, ed. *Private Vouchers.* Stanford, Calif.: Hoover Institution, 1995.

Molnar, Alex, et al. "Evaluating the SAGE Program: A Pilot Program in Targeted Pupil-Teacher Reduction in Wisconsin." *Educational Evaluation and Policy Analysis* 21 (1999): 165–177.

Morken, Hubert, and Jo Renée Formicola. *The Politics of School Choice.* London: Rowman & Littlefield, 1999.

Mosteller, Frederick, and Daniel P. Moynihan, eds. *On Equality of Educational Opportunity.* New York: Random House, 1972.

Mulhall, Stephen, and Adam Swift. *Liberals and Communitarians.* Oxford: Blackwell, 1992.

Muraskin, Lana, and Stephanie Stullich. *Final Report: Barriers, Budgets, and Costs Using Private Schools to Alleviate Overcrowding in Public Schools.* Washington, D.C.: U.S. Department of Education, 1998.

National Center for Education Statistics. *The Condition of Education, 1997.* Washington, D.C.: Department of Education, 1997.

———. *Private School Universe, 1997–98.* Washington, D.C.: U.S. Department of Education, 1999.

Neal, Derek. "The Effects of Catholic Secondary Schooling on Educational Achievement." *Journal of Labor Economics* 15 (1997): 98–123.

Nechyba, Thomas J. "Public School Finance in a General Equilibrium Tiebout World: Equalization Programs, Peer Effects, and Private School Vouchers." Working Paper 5642. Cambridge, Mass.: National Bureau of Economic Research, 1996.

Neito, Sonia. "Moving beyond Tolerance in Multicultural Education." *Multicultural Education* 1 (1994): 9–38.

"Note, Segregation Academies and State Action." *Yale Law Journal* 82 (1973): 1436–1461.

"Note, The Constitutionality of Race-Conscious Admissions Programs in Elementary and Secondary Schools." *Harvard Law Review* 112 (1999): 940–957.

O'Brien, Molly T. "Private School Tuition Vouchers and the Realities of Racial Politics." *Tennessee Law Review* 64 (1997): 359–407.

Ogbu, John U. "Class Stratification, Racial Stratification and Schooling." In *Class, Race and Gender in American Education,* ed. L. Weis, 163–182. Buffalo: State University of New York Press, 1988.

———. "Racial Stratification and Education in the United States: Why Inequality Persists." *Teachers College Record* 96 (1994): 264–298.

Orfield, Gary. "Unexpected Costs and Uncertain Gains of Dismantling Desegregation." In *Dismantling Desegregation,* ed. Gary Orfield and Susan Eaton, 73–114. New York: Free Press, 1996.

Orfield, Gary, et al. *Deepening Segregation in American Public Schools.* Cambridge, Mass.: Harvard Project on School Desegregation, 1997.

———. *The Growth of Segregation in American Schools: Changing Patterns of Separation and Poverty since 1968.* Washington, D.C.: National School Boards of Education, 1993.

Orfield, Gary, and John T. Yun. *Resegregation in American Schools.* Cambridge, Mass.: Harvard University Civil Rights Project, 1999.

Pangle, Lorraine Smith, and Thomas L. Pangle. "What the American Founders Have to Teach Us about Schooling for Democratic Citizenship." In *Rediscovering the Democratic Purposes of Education,* ed. Lorraine M. McDonnell, P. Michael Timpane, and Roger Benjamin. Lawrence: University of Kansas Press, 2000.

Parry, Taryn R. "Will Pursuit of Higher Quality Sacrifice Equal Opportunity in Education? An Analysis of the Education Voucher System in Chile." *Social Science Quarterly* 77 (1996): 821–841.

Patterson, James T. *Brown v. Board of Education: A Civil Rights Milestone and Its Troubled Legacy.* New York: Oxford University Press, 2001.

Payne, Kevin J., and Bruce J. Biddle. "Poor School Funding, Child Poverty, and Mathematics Achievement." *Educational Researcher* 28 (1999): 4–13.

Peltason, J. W. *Fifty-eight Lonely Men: Southern Federal Judges and School Desegregation.* New York: Harcourt, Brace & World, 1961.

Peshkin, Alan. *God's Choice: The Total World of a Fundamentalist Christian School.* Chicago: University of Chicago Press, 1986.

Peterson, Paul E., and Bryan C. Hassel, eds. *Learning from School Choice.* Washington, D.C.: Brookings, 1998.

Phillips, Derek L. *Looking Backward: A Critical Appraisal of Communitarian Thought.* Princeton, N.J.: Princeton University Press, 1993.

Putting Children First. 2 vols. Albany: Reports prepared for the New York State Special Commission on Education Structure, Policies, and Practices, 1993.

Racial Isolation in the Public Schools. Washington, D.C.: United States Commission on Civil Rights, 1967.

Rasell, Edith, and Richard Rothstein, eds. *Redesigning American Education.* Washington, D.C.: Economic Policy Institute.

Ratliff, Warren. "The Due Process Failure of America's Prison Privatization Statutes." *Seton Hall Legislative Journal* 21 (1997): 371–424.

Ravitch, Diane. *Left Back: A Century of Failed School Reforms.* New York: Simon & Schuster, 2000.

————. "Somebody's Children: Educational Opportunity for *All* American Children." In *New Schools for a New Century: The Redesign of Urban Education,* ed. Diane Ravitch and Joseph P. Viteritti, 251–273. New Haven, Conn.: Yale University Press, 1997.

Rawls, John. *Political Liberalism.* New York: Columbia University Press, 1993.

————. *A Theory of Justice.* Cambridge, Mass.: Harvard University Press, 1971.

Rinas, Erica J. "A Constitutional Analysis of Race-Based Limitations on Open Enrollment in Public Schools." *Iowa Law Review* 82 (1997): 1501–1534.

Rivkin, Steven, Eric A. Hanushek, and J. F. Kain. "Teachers, Schools and Academic Achievement." Working Paper no. 669. Cambridge, Mass.: National Bureau of Economic Research, 1998.

Robbins, Ira P. "The Legal Dimensions of Private Incarceration." *American University Law Review* 38 (1989): 531–852.

Robinson, Adele. "Risky Credit: Tuition Tax Credits and Issues of Accountability and Equity." *Stanford Law and Policy Review* 11 (2000): 253–265.

Rorty, Richard. *Contingency, Irony, and Solidarity.* Cambridge: Cambridge University Press, 1989.

Rose, Richard. "Charges as Contested Signals." *Journal of Public Policy* 9 (1989): 261–286.

Rosenbaum, Nancy, ed. *Liberalism and the Moral Life.* Cambridge, Mass.: Harvard University Press, 1989.

Rothstein, Laura. "School Choice and Children with Disabilities." In *School Choice and Social Controversy: Politics, Policy, and Law,* ed. Stephen D. Sugarman and Frank R. Kemerer, 332–364. Washington, D.C.: Brookings Institution Press, 1999.

Sander, William, and Anthony C. Krautmann. "Catholic Schools, Dropout Rates and Educational Attainment." *Economic Inquiry* 33 (1995): 217–233.

Savas, E. S. *Privatization and Public-Private Partnerships.* New York: Chatham House, 2000.

Schneider, Anne, and Helen Ingram. "The Social Construction of Target Regulations: Implications for Politics and Policy." *American Political Science Review* 87 (June 1993): 334–347.

Schneider, Mark, et al. "Institutional Arrangements and the Creation of Social Capital: The Effects of School Choice." *American Political Science Review* 91 (1997): 82–93.

Shokraii Rees, Nina. *School Choice 2000: What's Happening in the States.* Washington, D.C.: Heritage Foundation, 2000.

Singer, Joseph W. "The Player and the Cards: Nihilism and Legal Theory." *Yale Law Journal* 94 (1994): 1–70.

Skillen, James W. *Recharging the American Experiment: Principled Pluralism for Genuine Civic Community.* Grand Rapids, Mich.: Baker Books, 1994.

Smith, Kevin B., and Kenneth J. Meier. *The Case against School Choice: Politics, Markets, and Fools.* Armonk, N.Y.: M. E. Sharpe, 1995.

Spinner-Halev, Jeff. *Surviving Diversity: Religion and Democratic Citizenship.* Baltimore: Johns Hopkins University Press, 2000.

Steele, Claude, and Joshua Aronson. "Stereotype Threat and the Test Perform-

ance of Academically Successful African-Americans." In *The Black-White Test Score Gap,* ed. Christopher Jencks and Meredith Phillips, 401–427. Washington, D.C.: Brookings Institution Press, 1998.

Steinberg, Laurence, with B. Bradford Brown and Sanford Dornbusch. *Beyond the Classroom.* New York: Simon & Schuster, 1996.

Stick, Michael. "Educational Vouchers: A Constitutional Analysis." *Columbia Journal of Law and Social Problems* 28 (1995): 423–473.

Sugarman, Stephen D., and Frank R. Kemerer, eds. *School Choice and Social Controversy: Politics, Policy, and Law.* Washington, D.C.: Brookings, 1999.

Sullivan, John, James Pierson, and George Marcus. *Political Tolerance and American Democracy.* Chicago: University of Chicago Press, 1982.

Sullivan, Kathleen. "Parades, Public Squares and Voucher Payments: Problems of Government Neutrality." *Connecticut Law Review* 28 (1996): 243–260.

"Symposium: Constructing a New Federalism." *Yale Law and Policy Review* 14 (1996).

Tarcov, Nathan. *Locke's Education for Liberty.* Chicago: University of Chicago Press, 1984.

Texas Open Enrollment Charter Schools: Third Year Report. Austin: Texas Education Agency, 2000.

Tushnet, Mark. *Making Civil Rights Law.* New York: Oxford University Press, 1994.

U.S. Department of Education, Office of Educational Research and Improvement. *Parents and School Choice: A Household Survey.* Washington, D.C.: GPO, 1983.

Viteritti, Joseph P. "Choosing Equality: Religious Freedom and Educational Opportunity under Constitutional Federalism." *Yale Law and Policy Review* 15 (1996): 113–192.

Walzer, Michael. *Spheres of Justice: A Defense of Pluralism and Equality.* New York: Basic Books, 1983.

Wecht, David. "Note, Breaking the Code of Deference: Judicial Review of Private Prisons." *Yale Law Journal* 96 (1987): 815–837.

Weiss, Janet. "Policy Theories and School Choice." *Social Science Quarterly* 79 (1998): 523–532.

Willms, Douglas J., and Frank Echols. "The Scottish Experience of Parental School Choice." In *School Choice: Examining the Evidence,* ed. Edith Rasell and Richard Rothstein, 49–68. Washington, D.C.: Economic Policy Institute, 1993.

Witte, John F. "Is America Avoiding Race?" Paper presented at the annual meeting of the American Political Science Association, San Francisco, September 25, 1998.

———. *The Market Approach to Education.* Princeton, N.J.: Princeton University Press, 2000.

———. "Private School versus Public School Achievement: Are There Findings That Should Affect the Educational Choice Debate." *Economics of Education Review* 11 (1995): 371–394.

Witte, John F., et al. *Fourth Year Report: Milwaukee Parental Choice Program.*

Madison: Department of Political Science and the Robert M. La Follette Institute of Public Affairs, University of Wisconsin–Madison, 1994.

Wolf, Eleanor. "Northern School Desegregation and Residential Choice." In *The Supreme Court Review,* ed. Philip Kurland and Gerhard Casper, 63–85. Chicago: University of Chicago Press, 1977.

Woodhouse, Barbara Bennett. "'Who Owns the Child?': *Meyer* and *Pierce* and the Child as Property." *William and Mary Law Review* 33 (1992): 995–1122.

Wren, Jason L. "Note, Charter Schools: Public or Private? An Application of the Fourteenth Amendment's State Action Doctrine to These Innovative Schools." *Review of Litigation* 19 (2000): 135–166.

Index